Margaret Atwood: A Biography

Margaret Atwood:
A BIOGRAPHY

Nathalie Cooke

ECW PRESS

We acknowledge the support of the Canada Council
for the Arts for our publishing program.
This book has been published with the assistance
of grants from the Ontario Arts Council.

This book has also been published with the help of
a grant from the Humanities and Social Sciences
Federation of Canada, using funds provided by the
Social Sciences and Humanities Research Council of Canada.

CANADIAN CATALOGUING IN PUBLICATION DATA
Cooke, Nathalie
Margaret Atwood: a biography
ISBN 1-55022-308-9
1. Atwood, Margaret, 1939- – Biography. 2. Authors,
Canadian (English) – 20th century – Biography.* I. Title.
PS8501.T86Z58 1998   C813'.54   C98-931379-4
PR9199.3.A8Z58 1998

Cover photo: Charles Pachter, *Portrait of Margaret Atwood*
(detail), 1980. Adapted from an original painting.
Reproduced by permission of the artist.

Cover design by Guylaine Régimbald.
Imaging by ECW Type & Art, Oakville, Ontario.
Printed by University of Toronto Press, Toronto, Ontario.

Distributed in Canada by General Distribution Services,
30 Lesmill Road, Don Mills, Ontario M3B 2T6.
Distributed in the United States by LPC Group–InBook,
1436 West Randolph Street, Chicago, Illinois, U.S.A. 60607.

Published by ECW PRESS,
2120 Queen Street East, Suite 200,
Toronto, Ontario M4E 1E2.
www.ecw.ca/press

PRINTED AND BOUND IN CANADA

Never trust biographies. Too many events in a man's life are invisible. Unknown to others as our dreams.

— Anne Michaels, *Fugitive Pieces*

CONTENTS

ACKNOWLEDGEMENTS

My fascination with poetry began many years ago when, as a teenager, I sat on a beach near my home on Vancouver Island and read "Some Objects of Wood and Stone" from Atwood's first poetry collection, *The Circle Game*. I would like to thank Margaret Atwood for that moment, for the many subsequent moments of recognition, surprise, and delight her writing has given me, as well as for her honesty and careful consideration during the course of this project.

I also owe a very large debt of thanks to Charles Pachter, Dennis Lee, and Sarah Cooper. For their gracious help I would also like to thank Lenore Atwood, Joyce Barkhouse, Xandra Bingley, George Bowering, Brian Brett, Jerome Buckley, Mary Irving Campbell, Kay Cogswell, Matt Cohen, John Robert Colombo, Lorna Crozier, Peter Davison, Douglas Fetherling, Timothy Findley, James Ford, Robert Fulford, Gary Geddes, David Helwig, Helene Holden, Bev Hunter, Sandy Johnston, Doug Jones, David Knight, Joe Kronick, Patrick Lane, Phoebe Larmore, Chris Lloyd, Jay Macpherson, Alison Massie, Jack McClelland, Sue Milmoe, Hans Nygren, P.K. Page, Al Purdy, Jane Rule, Rick Salutin, Vivienne Schuster, David Sheps, Rhea Shulman, Mary Sims, Marylee Stephenson, William Toye, Germaine Warkentin, and Judy Wright.

Sheri Weinstein, Elizabeth Hay Steinson, and Darren Gobert signed on as research assistants and soon became partners in this project. Their invaluable support — both material and moral — raised the quality of the study and of the experience.

To Atwood scholars who have provided information and support, clarified details, alerted me to missing information and inconsistencies, I am very grateful: Donna Bennett, Russell Brown, Shannon Hengen, Earl Ingersoll, Lorna Irvine, Sally Jacobsen, Karen MacFarlane, Judith McCombs, Helmüt Reichenbacher, Jerome Rosenberg, and Sharon Wilson. Other experts on Atwood's writing were also particularly helpful: Janet Fetherling of Annex Books in Toronto; Bruce Whiteman; and all the staff of the Thomas Fisher Rare Books Library at the University of Toronto, but especially Edna Hajnal and Jennifer Ramlochan. Research was funded, in part, by a SSHRCC Faculty Research Grant and by a McGill Faculty Research Grant.

Thanks, also, to those who clipped articles, provided anecdotes, read drafts, and listened: Henri Audet, Jill and Harry Cherniak, Mark Cohen,

Julian Geller, William Graham, Don Naduriak, Johanna Schneller, David Sheps, and Rochelle Simmons. Special thanks to Susan Glickman, who, when I panicked, proved herself to be a real friend; to Chuck for coming through, as always; to Sara and Sharon for the precious gift of time; to Mary Williams for her calm conscientiousness; to Holly Potter for her kindness; and to my editor and colleague Robert Lecker for his unwavering support.

This book is for Sam and the boys for everything worthwhile. And for my mother, who, after reading *Alias Grace*, agreed that studying Atwood's work was worthwhile too.

PERMISSIONS

Diligent efforts have been made to contact copyright holders; please excuse any inadvertent errors or omissions, but if anyone has been unintentionally omitted, the publisher would be pleased to receive notification and to make acknowledgements in future printings.

Unpublished letter from Lenore Atwood to Margaret Atwood used by permission of the author. Excerpts from unpublished letters by Joyce Barkhouse used by permission of the author. Letters from Xandra Bingley used by permission of the author. Excerpts from unpublished letters by Professor Jerome Buckley used by permission of the author. Excerpts from unpublished letter from Mary Irving Campbell used by permission of the author. Excerpts from unpublished reader's report on *The Edible Woman* used by permission of John Robert Colombo. Excerpts from interview with Corinne Davies and Catherine Sheldrick Ross, originally published in *Canadian Children's Literature* 42 (1986), used by permission of Davies and Ross. Excerpt from *Man of Myth* and unpublished letter by Robertson Davies reprinted by permission of Pendragon Ink. Quotations by Peter Davison used by permission of Peter Davison. Excerpts from *Travels by Night* by Douglas Fetherling used by permission of the author. Excerpts from letter by Timothy Findley used by permission of the author. Excerpts from articles by Robert Fulford and from *Best Seat in the House* used by permission of Robert Fulford. Excerpt from *I Am Watching* by Shirley Gibson reprinted by permission of Stoddart Publishing Co. Limited. Excerpts from interview with Geoff Hancock reprinted by permission of Geoff Hancock. Excerpt from interview with M.T. Kelly reprinted by permission of Richard Ouzounian of Imprint and Leanna Crouch of Sommerville House Books. Excerpt from interview with Bonnie Lyons reprinted from *Shenandoah: The Washington and Lee University Review* by permission of the editor. Excerpts from "The Death of Harold Ladoo" as well as from unpublished letters reprinted by permission of Dennis Lee. Excerpts from "Novelist-in-Progress" by Roy MacGregor reprinted by permission of the author. Excerpts from unpublished letters by Jay Macpherson used by permission of the author. Excerpt from "Early *Cat's Eye* Stories" and "From 'Places, Migrations' to *The Circle Game*" by Judith McCombs used by permission of the author. Excerpts from interview with Elizabeth Meese used by permission of the *Black Warrior Review*. Excerpts from interview with Joyce Carol Oates, originally published in the *Ontario*

Review 9 (1978–79), used by permission of Ray Smith, editor. The "Ghost as Dry Rice" story is reprinted by permission of P.K. Page. Excerpts from letters by Charles Pachter reprinted by permission of the author. Excerpts from unpublished letters by Al Purdy, as well as excerpts from "An Unburnished One-Tenth of One Percent of an Event," used by permission of the author. "Egoist Agonistes" by Shakesbeat Latweed reprinted by permission of Margaret Atwood and Dennis Lee. Excerpts from unpublished letters by Mary Sims used by permission of the author. Excerpt from interview with Sue Walker reprinted by permission of *Negative Capability*.

★   ★   ★

Permission for written material by Margaret Atwood: excerpts from published articles by Margaret Atwood, as well as from unpublished letters and manuscripts by Margaret Atwood, used by permission of the author. Entry on the Writers' Union of Canada from *The Canadian Encyclopedia* used by permission of McClelland and Stewart, Inc., the Canadian Publishers. Excerpts from *The Animals in That Country* by Margaret Atwood used by permission of the author and Little, Brown (USA) and Oxford University Press (Canada). Excerpts from *The Edible Woman* by Margaret Atwood used by permission of the author and Little, Brown (USA), Andre Deutsch (Great Britain), and McClelland and Stewart (Canada). Excerpts from *Morning in the Burned House* by Margaret Atwood used by permission of the author and McClelland and Stewart (Canada), Virago (United Kingdom), and Houghton Mifflin (USA). Excerpts from *The Robber Bride* by Margaret Atwood used by permission of the author and Bloomsbury (Great Britain), Doubleday (USA), and McClelland and Stewart (Canada). Excerpts from *Second Words* by Margaret Atwood used by permission of the author and House of Anansi Press. Excerpts from *Two-Headed Poems* by Margaret Atwood used by permission of the author and Simon and Schuster (USA) and Oxford University Press (Canada). Excerpts from *Wilderness Tips* by Margaret Atwood used by permission of the author and Bloomsbury (Great Britain), Doubleday (USA), and McClelland and Stewart (Canada).

Foreword

This is not an authorized biography. Margaret Atwood and I did meet twice to speak about this project, and we exchanged letters and faxes off and on over a period of three years. I had broad access to the Margaret Atwood Papers at the University of Toronto, but quotation permission for previously unpublished material was more limited. As well, I had access to the Dennis Lee Papers at the University of Toronto, to Charles Pachter's private collection of the Atwood-Pachter correspondence, and to some of the *Northern Journey* and Contact Press Papers. Personal interviews with Atwood's friends, colleagues, and relatives were conducted between 1995 and 1998.

I take full responsibility for inevitable inaccuracies. I made every effort to check facts and to give those involved and affected the opportunity to review relevant passages and to respond to them. The analysis is my own, and I arrived at my conclusions independently.

Introduction

"Is it true that artists have to suffer to be creative?" asked artist Charles Pachter of his friend Margaret Atwood.[1] The year was 1968. Pachter was then twenty-six, Atwood twenty-nine. And for Pachter and Atwood, both acutely aware of the muse's demands, the question was a loaded one. I'm not sure why he asked the question in that particular letter. Perhaps because he was thinking of his portrait of Margaret Atwood (*It Was Fascination I Know* [1968]) and pondering the broader philosophical questions such a representation of one artist by another provokes. Perhaps because of his own artistic struggles — apparent in such pieces as his formidable and dark self-portrait *It's Only a Paper Mien* (1969). Or perhaps from sheer curiosity — the kind one close friend and collaborator has about the thoughts of another.

Atwood knew that the muse had exacted a high price from her colleagues and foremothers. Of some — such as Jane Austen in Hampshire, England, and Emily Dickinson in Amherst, Massachusetts — the muse was content to demand a tightly circumscribed existence in which the painful passing of days was communicated in oblique whispers. From the Brontë sisters, in exchange for the intensity of their novels, the muse took an even greater payment: the life of their mother, the lives of their two sisters due to the harsh environment they shared at the Clergy Daughters' School at Cowan Bridge, and the life of their dipsomaniac brother, who succumbed to alcoholism and opium addiction. In the twentieth century, Virginia Woolf walked determined, heavy stones filling her pockets, into a river. Her

1941 suicide was a gesture that signalled her own surrender to her inner voices and, to the world at large, the enormously high cost of creativity.

At the time of this exchange between Atwood and Pachter, the world was well aware that the suffering of some of its most talented women artists was reaching a crescendo. Poet Sylvia Plath committed suicide in 1963. Anne Sexton did the same in 1974. And there were equally dark lessons to be learned closer to home, in Canada. The death of poet Pat Lowther in 1975 closed a short and painful life. Gwendolyn MacEwen would later embark on a tragic path of alcoholism and depression that would lead to her death in 1987. Margaret Laurence would also suffer under the shadow of alcoholism.

For Atwood and Pachter the question of whether artists must — or even should — suffer in order to produce their best art was an urgent and potentially terrifying one. No wonder, then, Atwood pondered it carefully and at length. The answer she penned to Pachter in 1968, and, as I will show in this biography, the answer she scripted in her own life, were the same: a strong, defiant, and resolute "No."

> As for creativity & suffering: I think one goes through various stages (by "one" I mean me, as usual). I used to think (age 18–23 or 4) that one a) had to suffer, b) ought to suffer for being a poet; had to, probably from the Byronic-Poe version of the tormented artist, ought to probably some guilt thing (nice girls get married & have kids, they don't write poems; therefore if you do write poems you aren't a nice girl and deserve to be punished in some way). There's another version of that: artists suffer, therefore if you don't suffer you aren't an artist, therefore you deviously go about finding ways to make yourself suffer so you can write. And I did some of that too, (have you?) But basically I *don't like* suffering very much, so I evolved a rationale that permits less of it: everyone has neuroses, granted, but the artist has a way of working them out (his art) not available to those who ain't; the latter have to work

them out in their lives. Therefore the artist is likely to be better adjusted (to his own neuroses) than someone with an equivalent intensity of neurosis who isn't an artist. That's probably a lot of crap too, but I find it more viable than the suffering one. At least you don't feel guilty if you *enjoy* yr life or happen to have a *good* relationship with someone. And not all art is sublimated neurosis anyway, right? (Occasionally when people tell me how *sane* I am I feel I ought to be out there suffering; it's a hard habit to kick.) As for "paying a price": I think there's a bit more to that. That is, if there are certain conditions under which you can produce, and you have to make a choice between those conditions and something (a marriage, a job) that would disrupt those conditions, then obviously you pay some kind of a price. But that's different. You, for instance, have chosen not to take several jobs offered you, and paid the price of doing without that money; which isn't however the same as "suffering."[2]

That distinction between "suffering" and "paying a price" was a crucial one for Atwood. "Suffering," with all its connotations of dark, lonely garrets, suggests that the artist has no choice in the matter; "paying a price" implies that the artist makes a conscious decision about the costs and implications of creativity. The latter is much closer to Atwood's belief that the artist is a responsible citizen and not a passive victim. Atwood has based her career on this premise, labouring hard in the service of the muse and paying the necessary price. She has also worked to ensure that the price paid by her fellow writers is fair, involving herself with the Writers' Union of Canada, PEN, and Amnesty International. And, judging from her professional and personal achievements — which include producing a huge body of writing (poetry, fiction, criticism, and children's literature; some works have been translated into over thirty languages), receiving numerous honorary degrees, attracting international recognition for her humanitarian endeavours, and maintaining a fiercely loyal circle of family, friends, and colleagues — Atwood has proven the premise valid.

Atwood's 1968 letter was signed "Peggy Pupa," a jesting refer-ence to Pachter's portrait of "Peggy" Atwood and to the triumphant trajectory it suggested: from caterpillar to butterfly.

*   *   *

When, exactly, did Margaret Atwood become a writer? There are at least two answers on offer, depending upon whom you ask. Atwood herself will identify for you, with just the very tip of her tongue planted firmly in her cheek, the precise moment at which she knew she would become a writer. She was sixteen and walking across the football field at her high school. It came to her "with the force of a foregone conclusion" that she would be a writer.[3] As Atwood tells it, the thought descended as if from on high.

> I was scuttling along in my usual furtive way, suspecting no ill, when a large invisible thumb descended from the sky and pressed down on the top of my head. A poem formed. It was quite a gloomy poem: the poems of the young usually are. It was a gift, this poem — a gift from an anonymous donor, and, as such, both exciting and sinister at the same time.
>   I suspect this is why all poets begin writing poetry, only they don't want to admit it, so they make up explanations that are either more rational or more romantic. But this is the true explanation, and I defy anyone to disprove it.[4]

Atwood's graduating yearbook announced that her ambition was to write the "Great Canadian Novel"; she did not lose her sense of resolution.

Her family, though, might tell you that the idea had crossed her mind earlier. Her Aunt Kay, in particular, would date the announcement shortly after Atwood's fifth birthday:

> My sister and I had taken our children for a few days to the family cottage. . . . The other children were playing on the beach, but when I went upstairs I found Peggy sprawled

on one of the beds. "Oh, dear," I thought, "her feelings have been hurt."

"What are you doing, Peggy?" I asked.

"I'm writing a story."

"What kind of a story?"

"An adventure story."

"Oh, may I read it?"

"Yes," and she handed it to me.

"That's very interesting, Peggy. Are you going to be a writer when you grow up?"

"Yes."

I thought to myself, "There's one child who might make it." The spelling was atrocious, of course (strictly phonetic), but she had the beginning of a real story there — not your average five-year-old's. I could not forget that incident.[5]

Judging by the diligence with which Atwood practised the craft until the age of about eight and by evidence located among the Margaret Atwood Papers housed at the University of Toronto, Aunt Kay has a point. In her surviving childhood creations are found the seeds of Atwood's writerly ambitions.

So there are at least two versions of the story. Being a writer, after all, means different things to different people. Writing can be a profession — a way of spending one's days, of earning money, of gaining a reputation, of acquiring influence. It can also be a vocation — something for which one is chosen or to which one is called. In this sense, writing is a kind of responsibility, something a writer serves rather than something she is served by. (Remember the biblical story of the three talents?) Atwood is both these things: a writer by profession *and* a writer by vocation. Perhaps, then, she did become a writer at least twice; certainly as a writer she leads a doubled life.

Of course, Atwood also leads a doubled life in a more obvious way: as Margaret Atwood (poet and novelist, model of intellectual engagement and responsible citizenship, known for her pointed pen, her sharp wit, her distinctive monotone reading voice, and her impeccable sense of timing) and as Peggy Atwood (family member, stalwart friend, keen listener, known for her infectious laughter and good companionship). On very rare occasions a camera catches the exact moment Margaret Atwood breaks into laughter — the kind that starts inside and shines through the eyes. In those moments we glimpse the Peggy described by her friends and close associates, the Peggy who is both the source and secret of Margaret Atwood's phenomenal success as writer, solid citizen, and model of intellectual engagement.

Why this split? "To be larger than life," Lois Gould explains in her wonderful article about the world's formidable Margarets, "and still have fun, [the Margarets] have to call themselves Peggy. [*Not* Maggie; that's just Margaret trying vainly to lighten up. As in Thatcher.]"[6] Although Gould doesn't mention Atwood, the Margaret principle still applies. Margaret Atwood is serious about her writing; Atwood's saving grace is precisely that the Peggy in her doesn't allow Margaret to take herself too seriously.

I

Literary Apprenticeship

MARGARET ELEANOR ATWOOD was the second of three children born to Carl Edmund Atwood (BSA, MSA, Ph.D.), a professor of zoology, and Margaret Dorothy Killam, a former dietician and nutritionist. Margaret's elder brother, Harold Leslie, was born on 15 February 1937, in Montreal, where Carl Atwood was completing his Ph.D. at McGill University's Macdonald College. Margaret was born in Ottawa on 18 November 1939 at the Ottawa General Hospital. Her younger sister, Ruth Kathleen Atwood, was born in Toronto in 1951.

The Atwoods spent much of their time travelling due to Carl Atwood's research. After Margaret's first trip into the bush, when she was just six months old, the rhythms of her father's career as a government employee running a research station set up to study tree-eating insects (he was one of the first to insist that spraying wouldn't work) took her into the bush during the warmer months. Although Margaret's early years coincided with World War II, her father remained in Canada because, as a member of the forestry industry, his position was designated as "crucial." At a time when gas was rationed and there were fewer cars on the road, Carl Atwood had a car because of the requirements of his job. Travelling up Highway 17, the family would drive to Témiscaming and then follow a "one-track dirt road" into the bush. They would go north when the ice went out (although Margaret remembers an occasion when the ice was thick enough for them to go in on a horse-drawn sleigh) and return with the coming of snow. There they lived sometimes in tents, once in a rented cottage near Sault Ste. Marie (the summer when Margaret was four and a half), and, later, while Carl Atwood built a cabin, the family sheltered in the woodshed until construction was finished. The cabin itself was "on a granite point a mile by water from a Quebec village so remote that the road went in only two years before I was born." The road to the cabin was also constructed, with the aid of dynamite, by Margaret's father. (The Atwoods' cabin, by the way, was not finished until Margaret was twenty-seven. It still has neither phone nor running water.)[1]

Margaret remembers the cities of her early childhood — Ottawa, in particular — as snow covered. After all, she saw them only in winter. Early on, her parents struck a bargain: her father cooked breakfast in the bush, and her mother cooked breakfast in the city. In the early years — before Carl Atwood took up his job in Toronto — the bargain was to her mother's advantage.

Growing up in and out of the bush, travelling between Ottawa, Sault Ste. Marie, and Toronto, Atwood did not attend a full year of school until grade 8. "This," she told Joyce Carol Oates in an interview, "was a definite advantage."[2] Such a lifestyle allowed Margaret and Harold to spend plenty of time playing with each other and reading books. Their father would leave for work in a boat and might not return for a few days. Their camp was lit by kerosene lamps; wood stoves provided both heat and cooking surfaces. Books were a means of escape and entertainment. There were few alternative activities.

> We did not live in a small town or even a village, although we could see the covered bridge and white church spire of a tiny French-speaking hamlet a mile away by water. Thus my brother and I did not have many other children to play with. We could not go to the Saturday afternoon matinees so fondly remembered by some people my age, nor could we listen to the radio: although there was a radio, reception was so bad in those remote areas that the radio was turned on only for the weather, and for news of the War. There were no art galleries, special classes or plays, and television had not yet been invented. Books were it.[3]

Actually, television had been invented, but the Atwoods didn't acquire a set until Margaret was in grade 5.

While in the bush, Margaret and Harold's mother was their teacher. In the morning they spent time on lessons; they had afternoons off.[4] The pattern is reminiscent of that adopted by early Canadian pioneers: it is not one that many other people born in the mid-twentieth century have experienced. For instance, Catharine Parr Traill, well-known Canadian pioneer, literary figure, and sister of Susanna Moodie, tutored her children in the high room of their home, Wolf Tower, during the early mornings. They spent their afternoons walking and doing the chores necessary for survival.[5] But this was in the nineteenth century. It is small wonder that years later Margaret Atwood read the sketches of Susanna Moodie's life in the bush and recognized a way of life that was both quintessentially Canadian and strangely familiar. Indeed, there was something about the lives and struggles of the Strickland sisters — Susanna Moodie and Catharine Parr Traill — that captured Atwood's imagination and haunted her work as she, like them, strove to establish herself as a writer within the context of the Canadian landscape. Atwood would turn to Moodie's life and writings as she worked on at least three different projects: *The Journals of Susanna Moodie*; her play about Grace Marks, "The Servant Girl"; and her ninth novel, *Alias Grace*.

The ritual of moving into and out of the bush provided Atwood with a paradigm for the kind of doubled existence familiar to many Canadians. Very early on she developed an ability to separate one life from another, to organize and compartmentalize her activities.[6] Later, as she juggled various aspects of her career and family life, this ability to shift contexts served her well.

As well, the bush and her father's research subject provided Atwood with an example of metamorphosis.[7] But Atwood's strong sense that one thing can become another, can transform itself, comes not only from her experiences in the bush but also from her early reading, particularly of comic books. She learned to read so that she could read comics.[8] What does a young girl learn from comics? That superhuman ability has its advantages *and* its disadvantages. You can't have it both ways. Wonder Woman, for instance, may be beautiful and powerful, able to deflect bullets with her wondrous bracelet, evade enemies in her transparent airplane, or snare villains with her magic lasso. But in order to experience a mortal woman's joys — the kiss, the wedding — she has to give up her superhuman powers. Kisses make her weak in the knees. Tough choice.[9]

Another important source of information on roles and choices offered itself to Atwood in an unlikely form in 1944, just before she turned five. Atwood's parents ordered a collection of Grimm's fairy tales and, to their surprise, received the unexpurgated version: 833 pages long, containing 210 tales, published by Pantheon, and illustrated by Josef Scharl. Although their parents were rather horrified, Margaret and Harold were intrigued by the stories — spellbound. In them, men and women alike played a full range of roles, from stupid to intelligent, virtuous to evil. Not only did these tales provide the springboard for Atwood's *The Robber Bride*, but, as Sharon Wilson argues convincingly in her study *Margaret Atwood's Fairy-Tale Sexual Politics*, they also influenced a large portion of her writing in significant ways.[10]

Atwood was, and is, a voracious reader. Her parents read to her when she was young, serving up the classics: *Winnie the Pooh*, *Alice in Wonderland*, the works of Beatrix Potter. When she started to read by herself, she came across Edith Nesbit (*The Phoenix and the Carpet* and *Five Children and It*) and Edgar Allan Poe (who "terrified" her in grade 6). As well, she discovered Swift's *Gulliver's Travels*, Twain's *Tom Sawyer* and *Huckleberry Finn*, Rider Haggard's *King Solomon's Mines* and *Allan Quartermain*, Sir Charles G.D. Roberts's *Wild Animals I Have Known*, Alcott's *Little Women*, Montgomery's *Anne of Green Gables*, and the tales of Conan Doyle ("at about age ten or eleven I devoured all of Sherlock Holmes"). She read Orwell's *Animal Farm*, thinking it an animal story in the Canadian tradition, and admitted to being seriously disquieted by the horse's death.[11] Again expecting an animal story, she took on *Moby Dick*. "I skipped all the parts about people; I identified with the whale, and was not at all sad when it wrecked the whaler and drowned most of the crew and got away at the end. . . . [I]t was about time for an animal to come out on top."[12] In high school she scooped up *Wuthering Heights* and books by D.H. Lawrence and James Mitchener; these she took up to the garage roof to read. When she finished high school, she was presented with a copy of Austen's *Pride and Prejudice*.[13]

But Atwood's literary tastes were not always quite so lofty, and this, in the long run, has been just as crucial to her success as a writer, specifically to her ability to appeal to a mainstream audience. She loved the Dell pocketbook mysteries, "the ones with the map of the crime scene on the back and the eye in a keyhole on the front, along with the lurid picture of the strangled blonde in the red strapless gown."[14] (Atwood has a knack for capturing the precise image.) In the paperback club at school, she encountered some other rather trashy selections — for example, *Donovan's Brain* (about "an overgrown and demented brain which was being kept alive in a glass jar by scientists — a brain which was trying to take over the world").[15] And, also during her high school years, Atwood absorbed other popular stories: *Peyton Place*, *The Blackboard Jungle* (a novel transformed into the famous 1955 film starring Sidney Poitier).[16]

Both Atwood and her brother were avid comic book readers, especially early on; they would trade them back and forth on Saturdays. Each also wrote comic books and read them out loud to the other, testing their qualities and effects.[17] Harold's were full of war machines and strange planets. Margaret's had things like flying rabbits and, later, girls in ball gowns. She read whole series of comics — the Marvel ones as well as Batman, Superman, Captain America, Wonder Woman, Donald Duck, Mickey Mouse, and Little Lulu — but she admits that her favourite was *Plastic Man*, "who could transform himself into anything, but you could always tell because it was red and blue."[18] The possibility of transformation was the real fascination, it seems, behind all the comics and the Grimm's fairy tales.

A bit later, Atwood took to using her father's library in the basement, spending hours down there with her favourite snacks: crackers with peanut butter and honey, raisins, lime jelly powder. Yes, lime jelly powder. This was where she read Koestler's

Darkness at Noon, the romances of Sir Walter Scott, Orwell's *Nineteen Eighty-Four*. Her father was a history buff who amassed an extensive library that included anything from copies of the *National Geographic* to a biography of Rommel. Margaret took full advantage of the collection; she especially enjoyed Churchill's discussion of the war when she was fourteen or fifteen.[19]

What is Atwood's reading taste like now? Eclectic. In 1992 she listed the five Canadian novels she has read and reread as Anne Hébert's *Kamouraska*, Alice Munro's *Lives of Girls and Women*, Margaret Laurence's *The Stone Angel*, Robertson Davies's *Fifth Business*, and Timothy Findley's *The Wars*.[20] In the context of recent reviews of her work and talks she has given, it has been suggested that Atwood has also enjoyed the novels of Louise Erdrich, Toni Morrison, Chinua Achebe, and Nawar El Sadawi, as well as numerous biographies and works of nonfiction.

⋆ ⋆ ⋆

Crucial moments in Atwood's literary apprenticeship, then, occurred outside school. This was, in part, due to the fact that she did not attend school full time until the age of eleven, and so much of her early life was spent somewhere other than in school. In those early years Atwood started to "scribble," experimenting with words and her imagination. "If I were an archaeologist," she once mused,

> digging through the layers of old paper that mark the eras in my life as a writer, I'd have found, at the lowest or Stone Age level — say around ages five to seven — a few poems and stories, unremarkable precursors of all my frenetic later scribbling. (Many children write at that age, just as many children draw. The strange thing is that so few of them go on to become writers or painters.) After that there's a great blank. For eight years, I simply didn't write. Then, suddenly, and with no missing links in between, there's a wad of manuscripts. One week I wasn't a writer, the next I was.[21]

This "great blank" between age eight and age sixteen began with a rather grim school year for Atwood — she encountered "a horrific grade 4 teacher"[22] — and ended with the announcement to her parents of her intention to become a writer. Atwood jokingly refers to it as her "dark period," one in which the imaginary gave way to the pragmatic: "I abandoned writing and took up painting for a while at the age of eight or nine. Then, becoming more practical, I wanted to become a dress designer, and, becoming more practical yet, I wanted to be — I didn't want to be, but thought that I would probably go into Home Economics. And then when I found out how boring it was I went back to writing."[23]

Atwood spent her first six years in Ottawa. It was still wartime, so she would hear the occasional air-raid siren. In 1945 the family moved, for a year, to Pim Street in Sault Ste. Marie, where Carl Atwood was the director of an insect laboratory. Here Margaret wrote a book of poems called *Rhyming Cats*. It has been filed away in the Atwood Papers at the University of Toronto. As she was too young for grade 1, and as kindergarten was nonexistent in the postwar years because of teacher shortages, Atwood remained at home with her mother. She entered grade 1 at the Duke of York School the following year, 1946, when the family settled in Toronto and Carl Atwood took up a faculty position at the University of Toronto. That year, Margaret wrote poetry and a novel that "featured as its central character an ant." Between 1946 and 1948 the Atwoods lived at 111 Haddington Avenue in North York, which Atwood remembers as "a house in a field."[24] Worried about a gas station being built beside the house, Carl Atwood moved the family once again two years later, just after Margaret's eighth birthday. This time they settled into a permanent residence, just south of the eastern extremity of the Mount Pleasant Cemetery.

Although this final move marked the beginning of the "great blank" in Atwood's literary output, it does not seem to be an entirely bleak period. She spent grades 3, 4, and 5 at Whitney School. Peter Pearson, who would become a lifelong friend and colleague, was also at Whitney, but not in Atwood's year. It was at Whitney that Atwood was taught by Miss Macleod, whom she identified as "the good teacher in *Cat's Eye*. A holy terror; very eccentric Scotswoman."[25] And if grade 4 was coloured by the "horrific teacher," then grade 5 brought Atwood a "terrific" one: Katey Firstbrook, a "Brown Owl." That Atwood's tender devotion was reciprocated became obvious to her many years later. When Brown Owl was about ninety-four years old, Atwood visited her in a retirement home. "We had lunch and a nice talk. She had saved one of my Brownie projects from 1948. She didn't save anybody else's, just mine. And then she gave that to me. . . . Three days later I was in Montreal, and my assistant sent me a fax saying that Brown Owl had died on Saturday."[26]

As well as being a Brownie, Atwood took piano lessons and went to Miss Pickering's Dance School for ballet and tap. She recalls being the "centre cheese drum" in a production of *Anchors Aweigh*. Just in case you jump to the wrong conclusion that this is the source of the wonderfully funny mothball scene in *Lady Oracle* and, by implication, that the young Atwood is the young Joan, I should skip ahead a few years to make the case that Atwood — although not a star athlete or musician — was quite an accomplished all-rounder at school. No Joan Foster, in other words, by a long shot. Atwood has perfect pitch, so it should come as no surprise that she was in both the junior (grades 9 and 10) and senior (grades 11 and 12) choirs, as well as in something called the "Triple Trio" — a group of nine singers. She participated in the model UN the year her school represented Palestine. Sports weren't really her strong point, but she took the "Leaders Course" to learn game rules and acquire basic umpiring skills; she ran in the school relay one year, played on the basketball team ("if you can believe it," she adds), and "did — hah! — high jumping!" In grade 12, she represented the school, with Sally Hergert, in the "Consumers' Gas Miss Homemakers' Contest" (held at the Home Show, where the two girls were required to do domestic things with gas appliances: iron a shirt, bake a decent meatloaf), and she was in the school fashion show. And there were all the other things: singing commercials for the school prom, doing class writeups for grade 13, reporting on home-and-school initiatives for the bulletin.[27] In other words, as a school-girl, Peggy Atwood was accomplished and involved; she also demonstrated a healthy sense of humour and fun.

Atwood spent grades 6 and 8 at Bennington School, skipping grade 7. At that point the school had just opened. The first grade 8 class graduated four students (including Atwood's friend Sandra Sanders). Atwood's class (the second graduating class) consisted of eight students. All three grades — 6, 7, and 8 — were taught in one room. If the grade 1 and 2 students were rehearsing for a play at the same time, they would be put at the other end of the room. That first year they presented *Peter Rabbit*. And, just to prove it, Atwood sang a few verses to me.[28]

During the Bennington period, life changed dramatically for the Atwood family. Atwood's younger sister, Ruth Kathleen, was born in 1951. Atwood attended school full time beginning with grade 8 and started to spend less time up north in the summers — although a northern holiday in August was a ritual that she would maintain for the rest of her life. During winter weekends Margaret took a Saturday-morning class at the Royal Ontario Museum with her friend Meg Graham. (The Graham family lived across the street from Whitney School, and Atwood would spend hours playing in their attic.) By the time she was twelve, Atwood had become an expert at using her free time constructively. With a friend, she took a class and learned to make marionettes. "The real ones — with carved arms and legs," she says. "The heads were made from moulds." And, becoming interested in puppets (they were smaller, easier to make and manipulate), the two girls began to run the Bennington Heights Saturday Morning Program (when Atwood was twelve and thirteen — in grade 9) for neighbourhood children. The pair also formed a partnership and put together an act. In the early years they did birthday parties, supervising games and meals as well as performing with hand puppets. "We were a real deal for the parents," Atwood muses now. Later on, the girls found themselves an agent and, equipped with hand puppets and a folding stage, performed at company Christmas parties.[29] Although Doreen Kronick, Atwood's supervisor at the Bennington Community Centre, remembers her seriousness and acute shyness at this time, Kronick's actions suggest that there was another Atwood co-existing with the shy one, one who came to life through the voice of her puppets when the curtain went up.[30]

But Atwood's performances were not always successful. One embarrassing moment, Atwood says, took place in 1953, when she was fourteen and in grade 10. It was broadcast on television. With her pet, a "beautiful, green, intelligent praying mantis called Lenore (after the Poe poem, not after [her] future sister-in-law), which lived in a large jar, ate insects and drank sugar water out of a spoon," Atwood appeared on *Pet's Corner*, a television show produced for CBC by an Atwood family neighbour. Margaret did so well that she was invited back. Her second appearance, however, was disastrous. Her job was to be a prop. The "star" was a trained flying squirrel who was supposed to fly from its owner and land on Margaret. Terrified of the studio atmosphere, it flew to her but then scurried down the front of her school tunic.

> [I]t then began scrabbling around beneath, and could be seen as a travelling bulge moving around my waistline, above the belt. (Close shot.) But it was looking for something even more secluded. I thought of the bloomers, and swiftly reached down the front of my own neckline. Then I thought better of it, and began to lift the skirt. Then I thought better of that as well. Paralysis. Nervous giggling. At last the owner of the flying squirrel fished the thing out via the back of my jumper.
>
> Luckily the show went on during school hours, so none of my classmates saw it.[31]

Atwood was close to her brother while growing up, but their interests gradually drew them into different spheres during their teenage years. Both Margaret and Harold were good at science in school, and by the time they graduated from high school their marks were about the same in both science and English. Harold became a neurophysiologist who reads a lot. Atwood became a writer who reads "popular science as recreation."[32] However,

Margaret's eclectic taste and appetite for learning meant that a certain alliance between these two very talented young people was inevitable. Harold would "coach" his younger sister, trying to pass on the things he was learning. Once he tried to pass on the mysteries of Greek, which he was learning at school. The lessons proved unsuccessful.[33]

★   ★   ★

On weekends, both in the early school years and sometimes later on, Atwood attended Sunday school.[34] Her parents were not churchgoers, so she went to church with her friends and their families. Carl Atwood was a Darwinist by training. He encouraged his children to think and to question. He believed that children shouldn't be baptised; that choice should be a person's to make herself in adulthood.[35] The discussion between parent and daughter on the subject of faith and institutional religion is enacted in detail in both *Surfacing* and *Cat's Eye* (when Elaine decides to go to church with Grace Smeath and her family).

It was during her time at Leaside that Atwood started to attend the Unitarian Church — out of curiosity. Her friend Sandra Sanders and her family were members of the congregation there. As well, Atwood went to services at Saint Simon's Anglican, where her brother sang in the choir. Margaret describes Harold as having been "a talented boy soprano before his voice broke."[35] At church and at Sunday school Atwood learned about the evils of drink (as a teenager, she won a prize for an essay on temperance), about the Ten Commandments, about the Order of Worship.

But Sunday school was far from being Atwood's only source of religious knowledge. In the Canada of the 1950s, religion and the Bible were a central component of the educational system at all levels. Each day started with morning prayers in the institutions of the Protestant public school system, and at Leaside High School students took turns reading from the Bible. Students were also required to take a course in religious knowledge: Atwood's came in grade 8 and was taught by an Anglican minister —

Reverend Reisberry. (One of her classmates got the strap for calling him "Mr. Raspberry.")[36]

In a short fictional piece she wrote for Toronto's *Now* magazine, Atwood describes the religious musings of a young schoolgirl during morning prayers. The setting is Toronto in the 1950s:

> If Heaven is a good place and preferable to the earth, why is murdering good people bad? Wouldn't you be doing them a favour, since that way they'd get up there sooner? Only murdering bad people should be bad, since they weren't about to go to Heaven anyway. But if they were bad enough, surely they deserved to be murdered. So murdering both good people and bad people was actually quite good, all things considered: to the good people you'd be giving a helping hand, to the bad ones their just deserts.
>
> I told some of this to my friend S., on the way home from school, past the Bayview movie theatre with its ceiling pocked with spitballs, past Kresge's. . . . We wore pencil skirts then, shortie coats, velveteen ballerina shoes that caved out at the arches after a few wearings. . . . S. thought about the murder theory, but not for long. She did not think I was being serious.
>
> God is the good in people, she would say, from time to time.
>
> Like vitamins in milk? I'd say. So if everyone died that would be the end of God?
>
> No, she would say. I don't know. I need a cigarette. Don't make me dizzy.[37]

★   ★   ★

Having skipped grade 7, the girl who entered Leaside High School in grade 9 was one of the youngest in her class. Her friend Joan, luckily, was the same age; but the others were much older. "Shaving," as Atwood puts it. "That was when you had to stay in school until sixteen."[38] As of grade 10, though, the students were streamed, and Atwood became part of what was called an "extra options class." By grade 13, timetables varied according to which classes one took. Most of Atwood's friends from Bennington went on to other public schools in Toronto: to Jarvis Collegiate Institute (closer to downtown, with a more ethnically diverse student body — even then), to North Toronto (for the upwardly mobile), to Lawrence Park Collegiate Institute (where Atwood's friend Sandra went at first), or even to the University of Toronto School (for brainy students; an entrance exam was required). Leaside's student body was pretty homogeneous. With the exception of a few Armenian students, the Leaside crowd came from middle-class WASP homes. The student body was far less mixed than it had been at Bennington. Atwood remembers that Leaside was

> located in the middle of the middle class, in the mid-fifties, which were themselves in the middle of the century. It was a school of medium size, and was in fact so middling that the kids that went to Jarvis (cosmopolitan) and Forest Hill (rich) sneered at it. Leaside was not then the area of trendy boutiques and apparently desirable bijou houses that I'm told it is now. On the contrary. The walk home from it to my house — which was not located in Leaside proper, I would then hasten to add — led past such things as the Woolworth's, where girls who were indiscreet in the back seats of cars had to go to work after they quit school, and IDA drugstores and Aikenhead hardwares, and shops that sold discouraging women's clothing of middle quality. Remember baby blue nylon semi-opaque blouses?[39]

Although it was a public high school, Leaside had a real Scottish flavour. The school newspaper, for which Atwood wrote, was called *Clan Call*. And the principal was a character. Atwood, addressing an audience of Ontario teachers, described the Leaside environment:

> Our principal — whose name was Normie, which did not stand for normal but for Norman — was the founding

principal, and had constructed the entire school around a private fantasy of his own, which was that this was not a high school at all but a Scottish clan. His last name was McLeod, and darned if the school didn't have the McLeod tartan as its official tartan, and a Gaelic saying on its crest. The school magazine was called *Clan Call*, and every now and then we would have state visits from Dame Flora McLeod, head of the clan, and her two kilt-wearing, bag-pipe-playing grandsons. I thought nothing of it at the time; I must have assumed that all high schools were run along these lines; but in retrospect it does seem a little odd.[40]

Her favourite teacher? Not surprisingly, it was her English teacher, Miss Billings, despite the fact that Atwood did better in botany than in English composition in grade 13 because she was a poor speller (marks were deducted for spelling errors). Atwood remembers that Miss Billings "took literature seriously" and was "tolerant" of what Atwood calls her early "effusions."[41] It was on the recommendation of Miss Billings that Atwood eventually went to Victoria College.[42] Miss Billings's most famous quote is taken from her response to one of Atwood's early creative efforts. "I can't understand a word of this, dear," she told Atwood, "so it must be good."[43]

Other memorable teachers? Mr. Don McLeod, the history teacher who showed his students wartime propaganda films. "Fascinating," Atwood remarks now. Dr. Maura, the Latin teacher, who used to discuss predestination with her. Miss Smedley, the English teacher who, when "run to ground" by eager journalists, mentioned that she remembered Atwood as having "no particularly remarkable talent." Atwood recalls her "teaching Coleridge with her eyes shut"[44] and "whirling around as in 'Kubla Khan.' "[45]

In grade 13 Atwood wrote ten exams and achieved impressively high scores (remember, these were the days before mark inflation, when an A was 75 percent or above and a B was between 66 and 74 percent): English composition, 83 percent; English literature, 94 percent; French composition, 84 percent; French literature, 85 percent; Latin composition, 78 percent; Latin literature, 69 percent; history, 80 percent; botany, 92 percent; zoology, 86 percent; chemistry, 87 percent. During grades 10, 11, and 12 Atwood also took German lessons during the lunch hour; and, although she didn't take the exam, those lessons proved useful later on. Atwood's final standing was based on the average of her top nine marks. She finished with an extremely solid 85.4 percent average (a high A) and left Leaside with an English award, a university-entrance scholarship, and an award for good citizenship.[46]

⋆　⋆　⋆

In the late 1950s, Canadian literature was not really recognized either as a distinct body of literature or as worthy of much consideration at all. Although there was certainly a growing national sentiment, Canadian literature wouldn't be institutionalized until the late 1960s, and, of course, Atwood was to play a central role in the process. But during the Leaside years, she was introduced to very little Canlit. "[O]nce a year a frail old man would turn up and read a poem about a crow; afterward he would sell his own books . . . autographing them in his thin spidery handwriting. That was Canadian poetry."[47] The poet's name was Wilson Macdonald.

Atwood's classmates included Patricia Parker (who later married Sam Mitchell, prime minister of Saint Vincent), Helen Currie, Mildred Estona, Gregory Kasparian (school captain and an accomplished sportsman),[48] and Rosalie Kerbekian.

Although Atwood is remembered for being both shy and serious in high school, her papers suggest that there was another side to her — witty, mischievous, playful. In grade 12 she wrote "Three Cheers for Corona!" It was a sly piece about a woman who smokes cigars to the astonishment of her conservative, cigarette-smoking friends: "the smiles vanish when I slip my stogie out of my purse, lick it all over with my little yellow incisors, and light up."[49] Collected in *First Words*, this rhetorical exercise is a strong example of the Atwoodian sense of humour and the healthy scepticism with which she viewed conventional roles.

Another example of Atwood's wit, not to mention her sceptical attitude towards domestic roles, was a skit she wrote for her home economics class in grade 12, ostensibly "to get out of making stuffed animals."⁵⁰ The skit was donated to the University of Toronto by one of the seven performers, Atwood's classmate Dr. Helen Currie. The part of "Nylon" was played by Rosalie Kerbekian. Set to tunes from "Barcarole" in *Tales of Hoffmann*, Gilbert and Sullivan's H.M.S. *Pinafore*, and "Oh My Darling Clementine," the skit outlined a marriage of convenience between Princess Orlon of the new royal family of fabrics — the king, the queen, and their daughters Orlon, Dacron, and Nylon — and the outmoded aristocrat Sir William Wooley. Appropriately, the more modern princesses sing a rather fluffy theme song in three-part harmony, identifying themselves as "three little synthetic cuties / Who've hit fabric news with a bang." By contrast, Sir William's part is a rather formal one, indicating his pride of ancestry; it is a mark of honour to him that Cleopatra's royal robes were cut from his cloth. The chorus boasts a conspicuously Gilbert-and-Sullivanesque refrain. Needless to say, from the union issues, in short order, the offspring — "Woolorlene" ("Gabardine" is typed into the script and then crossed out). From the nurse's lips comes the relevant advertising slogan to the tune of "Oh My Darling Clementine," only the word "Woolorlene" is substituted for "Clementine."

There are much more serious pieces of writing from this period as well, the best of which can be found in *A Quiet Game* (Juvenilia Press, 1997) — a collection of two of Atwood's early short stories and an early poem, all three of which introduce some of the central themes of her mature work, including the rage and overpowering sadness lying just beneath the calm demeanour of the average 1950s Torontonian.

Another early example of Atwood's writing is the poem "A Representative," written about 1956 and published in her collection *First Words*. Through its use of a tightly controlled rhyme scheme and the repetition of sounds ("down / dark"; "sewerage of men / For one small spark . . . / Potential, silent, still and sad") and phrases ("lacks the power to use the power") the poem enacts the very tension it describes: to escape the crippling grasp of inertia.

When she first began writing seriously, Atwood was influenced by Poe and Shelley. She had read Poe well before high school and remembers the horror she felt at the encounter:

> I read the collected works of Edgar Allan Poe, which some fool had put in the school library on the assumption that anything without sex in it was suitable for young minds. This experience disturbed me in a way that *Grimm's Fairy Tales* had not, possibly because Poe is obsessive about detail and sets out to horrify. I had nightmares about decaying or being buried alive, but this did not stop me from reading on.[51]

The prose Atwood produced during this period was pretty bleak — "grit-filled," as she later described it. Her influences? D.H. Lawrence, certainly. Scribbled notes on the originals — "First North American Rights Only" — suggest hopefulness and a certain ambition. "I was not sure what 'First North American Rights' were," she later admitted; "I put it in because the writing magazines said you should."[52] One story, "A Cliché for January," describes the pain a mother endures when her daughter gets pregnant and is forced to marry. Another, called "The English Lesson," is about a middle-aged English teacher called Miss Murdock and has a distinctly D.H. Lawrence-like darkness and intensity. There are a few painfully awful phrases here ("I am a dried-up well, she thought, with dry dead moss around the edges"[53]), inspired, perhaps, by Lawrence's *The Virgin and the Gipsy* ("it's full of elderly women with moss around the edges," Atwood explains[54]). But the insight into the loneliness experienced by a woman who chooses her career over a marriage is highly charged. "To write. To write had been to live. To write she had saved and scrimped, scrimped and saved, rejected the bright, gay clothes she had once been so fond of, put herself through college, hating her poverty, waiting for the day she would be famous. . . ." Miss Murdock's failure is haunting: "She could not pinpoint the exact moment when her resolution had deserted her."[55]

It would be too easy to equate this story with Atwood's conviction, at age sixteen, that she would be a writer. Certainly the timing was right. But the moment for looking ahead to the practical implications of that decision, of that conviction, had only just arrived.

2

Family Values

WHEN THAT INVISIBLE THUMB descended on the young Atwood as she crossed the Leaside football field, it descended on an intelligent and well-read young woman who was prepared to meet the challenge. Others might have been crushed into the mud. That Atwood was well able to bear up under the pressure was the result of the firm footing her family had given her. She recognized that being a writer was a calling as well as a career choice, she committed herself to the hard work and dedication involved, and she stuck to that commitment: all of this was the result of the environment in which she was raised. From her family she learned to value hard work and to appreciate decisive individuals who take responsibility for their own actions.

★   ★   ★

Were the fiction to parallel the life, it would suggest that Atwood had experienced a pretty grim childhood. Dark holes. Ravines. Sombre thoughts. Familial dysfunction and childhood discomfort. The opposite is actually the case. "Life: I don't have a very promotable one, as am not in possession of anything picturesque like a beard or Unemployment Insurance. Have never been a lumberjack or a janitor. Had unfortunately a happy childhood. Am (alas) educated, but you'd better soft-pedal that as it's not fashionable."[1] From her parents Margaret Atwood inherited her intelligence — something her family encouraged her to use together with plain common sense. That Atwood takes her work

39

seriously while still retaining the ability to laugh — even at herself — is the result of her family's greatest gifts: high expectations and a healthy sense of humour.

Atwood traces her ancestry back to Massachusetts, New Hampshire, and Connecticut, until about 1780. Three branches of her family tree were comprised of "the second wave of the Puritan invasion"; a fourth, on her father's side, was Scottish.[2] She explains that her Puritan ancestors, Loyalists, came to Canada

> in search of a good cup of tea, thus becoming part of the brain drain; a drain, according to my father, from which the States has never entirely recovered. Canadian-American relations were a frequent topic of conversation in my grandmother's house. There were the Canadian relations and then there were the American relations, who lived mostly in Boston. That's what makes Canadian-American relations somewhat touchy at times: they *are* relatives. There's nothing that rankles more than a cousin, especially one with a Rolls-Royce.[3]

Atwood's parents left Nova Scotia during the Depression because there were no jobs there. But their sense of self was deeply rooted in the Maritimes and maintained through both anecdote and semiannual pilgrimages "back home," starting when Atwood was six and the period of wartime gas rationing had passed. All of this established for Margaret and Harold a sense of tradition and communal values.[4]

Carl Atwood's family lived on Nova Scotia's South Shore, a region of dark, coniferous forests and cranberry bogs. Their farmhouse was remote and lit by kerosene lamps. Cooking was done on a "wood range of great elegance," and water was pumped by hand. "My grandmother made butter in a hand churn and served it in moulds, not because it was picturesque but because that was the way to do it, and her patchwork quilts were not thought of as beautiful museum pieces or decorator's dreams but as bed-coverings."[5]

Atwood's maternal grandmother lived in a white house in the Annapolis Valley, and, across the North Mountain, she also had a cottage on a cliff overlooking the Bay of Fundy. At the cottage, the "hordes" were summoned to meals by the blowing of a conch shell. And pieces of raw amethyst, found along the shore, ornamented the mantle. These were, "for an inland child . . . almost shamanistic."[6] During the summer, the cottage would be full of the Killam clan; they dined on lobster, corn, and dulse. Through these family gatherings the two Atwood children grew very close to their Halifax cousins, the three eldest Cogswell children (David, Eric, and Elizabeth). The group known as "the big 5" would swim in the icy waters of the Bay of Fundy until they turned purple, investigate life-forms in the tidal pools, and examine local fishermen's nets. Later, the cousins made a sailing boat to take out into the bay.[7]

Grandfather Killam, Atwood's maternal grandfather, was a country doctor whom Atwood remembers best in his later years whittling wooden chess pieces. Within family lore, however, he was a heroic figure, a

> strict, awe-inspiring but lovable grandfather, a country doctor who drove around the dirt roads in a horse and sleigh, through blizzards, delivering babies in the dead of night, or cutting off arms and legs, or stitching up gaping wounds made by objects unfamiliar to me — buzz saws, threshing machines. Under his reign, you had to eat everything on your plate, or sit at the dinner table until you did. You had to go to church, every Sunday. You had to sit up straight. ("Father laid down the law," said my mother. And I could picture him laying it down, on the dining-room table, in the form of two great slabs, like those toted around by Moses; only his were of wood.)[8]

This grandfather was larger than life not only because Atwood heard such stories as a youngster, but also because the remembrances had been exaggerated by her mother, a woman with narrative skill and a lively imagination. She was a "raconteur," says Atwood, a "deadly mimic."[9] In one story, Atwood's mother explained how, as a child, she "thought that wings would grow out of her shoulder blades if she prayed for them, because you were supposed to be able to pray for things and get them. She cut little holes in the back of her nightgowns so that the wings would come out."[10] Indeed, Margaret Killam's strength of conviction was such that "having been told that faith would move mountains" she prayed and prayed for the South Mountain to move onto the North Mountain, "so that the Bay of Fundy would not come in and flood the Annapolis Valley."[11]

★   ★   ★

Strength of conviction was something Atwood's father had as well. In spades. Dr. Carl Atwood was a remarkable man, not only because of his professional success as a forest entomologist and, later, as a professor of zoology at the University of Toronto, but also because this success was achieved against considerable odds. Growing up in that isolated farmhouse (the family didn't get electricity until the 1950s) near Shelburne, Nova Scotia, Carl was one of five children. During his childhood, he learned "considerable backwoods skills" that, as Margaret Atwood points out, "are hard to acquire later in life."[12] He managed to get through high school by completing correspondence courses and took a teaching job at the age of sixteen in order to earn some money. Maintaining a frugal lifestyle, he was able to stretch the scholarship funding he received for university. Family lore has it that he lived in a tent for part of the time and made a little more cash by cleaning rabbit hutches. That Carl also managed to help put his siblings through school testifies to his strength of character and purpose; such characteristics are well entrenched on his side of the family.[13]

There is pride in Atwood's voice when she talks of her father — of "one match Atwood," the father who could haul and peel logs, who for two weeks kept his head while trapped with three friends in a tent in a rainstorm in the middle of a forest fire, and who, as a woodsman, advised M.T. Kelly when he wanted to choose a gun. With "a mind like Leopold Bloom's," Carl Atwood sometimes composed "doggerel" verses "filled with puns"[14] and whistled as he went about his chores. "I first heard Beethoven," Atwood writes, "because my father whistled it."[15] Scottish country dancer, fiddle player, collector of history books, Carl Atwood was able to take great pleasure from his reading and music.

Both Carl Atwood and Margaret Killam were strong-minded people raised during the Depression; accordingly, both were obliged to go it on their own. They prided themselves on being self-supporting, although this had necessitated both a long engagement and a move from the Maritimes to Ontario, where the jobs were. Not surprisingly, the couple raised their children to be independent as well. Margaret had her first bank account at age eight. Harold and Margaret did chores as youngsters — the normal things such as making their beds and tidying their rooms, dusting, polishing silver, cleaning bathrooms, mowing the lawn. When the family was in the bush, however, such mundane chores had to be done a bit differently. Margaret remembers doing dishes by floating them in the water and throwing stones at them.[16]

⋆   ⋆   ⋆

As a young girl, Atwood was subjected to one important lesson of the times: society expected women to choose between career and family. In fact, this was *the* lesson of the times, but somehow the Killam women had both acknowledged and ignored it. Ultimately, Atwood herself would reject it — after much careful consideration — largely because the extraordinary talent and drive of the Killam women showed her that it did not have to be an either/or option. Her mother was perhaps the most obvious example of a woman who could not be contained by the middle-class-Canadian-housewife stereotype. In fact, Margaret Killam — who took up ice skating at forty-six; who loved horses and considered becoming a jockey; whose stories were about escapades, scrapes, climbing fire escapes; who refused Carl Atwood's proposal the first time because she "didn't want to be tied down" — defied that stereotype. She "could use a gun, shot a bow and arrow, fished off the end of the dock, was left with two small children in the woods with nobody around for long periods of time. What with the bears and strange animals we're not talking helpless femininity."[17]

The Killam women were and are formidable: exceptionally intelligent, strong willed, and successful. Atwood paints a full portrait in "Great Aunts," a fascinating article about aunts who are "great" not so much in genealogical terms as in evaluatory ones. In the piece, the aunts are largely seen through the eyes of Atwood's mother, the eldest of the three Killam sisters. Hers is the voice of reason and maturity, the quietly confident voice of a woman who put herself through teacher's college, established herself in a career, and then had a family. She was a pragmatist, a raconteur, but no writer. Admits Atwood, with humour, honesty, and a healthy dose of admiration:

> She was not particularly literary; she preferred dancing and ice-skating, or any other form of rapid motion that offered escapes from domestic duties. My mother had only written one poem in her life, when she was eight or nine; it began: "I had some wings, / They were lovely things," and went on, typically for her, to describe the speed of the subsequent flight. The beauty of this was that whatever I came out with in the way of artistic production, my mother would say, more or less truthfully, that it was much better than she could do herself.[18]

Kay Cogswell, "Aunt K." in the article, was the brilliant middle sister. At the age of nineteen she gained an MA in history from the University of Toronto but decided not to take her father's offer to fund her through an advanced degree at Oxford. Instead, she married an Annapolis Valley doctor (in a double ceremony with her elder sister Margaret) and had six children.

> The reason, my mother implied, had something to do with Great-Aunt Winnie, who also had an M.A., the first woman to receive one from Dalhousie, but who had never married.

> Aunt Winnie was condemned — it was thought of as a condemnation — to teach school forever. She would turn up at family Christmases, looking wistful. In those days, said my mother, if you did not get married by a certain age, it was unlikely that you ever would. "You didn't think about not marrying," said Aunt J. to me, much later. "There wasn't any *choice* about it. It was just what you did."[19]

Atwood is not sure what her mother's point was, but she makes her own interpretation quite clear. "Unlike the stories in books, my mother's stories did not have clear morals, and the moral of this one was less clear than most. Which was better? To be brilliant and go to Oxford, or to have six children? Why couldn't it be both?"[20] Only Atwood could pose these questions without supplying the obvious answer: Because one would die of sheer exhaustion.

Joyce Carmen Barkhouse, "Aunt J.," was the third Killam sister (born in Woodsville, Nova Scotia, on 3 May 1913). She was to become a writer. Joyce married Milton Barkhouse in 1942 and had two children: Murray and Janet. Atwood wrote a poem for her uncle, entitled "Uncle M."; early drafts of it are called "For Uncle O., Banker, Dec'd."[21] Given my fascination with the plurality of Margaret Atwood's professional personas, I find it particularly interesting that Atwood describes "Aunt J." as a kind of doubled figure. "Underneath her façade of lavender-coloured flutter she was tough-minded, like all three of those sisters. It was this blend of soft and hard that appealed to me."[22] In making her life choices, Aunt Joyce also revealed herself to be a doubled figure, for she was (and still is) both a mother *and* a writer. As writer, wife, and mother, Aunt Joyce pulled off what young Margaret Atwood imagined herself pulling off: she balanced a family *and* a career. In Joyce Barkhouse's case, the family came first. Atwood, in the next generation, would restructure that juggling act: she would have a career first and *then* a family. In a revealing interview with Margaret Drabble, Atwood hints that this involved certain trade-offs. She acknowledges that she would like to have had children earlier in life, possibly more of them.[23]

What Atwood does not mention in "Great Aunts" is that she coauthored a book with Joyce Barkhouse: *Anna's Pet* (1980). She explains in an interview:

> I wrote it along with my aunt, who had been one of the first people to encourage my writing. So I thought it would be fun to do a book with her. She had the knowledge of how to write with a limited vocabulary for kids because she writes children's books. . . . [*Anna's Pet* is] based on a little story that she had written many years ago in phonetics because someone had asked her to do that. And she has based the story on my brother, who did take worms to bed and who hid snakes under his pillow and things like that. She had been visiting us at the time when my brother had taken a snake to bed and it had gone away, unknown to my mother. It had crawled into the wood stove to be where it was warm, so that when my mother opened the stove to light the fire in the morning, there was the snake. She said, "I think the snake would be happier outside."[24]

The encouragement Atwood mentions here is evident in the warm correspondence between the two writers; they so clearly enjoyed working together. Early on, Joyce Barkhouse took her niece under her wing. In 1958, for instance, Atwood attended her first literary conference, accompanied by her Aunt Joyce; it was a Canadian Authors' Association meeting. The letters the two wrote to one another later on impart a sense of collegiality, of a warm relationship between two like-minded family members. In hers, Atwood tells her aunt about books that publishers might be interested in[25] and, on a more personal note, offers Joyce her moral support. The affection and encouragement clearly flow in both directions. In a typewritten letter dated 26 October 1983, Joyce Barkhouse mentions showing one of Atwood's new poems to her daughter Janet. "Janet, too, read it and loved it," Joyce writes; "she believes you to be one of the *great* poets." A handwritten note at the bottom of the letter reads: "Janet and I bought *Bluebeard's Egg* in Ch'town — and are greatly enjoying it — although I'd read a few of the stories in periodicals — I like reading them again, and to have in my permanent collection of YOU—."[26]

Joyce Barkhouse has written a number of other children's books: *The Witch of Port Lajoye* (1983); *Pit Pony* (1990), a best-seller that has been made into a movie; *Yesterday's Children* (1992); and *Smallest Rabbit* (1996). A very active member of Nova Scotia's literary community, she has published stories and articles in periodicals and anthologies. Barkhouse is also a biographer, having authored *A Name for Himself* (1986), a biography of Thomas Head Raddall; *George Dawson: The Little Giant* (1974); and *Abraham Gesner* (1980).

As well as being wives and mothers, then, the Killam women managed to make their mark outside the home — in the world of writing (Joyce Barkhouse), in the academic realm (Great-Aunt Winnie and Kay Cogswell), and even in the bush (Margaret Killam). Standards were high in the Killam family; so were levels of support. And this pattern was set, a deep-seated sense of decorum and loyalty was instilled, by the head of the family: Grandmother Killam.

The story goes that Grandmother Killam — depicted by both Atwood and her mother as "distracted, fun-loving, bridge-playing" — was also quite formidable.[27] Atwood knew her as "an austere old lady, a Nova Scotia rural matron with stringent views on washing your hands before meals, a person you had to tiptoe around verbally; there were certain things — quite a few things — that could not be discussed in her presence. She did not smoke, drink, or swear, and she handled difficult social situations by talking about the weather. She was said . . . to have a sense of humour."[28] After Grandmother Killam's death at the age of ninety-four, Kay transcribed a diary she had written at sixteen; it provided ample evidence of that humour. But one of Atwood's anecdotes, in particular, proves Grandmother Killam's mettle:

> A certain amount of writing was tolerated [in the Annapolis Valley], but only within limits. Newspaper columns about children and the changing seasons were fine. Sex, swearing, and drinking were beyond the pale.

I myself, in certain Valley circles, was increasingly beyond the pale. As I became better known, I also became more widely read there, not because my writing was thought of as having any particular merit but because I was Related. Aunt J. told me, with relish, how she'd hidden behind the parlour door during a neighbour's scandalized visit with my grandmother. The scandal was one of my own books; how, asked the outraged neighbour, could my grandmother have permitted her granddaughter to publish such immoral trash?

But blood is thicker than water in the Valley. My grandmother gazed serenely out the window and commented on the beautiful fall weather they were having, while my Aunt J. gasped with suppressed giggles behind the hall door. My aunts and my mother always found the spectacle of my grandmother preserving her dignity irresistible, probably because there was so much of it to be preserved.

This was the neighbour, the very same one, who as a child had led my aunts astray, sometime during the First World War, inducing them to slide down a red clay bank in their little white lace-edged pantaloons. She had then pressed her nose up against the glass of the window to watch them getting spanked, not just for sliding but for lying about it. My grandmother had gone over and yanked the blind down then, and she was doing it now. Whatever her own thoughts about the goings-on in my fiction, she was keeping them to herself. Nor did she ever mention them to me.[29]

In "Five Poems for Grandmothers," published only a year before Grandmother Killam's death in 1979, Atwood offers a moving tribute to her maternal grandmother: a statement of close identification.

Sons branch out, but
one woman leads to another.
Finally I know you
through your daughters,

> my mother, her sister,
> and through myself:
>
> Is this you, this edgy joke
> I make, are these your long fingers,
> your hair of an untidy bird,
> is this your outraged
> eye, this grip
> that will not give up?[30]

Atwood's tribute also contains these lines: "Six children, five who lived. / She never said anything about those births and the one death; / her mouth closed on a pain / that could neither be told nor ignored."[31]

★   ★   ★

> I don't give a piss about generalized "roles." Never have. If I'd believed in "roles," espec. the ones being doled out in the 50's, I never would have been a writer. Would have been Betty Crocker instead. See Edible W. on the subj. of roles. (Rolls.) Why are people, espec. women, always being told they have Roles? It is not a play. The contribution you make as a writer can't be figured out ahead of time and then enacted by you. It doesn't work that way.[32]

Put bluntly, Atwood has come by her disregard for gender roles honestly. It is in her blood. Think of her mother, taking charge of two small children in the bush (approximately eighty miles north of North Bay, Ontario, on the Quebec side of the border), in the early 1940s. While women in the Allied nations were keeping the home fires burning, Margaret Killam Atwood was in the bush with her two small children providing Margaret with her first and strongest role model and defying her era's firmly established gender stereotypes. My favourite anecdote about Atwood's mother involves a bear (every Canadian has a bear story to tell). In it, a mother's victory over a wild creature provides impetus for a parable about the value of transcending society's rigid constraints:

> While I was growing up, my mother was an anomaly. The other mothers wore skirts and stayed in their houses. Mine preferred to be outdoors, in rapid motion if possible. . . . I must have been 6 or 7. We were living then north of Lake Superior, in a tiny cabin my father had just finished building. He'd gone off on a trip, leaving food for three weeks, which was still stored in one of the tents: we hadn't had time to move it into the cabin; we were going to do it the next morning. But we woke up to find that a bear had walked through the back of the tent, eaten everything he liked, and squashed or mangled everything he didn't like. He'd ripped open the tins and sacks, broken eggs, scattered flour and stepped on the tomatoes.
>
> My mother kept calm, which was one of her specialties. She had us look through the woods nearby for anything salvageable. There wasn't much, but the bear hadn't liked potatoes, so we managed to round up a few for breakfast. My mother was boiling them over the fire when the bear appeared, ambling quietly down the road; he was looking for more.
>
> My mother told us not to move. Then, she stood up and ran at the bear, waving her arms and yelling "Scat!" The bear was so startled that it bolted. Luckily, it was a wild bear and without cubs; otherwise, this story might have ended differently. If my mother had had a rifle handy, she probably would have shot the bear. She wasn't a bad shot.
>
> So when I think of my mother, I don't think of lipstick and feathers or the little woman or furniture polish or even five-course dinners. Because of her, I didn't grow up feeling that being female needed to mean having your feet bound. . . . My mother must have had to do some kicking to get the tight shoes off — my grandfather was an old-style patriarch — but she did get them off, as far as the times allowed. When I was younger, say 10 or 11, I had fits of

wishing that my mother was more average or at least looked
better in hats. But I've since concluded that life doled out
to me the perfect mother, although being the perfect mother
was, I suspect, never one of her goals.[33]

This is typical of Atwood's family anecdotes in a number of ways:
it refers to the bush experience, it describes a parent blessed with
strength of mind and will, and it features Atwood's characteristic
sympathetic yet analytical tone. But here I am most interested in
the pride with which Atwood establishes her mother's ability to
transcend cultural norms. "So when I think of my mother, I don't
think of lipstick and feathers or the little woman or furniture
polish or even five-course dinners." Rather, we are led to think,
she thinks of the bear and of a mother who is perfect precisely
because she does *not* try to be a typical mother, because she defies
the category. This pride appears again in other references to
Atwood's mother — the poem "Woman Skating," for example.
Margaret Killam Atwood was the kind of mother who made
pies from scratch, swam in ice-cold water, and paid little heed
to fashion.

My other favourite anecdote about Margaret Killam Atwood
is the one in which her daughters offer to take her shopping for
a new dress. "Why?" she asked them. "I already have one."[34]

*   *   *

One other ancestor on the Killam side needs to be mentioned:
the seventeenth-century Puritan Mary Webster (who appears in
Atwood's poem "Half-Hanged Mary"). She was hanged as a
witch in Connecticut, says Atwood, "for 'causing an old man to
become extremely valetudinarious'. . . . When they cut Mary
Webster down the next day, she was, to everyone's surprise, not
dead. Because of the law of double jeopardy, under which you
could not be executed twice for the same offence, Mary Webster
went free."[35] One can imagine Atwood taking a pause here,
preparing for the punch line. "Tough neck."[36] In a later interview
she offers a slightly less mythical and more scientific version,

explaining that the hanging occurred "before they invented the drop and therefore her neck was not broken."[37] But the point of the story is clear. Whereas in Mary Webster's time such defiance was rewarded by the death penalty, in Atwood's time it has become a source of pride. In her grandmother's time, of course, the jury was still out. While talking to me, Atwood smiled knowingly and remarked, "whether Mary Webster was or was not related was decided by Grandma's mood!"[38]

If Mary Webster provided one of the lessons of the Killam legacy — in order to survive, a woman must have a tough neck — then a different Webster, Noah, of the dictionary-writing branch of the family, offered another important lesson. Use words precisely. Margaret Atwood has taken both lessons to heart.

3

Professional Training

That summer I read *The Waste Land* and was completely
dismayed and discouraged by it. Because if that's what they
were going to study in university, I was obviously very out
of my depth.

— Margaret Atwood[1]

THE DECISION TO BECOME A WRITER was a comparatively
simple one — albeit a little unusual. Teacher or nurse were more
popular choices for girls in those days — or secretary, airline
hostess, home economist.[2] Atwood's close friends were a bit
unconventional, though. One, she recalls, wanted to be a doctor,
another an actress, a third a psychologist.[3] Later, Atwood would
become keenly aware of the obstacles strewn along her writerly
course. She would face a long apprenticeship, isolation in the
early years, and, equally difficult, popularity and close scrutiny
in the later years. Of more immediate concern to her, however,
was how she would tell her parents. After all, at some point she
was going to have to let on that she wanted to study arts rather
than sciences at university. Her announcement was followed by a
silence just long enough for her to hear, as she puts it, "the sound
of two tongues being bitten." Then her mother, always practical,
pointed out that perhaps she had better first learn to spell![4]

Harold went on to an extremely successful career in the sciences. He received his undergraduate degree in 1959 and, on 23
December of that year, married Lenore Mendelson. They would

53

have three boys: David Malcolm, Robert Carl, and Evan Douglas. By the time of his marriage, Harold was working on his MA at Berkeley (he completed it in 1960) and would go on to Glasgow for his Ph.D. (completed in 1963). He earned a doctorate in science in 1978, also from Glasgow. Harold has become a leading neurophysiologist. He lives in Toronto and, since 1991, has been a professor of physiology and the director of the Medical Research Council Group in Nerve Cells and Synapses. Before that he was professor and chairman of physiology at the University of Toronto. Author and coauthor of over 120 books and papers, he is a leader in his field.[5]

★　★　★

Margaret Atwood entered Victoria College at the University of Toronto in September 1957 and graduated with an honours English BA in 1961. She began her university career in philosophy and English on the assumption that it would be a less restricted program of study than English alone would be. Recognizing that the reality was quite the opposite, however, she completed an honours English degree with a minor concentration in philosophy and French, focusing on ethics and aesthetics.[6]

Through the years at Victoria College — during which she became involved in drama, debating, and journalism — Atwood built a network of literary friends and colleagues. These people would both witness and prompt the development of Atwood the writer and the emergence of Atwood the performance persona.

In 1957, the University of Toronto's system of colleges was quite rigid. All of one's classes were taken at the college to which one belonged; only a couple of hours a week would be permitted to study elsewhere. Of all the colleges, Victoria was the most homogeneous, the most solidly middle class. It was located south of Bloor Street on the east side of University Avenue, beside the Catholic Saint Michael's College, which attracted only the very serious scholarly types interested in the classics. On the other side of University Avenue were University College and Trinity College. University College, with its multicultural and — from the perspective of those at Vic, explains poet Dennis Lee — more "eclectic" student body, seemed more radical than Vic.[7] Trinity, an Anglican college where gowns were worn by students as well as faculty, seemed infinitely more formal. (Virtually all the professors at all the colleges wore gowns at that time.) The modern buildings that stand on the Victoria College campus today — the E.J. Pratt Library and the Northrop Frye Hall — were only just starting to be built during Atwood's last year there. She attended classes in the large stone building that dominates the circle and relaxed over coffee with other aspiring writers — "All 3 of them," she notes wryly — in the basement of Wymilwood.[8]

For a young university girl in the 1950s, Peter Pan collars, cashmere twin sets, and neatly coiffed hair were de rigueur. Atwood, with her wealth of curls, would gaze enviously at the long straight hair of her classmate Alexandra Johnston, who sat directly in front of her in American-literature class. She would tie her own hair back tightly (later she even cut it short) and, to augment the serious-academic look, would sport tweeds, horn-rimmed glasses (for those who needed glasses then, that's what was available), and an oversized brown coat. That enormous brown coat became her trademark. "Her drab coat," says Atwood's friend poet Jay Macpherson with a smile. "Which she scuttled about in," Macpherson adds; "she wasn't as interested in clothes then as she now is."[9] Perhaps, though, she was just dressing for a different effect. In Atwood's introduction to a book about her friend Charlie Pachter, she writes, "anyone who came of age as an artist in the Canada of the fifties and early sixties had need of some form of defensive armour."[10] She is referring to Pachter's use of irony — one significant part of Atwood's own defensive armour. Clothing was another.

Or perhaps Atwood's "look" wasn't the product of too much or too little interest on her part but simply the result of a student budget and a preoccupation with such things as course work, exams, and dressing warmly. Atwood is certainly acutely aware of the fashion statements she and others make; one of her real gifts is her ability to pick up on details — things that are said, the way that they are said (as evidenced by her ability to replicate dialogue convincingly in her fiction), and, especially, the things that people wear. Women, I think, tend to do that anyway — remember what they were wearing at an important event, say. Atwood can describe what others wear. The shape of a dress. Its colour. Its texture. And she can sketch it quickly on paper. (Actually, as I write this there's a little pink Post-it Note in front of me with three two-inch drawings of women in 1950s fashions, made by Atwood to illustrate a point.)

In a recent newspaper article Carol Shields is praised for her attention to "small, telling detail." Shields disagrees. "I can come home from a party and I won't know what anyone's worn," she says. "I have all these blind spots. Other writers don't — Iris Murdoch is always wonderful on hair. Anne Tyler notices a bracelet or a necklace."[11] Atwood is good on clothes. We know her characters by what they wear and by what they imagine themselves wearing. (We also know them by what they eat. This, by the way, is unusual. Writers often forget to feed their characters.)

The transition from Leaside to Victoria College was a pretty smooth one for Atwood. She rejoined old friends at Vic (Peter Pearson, for example, who had been at Whitney School, although not in her year) and quickly made new ones (Dennis Lee; her best friend, Gail Youngberg; Marielane Douglas; and, later, Jay Ford). The formal philosophy of the place, which included a respect for intelligence and integrity regardless of gender, suited her well. Extremely bright, she enjoyed lively discussion and debate for their own sake and found plenty of opportunity, both inside and outside the classroom, to engage in them. During the extra-curricular hours she spent developing skits and cartoons and offbeat parodies (this was the age of skits and parodies, the age of Wayne and Shuster), Atwood found an outlet for her humour and a circle of people who would help her to hone her skills.

In his memoir of the 1960s, a time of cultural renaissance in Canada, Douglas Fetherling writes:

> Sometimes it seemed [Atwood] had been at the University
> of Toronto with about half of the individuals I was coming

into contact with in my professional dealings: the magazine editors, publishing people and other writers who were all starting to get their first really important jobs now that they were in their early thirties. Peggy was loyal to all of them and they to her. She had many impressive qualities, including a level of justified self-confidence I had never encountered before (her parents must have loved her from the instant of her birth), but I think loyalty was the most attractive of her many attributes. It was the rarest and the one people would most like having themselves. When Peggy was your friend, she was your friend for life (and what's more, in a world of impractical poets and artists, she was worldly-wise in the extreme).[12]

Atwood interprets that "worldly-wise" remark to mean that she had a bank account. This was the 1960s.[13]

The University of Toronto was then teeming with the talented people who would go on to form Canada's cultural backbone. University College was home to David Helwig, Adrienne Clarkson, John Robert Colombo, David Louis Stein, Michael John Nimchuk (now of the CBC), Lawrence Garber, and Howard Adelman. John Sewell (later mayor of Toronto), Marie Kingston, Patricia Parker (Atwood's Leaside chum), Edward Lacey, and Robert Fulford were University of Toronto students as well. Lacey wrote the first book of poetry to be published under the Muddy York Press imprint; Atwood and Dennis Lee edited it. Fulford — now, of course, a renowned journalist, popular-culture columnist, and arts commentator — reviewed it in the *Old Bookseller*, calling it the first "explicitly gay publication in Canada."[14] Other bright lights on the University of Toronto campus at about the same time were actor Donald Sutherland (studying engineering and eclipsing most of his fellow amateur thespians with his arresting stage performances)[15] and journalist Barbara Amiel (who was involved in the *Varsity*, the university's student newspaper).

Atwood feels a genuine appreciation for her undergraduate training at Vic and has paid her alma mater a high compliment. Speaking about the inscription carved across the institution's front door ("The Truth Shall Make You Free"), she notes, "I thought at the time that the attitude towards the study of English at Vic — that it was supposed to make you somehow not only brighter but better, and that it should be undertaken in a spirit of friendliness and mutual cooperation — was the norm for English departments. I've found since that it's the exception."[16]

Also exceptional, yet harder to pin down and define, was the strength of the women at Vic in the 1950s as well as the atmosphere of collegiality and support they fostered. Writing in 1979, Atwood explained, "unlike the English Department at the supposedly radical and freethinking University College, [the Victoria College English department] hired women. I did not realize the value of this at the time, but it allowed me to witness the spectacle of women who were not only supporting them-selves, but thinking."[17] Today, that kind of atmosphere would be called "empowering," a 1990s word that speaks of the charged world that still seems to exist at Vic to some degree. There is certainly a critical mass of strong women there now, as there was in Atwood's time (Professor Eleanor Cook, whom Atwood mentions in the acknowledgements to *Alias Grace*, is one of them). Earlier, in the late 1940s and early 1950s, ambitious women had provoked enough discomfort to trigger a legendary (at least in the context of the college) battle between Coleridge scholar Kathleen Coburn and Principal Brown. Coburn had the good fortune to fall upon the Coleridge papers and obtain the permission of Lord Coleridge himself to take them to Vic. Although she was a leading Coleridge scholar, her promotions were notoriously slow in coming. By Atwood's time, however, Kathleen Coburn held a certain authority within the college system and was well recognized for her scholarship.

Another important woman, Jessie Macpherson, dean of women since the 1930s, was a partner and colleague of Coburn's. What seems ironic to me today, however, is that while Macpherson and Coburn were both extremely strong role models as single career women and, therefore, as women who challenged domestic stereotypes, Macpherson's goal seems to have been to turn the residence women into young ladies who conformed to, and excelled in, the traditional roles. "Every second week," Alexandra Johnston (now an English professor at Vic) recalls, "we had to eat in the dining room, and be served. Twice a year you would be summoned to eat with the dean. Once she would talk of nothing but the flower arrangement on the table, and students were required to take part."[18] Atwood never lived in residence. I am not sure that residence life and all its trappings would have appealed to her. But, in any case, it was never an option. In those days, you had to come from outside Toronto to be eligible to live in residence. Consequently, Atwood wasn't really a part of the Vic residence crowd, although, through her residence friends (Gail Youngberg, Alexandra Johnston, and Donna Youngblut) and through one particularly important mentor (Jay Macpherson), she was able to forge a connection.

During Atwood's time at Vic, Jay Macpherson was a residence don as well as an eclectic young lecturer. She was also a well-known and respected Canadian poet. Victorian literature was her field, and, "like all good teachers, she behaved as if it mattered, thus converting my surly contempt for the subject into fascinated admiration . . . [she] is one of my oldest and most appreciated friends."[19] Their friendship began during Atwood's undergraduate years. Classes were smaller than they are now, and relations between students and faculty members were, paradoxically, more formal and more relaxed. The two women had common interests: poetry and a delight in what Macpherson calls "Gothic elements."[20] It was an enduring friendship based on respect. In 1982 Atwood wrote that Jay Macpherson "reminds us that poetry is not a career but a vocation, something to which one is called, or not, as the case may be. She's still the best example I know of someone who lives as if literature, and especially the writing of poetry, were to be served, not used."[21]

This common interest — writing — is the subject of an academic paper that Atwood wrote for Jay Macpherson's course in third year. Not surprisingly, it's an excellent paper: "admirable," as Jay Macpherson notes at the end. But whereas most academic papers focus on the texts themselves — what is in them and how it affects the reader — Atwood employs such observations only as stepping stones to her real area of interest: she wants to explore the ways an author uses the supernatural for best effect. That is, she approaches literature as something one writes as well as something one reads. We can see the seeds of her method in *Surfacing* (the underwater vision), *Lady Oracle* (the astral body), and *Alias Grace* (the night vision) even in this undergraduate paper.

> The "natural" subjects of fiction — the social milieu, the living people, the physical realities — can stand to be treated in an expanded and detailed manner; they are rounded out by being seen from many angles and in many respects. But the supernatural subject must either be treated briefly or made ridiculous. There can be no morning after, no discovery that your mother's ghost was really only phosphorescent paint, or that the falling statue is worked from inside, with levers, by a little man. The supernatural, in the novel, must take the form of one or two concentrated incidents; if it recurs too often or is examined too closely, it has the numbing effect of too many gory murders in a drugstore murder mystery, or the amusing one of too many passionate love scenes in a copy of True Romances. When a situation loses its novelty, the reader becomes objective; and the supernatural has no greater enemy than objectivity.[22]

Needless to say, the quality of this analysis is exceptional for an undergraduate student.

During October of Atwood's last year at Vic, Jay Macpherson bought a small house at 15 Berryman Avenue in Yorkville. In those days Yorkville was still rather Bohemian; it hadn't yet become a chic and gentrified part of town. But, because of her role as residence don, Macpherson couldn't actually live in the house until after the academic year had ended. So that winter Atwood lived at Berryman. On weekends Macpherson would come to do odd jobs — stripping wallpaper and the like. The two would have long talks over coffee in the kitchen. Delving into Macpherson's home library, Atwood began to read a full range of Canadian literature. Macpherson had an extensive collection of poetry, including works by P.K. Page, Margaret Avison (Atwood reviewed Avison's *Winter Sun* while at university), James Reaney, D.G. Jones, and Douglas Le Pan. These were more than books of poetry for Atwood: they offered possibilities — proof that Canadians could write and publish. At that time, in Toronto, this in itself was important.[23]

★   ★   ★

Atwood enjoyed intellectual freedom during her years at Vic, but she also discovered that the college's academic programming was ordered, mannered, and rigorous. ("Yipee!" Atwood scribbles in her notes to me. "Let's go back to it!")[24] This, Alexandra Johnston now remembers (also approvingly), "provided a systematic preparation that marched you through the periods. It gave us confidence, a sense of being approved and respected."[25] Bibliography, a first-year course, was one of the more notorious hurdles. Atwood, because she began by majoring in philosophy, didn't have to take it. She did, however, take Old English, then Chaucer, then Milton, and so on. The class was small — about fifteen students. By the last year, only nine students were left in honours English, all of them girls except for Bill Wright.[26] (Dennis Lee took a year off to travel in Europe.) Jay Macpherson remembers them as a "lively bunch," "a diverse and interesting group who were more at the centre of things than classes since."[27] David Knight, who taught both bibliography and Elizabethan drama, qualifies this: "It was a class full of brilliant people but not necessarily a brilliant class. They are not the same thing. One of those recipes that doesn't come together as one thing."[28] Brilliant they were. The class included Dennis Lee (editor, critic, poet, and children's author), Donna Youngblut (Lee's first wife and Atwood's sparring partner), Gail Youngberg (Atwood's close friend who graduated under her married name, McConnell), Ann Macklem, and Alexandra Johnston, as well as Eleanor Feely, Katharine Ward, and Bill Wright. Loosely associated with the group through his close friendship with Margaret Atwood, although not in the same program, was Jay (James) Ford.

"In Honours English," says Atwood, "life was chronological and Milton came in the third year."[29] Even more formidable than Milton, however, was the famous professor who taught the great poet: the star of Victoria College, Northrop Frye. He was the reason Atwood had originally come to Victoria College. She once described him in action, teaching the "Bible" course for which he was well known. Atwood audited the course.

> It was done like this. He stood at the front of the room. He took one step forward, put his left hand on the table, took another step forward, put his right hand on the table, took a step back, removed his left hand, another step back, removed his right hand, and repeated the pattern. While he was doing this, pure prose, in real sentences and paragraphs, issued from his mouth. He didn't say "um," as most of us did, or leave sentences unfinished, or correct himself. I had never heard anyone do this before. It was like seeing a magician producing birds from a hat.[30]

Frye's reputation suggests that he would have been intimidating. But anecdotal evidence evokes a gentle, mild-mannered, well-loved man. Even during my own years at the University of Toronto in the 1980s, Frye was a familiar sight walking along Bloor Street near St. George, soberly dressed in conservative coat and hat, with a professorial air. His mind seemed focused on lofty things. Says Atwood of Frye's professional persona:

> I was more intimidated by the Philosophy professor who lectured with his eyes closed and could always tell when an extra person was in the room. It was hard, though, to be completely intimidated by anyone as easily embarrassed as Frye. . . . So lacking in intimidation was I, I recall, that I wrote and published a literary parody in which I applied archetypal criticism to the Ajax commercial, the eternal battle of the recurrent figure of the Housewife against the dark and menacing figure of The Dirt.[31]

Atwood's emphasis on myth, in her poetry and perhaps even more obviously in her critical work *Survival*, has often been linked to Frye's influence. But the reality doesn't fully bear this out. His shadow certainly did loom large over Atwood, but then it did over many aspiring writers, critics, and students of English, indeed over all students at Vic and, perhaps, over all English students in Canada at the time. Rather than acting as a direct influence on Atwood, then, I think that Frye offered her a formidable perspective on literature that impressed her deeply. She admits:

> I was never intimidated by Dr. Frye. The deadpan delivery, the irony, the monotone, the concealed jokes, the lack of interest in social rituals, may have seemed odd to those from Ontario, but to me they were more than familiar. In the Maritimes they were the norm. Puritanism takes odd shapes there, some brilliant, most eccentric, and no Maritimer could ever mistake a lack of flamboyance for a lack of commitment, courage or passion. Light dawned when I found out Frye had been brought up in New Brunswick. Not quite the same as Nova Scotia, where my relatives all lived, but close enough. A Nova Scotian joke of the thirties had been that Nova Scotia's main export was brains. Frye was an export.[32]

The irony in this passage is wonderful. A woman who is perhaps Ontario's best-known writer speaks about Ontario's best-known critic — and speaks as a Maritimer talking about another Maritimer. It puts a distinctly different spin on the popular impression of these two legendary Torontonians.

But surely, critics have argued, the myth and archetype in Atwood's poetry and prose owe a great deal to Northrop Frye. After all, Frye's *Anatomy of Criticism* — his touchstone critical text, which outlines his theory of symbols, myths, and genres — was published in 1957. Surely, their argument goes, Frye's influence was more direct.

But Frye did not have a monopoly on myth. This was the late 1950s–early 1960s: the era of folk songs and narrative ballads, of Robert Graves's *The White Goddess*. Atwood, having read her Grimm's fairy tales as a child, her comic books, her Bible (and, yes, having audited Frye's course on the Bible), her Virgil (she had also studied Latin in school), had already been exposed to the notion of myth and its extraordinarily powerful implications. Before Frye. Before listening to all the other academics who, in the 1960s and 1970s, became so keen on mythology.

Frye, Atwood maintains, had a specific, practical, and contained influence on her. For example, during a hallway session on career counselling, both of them shy and glancing at the floor, Atwood confessed to Frye that she planned to go to England, where she would waitress and write "masterpieces in a convenient garret at night. He said he thought it might be more productive to go to Graduate School, as I would have more time to write there. I said, Would that be ethical? He said he thought so. Anyway, he thought maybe a scholarship might be a less exhausting way of nurturing one's great works."[33] Practical advice, certainly. Not flamboyant. One Maritimer to another.

Atwood, in discussing Frye, does not make their contact seem more important than it really was. She is always careful to be accurate. There is a certain modesty in this. She talks of the man of mythic proportions and acknowledges that theirs was simply the kind of friendship that exists between a student and a professor whom she respects. But, as the 1979 article in which Atwood-the-Maritimer comments on Frye-the-Maritimer shows, Atwood was already comparing herself to this legend, watching the man closely to learn from his methods — as a student should. The "deadpan delivery, the irony, the monotone" (what David Knight would call Frye's "honking" monotone[34]) that Atwood noted when describing Frye became part of the speaking style she herself used when reading from her work at the Bohemian Embassy and when reading to audiences later in her career. A Maritime influence?

When Northrop Frye died in 1991, Atwood spoke at his memorial service. Interestingly, in this speech and in articles she wrote on Frye at the time, Atwood focused less on his scholarship and its influence and more on his humanity. In one of these articles she related an anecdote about her daughter, Jess. I include this here because I like it; it reveals a gentle side of both Atwood and Frye.

> [W]e had [Frye] to dinner and something burnt in the kitchen and the fire alarm went off, waking our young daughter. She wandered downstairs and got into a conversation with Norrie. Despite his well-known social shyness, he had no difficulty talking with a six-year-old, and she herself was enchanted by him. That interlude, not the high-powered adult conversation that surrounded it, was the high point of the evening for him.
>
> I think one of the sadnesses of his life was that he never had children. But there are many people, including some who never knew him personally, who will feel orphaned by his death.[35]

⋆   ⋆   ⋆

After classes at Vic, Atwood worked on the college literary journal, *Acta Victoriana*, and wrote for the college newsletter, the *Strand*. The *Acta* crowd hovered around the coffee shop in the basement of Wymilwood (it's there even today, called Ned's), no longer clad in tweeds: fashion now dictated they wear black. If you were interested in the arts, you simply *had* to dress in black. The rule still stands. Gail Youngberg was often responsible for producing the newsletter itself, for making sure that the final product got out. Atwood and Dennis Lee were the driving forces behind getting the articles written. By Atwood's last year at Vic, though, this cast of characters had changed. Lee, after his sojourn in Europe, completed his BA in 1962, a year later than his cohorts. Youngberg became busy with other things; she married a geography graduate student in her second year and had a child in her third.

Some of Atwood's early writing experiments published in *Acta* under various pseudonyms and the more formal and gender-neutral designation of "M.E. Atwood" provide the blueprints for her later work as poet, critic, and satirist. Among the most memorable articles were several written by "Shakesbeat Lat-weed," a pen name for the combined creative talents of Atwood and Dennis Lee. *Acta* provided a forum for students eager to test their writing skills and their wit. As you read the following example, keep in mind that this is pretty rarefied stuff. It was written for a very specialized audience: university students up on their literature and criticism, young people very familiar with the cast of literary characters that was being roasted. In "The Expressive Act," for example, Lee and Atwood challenge the shadow of Frye and his famous *Anatomy of Criticism*: "My earliest works have been branded by my detractors as 'obscure.' The blame for their apparent opaqueness must rest on the influence that literary criticism had on my young and easily fevered brain. 'Poems are made from other poems; a good poet steals more often than he imitates,' pronounced my oracle, *The Autonomy of Criticism* (or was it *The Anatomy of Melancholy*?) I became enlightened."[36] The hilarious result of this apparently extreme and mistaken philosophy — that writing authentic poetry is a form of borrowing — is a twelve-line poem with seventeen extensive and somewhat inaccurate footnotes. Footnote 17, for example (which appears at the end of the poem's concluding line), reads, "From *Songs of a Sauerkraut*, by Robert W. Serviceberry, a poet of the Canadian North. The last line assimilates the diverse cultures of the past with the reality of the present." The allusion, of course, is to the popular Canadian poet Robert Service and his collection *Songs of a Sourdough*.

EGOIST AGONISTES

I, Walt Whitman
While I pondered weak and weary over many an
Aprille with his shoures soote
    (The cruellest month,   lonely as a cloud)

I sighed the lack of many a thing I sought;
    but

Come into the garden Maude

It is the wish'd, the trysted hour
    (alas the Twilight of the Gods, The Childrens' Hour,

Mein Irisch Kind)

I never loved a dear Gazelle,

But I think you'll do just as well.

"The Expressive Act," which is, essentially, a short article on the anxiety of influence in Canada circa late 1950, goes on to cite the other central force in Canadian letters: the self-proclaimed prophet/poet Irving Layton. Although the name Layton never appears, the title of the "Prophet's latest, *A Yellow Doormat for the Moon*," is such an obvious inversion of Layton's title *A Red Carpet for the Sun* that any reader with a little knowledge of Canlit can identify him easily. Layton's poetry is formidable, but aspects of his persona are easy to spoof, in particular his kind of Dionysian reliance on women and song. The "Prophet," laments a less romantically successful Shakesbeat Latweed, "apparently, has only to say, 'I want to write a poem,' and snap his fingers, and a beautiful woman instantly appears, nostrils dutifully dilated, waiting to become grist for his mill. Such was not my case." The spoof ends with an appeal to yet another perspective, that of "John Dewley" (the spelling mistake is intended) in his book on aesthetics. Discovering that "the Artist was concerned neither with Literature nor with Life: he was only concerned with himself," the author approves of the notion of art formed by "the white heat, the inner fusion, the volcanic furnace of the Self-Expressive Act."[37] But the end result is a destructive fire rather than a creative one.

As a creative writer, Atwood also published in the *Acta Victoriana* and confesses that "It's hard to recall any piece of publication which has given me greater satisfaction than my first appearance in the pages of this magazine, with, as I recall, a story of medium awfulness."[38] Judging by the dates, the story must have been "A Cliché for January," written in 1959 when Atwood was nineteen.

In it, a dialogue between two women on a bus revolves around an unspoken event: the conception of a child out of wedlock. Atwood experiments here with narrative form, developing a tension between the women's superficial dialogue and the profound implications the issues they broach hold for women in general.[39]

*   *   *

Every era has its cultural landmarks. For arts students in the late 1950s, one of the most important ones was Robert Graves's *The White Goddess*. Subtitled *A Historic Grammar of Poetic Myth*, the book explores, among other things, the figure of the poetic muse and her relationship to the Moon Goddess. Graves argues that she was a "historic character: the goddess of love and battle, the goddess of life and death, who rules Europe long before any male gods appeared here." As such, she was rather a dangerous figure, alternatively nurturing and destructive. The kind of woman a mother wouldn't want her son mixed up with. In California this very alluring goddess-figure-cum-poetic-muse became the centre of "wildwood celebrations."[40] Not surprisingly, in Toronto the response was more conservative.

Within the context of Atwood's own imaginative sphere, we can find traces of Graves's influence — in her poetry, especially, but also in her novels, in the moon symbolism in *Surfacing*, the triple-goddess figure in *Lady Oracle* and *The Robber Bride*. But if the White Goddess functioned rather nicely as an inspirational figure for a male poet, then she was a particularly awkward construct for a female poet: limited in gender and nature, and therefore limiting both as a model for a female poet and for her muse. But *must* the muse be a woman? (The thumb that bore down on Atwood as she crossed the football field, you will remember, gave no clue as to the gender of its owner.) And, if female, would the muse be like the White Goddess? Not older? Perhaps motherly? Perhaps wise and wrinkled rather than mythic and seductive? And couldn't the muse change? Graves's White Goddess was, at the very least, an awkward figure for an aspiring female poet. But she was also a formidable presence in that era and hard to overlook:

> A woman just might — might, mind you — have a chance of becoming a decent poet, but only if she too took on the attributes of the White Goddess and spent her time seducing men and then doing them in. All this sounded a little strenuous, and appeared to rule out domestic bliss. It wasn't my idea of how men and women should get on together — raking up leaves in the backyard, like my mom and dad — but who was I to contradict the experts? There was no one else in view giving me any advice on how to be a writer, though female. Graves was it.
>
> That would be my life, then. To the garret and the TB I added the elements of enigma and solitude. I would dress in black. I would learn to smoke cigarettes, although they gave me headaches and made me cough, and drink something like absinthe. I would live by myself in a suitably painted attic (black) and have lovers whom I would discard in appropriate ways, though I drew the line at bloodshed. (I was, after all, a nice Canadian girl.) I would never have children. This last bothered me a lot, as before this I had always intended to have some, and it seemed unfair, but White Goddesses did not have time for children, being too taken up with cannibalistic sex, and Art came first. I would never, never own an automatic washer-dryer. Sartre, Samuel Beckett, Kafka, and Ionesco, I was sure, did not have major appliances, and these were the writers I most admired. I had no concrete ideas about how the laundry would get done, but it would only be my own laundry, I thought mournfully — no fuzzy sleepers, no tiny T-shirts — and such details could be worked out later.[41]

Needless to say, Atwood went on to become a successful writer who would own and operate household appliances. That her story goes against all those other ones about suffering artists and garrets is part of its interest to aspiring writers. Atwood's imitation of the White Goddess was short-lived, then, nothing more than a phase; but her fascination with mask and persona has been lifelong, and, even today, I think Atwood would say that her muse is female. But I suspect that her muse's power derives from wisdom and age, not allure. And her secret weapon, like that of a comic book heroine, is her ability to transform herself.

★   ★   ★

During her second year of university, Atwood began to read her poetry at the Bohemian Embassy, a small coffeehouse at 7 Nicholas Street. The Embassy was the only place in Toronto where poetry was read on a regular basis. Located at the top of a rickety flight of stairs, it was a place where, Atwood recalls, a poet's most "poignant lines" were often accompanied by noises emanating from the establishment's single espresso machine or the toilet, the door of which opened into the main room. The Embassy was the proving ground for some of Canada's best poets. "I've since felt," Atwood explains, "that any reader of poetry who could survive that could survive anything."[42]

Many of Atwood's Vic friends never ventured across the threshold into that other, more Bohemian world, even though it was located within easy walking distance of the campus. Atwood herself lived on the threshold of two worlds — academic and creative — fascinated by poetry but unwilling to risk all for it. In photos taken during her early Embassy readings, she looks almost businesslike in her crisp white shirt and cardigan, hair pulled back into a neat ponytail. But Atwood notes that this look was created for effect on a particular night; more often, she would appear in black, *the* colour for the younger poets. Trying to give me a sense of the place, Atwood talked of two "styles": "hot" and "cold." "Milton Acorn," she explained, was " 'hot' — but people younger than him went more in for 'cool.' "[43] Irving Layton would have been hot, Atwood and Gwendolyn MacEwen cool.

"She had intelligence and taste as well as talent," remembers John Robert Colombo, "and that was obvious."[44] But Atwood remembers having the jitters. She would gulp coffee before her readings and recalls feeling a bit "green and queasy." She later found out this was partly the result of a coffee allergy, not simply stage fright. "I understand why Dylan Thomas used to get drunk beforehand, but getting drunk is not yet socially acceptable for female poets," Atwood writes. "Also, I'm allergic to alcohol."[45]

The Bohemian Embassy was then one of the only places where poetry was being read and taken seriously. Tucked into a small lane near Gerrard and Yonge, the unpretentious little place belied its rather grand-sounding name. Although it had no liquor licence, the Embassy served coffee and espresso and hot mulled cider. Colombo, today a well-known man of letters (editor, anthologist, translator, poet, book reviewer, and storehouse of information on Canadian literature and culture), was then a University of Toronto student and the organizer of the Thursday-night poetry venue. He remembers that in winter, due to the Embassy's faulty heating system, the poets' warm breath left "vapour trails" in the air.[46] Coffeehouse manager Don Cullen struck a deal with Colombo: on the Thursday nights they earned a profit, Colombo would be given five dollars for his efforts. In other words, Cullen and Colombo were not in it for the money.

Regular Embassy performers were poets George Miller, Milton Acorn (one of the Embassy's central figures, who came to Toronto via Montreal), Gwendolyn MacEwen, and Atwood herself. Atwood was twenty by then, and MacEwen only eighteen. MacEwen had left school to write and, noted Atwood, had "a fully formed style and a manner of presentation that was completely professional."[47] Atwood, too, had developed a particular presentation style. Remembers Charles Pachter, "She would 'drone on' with 'no inflexion in her voice' — and you could hear a pin drop. It made you think about the words." Pachter suggests that Atwood was watching MacEwen closely and, noting her style particularly, her stage persona. And yet the words Atwood used to describe Frye's teaching style, the "deadpan delivery, the irony, the monotone," come back to me here and suggest that she was drawing from a wider sphere of influence than that formed by the small crowd at the Bohemian Embassy.[48]

As critic Judith McCombs points out, Atwood's presentation style has changed during the course of her career. Whereas the early "deadpan" delivery conformed to "Atwood's theories of evocation," McCombs explains, by 1984 her style was more modulated, more "charming" to the audience. In her prose delivery, Atwood has always had a wonderful sense of timing — which not only allows her to build a strong rapport with her audience but also enables her to set up punch lines like a "straight man" and then pull them off.[49]

The character of Selena in Atwood's story "Isis in Darkness" is based on Gwendolyn MacEwen. In creating the setting of the story, the Bohemian Embassy, Atwood uses accurate details.

> It was called the Bohemian Embassy, in reference to the anti-bourgeois things that were supposed to go on in there, and to a certain extent did go on. It sometimes got mail from more innocent citizens who had seen the listing in the phone book and thought it was a real embassy, and were writing about travel visas. This was a source of hilarity among the regulars, of whom Richard was not quite one.
>
> The coffee-house was on a little cobbled side-street, up on the second floor of a disused warehouse. It was reached by a treacherous flight of wooden stairs with no bannister; inside, it was dimly lit, smoke-filled, and closed down at intervals by the fire department. The walls had been painted black, and there were small tables with checked cloths and dripping candles. It also had an espresso machine, the first one Richard had ever seen. This machine was practically an icon, pointing as it did to other superior cultures, far from Toronto. But it had its drawbacks. While you were reading your poetry out loud, as Richard sometimes did, Max behind the coffee bar might turn on the machine, adding a whooshing, gurgling sound effect, as of someone being pressure-cooked and strangled.[50]

When Selena appears in the story, her similarity to MacEwen is startling.

> She was slight, almost wispy. . . . [S]he had long, dark hair
> with a centre part. Her eyes were outlined in black, as was
> becoming the fashion. She was wearing a long-sleeved,
> high necked black dress, over which was draped a shawl
> embroidered with what looked like blue and green dragon-
> flies. . . . Then the voice hit him. It was a warm, rich voice,
> darkly spiced, like cinnamon, and too huge to be coming
> out of such a small person. It was a seductive voice, but not
> in any blunt way. What it offered was an entrée to amaze-
> ment, to a shared and tingling secret; to splendours.[51]

The story from which this portrait is taken is one of those
collected in *Wilderness Tips*, published four years after Mac-
Ewen's untimely death. It is a tribute of love and respect from a
friend, from one poet to another.

As Rosemary Sullivan explains in *Shadow Maker*, her biography of Gwendolyn MacEwen, Atwood and MacEwen were two
young, talented writers who were just starting to explore creative
possibilities in a male-dominated world. Atwood sums up:

> It was the early sixties, the years in which *Playboy* was very
> big among men. That women's liberation thing started with
> men spitting on women. If you go back and read *The Ginger
> Man*, it's all there; or *On the Road*. The perfect woman
> in *On the Road* is a woman who lets her man come and
> go as he pleases and smiles all the time. Now *that's* a
> woman! What woman could actually *be* that? Or who
> *wanted* to be that?[52]

Perhaps this explains the opening of Atwood's *Surfacing*; the
female protagonist finds herself "on the road again," and the narrative slowly undermines the macho myths of Kerouac and his
cohorts. Atwood needed to define her role as a female writer in
a world of male literary paradigms. *The White Goddess*, *On the
Road*, and *Playboy* provided few workable answers.

A publicity flyer for one of those Thursday evenings at the
Bohemian Embassy reads, "From 9:00–1:00, Admission $1.00

only." On Thursday, 17 November 1960, one dollar would have bought you the opportunity to hear three poets in ascending order of rank: John Higgins ("18 years old, from Brampton and unpublished so far"); M.E. Atwood ("a 20 year old student at the University of Toronto, and better known as Peggy Atwood"); and Milton Acorn ("who needs no introduction to the audience at The Bohemian Embassy"). The flyer's description of Atwood's poetry reveals the Embassy's credo: "She writes in a traditional fashion which should contrast with that of John Higgins, but her poetry has an immediate relevance to the Toronto scene."[53] That "but" indicates the mood of the early 1960s: a general distaste for tradition was on the rise; people were beginning to crave relevance, to call for experimentation.

Given this context, the poems of Atwood's first chapbook, *Double Persephone* (for which she won the E.J. Pratt Medal in 1961), seem not only strong but also courageous. They are also very much a product of the times: these tightly controlled classical poems emerged from Atwood's formal literary training at Vic and her early exposure to the power of myth; the chapbook was generated by confidence, energy, youthful enthusiasm, and talent. Atwood laboured over this collection with fellow poet and one-time fiancé David Donnell. She wrote the seven poems and designed the cover; with Donnell, she set the type and printed 250 copies of the little chapbook on a flatbed press in Colombo's basement. Atwood distributed them to local bookstores, selling them for fifty cents each. Today they trade for $1,800.[54]

The poems themselves, in their classical formality and their exploration of myth, are reminiscent of Jay Macpherson's work.[55] I asked Macpherson if she had ever felt a shudder of recognition when reading Atwood's poetry, if she had ever experienced a moment of confrontation with her own influence on the younger poet. "I did feel it, once, with the small early book," she admitted. "And I closed it quickly. But," she added, "it's not a reading I encourage."[56]

Atwood gave a copy of *Double Persephone* to poet Margaret Avison. In January of 1961 Atwood had published a very positive review of Avison's own first collection, *Winter Sun*, arguing that it was "a book not to be read, on any account, just once."[57] In response to Atwood's gift, Avison dropped a handwritten note through the door of 15 Berryman Avenue. It said: the "precision, full air, verbal coefficients, all delight a reader. Every smallest part belongs where it is and largeness comes of it . . . and so far I show no signs of tiring, however often I re-read, bless you." She signed off with "Best wishes for next year — and may your voice serve learned and vulgar alike forever amen —."[58]

As well as publishing the chapbook, Atwood had started to submit her writing to various literary magazines. Her first poem to appear in a noncollege publication was "Fruition"; it was published in the September 1959 issue of *Canadian Forum*. "Small Requiem" came out in the same magazine two months later. "Woman in the Subway" and two other poems appeared in the autumn 1961 issue of the *Tamarack Review*, which was edited by Robert Weaver. "Nothing has since matched the thrill of opening the acceptance letter," Atwood confided years later.[59]

⋆   ⋆   ⋆

Throughout these years, Atwood's commitment to her craft and vocation, as well as the sheer momentum she managed to maintain, were daunting to witness. There was a profound seriousness about her; it was as if, because she had chosen literature and the arts over the sciences as her family might have expected, she had to justify herself. This was a manifestation of the practical and responsible side to her nature: Margaret Atwood the professional writer. All this time, the poet in her was being driven to find a voice and a medium through which to express the ideas and observations of her perceiving self. Hence the enormous shifts in tone from the skits and parodies of *Acta* to the controlled eloquence of *Double Persephone*. Atwood was earnest, careful to purge her strong and quirky sense of humour, her sharp and incisive wit, from the early poems and stories. Although the literary productions of Shakesbeat Latweed were probes, tentative gestures towards incorporating humour into serious art, it was only with *The Edible Woman*, I think, that Atwood found

"Portrait of the Artist as a Young Cipher."

COURTESY *UNIVERSITY OF TORONTO MAGAZINE.*
REPRODUCED BY PERMISSION OF MARGARET ATWOOD.

a form for that successful integration: the contemporary social novel.

Not that Atwood didn't let off a bit of steam now and then. She found safety valves, safe outlets for humour and fun. *Acta* was one, of course. Another was drama: she participated in the Bob Revues, a series of dramatic sketches put on at Vic. Atwood never really commanded the kind of attention in these productions that, say, Dennis Lee did. His *Mushroom Malady*, the Bob Revue of 1962, was a highlight of the series.[60] Rather, Atwood was part of the team. Her involvement was informal; she was performing a kind of pleasant community service. She roped her friend Peter Pearson into the act and wrote the lyrics for a number of the songs, such as those that were part of *The Big F* in 1959. In this production she played "a young poetess" in the number "Portrait of a Poet as a Young Goat." Her drawing talents were put to good use (she provided sketches and cover designs for a number of the play leaflets — for *The Pirates of Penzance* in 1959, for *Epicene; Or, The Silent Woman*, for *The Mikado*, and for *The Yeomen of the Guard* in 1961). The dramatic roles she played were secondary. She performed the role of "Specksy" in the 1959 skit *Hilda*, for instance, and played "Lady Haughty" (collegiate president) in *Epicene*.

Her real outlet for humour, apart from the spoofs of Shakesbeat Latweed, was the comic strips she had begun to draw. But it was not until the 1970s, when she was drawing a comic strip series for *This Magazine* under the name "Bart Gerrard," that this hobby gained momentum and credibility. By the time Atwood drew *Portrait of the Artist as a Young Cipher* in 1977, a comic strip about her years at Vic, her ability to develop irony through the juxtaposition of word and image had become sophisticated. This strip reflects the powerful influence of Ronald Searle's *Portrait of the Artist as a Young Rake*; but the humour, the incisiveness of the observation, and the precision of the irony are vintage Atwood.

4

Growing Concerns About Nature

ATWOOD'S EARLIEST WORK reflects a number of concerns that have remained central to her oeuvre: a profound respect for the natural world, a commitment to Canadian culture, and a firm belief in the rights of the individual. In her work, such concerns can be traced in the themes of nature's triumph over civilization, Canadian nationalism, and feminism. They emerge from Atwood's own experience as well as the times in which she has lived.

Atwood's love of the natural world, of the wilderness, is quite obviously rooted in her childhood. During her early university years, however, Atwood worked each summer as a camp counsellor; and the experience linked her respect for the wilderness with a growing social conscience.

*   *   *

Those of us who inhabit Canada's colder regions by necessity lead a double existence: we have a winter life and a summer life, marked by differences in clothing and attitude. "Canadians really appreciate summer," a friend who had come to Toronto from Florida commented to me recently. Of course he's right. Canadians relish those few short months when the air finally warms. Each year a human migration occurs: Torontonians go north on the Victoria Day weekend in May and come south again on the Labour Day weekend at the beginning of September. Atwood's childhood was exceptional not because she went north but because she went farther north than most and for longer than most.

The destinations of these ritual journeys vary: Muskoka (relatively luxurious, with flagpoles and covered slips for the boats), Georgian Bay (rocky, open water), or Haliburton and the Kawarthas (smaller lakes, not so posh). Some vacationers head for the more remote areas where canoes outnumber motorboats: Algonquin Park (no electricity, no loud motors), Killarney, Temagami. The area in which Atwood spent her childhood, near Témiscaming, was at the northeast tip of all these points, deep inside a world of canoes and kerosene lamps. But there's a common vocabulary to all of cottage country, and it became very clear to Atwood when she taught Canadian literature in Alabama. Some words completely baffled her students, words that were common currency in Ontario: "blackfly," "loon," "portage," "Wendigo."[1] Although most Ontarians could do without the blackfly (which plagues cottage country in May and early June), a summer without the graceful loon and its plaintive cry is, as Atwood writes, "unthinkable." In a short 1987 article decrying the onslaught of civilization and pollution, she asks, "but how do you tell that to people who don't know it because they've never had any to begin with?" The old song that goes "land of the silver birch / home of the beaver / where still the mighty moose wanders at will" was transformed in Atwood's article into

> Land of the septic tank,
> Home of the speedboat,
> Where still the four-wheel drive
> Wanders at will,
> Blue lake and tacky shore,
> I will return once more:
> Vroom-diddy-vroom-vroom
> Vroom-diddy-vroom-vroom
> Vroo-OO-oo-oom[2]

The north is in Atwood's blood. As a child, she travelled in the bush. As an adult, she continues to take these summer treks, often in the wilderness of Temagami. But another aspect of her northern experience was gained when she worked at summer camps in and around Haliburton, Ontario.

★   ★   ★

During grades 12 and 13, Atwood worked at the Sportsman's Show — an enormous trade show featuring camping, fishing, and hunting gear, which was held at downtown Toronto's CNE site. She handed out the arrows at a target-practice booth. This particular job inspired the comic scene in *Lady Oracle* where Joan Foster's enormous rump suffers the consequences of a bowman's bad aim. (For the record, no one ever shot an arrow into Atwood.)

Finishing grade 12, Atwood went to work at the Crippled Children's Camp (which provides the setting of "Training" in *Dancing Girls*). Graduating from grade 13, she took a job as a waitress at Camp Hurontario (the inspiration for "True Trash" in *Wilderness Tips*). Camp Hurontario, located on an island, was a pretty rugged place. Hot water was a rare commodity. Hurontario was a tripping camp: its staff taught campers how to canoe and portage, how to survive, and even enjoy, an extended trip.[3] Robert Fulford's characterization of Atwood — "Deep in her soul, Margaret Atwood is still a camp counsellor" — derives, in part, from her involvement with Camp Hurontario's production of a play called *The Tragedy of Moonblossom Smith*, in the course of which John Sewell performed a ballet number with four rolls of toilet paper on a broom. (For Fulford, of course, the incident is wonderful: John Sewell is part of Toronto lore; the absurdity is irresistible.)

Most of Atwood's camp capers took place at Camp White Pine in Haliburton, where she spent three summers. Here she met a crowd of people who, creative in their own right, would become lifelong friends and colleagues: among them, Charles Pachter, Rick Salutin (editor and writer), and Beryl Fox (known for her work on the fine television program *This Hour Has Seven Days* and the Vietnam documentary *The Mills of the Gods*). Another close friend, Rosalie Abella, now Madame Justice of the Supreme

Court of Ontario, was also at White Pine, but after Atwood had left. The two didn't meet until the 1970s.

Camp White Pine was and still is one of the largest children's summer camps in Canada. Situated about six kilometres west of Haliburton (or three hours north of Toronto) on Hurricane Lake, and run by Joe Kronick, it provided campers with programs in music, horseback riding, and a number of sports. Atwood was hired by White Pine because Kronick's wife, Doreen, had been the director of the Bennington Heights Community Centre when Atwood worked there. Doreen Kronick realized that Atwood's experience in the bush would equip her wonderfully to be a nature and campcraft counsellor; Atwood was someone who could deal with the insects, work well with the campers, and handle a canoe.

Wages for camp counsellors were, and still are, low: the attraction is the lakeside setting and the camaraderie. What keeps campers and staff coming back is a strong sense of community and tradition. Camp White Pine, where the "sun will always shine," has all of these attributes. Camp culture is part and parcel of Ontario culture. The raison d'être of summer camps is to instil in young campers — generally from urban centres — a healthy sense of fun, love and respect for the outdoors, and some basic skills. Each camp has its own emphasis: ecological awareness, for example, sports, arts. During Atwood's tenure, White Pine's emphasis, not surprisingly for a predominantly Jewish camp in the post-World War II era, was on community and political awareness. Social conscience.

One lovely tradition was the playing of subdued music just before sundown each Friday night as a way of ushering in the traditional Sabbath dinner. Atwood must have felt a bit out of place her first year at White Pine. She recalls:

> This was a reformed, liberal Jewish summer camp, and they hired a certain number of non-Jewish people every year to expose the children to them, because the children were from a quite rich area of Toronto which they never went out of and they just didn't see people who weren't Jewish, except

the cleaning ladies. One of the first things the seven-year-olds asked me was "Are you Jewish?" I said, "No." And they said, "Are you the cleaning lady?"[4]

The punch line here is a strong one, and it exaggerates the social and cultural distinctions, for Atwood quickly became part of the White Pine community and returned for the next two summers.

But Atwood was aware of the cultural issues that concerned the camp community, even when they were not discussed explicitly. With World War II a very recent memory, there were many open wounds. "In the '50s," Atwood remembers, "people didn't talk about the war or the concentration camps. . . . There was a man who peeled potatoes for the [White Pine] kitchen. He did nothing but peel potatoes. And he had a number on his arm. He was obviously a shell-shocked survivor that the camp had hired. Everybody knew he was there. Nobody talked about him. He was the 'forbidden man.' "[5]

*   *   *

When I met Joe Kronick in 1995, he spoke with well-deserved pride about his camp. It was founded in 1956. When Atwood arrived in 1959 there were already about 350 campers. For Kronick, Atwood is but one of many very talented White Pine "alums." Her contemporaries at White Pine, for example, included Mark Phillips (a CBC correspondent), Mickey Cohen (onetime deputy minister of finance and CEO of Molson Breweries), Jerry Grafstein (a senator), Marty Frieland (former dean of the University of Toronto Law School), Gerry Caplan (a political commentator), Arthur Pape (a human-rights advocate), as well as the close friends I have already mentioned — Salutin, Pachter, and Fox. Kronick seemed quite used to being asked about famous former campers. The next day, he was expecting a German film crew from Next Step Productions who were coming to film the camp for a documentary on Atwood.

Together, the Kronicks watched Atwood develop from the young girl who ran the puppet show on Saturday mornings at

Bennington Heights into a university student. Doreen Kronick mentioned that as a teenager Atwood was "always mature, beyond her years really," "capable," but "shy" to the point of awkwardness. Once Atwood found herself at White Pine, however, she began to blossom; as Joe Kronick explained this, his cupped hands mimicked the opening of a flower.[6] Camp White Pine played a large role in that development.

The camp served as backdrop for a summer romance between Atwood and a blond artist who did maintenance work around the camp property (he was an "older" man, being all of twenty-eight at the time). Camp White Pine also provided Atwood with some very practical lessons in child psychology. One, in particular, was still vivid in the minds of a number of the campers with whom I spoke. Each section of the camp was named after an exotic animal or bird. The Kiwis were the youngest campers, the eight-year-old boys. They were named after a bird that, as Joe Kronick says, "thinks it can fly but can't." Her first summer, Atwood was den mother (with Bernice Eisen) to this group of approximately ten little campers. Any counsellor obliged to deal with this age group will tell you about the disciplinary dilemmas that inevitably result. For Atwood, one such dilemma arose from the fact that there was no washroom in the cabin. Young campers, terrified of venturing outside in the dark in the middle of the night, were inclined towards accidents. One morning, Atwood discovered, on the middle of the floor, the remains of "a major accident — a number two." Not knowing quite what to do, she went to speak to the late Dick Lehrman (at that time a senior counsellor) about it. He went straight to the cabin and approached the occupant of each bed individually, quietly suggesting that he should be mature enough to tell the truth, to confess. That is, Dick made confession sound like a good thing — the mature thing. So, quite naturally, four Kiwis owned up (four, at least, in Salutin's account; all of them in other accounts). According to Salutin, the penitent campers wanted "to be respected." But there was another lesson to be gleaned here: counsellors aren't the only ones who understand child psychology — children do too.[7]

The next summer, after her second year of university, Atwood was given the job of nature and campcraft instructor. "In practice," she has written, "this meant identifying squashed caterpillars and stepped-on mushrooms, and teaching small boys to light fires with one match."[8] "[T]he kids would catch [small creatures] and they would come up to me and say, 'Look what I caught,' and there it would be, all over their hand. I spent a lot of time rescuing creatures from kids who clutched them too tightly."[9] "Peggy Nature," as she was called, presided over the old icehouse that, once the horse manure had been cleaned out of it, served as the headquarters for the nature program.[10] Pachter recalls that the building was a "shack in a swampy field. Really quite sordid. When it was wet, your boots would squish in. [Atwood] looked a bit like Jane Goodall: rubber boots, shorts, maybe even a machete at the side, 'shmata' on her head. She curled her finger to me and said that I would be a 'test.' I was made to hold a toad so the kids would see I wouldn't get a wart."[11]

"She was as happy as a pig in a pile of manure," says a beaming Joe Kronick, remembering that summer.[12] After so many summers in the bush, Atwood must have been at ease with the "Peggy Nature" persona. The stories she has written about this time support the notion that she was truly in her element at White Pine. Typically, though, these stories also suggest that the persona Atwood revealed to the community at large — that of a cautious young girl with an "air of nerdish innocence"[13] — concealed a real and rather impish prankster quite capable of holding her own in the camp atmosphere. Setting the scene in a 1991 anecdotal piece called "Capering," Atwood describes White Pine in a way that Joe Kronick did not when speaking to me. Her perspective is supported, however, both by accounts I have heard from other campers and by the late-night laughter that would drift across the lake from White Pine to the summer cottage my family used to rent. "White Pine," writes Atwood, "was a co-educational Jewish camp, run by a man named Jo-Jo Kronick, who was something of a kibitzer himself, and took on the entire male staff every summer in a ketchup-and-mustard squeeze-bottle fight in the dining room; so he could hardly object to the occasional prank pulled by the staff on one another. The only rules were: i) no murders, and ii) the campers were not to be involved."[14] Atwood goes on to describe a prank she pulled with partner-in-crime Beryl Horses (Beryl Fox, then the riding instructor). It involved sneaking into the trip cabin where the male tripping staff lay sound asleep, gluing their shoes to the floor, filling them with horse manure, covering the door handle with shaving cream, and then, just for good measure, spreading the remaining horse manure on the porch. Still, this isn't the real prank. From Atwood's perspective, the ultimate prank was getting away with the caper: she managed to maintain an air of "nerdish innocence"; she pulled off an excellent "wakened-from-slumber crabby act" that saved her from the closer scrutiny of a rather smelly and angry posse of trip leaders. So the next day Peggy Nature was left in peace while Beryl Horses (a suspect, presumably, because of the horse manure element of the crime, if nothing else) had raw egg rubbed into her hair and was forced to take a dip in the lake. Atwood ends the anecdote with a farewell note: "Now you know, folks: it was me, all along."[15] Whether or not Atwood really did pull it off only Beryl Fox knows ("'Course I did," wrote Atwood in my margin, "ask Beryl!"[16]); but she certainly executed the prank successfully in print.

There are two more lessons about camp culture to be learned from Atwood's story. First, campers don't tattle. Beryl Fox knew that. Second, campers are pranksters: it's a source of pride. Peggy Nature knew that. But, of course, it is Margaret Atwood the writer and not Peggy Nature the counsellor who knew how to transform a "nerdish innocent" into a champion prankster. The transformation is reminiscent of those performed by the narrator mother in the *Bluebeard's Egg* story "Significant Moments in the Life of My Mother." She describes herself as simultaneously shy and courageous: double.

5

A Canadian
Nationalist Abroad

Harvard is sort of like anchovies. An acquired taste.
— Margaret Atwood[1]

CANADIAN NATIONALISM is perhaps the most obvious cause célèbre of Atwood's early fiction. Ironically, it was prompted by her time studying in the United States. In the fall of 1961, she left Toronto and travelled to Cambridge, Massachusetts. There, at Radcliffe, she would do graduate work in literature supported by a Woodrow Wilson fellowship in the first year and a Canada Council grant in the second. The attractions for Atwood were a professor named Jerome Buckley, an expert in Victorian literature, her chosen field; the spectacular Widener Library; and the prestige of the institution. Naïvely, and not surprisingly, Atwood expected to find at this institution the same supportive and exhilarating environment she had found at Vic — only more so. This was Radcliffe, after all, and she was bright and ambitious.

The reality was quite different. As it turned out, the years Atwood spent in Cambridge tested her staying power, her ability to see things through to the bitter end. Compared to Vic, Radcliffe was mired in tradition, and the ambience was so cold that it often felt quite hostile. Compared to Toronto, Boston was dangerous. ("These were the days of the 'Boston Strangler'" recalls Atwood's roommate, Mary Irving Campbell.[2]) Compared to Canada, the United States was, for Atwood, too familiar to be exotic and too unfamiliar to be comfortable.

These inconsistencies led first to disappointment and then to a growing resolve about who she was and who and what she wanted to be. If Atwood entered Radcliffe expecting to pursue an academic career as a way of supporting and nurturing her writing, then she left Harvard — for Radcliffe had become part of Harvard by 1963 — firmly convinced that she would be first a writer and specifically a *Canadian* writer. But, coming from the Atwood-Killam clan, she was compelled to finish any project she had started: despite her remarkable early success as a writer, she continued to work doggedly on her doctoral dissertation. Years later, after she had tackled and completed works more closely related to the direction of her life and writerly ambitions, and after she had won Canada's top literary honour for *The Circle Game*, she would still write letters to her dissertation typist — making corrections, rearranging chapters, planning the completed thesis. Ultimately, the thesis was never finished to her satisfaction, but it wasn't for lack of trying. Her supervisor, Professor Jerome Buckley, explains that "her rapidly accelerating career as poet and novelist soon diverted her from the routine of critical scholarship, and in any case before long she had acquired so many honorary doctorates that an academic Ph.D. must have seemed superfluous."[3] The manuscript that finally emerged from her time at Harvard was a fictional one. It became a watershed in her literary career. *The Handmaid's Tale*, a dystopian fiction set in an imaginary and futuristic New England, was a crucial element in Atwood's transformation into an international best-selling writer. With that novel, she laid her ambivalent feelings about Harvard and Cambridge to rest in the same way that she purged similar feelings about her childhood with *Cat's Eye*.

★   ★   ★

Buckley is known for his critical book on the bildungsroman, the coming-of-age novel. The best-known examples of this genre are Charles Dickens's *Great Expectations* and James Joyce's

A Portrait of the Artist as a Young Man. During Atwood's time, Buckley taught a large undergraduate lecture class (of 350 to 500 students) on the bildungsroman, which covered "Dickens through to Joyce and Woolf."[4] When I contacted Professor Buckley, I expected him to tell me that Atwood, as a graduate student, had been a teaching assistant for that course — which he did. Technically, though, as a Canadian, Atwood was not eligible to work in the United States, even as a teaching assistant. She was, however, a student in Buckley's graduate course on Victorian literature and in his Tennyson seminar. Her own novels reveal her engagement with Buckley's ideas.

Precisely because *Cat's Eye* and some of Atwood's other novels utilize the bildungsroman form as Buckley defined it in his important critical text *Season of Youth* and his Harvard lectures during the 1960s and 1970s, I asked him if he saw any traces of his approach in Atwood's creative work. In many ways, of course, my question was rather awkward for him to answer, but his response was eloquent and generous, in keeping with the tone of his correspondence with Atwood over the years: "[Atwood] may, as you say, have drawn some notion of the scope of the 'novel-of-development' from the Bildungsromane she taught, but of course, [she] has such a fertile imagination of her own that it is hard to say what themes or techniques she has borrowed."[5]

While at Victoria College relationships between faculty and students tended to be strong and open, at Harvard such interactions were more formal. Buckley was unusual in that he and his wife would welcome students into their home. Each year at American Thanksgiving, for example, the Buckleys would invite foreign students for a traditional turkey dinner. As a Canadian, of course, Atwood celebrated that holiday earlier in the season and would be unlikely to travel home for this long weekend. Like other students from more distant countries, she would find herself in Cambridge on an important American holiday weekend with no holiday to celebrate.

A holiday dinner — actually based on several such gatherings at her own home in Toronto over which her professor father presided — is the basis of a scene in *Cat's Eye*. It is a Christmas dinner during which a discussion about the cultural ritual of turkey eating takes place between the father of young Elaine (the protagonist) and his guest, a foreign student from India by the name of Bannerji. Elaine feels a kinship with the gentle Mr. Bannerji; she senses his unhappiness and his displacement, which mirror her own. The seeds of this compassion were planted in Cambridge.

⋆   ⋆   ⋆

Foreign students don't always come off so well in Atwood's work, though. Christine, the protagonist of "The Man from Mars" (collected in *Dancing Girls*), finds the awkward persistence of one male student positively threatening. At different points in the story, both Christine and "the man from Mars" lose sight of the other's humanity. That sense of threat — urban fear examined from different angles, as in "Rape Fantasies" (also from *Dancing Girls*), with something akin to fascination — emerges in the fiction Atwood wrote after leaving Cambridge. *The Handmaid's Tale*, of course, is an extended exploration of this idea.

Learning to recognize the threat inherent in the American urban environment for what it is — fear — became an integral part of Atwood's Harvard experience. The transition from Toronto of the late 1950s, where the streets were safe at night, to Cambridge of the 1960s was dramatic. The mundane reality of the threat that thrives in an urban environment struck home one day when Atwood was in the bath and saw "a hand appear through an open window, grope around and then disappear."[6] In fact, the fire escape at Atwood's dorm — a Radcliffe women's residence at 6 Appian Way — attracted at least two peeping Toms, one of whom Atwood helped to corner and against whom she eventually testified in court. Writes Mary Irving Campbell, "I think part of that adventure is re-captured in *Bodily Harm*."[7] Certainly, a sense of threat permeates the novel.

The Appian Way women's residence (since replaced by the Education Building) was a large, white, clapboard affair approached by brick sidewalks. Atwood would climb to her garret room by clinging — literally — to a rope that served as a makeshift handrail.[8] The building was home to about fifteen female residents, all of whom shared a kitchen. Atwood and Mary Irving cooked and ate meals together that year and shared a bathroom, on the third floor, with "two vivacious bio-chemists . . . who were studying herpes." Mary Irving Campbell remarks that "those were the Timothy Leary days at Harvard and on the second floor at 6 Appian Way were two psychology students who were attending LSD sessions. Jim Watson, who won the Nobel Prize for DNA discoveries, lived in the house next door." As a roommate, Campbell found Atwood "ideal": "quiet, studious, orderly, private, but also lots of fun, witty beyond compare; a great conversationalist and deep thinker. . . . She could concoct hair-raising ghost stories and spin them out in a most dramatic and fearful oration."[9]

Atwood remained faithful to David Donnell, her fiancé back home (the young poet who had helped Atwood to print *Double Persephone*), and so her social life during the first while at Radcliffe was limited. She led the life of a typical graduate student: procrastinating when it came to finishing her papers; staying up late and taking "no-nods" when deadlines were looming so large that they couldn't be avoided. The difference between the average student's periods of procrastination and Atwood's was that hers were productive: she wrote poetry to avoid writing term papers. Notes Campbell, "I am not surprised that she has become a successful writer since her commitment, drive and ambition were quite evident. And enormous talent. I was aware of her early feminism, her patriotic spirit and the fact she would jump out of bed in the middle of the night to write a poem."[10]

Another 6 Appian Way resident was the late Ilsa Sedriks, a student from Latvia. She had lovely red hair and red petticoats — the kind of red that is vivid enough to be shocking. (That hair would one day end up on Joan Foster, the protagonist of Atwood's *Lady Oracle*.) Ilsa and Atwood took a weekly tutorial in the men's residence, and one day the porter there almost refused them entry, so convinced was he that Ilsa, and presumably her companion, were ladies of the night. The red petticoat must have peeped out from beneath the hem of Ilsa's skirt.[11]

Mary Irving was from Winston-Salem, North Carolina, and had a thick "accent — the kind you could cut with a knife." The daughter of a liberal lawyer who had actually run for local office on an integrationist platform, she was planning to teach at a black college in the South after graduating. Having acquired an English degree from Duke University, she had come to Radcliffe to do graduate work in fine arts. Wrote Atwood, "Harvard has a top star in Art History and Criticism, but there's only one practising artist on the staff. The feeling one gets about Boston, in general, is that although there is a lot of dead, pickled and preserved art around, there is not much going *on* here. We learn about it but we're not supposed to do it: sort of like a class in Comparative Anatomy!"[12] In November of 1962, Mary Irving was married in her hometown of Winston-Salem. Atwood flew down for the traditional Southern wedding, held in an Episcopal church. "Peggy was delightful," says Mary Irving Campbell. She "wrote all the toasts for the rehearsal dinner and seemed to enjoy all the Southern brouhaha of weddings."[13] Campbell's parents also took Atwood to a tobacco auction, so that she could "experience life in Winston-Salem." But Atwood's own engagement to David Donnell and their long-distance relationship were broken off before May of 1962.[14]

★　　★　　★

Students in the graduate program at Harvard began by taking courses grouped loosely around the categories of English and American literature. These courses prepared them for five comprehensive exams: three in English literature, one in American, and one identify-and-give-the-significance-of kind of exam that tested coverage. The students were also required to write three foreign-language exams (Atwood did French, German, and, from 1965 to 1967, Latin). Finally, they wrote a doctoral dissertation. As a Canadian Atwood didn't have much background in American literature, so she took three American courses: The American Puritans and The American Revolutionary Period with Alan Heimert; and The American Romantics with Perry Miller. Her

English-literature courses included The Eighteenth-Century Sentimental Novel; The Metaphysical Poets; a Keats seminar with David Perkins; a Tennyson seminar and a Victorian-literature course with Jerome Buckley; and a Victorian-humour course with Harry Levin.[15]

Atwood was surprised at a certain double standard she found in existence at Harvard. In Victorian Humour, a course she took in her first year, there was a break during the class period. The female students would serve tea and cookies.[16] In itself, this ritual could be put down to social convention, but there were several even more substantial discrepancies between the way in which male and female students were treated in the institution. For instance, women weren't allowed into the Lamont Library, where all the modern poetry and records were kept. "So," comments Atwood,

> I always felt a little like a sort of wart or wen on the great male academic skin. I felt as if I was there on sufferance. Harvard, you know, didn't hire women to teach in it, so the male professors were all very nice. We ladies were no threat. There was a joke among the woman students that the best way to pass your orals was to stuff a pillow up your dress, because they would all be so terrified of having parturition take place on the Persian rug that they would just ask you your name and give you a pass.[17]

In her second year, Atwood took a course called The Classical Tradition in American Literature, with Perry Miller. Here, again, she was acutely aware that her gender put her at a disadvantage. After all, she was learning that between 1630 and 1900 there were only two women writers worth their salt in American literature: Ann Bradstreet and Emily Dickinson. No wonder when she told her fellow women graduate students of her writerly ambitions they were shocked — not because she planned to be a writer (that alone would shock Atwood's fellow Canadians) but rather that she was a *woman* who planned to be a writer. Explains Atwood, "It was like saying you were going to pee in the men's washroom: either daring or in bad taste."[18]

However, the fact that Atwood noticed this significant gap in the canon (that is, the virtual absence of women writers) and understood its implications owes much to the central thesis of Perry Miller's lectures. Atwood was becoming increasingly aware of the political nature of literature: words have power, and it matters who speaks them and to whom. For this reason, she dedicated *The Handmaid's Tale* to Perry Miller.

> The classical tradition in America is political. I studied this with Perry Miller. It was a big eye-opener to me. But from the Puritans on down, practically until the '50s, there was a great deal of what would now be called "political." *Moby Dick* was a political book. Thoreau, Lord knows. Whitman. You know, the classics. You can't say that those had no political interests, no vision. And what do we mean by "political"? What we mean is how people relate to a power structure and vice versa. And this is really all we mean by it. We may mean also some idea of participating in the structure or changing it. But the first thing we mean is how is this individual in society? How do the forces of society interact with this person?[19]

This statement, made by Atwood in an interview, serves as an extremely concise summary of the politics of *The Handmaid's Tale*.

★   ★   ★

Perry Miller's course, as well as those taught by Alan Heimert on the American Puritans and the American Revolutionary period, also stirred in Atwood feelings of nationalism. She wrote a paper on Charles Mair's dramatic verse *Tecumseh*. (Which, presumably, was unfamiliar to Perry Miller — right period, wrong country.) Atwood got a B, as much, I suspect, for her choice of topic as for the quality of the paper.[20] Atwood was becoming indignant about all the American work she was studying. "[I]f one can study this in a university, I thought, why not Canadian literature?";

"(you must understand that at that time Canadian literature was simply not taught in high schools and universities in Canada)."[21] Gradually, then, Atwood was developing a sense of her place of origin, prompted by the lack of awareness of Canada evident in those around her. It was the pre-Vietnam period. The Americans she met thought of Canada as "the blank area north of the map where the bad weather came from."[22] Consciously seeking out differences between America, a place that in climate and landscape is very similar to Canada, and her native land, Atwood started thinking seriously about Canada as having a shape and a culture of its own. This search would ultimately result in her first book of nonfiction, *Survival*, and lead her to be instrumental in the Canadian quest for a national cultural identity.

⋆ ⋆ ⋆

Always, always, though, Margaret Atwood the writer was reading, and scribbling, and observing, and thinking. Finding pockets of time in which to write. Her Radcliffe roommate recalls how Atwood would leap out of bed to write a poem. She also remembers, in 1962, helping Atwood to lug an "enormous suitcase packed with books to the [Massachusetts Transit Authority Station] so she could catch a plane (or train?) to New York City and stay in a YWCA all alone. The suitcase wasn't her only piece of luggage, but certainly the heaviest; we had to stop every 100 yards to rest from the exertion. She could not be discouraged from that adventure by any words of caution and apprehension I could think of."[23] The whole idea of such a trip — the young graduate student travelling to spend a weekend alone with her thoughts and her books — is the subject of one of Atwood's stories: "Hair Jewellery." The story (collected in *Dancing Girls*) is set in Salem, Massachusetts, where the protagonist spends a few melancholy days researching a paper on Nathaniel Hawthorne before returning to Boston. (Salem, of course, site of the witch trials, was a place where someone like Hawthorne's Hester Prynne might have been condemned to wear that odious scarlet letter and where Atwood's own ancestor — Mary Webster — might have been hanged). In such a setting it's not surprising that the story's protagonist begins to feel distinctly disempowered long before she finds evidence that her love is, as she had feared, unrequited.

Throughout Atwood's time in Cambridge, her mind turned to poetry. Poems from this period, and ideas about poetry, scribbled on pieces of paper may be found among the Atwood Papers. One handwritten note dated 29 October 1962 is of particular interest to those interested in the development of Atwood's poetry. Atwood clearly wrote it to herself, and it outlines certain ideas about the poets she was reading and the relation of their work to her own. The page is headed with the words "My Poetic Principles." It records her thoughts on the difference between horizontal and vertical poetry: Daryl Hine, she notes, is both; Gwendolyn MacEwen, vertical; Milton Acorn, horizontal. It contains observations on poetic technique — "the iamb is still basic for lyric poetry" — and the use of the arbitrary stanza. Jotted in shorthand. Vehemently honest. Here, as in the poetry she wrote at the time, Atwood renounces both end rhyme, on the one hand, and the lack of rhyme, on the other.[24] Then, as now, Atwood's poetry often enacted on the technical level the very conflict it describes: between control and lack of control, between control and discomfort over its practical and ethical implications.

Four-year-old Margaret
Atwood with the day's catch

PHOTO BY CARL ATWOOD.
COURTESY MARGARET ATWOOD.

The Three Belles.
From left to right: Joyce,
Margaret, Kathleen Killam

PHOTOGRAPHER UNKNOWN.
COURTESY MARGARET ATWOOD.

The siblings together in the early 1980s.
From left to right: Ruth, Harold, Margaret Atwood

The Atwood family with a friend (Lloyd Sharpe), on a picnic (1945)

Margaret Atwood at age twelve (1951)

Margaret Atwood at age thirteen (1952), Niagara Falls

It Was Fascination, I Know (1968)

Déjeuner sur l'herbe. *From left to right*:
Margaret Atwood, Graeme Gibson, Charles Pachter (1988)

Margaret Atwood bending over a campfire (1971)

A quiet moment: Margaret Atwood reading at her country retreat (1971)

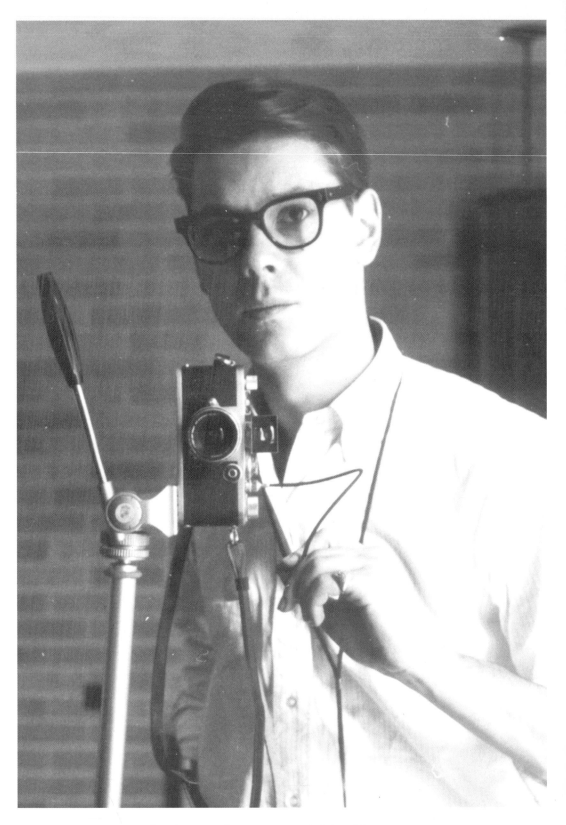

The photographer, James Ford, behind his camera

6

Feminism

THE PRECISE ORIGIN of Atwood's feminism is hard to pin down. But certainly the strength of the Killam women had a lot to do with her starting premise: women should be respected as capable individuals. Harvard had something to do with it as well. Serving cookies. Not getting into the right libraries. And then there were the times themselves. The times, so the song goes, they were "a-changing." Feminist ideas were in the air in the 1950s and 1960s, a time when social convention was holy writ for some while others saw it as begging to be challenged. Still others took both approaches at the same time: think of the Smothers Brothers, two comedians in tidy suits and well-brushed hair taking aim at the establishment. But people had not begun to use the term "feminism" — yet.

★   ★   ★

After her first year at Harvard, Atwood returned home and found a job as a cashier in a Toronto restaurant. It was the summer of 1962. She worked in the coffeeshop of what is now the Venture Inn on Avenue Road, just north of Bloor. She didn't last long. The job description was predictable: milkshake making, coffee serving, filling counter and room-service orders (which were communicated via intercom to the short-order cook). Remembers Atwood, "Only an octopus would have been able to do all these things at once, even if it knew how to work the cash-register, which I did not." An MA from Radcliffe had not prepared her for this.

Immediately I was caught in the Lunchtime from Hell. Milkshakes and spilled coffee puddled on the counter. My hair unravelled. A line of irate customers formed behind the cash register, waiting for their change, while I fruitlessly pushed buttons and the little drawer shot in and out, locking itself at will. From time to time my boss would stop by with regular customers to show me off. "She has an MA," he would say proudly, as I frazzled around like a trapped Junebug, shedding hairpins, dripping cloth or filthy plate in hand.[1]

This younger, Erma Bombeck-like protagonist shows up, of course, in *Lady Oracle*. Remember Joan Foster, working as a waitress, trapped by a marriage proposal? Atwood found herself in a similar predicament with the short-order cook, whose intercom messages became increasingly amorous. Seriously so. He was Greek and had enough money to open a restaurant. Atwood's command of the English language and her cashiering abilities attracted him. "Our religions are different," she told the cook. "That's all right," he replied, "You can change yours." The conversation took place over lunch.[2]

The final straw for Atwood came when swarms of loud men in burgundy velveteen hats took over the Venture Inn. Shriners conventioneers. Phoning down for ice buckets. "I quit," remarks Atwood in her article "Case of the Crazed Cashiers," "taking away with me one gravy-stained white dress and an enduring respect for cashiers."[3]

She spent the rest of the summer working as a "checker" for grade-13 examinations. At that time, students graduating from high school took a whole series of exams; the scores determined their university placement. The stakes were incredibly high: if a student was deathly ill on exam day and, therefore, scored poorly, then she or he could take the exam again, but the final mark would still be an aggregate of the two scores. Consequently, the exams were marked *and* checked. For Atwood, this task of checking was an exercise in precision. In that sense, it prepared her for her next summer job.

In the summer of 1963, after two years of graduate school, she returned to Toronto to look for work. She planned to take a year off school, earn some money, and write. Clearly overqualified for the jobs she was applying for, Atwood was, as she once quipped, refused work by some of the best companies: Bell Canada, McClelland and Stewart, and Oxford University Press.[4] She was hired by Canadian Facts Marketing, a firm that designed and carried out consumer surveys — about one hundred each month. Her job was to word the survey instructions so that both the person asking the questions and the person responding to them understood what was involved. "One of my early jobs," she explains, "was taking those recondite, verbose market-research interviews written by psychologists and translating them into language that the average person interviewed could understand. So it was breaking down 'psychologese' into simpler units that could be understood by somebody not a professional in the field."[5] Atwood was quick at the job and displayed a certain flair, a sense of humour, while performing it. She would add instructions to the information manuals: "pay yourself 25 cents when you reach this point," she interjected in an effort to encourage field-workers to read the instructions and to see if any of them actually did.[6]

This was the heyday of domestic innovation, the era of Tang and Pop Tarts. Atwood's boss, Mary Sims, and her team were committed to thinking up ways to test these new products, allowing the least room for disaster. But, inevitably, despite their best efforts, some awful things did happen. Flies in the cereal, for example. Atwood drew on her Canadian Facts Marketing experience in writing her first published novel, *The Edible Woman* (which appeared in 1969), but if those marketing disasters were laughable in the fictional world she created, they were not quite so much fun to handle in real life. "It was a job," said fellow employee Chris Lloyd, "and it was pretty intense."[7] Lloyd, who hired and trained the surveyors, and Atwood were hired at the same time, along with Bev Hunter, who costed the questionnaires. All three were well-educated, intelligent women who would develop a lasting friendship.

A classic story about this summer of surveys is told by both Atwood and Hunter, although both — wisely — refuse to supply a name. Hunter worked beside another woman at Canadian Facts — a blonde, gum-chewing woman whom she describes as being more "with it" than the rest of the team. "She wore that pink, pink lipstick," Hunter explains, "the kind worn by the Barbie-doll women in the James Bond films. You know, that mauvish, silvery pink." (I did know — exactly.) When Atwood arrived on the scene, this unnamed lady passed a quick judgement. "I don't think the new girl is too bright," she said.[8]

"I practically fell off the chair," says Hunter, laughing. "I thought Peggy was utterly fascinating, with those tight, tight corkscrew curls all over her head — she reminded me of a character in an old children's book of mine . . . Amelia Anne Stiggins. Those amazing blue eyes. And her skin, like warm rose petals." Gradually, it became clear that Atwood and Hunter, though eight years apart in age (Hunter had four children ranging in age from thirteen years to six months by the time she came to work at Canadian Facts), shared a certain attitude towards life, despite their diverse situations and experiences. "She was the first person I had met in my entire life," remarks Hunter, "who came from the same precise ethical base as I."[9]

Atwood, as described by Hunter, stood out from the others at Canadian Facts; she appeared to be someone who was very "contained." "She had this little desk — nothing lavish about this hole-in-the-wall, let me tell you," Hunter adds with a note of genuine fondness, "with a sign saying 'out to lunch.' That meant: 'don't approach'; 'don't talk.' When she took the sign down, people could come and talk. She was incredibly focused. There were times you could talk to her and times when you couldn't. When she was working she was absolutely engaged in what she was doing."[10]

Presumably, Atwood put that little sign up when she was rushing to complete her assigned task for the day. She could usually get through it all in a few hours, which left her with hours of free time. Recalls Mary Sims:

At such times she would pull out a paper-back and read it. This terrified me — I was afraid that Mr. Severs, who acted as Office Manager when he was not wearing his Accounting or Tabulation hat, would walk past, see her, and decide she was supernumerary. Then I'd lose the fastest and most literate help I'd ever imagined. I tried, "Why don't you help out with checking the interviewers' work when you run out of stuff to do?" But no, she said she didn't like doing that kind of thing (who could blame her?). I finally told her that I didn't mind her reading if she ran out of work, but please make it *look* as if she was working at something, and somehow she managed it.[11]

This innocent masquerade suited the young writer very well, because she was able to spend her downtime working on a novel. Reading paperbacks looked too much like slacking off, but typing looked like work. Interestingly, Atwood wasn't writing *The Edible Woman*; rather, she was drafting her first novel, "set north of Lake Superior. It was very Existential. People drowned."[12] "Up in the Air So Blue," as it was titled, has never been published. It was

set near a swamp. . . . There was a lot of marsh gas in it. People committed suicide and also drowned. . . . I paid a friend of mine to type it for me, since I could not touch-type, a handicap I acquired by having foolishly taken home economics instead of typing in school. (My zippers are a marvel. My punctuation is hell.) My friend said my book was "very mature," but nobody wanted to publish it; probably just as well. However, I was downcast at the time.[13]

By 1965, Atwood had recognized this early novel's flaws. "I would not want it published now without considerable alteration," she wrote to literary agent Hope Leresche. "It was my first literary effort . . . and was written with strain — which is evident in the prose."[14] Atwood submitted this mature appraisal after she had received Leresche's own frank summary of reader responses to the novel and after she had written her next novel.

Summarizing the readers' reports, Leresche's comments on "Up in the Air So Blue" were mixed. She praised the portrait of Mrs. Hunter, as well as the intensity of the novel — the way its "interwoven" imagery and "tightly packed" plot ("such as it was"), together with flash backs that "built up with increasing tempo," worked towards a crescendo. But Leresche also pointed to moments when the momentum of the novel was broken — for instance, when the "castration theme" seemed a bit too "clinical" or "overt" — and argued that the opening scenes did not adequately grasp the reader's attention. The novel's title, she added, was not really "in keeping with the seriousness of the book."[15]

The manuscript was ultimately rejected by both the Ryerson and the Macmillan publishing houses. In the spring of 1965, Atwood was taken out to lunch at the Canadian Pacific hotel in Vancouver — "the one with the green roof," Atwood remembers — by one of the editors at Macmillan. "If only you *had* changed the ending," he began.[16]

> He was an ex-military man, a colonel, I do believe. He asked if I could change the ending, because everybody found it too gloomy. I said I could not. The ending, by the way, involved the heroine and hero on the roof and the heroine deciding whether or not to push the hero off, and in 1963 this was considered quite strange. So he asked if I would change it, and I said no — and he leaned across the table and patted my hand and said, "Is there anything we can do?" Making the autobiographical assumption.[17]

The wrong autobiographical assumption.

7

The Right Balance

IN ATWOOD'S LIFE, the business of being a writer has been an intricate balancing act between obeying inner voices and fulfilling professional obligations. Atwood is deadly serious about her writing, but she manages not to take herself too seriously, and during the early 1960s she managed to maintain a precarious balance between her allegiance to the muse and the normal demands of life for a working woman in her twenties.

★   ★   ★

This balancing act began with her very successful novel *The Edible Woman*, which itself achieved a fine balance between weighty ideas and wit. In many ways, the novel was a watershed for Atwood. The "strain" that she had noted in "Up in the Air So Blue" had disappeared. *The Edible Woman*, by contrast, relies heavily on plot and character for its satire. Written in 1965 and published in 1969, *The Edible Woman* was set in Toronto at a time when it just wasn't *done* to set a novel in Toronto. All well-read Canadians knew that great stories took place elsewhere. Atwood knew this too, and, because she was young and ambitious, she changed the names of the neighbourhoods — slightly. Later, when she had gained more confidence in herself and the Canadian literary tradition in which she wrote, she would refuse to make such concessions.

As I have said, Atwood turned to her experiences at Canadian Facts Marketing — where she worked from the summer of 1963 until the spring of 1964 — to find inspiration for the setting of *The Edible Woman*. In the novel, the company is called Seymour Surveys. Canadian Facts was located at the corner of Bay and Wellington, today the heart of Toronto's business district. Then it was an area in transition. Its small shops — tailor shops and clothing stores, mostly — were starting to be ripped down. Skyscrapers sprouted in their place. Atwood and her coworkers — Bev Hunter and Chris Lloyd — watched as a hole was dug for the Toronto Dominion bank tower, the city's first skyscraper and still one of its highest. Debate over the newly minted Canadian flag was raging, and Lloyd remembers that Toronto Dominion erected the red-and-white banner on the building site before the tower even went up.[1]

The Canadian Facts field office consisted of about twenty staff members. Mrs. Mary Sims, the boss, sat at one end of the room. Atwood, Lloyd, and Hunter sat nearby in their own cubicles, and at the far end a number of older ladies transcribed survey responses by hand. At break times, Atwood, Lloyd, and Hunter would leave the building by the side entrance on Bay and nip across the street to the Mercury Café (which was next door to the Press Club). Here Lloyd would quibble over the raisins in her Danish, much as Lucy does in the novel.

Atwood was at Canadian Facts for a number of important marketing breakthroughs (remember those Pop Tarts?) and disasters (the early version exploded). She was there for the testing of canned rice pudding (in three "grisly flavours") and "the bran breakfast cereal with raisins in it." This cereal had "so many squashed flies masquerading as raisins" that "sharp-eyed and irate testers" kept turning them in.[2] Notably absent from Atwood's description is the brand name of the pudding.

The link between life and art in *The Edible Woman* is important because it is both obvious and indicative of Atwood's use of character and setting. Protagonist Marian McAlpine's work environment is taken almost directly from Canadian Facts: the glass cubicles, the ladies working at one end, the office manager at the other, the men upstairs. And the novel's characters (with, I believe, the exception of Millie) reflect aspects of Atwood's

Canadian Facts colleagues. Chris Lloyd, for example, says, "I think I am Lucy. With the painted nails. Picking the raisins out of the danishes."[3] Emmy seems to have some of Bev Hunter in her. And Mary Sims declares, "I am Mrs. Bogue in *The Edible Woman*."[4] What they all know, however, is that although *aspects* of the novel's characters are borrowed from real life, they are ultimately characters — figures created by Atwood to be used in the service of a larger narrative point. (Atwood's critics have made a convincing argument that the "point" of *The Edible Woman* is, most obviously, a feminist one.)

An example of the distinction between fictional character and real person: Mrs. Bogue is a solid type in the novel — earnest, hard working, with little time and inclination to laugh. She plays a particular part in the narrative drama. If Mary Sims "is" Mrs. Bogue, she is also very different from her. Sims, for example, was capable of such creative acts as fabricating a "voodoo doll for the Montreal branch manager, made of wax and complete with an assortment of pins."[5] In fact, Atwood phoned Sims after *The Edible Woman* came out to explain that she didn't really think of her former boss as the "Helen Hokinson" type she had portrayed in the novel: "a novelist ha[s] to take certain liberties for the sake of a good story," Atwood maintained.[6] Unlike Mrs. Bogue, Mary Sims is quite a character; it comes through even in her letters. After identifying herself to me as Mrs. Bogue, she continued:

> The character I should have liked to be is Aunt Lou in *Lady Oracle*. Once again, Peggy telephoned me when Aunt Lou appeared, to tell me that she had borrowed an incident from my early married life to flesh her out a bit; the story where Aunt Lou ordered a pound of *everything* — flour, pepper, sugar — by phone from the grocer, as I had done. I wish she had remembered the pound of bay leaves. It stood three feet high in its bag, and lasted eleven years. I loved Aunt Lou, a real kindred spirit.[7]

When I told Atwood this, she chuckled. "Of course," she responded, "she *is* Aunt Lou."[8] That she can be both and neither owes everything to the craft and imagination involved in fiction making.

That craft is carefully controlled. When Atwood wrote *The Edible Woman*, for example, on University of British Columbia exam booklets, she pencilled details in the margins related to what each one of the characters did that day. "Every day I would ask myself, What is going to happen today to these people? In the place where you plot out your exam question, on the left hand side, I'd make a list, a few notes, on what she does today. Then I would write the chapter."[9]

If careful planning makes characters realistic, then it can sometimes anticipate reality itself. For example, one of the most memorable questionnaires that Seymour Surveys concocts involves listening to the commercial jingle for Moose beer. "I thought that I was making up that product," remarks Atwood, "and I made up this ad, and when I went to New Brunswick, everybody was just overjoyed to see me. There is a beer there called Moose Head Beer, and it has a moose on the label, and they got one of those labels and presented it to me. So truth and fiction are not always that different."[10]

*   *   *

During her year at Canadian Facts Marketing, Atwood lived in a rooming house on Charles Street just east of Victoria College. For sixty-seven dollars a month, she had fresh sheets and towels each week and a small space to call her own. Her room was not much bigger than a cupboard. Atwood kept her food (bread, butter, Kraft Dinner) in a dresser drawer and cooked on a one-burner hot plate. Sometimes she'd boil plastic packages of peas or corned beef. Her coffee was instant. And, because this was Canada, her kettle was electric. (Have you ever noticed that these kettles only seem to be a standard item in Canadian kitchens?)[11]

Shared bathrooms were one serious drawback of tenement living. Again and again, in Atwood's commentary and stories, we hear of the bathtubs littered with bits of macaroni (dishes were washed in the tub, apparently) and the bathroom residue of other tenants (think of the story "Dancing Girls"). Although, in *The Edible Woman*, Marian and her roommate Ainsley occupy the top floor of a house, they don't have a bathroom to themselves; this accounts for "the low rent."[12]

Atwood was quite an earnest young woman at this point. Although these were the very early days of pot and blue jeans, of Yorkville Bohemia and the coffeehouse scene around Avenue Road, Atwood socialized conservatively. But the atmosphere of her first (unpublished) novel — so dark that a concerned publisher, making the autobiographical assumption, asked if there was anything he could do for her — fails to reflect the atmosphere Peggy Atwood inhabited during this period. "She had a really ribald sense of humour," recalls James (Jay) Ford, Atwood's friend from her Victoria College days, then a resident at Massey College pursuing graduate studies in philosophy. "All of her friends knew this and enjoyed it. Peggy could drink like a trooper. You could take her to the Park Plaza and the stories would fly thick around the table. . . . A much bleaker picture emerges in her writing than that which she, as quite a young person, held." Ford does not suggest that Atwood's humour detracted from the seriousness with which she pursued her craft: "She worked at her writing very diligently," he remarks. "If she was away for the weekend she would swim, boat, and so on. But she always had a pencil and a pad of paper. Never ostentatious about this. Never 'be quiet, I'm thinking great thoughts.' Part of Peggy really."[13]

★ ★ ★

Feminism was in the air in the mid-1960s. A revolution was at hand — driven, in part, by the advent of the birth-control pill. A generation of woman would come to know a form of sexual freedom that had previously been unattainable. *The Edible Woman*, which locates its protagonist's discomfort in specifically feminist concerns and details the symptoms of an eating disorder — anorexia nervosa — that would only become familiar in the next decade (although its neurological cause still remains unknown), clearly demonstrates that Atwood was by now acutely conscious of feminist issues. Ford remembers her feminism (she was "very touchy about people regarding women as intrinsically inferior and she could be quite easily provoked if goaded in this direction") but quickly points out that there was "no stridency about it. Nothing suffragette about it; she wasn't chaining herself to the gates of Massey College."[14] Certainly Mary Sims remembers no stridency. In fact, she suggests that Atwood did not seem to be deeply concerned with political issues at the time:

> at one point I suggested to Peggy that she might become more interested in social issues (or perhaps expressed surprise that she was not).
> She explained to me that she was much engaged in her writing, and that she did not feel that she could handle both writing and political activity at the same time. I am sure that was a wise decision for her at that time. I was happy when I could see from her books at a later period that she was now waking up to the way the world was going.[15]

Although Atwood was not actively voicing her political concerns, she was certainly looking very closely at what was happening around her and tuning in to its political significance. I'm thinking more of small-p politics here — a growing sense of feminist awareness — than the capital-p politics Sims had in mind. Although Chris Lloyd says that feminism wasn't "a wild issue" for Atwood, she does assert that feminism was "more obvious in Peggy's whole disposition."[16] When I asked Lloyd what she meant by "feminism" in that context, she told me another Canadian Facts story.

She had decided to ask for a raise. With knees knocking, she had approached the company president, and her annual salary had been bumped up to four thousand dollars.

> But, [the president] added, "You understand, of course, we have to pay the men more because they have families to support." And I did accept that as an explanation. I am

not sure Peggy would have accepted that. She was ahead of me in her thinking about equalities of men and women. I don't think we talked about it in terms of feminism or equality. Rather, "rights to have a job." At that time employers expected that, for women, jobs were a transition to marriage. That would not have been Peggy's view. She was more on the cutting edge of such issues for women than I was at that time.[17]

Curiously, Marian McAlpine seems to be even more on "the cutting edge" than Atwood herself was. Like Atwood (and so many other young women of that era), Marian is profoundly ambivalent about marriage; unlike Atwood, she develops a severe eating disorder. It is the outward, physical manifestation of her turmoil. That is, Marian literally stakes her life on her political (again, small-p) beliefs. Now, of course, we know that what Marian is suffering from is anorexia, an all-too-familiar disorder. But eating disorders weren't widely understood then. It is as though Marian — once created — directed her creator to outline the disease in detail and then to demonstrate its causes.

Marian's cure, which involves baking a cake in her own like-ness, provides one of the most startling images in all of Atwood's fiction. The idea came to Atwood as a result of her early curiosity in the rather odd rituals of cake baking. "About the cake in the shape of a woman — all I can tell you is that I used to be a very good cake decorator and was often asked to reproduce various objects in pastry and icing. Also, in my walks past pastry stores, I always wondered why people made replicas of things — brides and grooms, for instance, or Mickey Mice — and then ate them."[18]

⋆   ⋆   ⋆

Having spent much of the summers of 1962 and 1963 in each other's company (often at their families' cottages), Atwood and James Ford became engaged. This happened at the end of August, 1963, the year Atwood was at Canadian Facts. (Perhaps this influenced Atwood to take a year off and work in Toronto.) At Christmas, Ford's present to Atwood was an engagement ring. But by Easter of 1964 a strain had developed in the relationship, due partly to Ford's workload at Massey (he was teaching two courses and preparing for comprehensive exams), and the engagement was broken off. So Ford only read *The Edible Woman* (the setting of which owes so much to the Canadian Facts era in Atwood's life) a couple of years after its publication; he thinks it must have been in 1970 or 1971. One of his friends suggested that he read it. When he did, he found it "immensely amusing, especially since some of the characters could be easily identified as people we knew and many of the incidents are . . . only slightly altered." Ford now recalls that Atwood had written to him when she started working on the novel, "tipping him off" in the "friendliest terms." "Please don't take this personally," he remembers her saying — meaning, presumably, the way she used some real-life details in the service of fiction and the way she distorted some things, including the character Peter (who shares many of Ford's characteristics), and pushed them to an extreme, in order to serve the novel's purposes, both ideological and humorous.[19]

★   ★   ★

Although Atwood submitted the manuscript of *The Edible Woman* to McClelland and Stewart in the fall of 1965, she heard nothing about it until two years later. During that interval the status of the manuscript became something of a mystery. Atwood secretly wondered if the publishers were holding it hostage, the ransom being her next manuscript.

Finally, in 1967, she received some readers' reports. The first was written by John Robert Colombo; he identifies himself early in his report by making a reference to the poetry published in his anthology *Poetry 64*. Colombo was responsible for sorting through the "over the portal" manuscripts at McClelland and Stewart. It was an enormous job. The company was getting nearly a boxful of unsolicited book manuscripts every couple of days.

Colombo had to sort through them, flag any promising ones, and pass them on to an appropriate set of readers. That his reading of the novel was somewhat cursory is evident in his references to "Marian *Moorehouse*" and to "Ainsley *himself*." Although *The Edible Woman* was not really to his taste, Colombo sent it on, explaining that it deserved another (and more sympathetic) reader: "a female reader who goes for Lawrence Durrell and Mary McCarthy and Doris Lessing." His own basic assessment was that "The novel is very much a pastiche in the tradition of pastiches written by Daryl Hine, whose work [Atwood] very much admires. I'm extremely unsympathetic to this kind of novel and feel there should be a narrative worth recounting before the author can expect a reader to spend three hours pouring over so much prose."[20]

The three subsequent readers' reports are anonymous and conflicting. One can imagine Atwood's dilemma as she sat down, in 1967, to revise the manuscript along the lines they suggested. The first of the three readers liked the "fine manuscript" and found it "practically flawless." But he or she did point to the rather puppetlike portrayal of both Peter and Ainsley. "If Peter could be made into a character instead of a puppet the way he is at present — a sympathetic, believable character that Marian has strong affection (perhaps even love) for, then the novel would gain strength. As it is Peter is a nothing — a tailor's dummy — almost a caricature and there seems no reason why Marian agrees to marry him in the first place."[21] This reader also noted one technical difficulty: Ainsley gets Ben into bed in late November and has her pregnancy confirmed by early December.

The second reader enjoyed the " 'flip' style" and "caustic humour" but added: "Why 'Gorunto' and 'Rosevale' etc.? The city of Toronto is no longer a village and the need for disguise is no more real than in the case of writing in London or New York." This reader also objected to the shift in narrative voice. "Miss Atwood is far better at writing in the first person than the third. I would think that the switch in Chapter Twelve was an effort to be original, but my own feeling is that the first person part of the book is far better." Finally, this reader remarked that, with the exception of Duncan (who "ought to be either more brilliant, or more charming, or more obviously appealing"), the novel's characters were so well drawn that "each one was real."[22]

The third reader found the book "simply too young" and lamented the fact that "the central young lady and her young man are a bit dim compared to some of the others" (making me wonder *which* others). "[B]ut," the report continues, "I don't think broadening them would do much good." Despite the "great interest" and "pleasure" with which this person read the manuscript, the report suggests that it was not publishable.[23] Still, of course, *The Edible Woman was* published. And it met with enormous success.

8

The Demands of the Muse

THE YEAR ATWOOD SPENT at Canadian Facts was, overall, a pleasant one. She made a comfortable niche for herself at the office. She was able to be with her family and renew her contacts with other young writers. Gwen MacEwen, whom Atwood had first met at the Bohemian Embassy, was living on 2nd Street on Ward's Island with Bob Mallory.[1] Ward's Island was, in the early 1960s, a fairly remote place. Although a few literary types lived there year-round — the poet Victor Coleman and the antiquarian book dealer David Mason — most of its population spent only the summers there.[2] Peter Gzowski (the beloved CBC Radio personality) and Robert Fulford were among those who rented their small houses out during the bleak winter months.

Doug Jones remembers Atwood taking him over to the island to visit MacEwen on a "summery Saturday or Sunday." "What impressed me," says Jones, "was the fact Gwen was wall-papering her cottage with brown wrapping paper." MacEwen's persona and the whole atmosphere of the island rendered exotic her brown paper and the hot dogs she served that day. "The Island then had no great recreational facilities; it was truly like visiting a sort of wilderness suburb, clusters of cottages that had drifted off from the mainland."[3]

By the time the summer of her Canadian Facts year had rolled around and her engagement to Ford had been broken off, Atwood needed to get away. She spent the summer of 1964 living with a friend named Alison Cunningham in London, England, and travelling in France. In an article entitled "The Grunge Look," she describes that sojourn in hilarious detail. The fashion scene, she recalls, then favoured the "bubble-cut":

> women rolled their hair in big bristle-filled rollers to achieve a smoothly swollen look, as if someone had inserted a tube into one of their ears and blown up their heads like balloons. I indulged in this practice too, though with mixed results, since my hair was ferociously curly. At best it resembled a field of weeds gone over with a lawn roller — still squiggly, though somewhat mashed. At worst it looked as if I'd stuck my finger in a light socket. This silhouette was later to become stylish, but was not so yet. As a result I went in for head scarves, of the Queen-at-Balmoral type. Paired with the slanty-eyed, horned-rimmed glasses I wore in an attempt to take myself seriously, they were not at all flattering.[4]

Atwood took along a suitcase (backpacks were not yet in). She wore a grey-flannel jumper with a Peter Pan-collared blouse and Hush Puppies — the same ones her Harvard roommates would later remark upon. Her introduction to London was much like that of any other young North American woman arriving there for the first time in the mid-1960s. She visited a dizzying number of cultural sites (unfortunately, a sprained ankle slowed her down a bit). Her Paris interlude was also a fairly typical one. Atwood and her friend stayed at a cheap pension on the Île de la Cité. Poor as "rats," they lived on baguettes and cheese, consuming an orange here and there to ward off scurvy.[5]

In Atwood's own estimation she returned to Canada a changed woman. "Changed" meant, among other things, that the grey-flannel jumper had been replaced by a brown suede vest bought at Liberty's, and there was an "addition of a lot of black and some innovation with the hair."[6]

In September of 1964, Atwood joined the teaching faculty at the University of British Columbia. To her new colleagues, she appeared a serious young woman, despite the Liberty vest and the hair innovation. One of those colleagues was writer Jane

Rule, whose verbal portrait of Atwood at UBC belies Atwood's own sense of herself as transformed: "Tweed skirt suits. (There were miniskirts then, but you wouldn't see Peggy in them.) Hair pulled back in a bun. Horn-rimmed glasses. Low heels. Very low-key. Not stylish. Somebody inside a chrysalis. Quite shy and uneasy in groups of people she didn't know. She still is." Rule perceived Atwood as a young woman just on the verge of realizing her personal power. Still a bit isolated. Focused. "Peggy was intense and self protective in those days. Humour then was sharp, and associated with protecting herself. Distancing herself from people. She read tarot cards. I had a palmist friend once who said that she read palms because she liked to hold hands."[7]

Atwood began work as a lecturer. During the year she spent at UBC, she made some hard decisions about her personal and professional future. Driven by a powerful creative energy and torn between two suitors, Doug Jones and Jim Polk, both of whom were far away (Jones in eastern Canada and Polk at Harvard), Atwood now experienced one of the most productive phases of her career. In her Vancouver apartment, which boasted a 180-degree view, Atwood worked at what she would call "white heat." She made the very early notes for *Cat's Eye*, drafted *The Edible Woman* (in 1965), and completed a libretto to accompany John Beckwith's music called *Trumpets of Summer* (performed on CBC Radio in 1964). She also wrote fourteen stories in 1964 as well as the beginnings of *Surfacing*.[8] This writing streak also produced, in the fall of 1964, at least twenty-five new poems and, in the first half of 1965, twenty-eight more. Exhausted, living on caffeine, Kraft Dinner, and frozen peas, Atwood lost weight and developed spinal neuritis.[9] But she had achieved a momentum in her writing that would carry her to the first stage of literary success.

Atwood submitted her new poems and some earlier ones, collectively titled "Places, Migrations" to Ryerson Press in December of 1964; this sequence of forty-two poems was rejected in 1965. Unlike "The Journey," a poetry sequence submitted to Contact Press in 1963, "Places, Migrations" was carefully revised — transformed — and was eventually published in 1966 by Contact Press as *The Circle Game*.

Perhaps the best, and certainly the best-known poems of *The Circle Game*, were already written before the fall of 1964: "This Is a Photograph of Me," "After the Flood," and "The Circle Game" sequence itself. But twenty-five of the forty-two poems in "Places, Migrations" were written during the fall of 1964, and most of these, Judith McCombs argues, were female-identified. As McCombs explains, in twelve of the poems, "women are central characters, have power over others, are allied with primitive or with Edenic natural powers, are fertility goddess, harpy, Euridice, seer." Another six of the poems, McCombs thinks, are "covertly female-identified." (Was Atwood's growing feminist sensibility the result of her exposure, at Canadian Facts, to such strong women? A reaction to such a male-centred business world? Or, rather, did it emerge from the environment at the University of British Columbia? The answer, surely, is all of the above.) Many of the "female-identified" or "female-empowered" poems were, McCombs notes, removed from the collection at the insistence of the publisher, who was concerned primarily with "communicability, humanisation, and . . . communicating something the reader can share."[10]

In the early months of 1965, Atwood wrote another twenty-eight poems, including "A Descent through the Carpet," "Camera," and "Explorers." Of these, McCombs argues, twenty-six are female-identified poems, and twenty are overtly so. "Why," then, McCombs asks, "is the female *I* in the final *Circle* confined to seer, victim and lover roles *vis-à-vis* the male?" Why is she never fully empowered? McCombs proves that it is, in large part, the result of the publisher's pressure.[11]

The award-winning collection, however, is also the result of the publisher's nurturing and especially the advocacy of Peter Miller. Often that nurturing involved financial support; that is, at Contact Press, the editors frequently dug deep into their own pockets to support the publication of books they felt strongly about.[12] At other times, as with Atwood's manuscript, that advocacy was rhetorical. "Most of this ms shows a great advance towards approachability," Miller wrote to his colleagues as if attempting to anticipate and forestall the kind of criticism that had prevented them from publishing Atwood's earlier effort. "The most important factor, however, seems to me that Margaret's sincerity, development, style, imagination and genuine talent . . . should not and cannot be ignored or sold short by a firm of publishers whose sole aim is the encouragement of deserving young talent."[13] In the same letter, Miller suggests the collection's final title, thereby opening an editorial dialogue that closes with a poetry sequence that enacts the very structures it examines: mirrors and circles. In 1967, when Contact was in the process of closing down its operations and passing the torch to other small presses such as Coach House in Toronto and Delta in Montreal, Miller accompanied Atwood to Ottawa to receive the Governor General's Literary Award for *The Circle Game*. "This well-deserved tribute to her poetry," he wrote in 1997, "also crowned the publishing efforts of Contact Press. We went out in style."[14]

Atwood's first real break came in the form of *Poetry 64*, an anthology of the best poems published in 1964. It was edited by John Robert Colombo. *Poetry 64* emphasized the work of four talented new poets: Gwendolyn MacEwen, Margaret Atwood, John Newlove, and George Bowering. MacEwen and Atwood had ten poems each in the anthology, evidence of their rank as "serious" poets. It was a turning point for both women. "I think I chose the best of the early Atwood," reflects Colombo.[15] His selection placed less emphasis on the Atwood poems that featured figures of myth, although these figures were a key component of her early work (look at her collection *Double Persephone*). Colombo's choices did, however, play with certain personae: the dwarf, the mad mother. Atwood's concern for women in society, and the horror she felt when contemplating the middle-class-marriage trap, emerge very strongly in *Poetry 64*: witness "The City Girl," "The Mad Mother," "Woman on the Subway," "The Lifeless Wife." "Houses" introduces Atwood's powerful trademark: the first-person voice.

Atwood garnered more professional recognition when, in November of 1964, *Trumpets of Summer* was performed. This choral suite for a mixed chorus of four soloists — one male speaker and six instruments — combines John Beckwith's music and Atwood's text. The suite was commissioned by the CBC for the Shakespeare Quartercentenary. The text explores various responses to Shakespeare and outlines a child's ignorance of Shakespeare's work, that child's subsequent introduction to Shakespeare during a high school play, an adult's appreciation of the bard's stagecraft, and a learned man's theoretical discussion. The text concludes with an epilogue, an evocation of a city and a theatre left empty once the summer is past, and the words of Shakespeare — the Swan of Avon — are merely an echo in "this particular chilly / space and time."[16] For a writer as young and untried as Atwood, creating such a tribute was a real challenge. That she was asked to confront such a challenge at all testifies to the fact that her reputation was growing in Canada.

*　*　*

In Vancouver, Atwood rented a spacious Point Grey apartment (at 3886 West 11th) for ninety dollars a month. The bathroom was done in mauve and "hemorrhoid pink"; the bedspread was a green-satin concoction; the wallpaper was "something else."[17] To her friend Charlie Pachter she wrote:

> You should picture a room with papers strewn all over the floor and in piles that only I could make sense of, and an apartment with hardly any furniture in it because it was only partly furnished and I didn't have the money to buy any other furniture. My dining-room table was a card table lent to me by Jane Rule, bless her. She lent me the plates too. And there I was with my pencil. These were poems written in pencil, scribbled, as like as not, not on the lines but diagonally across the page. That tells what an optimist I am: I start at the left and I slant up.[18]

While that optimism issued from her youthful drive and ambition, Atwood's interest in graphology was prompted by her former boss, Mary Sims, who was fascinated by it.

So Atwood lived alone, writing late into the night and rising early to lecture. The inhabitants of the apartment below hers, apparently, weren't too fond of her schedule; the late-night typing, from their perspective, sounded like "termites."[19] But Atwood was unstoppable. The pace she maintained was frenetic, but she still managed to enjoy teaching (especially her first-year class) and living in Vancouver ("the mountains are worth everything").[20]

Jane Rule and Helen Sonthoff, both faculty members in Atwood's department, welcomed her into their ranks. That year, there were two new faces: Atwood and Shelagh Day (today one of Canada's foremost human-rights experts). With Warren Tallman, Sonthoff ran the poetry committee; they took turns hosting parties and would invite young writers, Atwood among them, to attend. Both Tallman and Sonthoff had come from the United States and were interested in facilitating an exchange between the Canadian and American poetic traditions. Remembers Rule, "the Black Mountain group would come, for instance. The whole community was really interested in poetry. Hundreds of students would come out."[21] In this charged and creative atmosphere where students were truly excited about poetry, Atwood made a place for herself.

Earle Birney, already a well-known Canadian poet, was also active in the UBC creative-writing scene. He was deeply committed to the idea of creating a specifically Canadian writing movement. Atwood recalls that Birney asked her to sit in on his creative-writing class — "one of the first in Canada — and to express my callow, virtually unpublished opinions."[22] Poet Dorothy Livesay was also at UBC, but she wasn't quite as open to the new challenges and ideas that Atwood had brought with her.

When she wasn't caught up in this world of creative writers or hard at work, Atwood spent quite a bit of time with a former camp contact, Larry Cohen, who was studying law at UBC, and his roommates: David (the autoharpist), Steve, and God. "God" was Steve's monkey. Atwood remembers the creature clambering around the wainscotting. "Preferred women to men," she says. "More hair. Was fond of the charcoal on the end of matches. Steve had to give it away when it was full grown. It had to be with other monkeys."[23]

Atwood taught two courses that year: "the whistle-stop" course from Chaucer to T.S. Eliot and grammar to engineering students, at 8:30 in the morning, in a "Quonset hut — left over from WWII." (Those huts still stand on the UBC campus.) That was the only time Atwood ever smoked. She took it up when confronted with her "first batch of undergraduate compositions."[24]

Atwood remembers herself in those "writing days" as being "grubby and bespectacled." Speaking on the condition of being a writer in the early 1960s, she has said:

> Poverty and obedience — not to external powers but to your inner voices — would be your lot. (Chastity was not required but if you wanted to get anything accomplished you had to have a certain amount of that, as well.) The Muse would not reward you with a two-car garage. But you would have a sense of community with others of your kind (those with the black turtlenecks, as distinguished from those with the suits) and you would share the clandestine sense of excitement that came from feeling you were part of an enterprise that had really — in historical terms — just begun.[25]

In the midst of demonstrating her strenuous devotion to the muse, Atwood maintained her characteristic good humour. "She would bring work," Rule recalls, "and we would talk." Once, she went to Rule with a great pile of poems. " 'Peggy,' I said, 'there are too many people-eating-people poems. Let's make a pile of them, and pick the best.' And we did."[26]

Doug Jones courted Atwood during the early part of her year at UBC. He travelled to the West Coast quite often to read his poetry. He was reading at noon on the day John F. Kennedy was shot. The reading resumed after a moment of silence, with Jones and the audience still in shock.[27] But that was before Atwood had come to UBC. She had been at Canadian Facts that day and had heard the news in the elevator, thinking at first that it had been just a bad joke.[28]

One of the poets invited to speak to Atwood's class at UBC was Al Purdy. When he came, says Doug Jones, he was asked to

explain how he had first met Atwood, and the answer involved
Jones himself. The setting had been Jones's cottage on Paudash
Lake in Ontario (fifteen miles from Bancroft on the road to
Peterborough), where Atwood happened to be visiting. Confirm-
ing the date and location, Jones notes, "I do have a vivid image
of Al Purdy's car bouncing in over the grassy stretch in front of
the cottage on Paudash — before coming to a rocking halt. At
which point Al emerged and hoisted a case of beer from the
trunk."[29] Purdy remembers dropping by with his wife, Eurithe,
for an unannounced visit. Jones can't remember Eurithe being
there at all. But both men agree on the details of the amicable
Atwood-Purdy fracas that ensued. Writes Purdy:

> Greetings were exchanged with no obvious lack of cor-
> diality. Beer being available, we drank some; small talk
> was interchanged, among which there must have been at
> some point a serious shortage of communication (as Paul
> Newman was understood to say in *Cool Hand Luke*).
> Peggy, in error of course, understood me to say something
> quite disparaging about academics: of which learned legions
> she is one. Now it must be understood forthwith: I love
> academics. Some of my best friends? Best-loved enemies?
> Peggy, in the normal tenor of her ways, would never have
> such a misunderstanding again, of this I am sure. She just
> made a mistake, and I forgive her for it.
>   At the time she appeared calmly enraged, or perhaps
> a little mentally disturbed. The obvious retaliatory wea-
> pon was close at hand: namely, beer. Now I deplore such
> wasteful misuse of good Canadian beer, but there was no
> dissuading Peggy from her obvious intention: to swizzle a
> half-full bottle in her hand until the contents achieved con-
> siderable muzzle velocity and then douse me with the stuff.
>   And she did.[30]

Purdy's tale continues with the two writers pursuing each other
along the shoreline, armed with bottles of foaming brew. When
Jones tells the story, he calmly remarks: "Just the right sort of
physical contact to get them back into their chairs in amicable

intimacy."[31] Purdy counters: "Hell, no! We grabbed each other, in the lake shallows, in order to protect ourselves from the other. When we sat down, there was an amused suspicious slightly obsequious feeling in myself, and I guess in her too. We had added a dimension to each of our characters."[32] Jones concludes, "And the rest of the afternoon proceeded without incident."[33] But, of course, the incident gave rise to Purdy's story, which he says he "saw" taking place in his mind on paper.[34]

$\star$ $\star$ $\star$

Atwood wrote *The Edible Woman* between April and August of 1964. The length of the chapters was limited by how much she could fit, writing longhand, into an exam booklet.[35] The novel was revised in the early fall and submitted to McClelland and Stewart in October.[36] While Marian's experience is not, of course, that of her creator, Atwood herself was certainly feeling pressured during her year at UBC. In 1987, she wrote:

> I had never had, or even heard of, anorexia — in 1964 it was not yet fashionable — so Marian's eating disorder had its genesis in speculations that were symbolic rather than personal or medical. However, the result for me was a marked queasiness in the face of my morning egg. (After anorexia hit the glossies, I found myself deluged with clippings and letters, and Marian even appeared as a case study or two, but that was much later.)
>
> I've looked at steak differently since seeing it through the eyes of Marian — which was how I first learned that writing fiction is a two-way street. If the author gets too bossy, the characters may remind her that, though she is their creator, they are to some extent her creator as well.[37]

Until mid-July, she stayed on in Vancouver, taking German lessons. Then Jim Polk came up from Montana and accompanied her, by train, back to Toronto. This trip, ostensibly planned with the purpose of introducing Polk to Atwood's family, was a great success and opened a new chapter in Atwood's life.

9

Atwood as Muse

She was my muse.

— Charles Pachter[1]

SOME OF ATWOOD'S most candid reflections on writing — why she became a writer, what she has accomplished as a writer, what success has meant for her as a writer — appear in a poem called "Owl and Pussycat, Some Years Later." She sent a copy of this poem to her close friend and collaborator, the artist Charles Pachter. He is, after all, the owl in the poem — with the bifocals, minus some hair now. Atwood is the pussycat.

In this poem, the speaker muses about the artistic success of these two creatures several decades after their first meeting, measuring their hard-won achievements ("prizes," "trophies") against their earlier ambitions (to "change the world"), questioning the size and value of their artistic talent (perhaps theirs is only "small talent," "rubbed" and polished like "silver spoons"), gauging their audience and their impact. Has the world been changed for the better by their singing? Their art? Perhaps. And that, of course, is why the poem urges "moulting" owl and "arthritic" pussycat to "sing on" by the light of the moon: just in case they can do more.[2]

"When we were young," says Pachter, "we were like [Betty] Comden and [Adolph] Green: music and lyrics. She made me feel as though I was the only one. Perhaps she worked with other people that way. Connected. We hooked into each other."[3]

★   ★   ★

When they first met at Camp White Pine in 1959, Atwood and Pachter struck up an instant friendship. Camp comrades, fellow pranksters with lively senses of fun, they clicked. "Peggy had a way that was sort of genteel, waspy-kind," says Pachter.

> I'd go to her house, and we'd sit down and have cookies and milk. It was like a ritual — her mother would put out the cookies and then the milk — and everybody would say "please" and "thank you" and I would sit there in awe. It's her way. I just found it very comforting, in some way. In our house it was boom, and boom, and boom, and boom, and everything on the table, and everybody talking at once.[4]

However, as their careers began to take off — Atwood's as a writer and Pachter's as a painter and illustrator — their friendship took on another dimension. It rapidly became a collaboration between two artists well endowed with professional ambition and creative drive. They carried on an extensive correspondence over the years, which ranged dramatically in tone and subject matter and detailed much of what was going on in their lives and in their thoughts. The letters they exchanged during the mid-1960s outlined the genesis and progress of a number of important artistic collaborations: Pachter provided illustrations for a range of Atwood chapbooks, among them *The Circle Game*, *Expeditions*, *Kaleidoscopes Baroque*, *Speeches for Doctor Frankenstein*, and *Talismans for Children*. Pachter's illustrated *Journals of Susanna Moodie* would not appear until 1980, by which time Oxford University Press had already published the poems with illustrations by Atwood. A reprinted version was published in the fall of 1997.

Although the correspondence traces one of the most significant artistic collaborations of the period, it is filled with quips and jokes — evidence, once again, of the balance Atwood maintained between humour and high seriousness. "Yesterday I found this piece of paper with some holes punched in the centre of it," wrote

Pachter, setting up the kind of joke that often punctuated their letters. "When I opened it there was a message inside which said, 'You have just been SINGING ALONG WITH HELEN KELLER.'"[5]

*   *   *

Atwood completed a series of poems in 1963 and submitted the manuscript to Contact Press under the provisional title "The Journey." Contact first accepted the collection but later retracted that acceptance.[6] The editors were divided in their assessments of the collection, so much so that in December Raymond Souster — who had founded the press with fellow poets Irving Layton and Louis Dudek in 1952 — acknowledged his frustration. "I know it's so damn good that you won't have too much trouble placing it elsewhere."[7] Atwood had also sent some of the poems, including "The Circle Game," to Pachter, who, at this point, was working on his MFA degree at the Cranbrook Academy of Art near Detroit; he was exploring papermaking techniques, as well as "typesetting, lithography, etching, silkscreen, book design, and painting."[8] Pachter started work on making lithograph illustrations for the poems almost right away. But soon he was floundering. To Atwood he wrote:

> Everything I've done ends up not at all the way I originally drew it on my stone. My greys turn black, and my blacks are wishy washy. My crayon lines bleed and my washes go solid. Today, I just about smashed a stone on the floor. I had worked on it for a whole week, etching and re-etching, cleaning the pores, inking it just right. So what do you think happened already? It goes black on me. Why? If I knew would I be asking you? I see now why Picasso never printed his own stones. He just drew on them and let the master printers take over. The chemistry involved in lithography is so subtle that you have to work for years in order to judge what effects you'll get under different circumstances. I plunged right in knowing nothing, and what did I get? NOTHING. . . . If I fail next time I'll go to medical school.[9]

In this letter Pachter also asks about the spelling of certain words (spelling is Atwood's Achilles' heel): "anenomes," "argueing," "memorizor," "wellknown." Atwood's reply, acknowledging errors where appropriate but demonstrating that she was quite able to hold her own in the humour department, was addressed to "Chawles (sic)."[10]

Needless to say, Pachter didn't go to medical school. Instead, he sent his artwork to Atwood in early November, and she responded, "I'm ecstatic about your prints."[11] By mid-November Pachter was hard at work on "The Circle Game" poem cycle itself. He wrote to Atwood, setting down his thoughts on certain practical aspects of typesetting — specifically, how to deal with the overabundance of "g"s — before describing his moment of victory. He had executed two lithographs — one of a ring of children and one of a room's interior — of which he was very proud. The first

> looks so marvellous and you know when I set each word by hand it gave me a chance to really think about those children going around and around. I have only taken proofs but it's going to be great.
>
> I have to tell you about the lithos themselves. My conception for the children came immediately. I drew it and re-drew it for days but when I got to doing it on the stone I froze up. Four times I drew it and re-ground down not thinking it was right for the poem. I gradually began to be aware of the difficulties involved — words and illustration must complement each other not detract. Poem must be enhanced by drawing and drawing shouldn't need poem to complete it. I don't want the spectator to enjoy the drawing until he has read the poem and I'm telling you all this because tonight, thank God, I finally got what I wanted. I worked all day and my back and fingers and hands [are] sore and swollen (our press is old and lousy) but I feel exhilarated. I've pulled an edition of twenty hoping to get a final total of fifteen. Also I finished the illustration for number two. The room reminded me so much of yours on

Charles Street, transom, wardrobe, etc. I'm so happy with the first two, I hope I'll have as much pleasure from the next ones. . . .

It's now 2:30 a.m. Goodnight, Peggy.[12]

Atwood wrote back, enclosing two new poems based on excursions she had taken with their mutual friend Larry Cohen. One was "Skier in a Cave," which was omitted from the final published collection. Although Atwood notes that it is about "space and time,"[13] she admits that, unsure of how Larry Cohen would react, she had not yet shown it to him. On 8 December, Pachter wrote triumphantly: "Well, it is finished. I've never felt so good about anything in my life as I do now. . . . God, how I wish I could be there when you get it."[14] Atwood was thrilled with his work. "I'm ecstatic upon receipt of the fifteen copies," she wrote, and then added a note of warning: "But it would not, I repeat NOT, be a good idea to show it to my parents. The subject matter of the poems would disturb them. . . . They're very nice people and I like them to be happy but I don't think these poems would contribute much to their peace of mind."[15] Ever practical. Just after the New Year, then, Pachter completed his illustrations and published *The Circle Game* himself. It took the form of a limited-edition folio and bore the imprint of the Cranbrook Academy of Art, where Pachter was studying. Each sold for about $150; today, a copy can fetch approximately $12,000.[16]

Although Atwood often provided Pachter with details about the contexts of her poems, she was extremely careful about her timing. That is, she scrupulously avoided influencing his interpretation of the work. For example, when Pachter probed the identity of the man in the "Circle Game" manuscript by asking the colour of "Jay's eyes" (Jay Ford, that is), Atwood answered only *after* she knew that Pachter's illustrations were finished. The room she evoked in the poem, Atwood explained, was a composite: drawn from a room in Paris (reminiscent, presumably, of the Parisian *pension* she occupied during the summer of 1964), although it had (as Pachter had pointed out) much in common with her small room on Charles Street. And the man? Also a composite. Far from being an unmediated transcription of real-life events, the published version of *The Circle Game* is carefully mediated and controlled, a "centred, symmetric, and mirroring structure."[17] In real life, Atwood admits, the eyes (Jay Ford's) were brown.[18] But the eyes in *The Circle Game*, which fix, "transfix," the poem's speaker[19] at that central moment in the poetry sequence, are "cold blue thumbtacks."[20] One "can't" have cold *brown* thumbtacks, Atwood explains in a letter to Pachter.[21] Not at all poetic.

The brown eyes suggest that the book's dedication — for "J" — was in part a reference to Jay Ford. Atwood wrote to Peter Miller of Contact Press: "Note: this is handy, as everyone I know begins with J."[22] Indeed, there were many important "J" people in her life: (her mentor) Jay Macpherson, (her university beaux) Jay Ford, Doug Jones, Jim Polk. In Atwood's most recent novel, *Alias Grace*, that important initial crops up again. Protagonist Grace Marks is told that she will "cross the water three times and then get married to a man whose name began with a J."[23] The prophecy is fulfilled for Grace, just as it was for Atwood herself.

Atwood received the finished product, Pachter's edition of *The Circle Game*, in January of 1965. "IT arrived yesterday," she wrote, "and I was so excited that I just took IT out into the hall and undid 'mummy' like wrappings for half an hour until I finally uncovered IT. And is IT ever a STUNNER. It functions so well as a unit. The type is just right, and you managed to include so much detail from the poems. . . . So you get 2,000 gold stars."[24] When Pachter wrote back on 23 January, he was still excited. He reported that he had shown it to Jay Macpherson.

> Peggy, she was great. She was so excited about how well the poetry and illustrations went together. She said they *needed* each other. Also she asked me several questions about my intended symbolisms and was also interested in the ear-sink picture. Also she loved the last one. A propos, did you notice the couple still arguing in the next room, and the teeth and the children melting and the woman trapped in the womb-like mass? . . . The end papers are made from

12 cotton shirts, 1 linen table cloth & 1 pr. faded jeans — it makes a very rich blue which embosses well.[25]

In the same letter, Pachter also told Atwood that he had just finished illustrating and printing yet another of their collaborative efforts: the chapbook *Kaleidoscopes Baroque*:

I worked on it 2 weeks solid all day and evg's till 12. It's almost miniature — about 4 x 5", all on hand-made paper (from all linen) and it's illustrated with colour woodcuts (teeny ones). People here are beginning to revere me and suspect me at the same time. Looks like I set a record — 2 books in 1 semester but they wonder what secret power your poetry has to "inspire" me so. . . . My instructor wanted to know just what was between us. Tee hee. . . . I guess I'm just lucky that the Atwood mind is so chock full of things that strike my fancy and that set my wheels a-turnin'. THANKS![26]

Atwood had the book in hand by February. "Got the little book," she wrote, "It's a honey (particularly the hairs and upside-down picture of the man in the eye and the little things from the title page coming apart in the last one)."[27]

By early 1966, Pachter was hard at work on a new set of lithographs. They would be used to illustrate the next Atwood-Pachter collaboration: the chapbook *Expeditions*. The hitch this time was a misspelled word. Atwood acknowledged the mistake; Pachter was able to correct it by hand. "I tried hand-lettering in ice and honest it's virtually indistinguishable from the litho-d stuff so I can go ahead and put it in without endangering the visual effect. O.K. with you?"[28] If you look closely — very closely — at the limited-edition chapbook, you will just barely be able to see the correction to the word *ice*. Of course, it adds character to the piece and is a very tangible reminder of the practical considerations that go into book production. Pachter himself kept reminding Atwood of these considerations in his letters. In one, dated 23 February, he included some mirror writing.

"This is how I had to do your poems," he declared, meaning that he had to write out her words backwards so that they would come out reversed — and therefore legible — in the final lithograph.[29]

Not only did Pachter complete *Expeditions* in early 1966, but on 20 April 1966 he also completed the chapbook called *Speeches for Doctor Frankenstein*, which contained a long poem that would become, as well, part of Atwood's next collection, *The Animals in That Country*. Containing ten illustrations, each with eight to ten colours, *Speeches* was finished in just over three weeks. Fifteen copies in all. The range of colours and textures this chapbook encompasses is absolutely spectacular.

In an undated letter to her grandmother that was likely written at about this time, Atwood mentioned Pachter:

> Do you remember my young friend Charlie? He came in once while you were visiting in Toronto with some second-hand clothes he had just bought to use as costumes for camp plays. He was here visiting about a week ago; he has a scholarship at Cranbrook Academy in Michigan, where he is studying graphic art. He brought several new books to show me; very good work. He designs and prints them himself, and even makes the paper — out of various kinds of cloth, which he dissolves in water and mixes up and dries on screens. He has made a lovely shade of blue out of a pair of blue-jeans, a pastel orange from a towel, pink from a red checkered tablecloth; for one book he chopped off some of his own hair and added it to the pulp, for the "texture" as he says (that's what I call putting a lot of yourself in your work!).[30]

The creative electricity passing between these two artists was powerful. It was based on a shared sense of humour, a shared understanding of the dynamics that fuel artistic energy and ambition, a solid friendship, and mutual trust. When Atwood showed the precious chapbooks to her friends, it was no wonder that they misunderstood the relationship. "I showed the book to a poet here to-day," she told Pachter in a letter, "and he . . . said,

'Is he in love with you?' "[31] "Inspired by you" would have been a better way of putting it. Pachter began his conversation with me by saying, point blank: "From the earliest time, she was my muse."[32]

★   ★   ★

In 1968, when Atwood was married to Jim Polk and living in Edmonton, Pachter began a portrait of her. The famous result was called *It Was Fascination I Know*. In *Charles Pachter: The First Thirty Years*, Bogomila Welsh-Ovcharov describes this work — which uses both lithograph and silkscreen techniques — as having a "whimsical component" and as reflecting "the continuing influence of Pop Art" during an otherwise dark period in Pachter's artistic career. "It depicted an 'insectomorphic' Margaret Atwood proffering a caterpillar on a twig to the artist as she sprouts butterfly wings. This image also recalls her role as nature instructor at the summer camp where Pachter first met her."[33] Welsh-Ovcharov also notes that it borrows its title from a popular song of the time. But I remember that the tune also contained the line "it was *magic* I know." Both words — magic and fascination — describe their subject well.

Had I not seen the original slide on which the portrait was based, I wouldn't have believed that it was derived from a particular image. But there was Atwood in the slide, wearing enormous plastic-framed glasses, smiling, displaying a caterpillar on a twig. The snapshot was taken in front of Pachter's farmhouse in northern Ontario. *It Was Fascination I Know* portrays a smiling Atwood, rendered in bright yellow, sporting those same huge glasses. The shape of the glasses echoes that of the insectlike wings sprouting from her shoulders. The caterpillar she offers is a green that is just a shade darker than the portrait's almost lime-green background. During the days I spent looking over papers at Pachter's residence, a copy of the portrait was always in front of me, as were a number of the artist's other prints. I find it hard now to think of the Atwood-Pachter letters without thinking of this image of growth and transformation, of energy, magic, and fascination.

When Pachter was ready to unveil this image to the source of its inspiration, he added this note:

I hope the initial "scariness" [of the portrait] has worn off. Having worked with it for so long I guess I didn't bank much on its apparent shock value, but it just kept growing. I'm glad you realize that it has lost its personal identity for all intents and purposes, though it was based on a split-second you at a given distance. What later resulted was the work of my devious imagination, and you're not azz-posed'ta ask yourself do I really look like this beCAUSE you DON'T. I think I got excited about the powertransference image from you to the caterpillar, or that by some mystery you were absorbing its ability to transform, or maybe taking on its beautiful characteristics as a Butterfly.[34]

In a 1969 photo, Atwood poses in front of her portrait. She is clearly pleased with it.

★   ★   ★

By April of 1969, Pachter's illustrations for *The Journals of Susanna Moodie* were coming together successfully. "Chère Madge," he wrote to Atwood from deep inside the creative process. "Wake up often in cold sweats over Susanna and run down to studio to get things down on paper. Oh, it's happening. Oh, mémoire."[35] But it didn't last. By May, Pachter was absolutely frustrated:

I'm going mental over Susanna, mostly because I have to work according to SOMEONE ELSE's specifications. I can't stand it when they make suggestions such as "Why don't you do page sixteen in brown, it will save money because it matches with page thirty-one. And while you're at it, try not to do too many colours as we want to keep it down, etc., etc." Someday, in my dreams, they will give me *carte blanche* and say, do whatever you want and we'll work it out technically. Alas, not yet. I'm only hoping I can come

thru with it. Each time they notify me of a new limitation,
I see the original idea getting further and further away. But
I'm determined to do it. . . .[36]

By October 1970, Pachter had decided to "pass" on Susanna until
he could be given more freedom.

One hundred and twenty folio-edition copies of *The Journals
of Susanna Moodie* appeared in 1980; they were silkscreened by
Manuel and Abel Bello-Sanchez, who worked together with
Pachter for nine months on the project. A more affordable reprint
was published in the fall of 1997. When the first edition of the
Journals was put out by Oxford University Press, Atwood gave
Pachter a copy inscribed, "With regret, but hope for the future."
She had made a special arrangement with Oxford's William Toye
to allow for a different edition, containing Pachter's illustrations,
to appear at a later date. Pachter had initially asked the Canada
Council for a six-thousand-dollar grant to support the venture;
he was refused. Ten years later, he did the job for $200,000.
The original drawings were executed by Pachter himself, while
Manuel and Abel Bello-Sanchez "silkscreened the poems and
images in an old warehouse on Niagara Street. The work was
completed in nine months. . . ."[37] Pachter sold twenty-six copies
at six thousand dollars each. Then the recession of 1982 hit, and
he found himself backed into a corner. His bank was demanding
that he pay the interest on a sizeable loan he was carrying. Pachter
finally settled the matter by compensating the bank with various
pieces of art and six copies of the limited-edition *Journals*. He
piled the remaining copies on the floor and used them as a base
for a bed, "because they were so heavy." Atwood remarked,
"that's the best use made of them so far."[38] The price tag for those
bed supports is now ten thousand dollars each.

10

Writing and Harvard

[Jim Polk and I] went through Harvard grad school together, which is sort of like having been at Dieppe.
— Margaret Atwood[1]

WHEN ATWOOD RETURNED TO HARVARD in the fall of 1965, she found that little had changed. Major reforms were not instituted in American universities until the late 1960s, although the rumblings of unrest — massive protests and sit-ins — began during the late 1950s. Atwood herself had changed; her writing career had developed substantially since her 1963 departure from Cambridge, and although she was now living in the United States again she would remain part of the rapidly developing Canadian literary scene. There were a few small financial rewards for her increasing prominence — enough, at least, to provide her with a bit of pocket money. Strapped financially, she started to think of selling her papers — including the Pachter correspondence — as early as March of 1966. In 1967 she wrote to her old high school English teacher, Miss Billings, and mentioned that it would be worth hanging on to her old papers — just in case.[2]

With the publication of *The Circle Game* in 1966, Atwood became a "known" poet. When John Robert Colombo, in his capacity of "provisional coordinator" of the League of Canadian Poets (part lobby group, part trade union, with the aim of promoting poetry in Canada) sent out approximately eighty invitations to join the group, he included Atwood on the mailing list.[3]

In early February 1967, Atwood was flown out to Vancouver to do a reading. "The reading was an ordeal for me," she wrote to Pachter; "stomach kicked up, thot I would barf on stage, but didn't. Have another in Toronto on March 10th. Have to figure out some way of coping with the public image thing, I guess."[4] Nervous before live audiences, anxious about her publishing initiatives, Atwood was also feeling cut off from home.

During this period Rick Salutin was in New York, so Atwood and Polk would see a bit of him. Salutin was caught up in a failing marriage, and Atwood was pretty miserable in Boston. "We talked of that," Salutin remembers: "being miserable."[5] Salutin was also involved in left-wing politics, which were just beginning to heat up. Such concerns didn't really touch Atwood, who was still grappling with a very conservative department in a very conservative institution, trying to play by the rules — and succeed.

On the publication front, succeed she did. Peter Miller of Contact Press was advocating *The Circle Game* (at this point still called "The Winter Sleepers"; in fact, it was Miller who suggested the final title in a memo to Souster and Dudek, preferring it to the other two titles suggested by Atwood: "The Winter Sleepers" and "Journey into the Interior." "[W]ould the work not sit better," he asked, "under the title of a more important poem — say, *The Circle Game*?")[6] Atwood had revised the manuscript since first submitting it to Contact, and this time Raymond Souster was won over: "I vote a very emphatic 'yes' to what I believe will be (if published) one of our most discussed titles, *The Winter Sleepers*."[7] Miller's own comments reflect his awareness of Atwood's growing reputation. "Atwood is a person to be reckoned with," he writes, "a poet who has developed even since her recent ms, and who is capable of much further development. As one of Canada's best young poets (and a fine stylist by any standards) she should probably be given practical encouragement."[8] The delay in publishing this collection was largely a function of editor Louis Dudek's discomfort with the early version. But after reading this second manuscript, even Dudek became committed to publishing Atwood.

Dennis Lee has always been a trusted first reader of Atwood's manuscripts. His response to this Contact Press submission was measured. In a handwritten note, he cautiously praised the first three-quarters: "some I liked, but my overall impression was of very gifted piece-work."

> The last quarter was a revelation to me. This is the real article — a gathering that makes all the rest make sense, and works in ways I didn't ever know about. Though I don't tend now to end things I write with [the note has a sketched hand with index finger pointing forward here] Affirmations [another sketched hand, this time with index finger pointing backward]. I still don't trust my reaction altogether to poetry that is affirmative.[9]

Even Lee, however, could not have estimated the success of the volume. As it turned out, Contact Press did a relatively small production run, and House of Anansi, the press that Lee was running, would release *The Circle Game* again in 1967. Early in 1966, Atwood made the final changes to the manuscript. She eliminated the reference to her "esteemed father," nervous about whether he would approve of the book's contents and careful to keep her writing and her private family life separate. (Was she guarding her writing from her family or her family from her writing?) "They are from N.S.," she wrote, and "have no vices; would rather I had been a scientist."[10]

Things were starting to move very quickly. In October of 1965, Atwood finished typing the manuscript of *The Edible Woman*. "Have just, at last, finished typing ms of the Hard Novel — shriek, shriek! For me, the agony of creation I'm going to buy an electric typewriter; and when really rich, an electric secretary."[11] The following June, Atwood won the President's Medal of the University of Western Ontario for her poem "The Settlers" (which was selected from every poem published in Canada during 1965).

She spent the summer of 1966 in a sublet apartment, which became the scene of a poem included in *Procedures for Underground*. It had an antique gramophone and two rooms, one of which was the bathroom. No kitchen. She did her dishes in the tub. "Not the first time," wrote Atwood.[12]

Atwood spent the first month of the Harvard academic year living in an anthropologist's front parlour before moving on to 340 Broadway. On Broadway she inhabited "a large room that has a kitchen at one end and a good desk, and an earth-mother landlady."[13] Today, Broadway is a very staid, tree-shaded street lined with spacious homes. The sidewalks are cobblestone. Walking from 340 Broadway to Harvard Yard, you will notice plaques of historical interest indicating such things as "Revolutionary Earthworks: Site of a fortification erected to protect the patriot encampment from attack by the British Army — 1775."[14]

Her Broadway apartment, Atwood told me, was the setting for the story "Dancing Girls." Atwood also provides a powerful sketch of the 340 Broadway atmosphere in "The Landlady"; the poem is full of consonants that seem to harangue the reader as the speaker is harangued by her landlady.

> This is the lair of the landlady.
>
> She is
> a raw voice
> loose in the rooms beneath me,
>
> the continuous henyard
> squabble going on below
> thought in this house like
> the bicker of blood through the head.
>
> She is everywhere, intrusive as the smells
> that bulge in under my doorsill. . . .[15]

By comparison, Jim Polk's domestic life with "the singing nun" — a small mouse he kept in a goldfish bowl — must have seemed tranquil. Polk, a trained and skilled musician, took up yoga at about this time. By contrast, Atwood was finally driven out of her place by "wild Arabian orgiasts."[16] (I am quoting Atwood herself here, although the phrase could just as easily have come from "Dancing Girls.") She took temporary refuge in another apartment in June: apartment 3A, at 19 Agassiz. It was near the chic stretch of Massachusetts Avenue that is lined with small shops and boutiques. It was also just on the border of Somerville, an area of low-rent housing and cooperative living arrangements, which became a popular alternative to Cambridge for Harvard students in search of digs. The building at 19 Agassiz overlooked a historic Cambridge residence: the Cooper-Frost-Austin House, the oldest residence in Cambridge, built in 1690.

Atwood's letters from this period comment very little on her graduate studies in English. Rather, she talks about the novel that insisted on being written. She wrote to literary agent Hope Leresche saying that she planned to write a play — "The Loons" — and to begin another novel — "The Deaths of the Animals" — in January of 1966. But by 7 December she was reporting to Leresche that she had started a novel "which insisted on being written before the play. So far it is quite embryonic. It will take longer than the last one did, as it is a multiple-stranded rather than a single-stranded construction."[17] As September drew to a close, she had completed twenty chapters.[18] But, eventually deciding that there were just too many characters, too many different points of view, Atwood abandoned the project.

This second unpublished novel (the first being "Up in the Air So Blue") was called, alternatively, "The Deaths of the Animals" or "The Nature Hut." In the Atwood papers at the University of Toronto, there is a page containing a small sketch of a crescent-shaped island with houses, harbour, and swimming beach (the novel's setting?) marked on it. Below the sketch are two matrices — one circular, the other rectangular — representing the social order (the plot?). And in the top right-hand corner of the page are a few doodles: the watchful eyes of two women's faces, an hourglass, a dragonfly, and a pair of lips (the novel's themes?).[19]

When she returned to Harvard in September of the following year, 1966, Atwood took up residence in yet another apartment: number 6, 333A Harvard Street. But again her domestic arrangements didn't exactly click into place. This time, Atwood would have two roommates. One was named Sue Milmoe. When Sue's mother showed up with a car full of furniture, she was told that there had been a mistake; the landlord had let the apartment go. Luckily, she had a signed copy of the lease and a forceful personality. "That's impossible," she insisted, waving the lease. "I understand that you have a problem, but it's not the girls' problem." The realty office where this exchange was taking place was itself housed in an apartment of approximately the same size. So, looking around the room, she added: "I'm sure that the girls would be happy with this one, and the boys can go ahead and move the furniture in." The realtors knew that they had met their match in Sue Milmoe's mother; the furniture was duly moved into the right apartment, and on schedule. There was only one hitch: layers of "grease and slime cover[ed] every available surface."[20]

The Harvard Street apartment was quite close to Harvard Yard, about a ten-minute walk. The street was a busy one but residential and very staid. The apartment itself was in a large red-brick building, but the quarters were tight for three girls. They used the entrance hall as a living room — furnishing it with a straight-back chair, a table, a cot frame they found on the sidewalk — and the living room as a bedroom. They usually ate in the kitchen.

The household had taken shape like this. In the days before answering machines, Sue, working in New York City and about to start graduate school, placed an ad seeking a roommate in the *Harvard Summer School News*. An old roommate of hers, Fay, now married and living in Cambridge, fielded the calls the ad elicited. Atwood was one of the callers who made it onto Fay's shortlist. Karen, another caller, was signed up sight unseen. In her letters to Pachter, Atwood described her as "Karen the crystallographer." Actually, she had come from Wisconsin and had just spent a year in Germany studying chemistry on a Fulbright scholarship. She was to spend a year studying in the chemistry department. Sue, whom Atwood identified in her letters as "the Group Psychologist from New York,"[21] was in a department called "social relations," her field being social psychology. Both Sue and Karen received about two hundred dollars a month in scholarship money (a healthy amount at that time); Atwood, by comparison, was very poor.

Milmoe remembers that she and Karen thought of Atwood as "the senior citizen" because she was four years older than they were. "She used to wear the most relentlessly sensible shoes, a kind of rat-grey pair of Hush Puppies, which had not been improved by two years of slush and damp. Just dreadful." But, in hindsight, Milmoe wonders whether Atwood's rationale for continuing to wear those Hush Puppies was financial rather than aesthetic. Atwood's student visa did not permit her to earn much money, and in any case female graders were paid "a pittance." "In many departments," explains Milmoe, "guys were teaching fellows . . . girls were graders."[22]

At first, Milmoe recalls, she considered Atwood to be a "mouse — with the hush puppies"; however, the three "quite good looking guys who helped to move [Atwood] in" impressed her.[23] They were Jim Polk and his two roommates. "We all had carefully suppressed crushes on Jim," says Judy Wright, a friend who camped out in the Harvard Street apartment for a few weeks.[24]

Although they had started out as virtual strangers and were forced to share cramped quarters, Sue, Karen, and Peggy were soon getting along very well. "Atwood was a marvellous cook and housewife," laughs Milmoe. She would make bread and a good pork-chop dish. She had a "decent" scallop recipe, Milmoe recalls. "You had to cook them for ten minutes; that's how one cooked then."[25] The trio entertained quite a bit too. When Harold, Atwood's brother, came to visit, Atwood baked him a wonderful cake decorated with elaborate insects. Insects, after all, were an Atwood family favourite. Ruth, Atwood's younger sister, visited that year as well, during spring break. Polk spent quite a bit of time at the apartment, as did his roommates, Mowbray Allen and Charles Matthews (both of whom ended up teaching English in the American Midwest). A few others also managed to squeeze themselves into those small rooms on Harvard Street. Judy Wright lived there between March and mid-April, so she was on hand when Atwood received the momentous news that she had won a Governor General's Literary Award. (More about that later.) "I am very, very fond of Peggy," says Wright, "and from the first, quite worshipful — she and

Jim were impenetrable, hilarious, iconoclastic, quite perfect."[26]

Atwood then, as now, had a sharp wit and a willingness to use it. "Sometimes she made points by being ruder than other people were willing to be. I don't know if that's insecurity or great confidence," muses Milmoe now. Once, she was particularly rude to one of Milmoe's boyfriends, mimicking his way of talking — the "goshes" and "gollies" and other interjections that punctuated his phrases. Karen and Sue didn't speak to Atwood for two days afterwards — not only because her rudeness had verged on the malicious but also because it had been, as Milmoe says, "rather like swatting a puppy."[27]

That said, Atwood's strength of character had an impact on life at Harvard Street — from the apartment's decor (an enormous poster whose message — "Fuck Communism!" — took up half the living room wall), to its ceremonies (Atwood insisted on reading tarot cards for any "beau" brought into the house), to its daily rituals (she liked the bath mat hung over the tub rather than spread beneath the sink, as Milmoe would have done). Laughing, Milmoe told me that she still hangs the bath mat over the tub.

Ph.D. orals were scheduled for both Atwood and Polk in January of 1967. Atwood's were relatively simple, and her committee "chivalrous," as she put it in a letter to Daryl Hine. Jim's proved more difficult because of some unpredictable questions — such as, "What Shelley scholar died of alcoholism?" To celebrate getting out alive, they dined on lobster and went to the movies. Then they began to think about the next scholarly hurdle: the thesis topic.[28]

By that January Atwood had decided to marry Jim Polk,[29] "after five years of equivocation." "We've been through so many Horrible Things together I figure we have a good survival chance."[30] A June wedding was planned to coincide with the completion of Atwood's novel (which she hoped to wrap up by the end of May) and to allow for a trip out West, to Montana, to visit Jim's family. The couple announced their good news to friends and family via letter on or around the date of Atwood's Ph.D. orals: 5 January. On 11 January she received an advance payment for her papers, which she had sold to the University of Toronto. All in all, Atwood's life seemed to be in order. Even the previously troublesome novel was now allowing itself to be wrestled into shape. By 27 February, Atwood told Pachter that it was finally at the "point of break-off with the real world and becoming its own thing."[31] The problem was that publication of *The Edible Woman* was being delayed. But this obstacle would soon be overcome.

★ ★ ★

It began with a phone call. The ringing woke Milmoe — the phone was right outside her room — and then she heard the shriek. On 17 March 1967, Atwood won Canada's top literary honour — the Governor General's Literary Award — for *The Circle Game* (beating out such revered Canadian poets as F.R. Scott, Earle Birney, and Miriam Waddington).

After the initial excitement had subsided, Atwood's roommates took her firmly in hand. Her wardrobe needed serious attention. The Hush Puppies, they insisted, had to go. Atwood, presumably too thrilled to care much about such things, and quite a bit wealthier, didn't mind. The award came with a cheque for $2,500, enough to buy the electric typewriter she had set her sights on. And contact lenses. So Sue and Karen rolled up their sleeves and began to prepare Atwood for the awards ceremony. Atwood would wear Sue's dress, "bought for $7.99 in Filene's Basement, beige crepe with a drawstring neck." Milmoe had worn it to a dinner with Nobel Prize-winning biologist Jim Watson at Jimmy's Harbourside in 1965, so it was definitely a dress for important occasions. "Somehow the neck was never quite right on me," Milmoe confesses, "but it suited Peggy awfully well." Next came the shoes. Atwood borrowed a pair of Judy's. Finally, Judy was recruited to set Atwood's hair on "orange-juice cans. Those were the days of straight hair." Then she adds, thoughtfully, "Judy was good with hair."[32] Judy denies this particular story detail. "I remember brush rollers," she says. "Setting her hair so it wouldn't be too curly (lord . . .) was a big ordeal." But, she adds, "remember, count on Susan." By this, she means that Sue Milmoe, like Atwood, "has a talent for storytelling and drama which has kept me enthralled for thirty years."[33]

Atwood asked Peter Miller to accompany her to the awards ceremony, as the representative of Contact Press. The award was an incredible honour, and the presentation itself was quite formal. It was held at Government House in Ottawa on 2 June at 6 P.M. A very nervous Atwood, clad in a borrowed dress, was presented with a special edition of her book and invited to a reception and dinner in honour of the award winners. This was held at the Country Club, Aylmer Road, Quebec.

"Well, guess *all* my friends will hate me now," Atwood wrote to Pachter; "at first I thought it was *you*, playing a practical joke."[34] But this award was clearly no joke. Years later, Atwood would say that she won the Governor General's Literary Award for 1966 because it "was the 'turn' of a younger poet";[35] but we now know that the award marked the emergence of a formidable literary talent.

⋆   ⋆   ⋆

Soon after this coup, Atwood was contacted by Jack McClelland of the publishing house McClelland and Stewart. She also began the process of establishing strong ties with other Canadian publishers.

Early in 1967, William Toye, editorial director of Oxford University Press Canada, phoned Atwood and told her that Oxford would like to publish her further collections of poetry. They had lunch soon after, and that meeting led Atwood to a strong publishing relationship with Oxford and a lasting friendship with Toye. She asked Toye what his birth sign was. "I'm a Gemini," he explained to me; "she's a Scorpio. I know nothing about astrology, but she must have decided that the combination worked well." It did. Atwood and Toye, off and on, over a period of twenty-nine years, have worked together on thirteen different books, including three anthologies. Toye stresses Atwood's consummate professionalism and says that their association has been "a privilege, and represents the highlight of my own long career in publishing."[36] The first book to result from this was *The Animals in That Country*, published by Oxford in 1968.

House of Anansi, a new press cofounded by Dennis Lee and Dave Godfrey, approached Atwood about reprinting *The Circle Game*. After all, the enormous success of this collection had taken Contact by surprise, and its print run had been small — just 450 copies. Atwood quickly wrote to Peter Miller, ostensibly to ask his advice but also to let him know about Anansi's invitation. Miller graciously urged her to republish with Anansi.

Also as a result of her Governor General's Literary Award win, Atwood was being sought out by interviewers. This situation has never abated. Some of the early interviews she did were disastrous. They were also hilarious. The first newspaper interview was conducted in Cambridge while Atwood was still an "impoverished graduate student." She recalls, "We slogged through the interview as if through knee-deep mud, until finally, in exasperation, he said, 'Say something interesting. Say you write all your poems on drugs.' "[37] Since then, of course, Atwood has learned to inject interesting nuggets into her interviews. That she wrote all her poems on drugs has not been one of them.

John Robert Colombo remembers seeing a *Toronto Star* interview in which Atwood mentioned that she was busy writing a novel. As he read, the thought crossed his mind that had he been a publisher he would have followed up immediately. At precisely that moment he received a phone call from Marge Hodgson, Jack McClelland's assistant at McClelland and Stewart, who wanted to know if he had Atwood's number.[38] The call Atwood received from Jack McClelland must have come shortly afterwards.

By the time Atwood actually spoke to Jack McClelland, she was feeling extremely frustrated with McClelland and Stewart. She suspected that the publishing house had lost the copy of *The Edible Woman* manuscript she had submitted and was maintaining a mysterious silence about the whole thing. In a letter dated 16 February 1967, Atwood mischievously told Roy MacSkimming of Clarke, Irwin that her novel was being "held hostage" by a publisher; the ransom was her second novel.[39]

A more likely scenario was that the manuscript had gotten lost in the shuffle somewhere at McClelland and Stewart. Since the readers' reports on the novel are undated and anonymous, it is almost impossible to determine what happened with greater accuracy. When she finally summoned up the nerve to phone McClelland and Stewart and demand the return of her manuscript — feeling strengthened by her recent success — the man to whom she had to speak was out. Instead, she received a call from Jack McClelland himself, complimenting her on the *Star* interview. As Atwood reported to Pachter, McClelland then explained that, after reading the *Star* piece, he had sat down "and dictated a long, enthusiastic letter to me asking to see my novel!!! He went on to say that he had a terrible thought that he actually had my novel already so he tried to assemble a file on me and to find out what had been going on and was overcome with embarrassment. . . ." But now the wayward manuscript had apparently been found. McClelland "pleaded with me (tee, hee) to bear with them a little longer, so I asked for a copy of the manuscript which was whisked to me by cab, and I'm now supposed to be altering it, though I haven't had the guts to open it yet. That's his story anyway; don't know how much I believe."[40] Atwood was on her way to spend three weeks at the family cabin. She calmly told McClelland that she would contact him upon her return.[41] Had she spoken to him before winning the Governor General's Literary Award, she might not have felt quite so calm.

II

A Wedding

IN MAY OF 1967, Atwood went apartment hunting in Montreal. She needed to find a place to live for herself and her new husband, Jim Polk. They would be arriving as the fall term began. Atwood settled on number 5, 17 avenue de l'Épée.

The wedding itself was not until mid-June. Since Polk's mother was a Catholic and Atwood's family didn't have strong religious affiliations, the couple decided on a civil ceremony. They thought that Mrs. Polk's sensibilities would be less offended by a City Hall wedding than by a ceremony performed in a church of another denomination. City Hall actually was their first venue choice, but Sue Milmoe came up with a better idea. She managed to wangle a room at Radcliffe's grad centre, near a garden. After all, Atwood had been a Radcliffe student and had lived in residence when she first came from Toronto. Polk found a justice of the peace in the yellow pages who agreed to perform the ceremony.[1]

Most Massachusetts justices of the peace preferred to conduct marriage ceremonies on their own premises. Technically, they were only licensed to perform ceremonies in their jurisdictions. So they often performed a bare-bones ceremony within their own jurisdiction prior to the larger ceremony held elsewhere. Atwood and Polk's justice stipulated that the couple go to his house in Jamaica Plain beforehand to sign the papers — or so they thought. Instead, when they got to the house — which boasted plastic Buddhas on the mantlepiece and such other curiosities — a rather exotic ceremony was performed. With Atwood's parents and sister as witnesses, rings were passed over the two statues of Buddha. "It's all in the book," says Milmoe, referring to the wedding ceremony in *Lady Oracle*. The couple received a shopping bag full of souvenirs and handouts from various Chinese restaurants (the justice of the peace himself was Chinese), including the printed motto "Love each other for what you are; forgive each other for what you ain't."[2] Not bad advice, really, but the turn of phrase lacked the usual formality. Atwood and Polk returned to Boston somewhat shaken and decided *not* to invite the justice of the peace to the Radcliffe garden party.

Everybody helped with the party. Karen shopped for the food. (Atwood was mildly upset later because she had used the money to buy expensive mixed nuts rather than cheap peanuts.) Polk's friends Robert and Pamela Kirkpatrick lent silverware. Milmoe baked the cake. She remembers that she bought the cake pans of graduated sizes but, at the last moment, unsure about how to make stiff icing, decided to make the fluffy kind. Mrs. Atwood, a very good cook who had trained as a home economist, commented quietly: "My, I've never seen a wedding cake frosted in seven-minute icing before." The weather was very hot, and the icing was decidedly "soupy." As they transported Sue's concoction in Judy Wright's fire-engine-red convertible Volkswagon "with a martyred front right fender," Judy driving incredibly slowly in an effort to head off disaster, "the layers started to slide."[3] Polk, the day before, had said that he wanted a plastic bride and groom on top of the cake rather than fresh flowers. Unfortunately, no plastic bride-and-groom sets were to be had that day. "Had I found them," Milmoe laughs ruefully, "perhaps things might have turned out differently."[4]

Atwood wore a white Mexican-cotton dress to the garden party. She "tried to get away with wearing the beige shoes (borrowed for the Governor General's Awards ceremony)," recalls Milmoe, but her roommates put their feet down, so to speak. "No," they said. "*White* shoes."[5] So Atwood went out to buy a pair of shoes.

After the wedding, the newlyweds travelled to Montana to stay with the Polks before heading up to Toronto for a 7 July celebration in the Atwood backyard. Only after all of this did Atwood and Polk get a chance to have an interval of peace and bird-watching at the Atwood cabin.[6]

12

And Teaching Too

MONTREAL PLAYED HOST IN 1967. It was the year of Expo, the world's fair. A mood of celebration prevailed, and the city was at its best. In fact, Canada was at its best. Optimistic. Forward-looking. Proud. Atwood returned to her country as it hit a high point.

Miniskirts were in; so were bell-bottom pants and dead-straight hair. The newlyweds arrived just after the Expo festivities had wound down, Atwood to take up a faculty position at Sir George Williams University, and Polk to complete his Harvard doctoral dissertation.

Sir George Williams had advertised a full-time tenure-track position with a primary field in Victorian and a secondary field in American literature. Atwood was hired on the basis of her academic work. It was common practice in those days to hire academics who had not yet completed their doctorates for such positions, the assumption being that they would complete their dissertations during their first couple years of teaching. Incredibly, it was (and continues to be) normal to view a person's creative writing as not particularly relevant or helpful to the academic profession. The study of English, or so the thinking goes, involves critical rather than creative writing. And when Atwood joined the faculty of the Sir George Williams English department, the Governor General's Literary Award would not have carried the prestige it carries today in the academic milieu. A number of her new colleagues were likely unaware of the honour she had just received.

During the 1967–68 academic year, Atwood taught two literature courses: Victorian (English 436) and American (English

445). Her name appears in the course calendar for 1968–69, but this is a function of publication deadlines and is not accurate. She and Polk rented an Outremont walk-up at the foot of Mount Royal (the wealthy inhabit the mountain's slope) near a Greek bakery. That year, Atwood taught four classes (two during the day and two at night), marked stacks of papers, finished *The Animals in That Country*, started *The Journals of Susanna Moodie* and *Procedures for Underground*, and made the final cuts to *The Edible Woman*. She travelled to work on the subway, hauled groceries home on the bus, and recalls that she was "always running." By the end of the year she had lost twenty-five pounds. Her friends told her that she looked like a "model." What they meant, Atwood explains, was that she looked "gaunt."[1]

Although her office was small and lacked a source of natural light and fresh air, Atwood enjoyed the teaching. Enthusiastic, she drew charts to illustrate her points, brought Aunt Jemima pancake boxes to class to "demonstrate racial stereotyping," and introduced James Whitcomb Riley to her Victorian classes "to show them that Tennyson was really very nice by comparison."[2] She especially liked the evening classes, the domain of mature students who wanted to be challenged, who demanded more from their instructor. The daytime students were more interested in marks.

> My biggest problem . . . was "The American Project." Thinking that I would be giving the students a chance to be creative and express themselves, I told them I'd give them 10% of their marks for a project which they were to think up themselves. It could be anything, I said, thus releasing clouds of *angst* which were to follow me around all year. What *kind* of thing, they wanted to know. What did I expect? I told them my mind was open. So, as it turned out, was theirs: on the due date, scale models of Salem, collages, dolls dressed as Puritans, . . . scrapbooks, dialogues from the points of view of Hester and the Scarlet Letter, a small clay whale, lovingly modelled and baked, and a couple of wall murals arrived in the classroom. Plus a slogan button,

which is finally what I remember most clearly about my year at Sir George:

MOBY DICK IS NOT A SOCIAL DISEASE.[3]

But Atwood really found her niche at Sir George Williams with a group of people interested and involved in creative writing. She was still, of course, first and foremost a writer. "That she was seeking a career as a Canadian writer was always clear," remarks David Sheps, a Sir George Williams colleague.[4] Montreal's community of English-language writers was a vibrant one at this point. Atwood remembers:

> Frank Scott was alive and well. He came out from behind a curtain once, playing the ocarina. Buffy Glassco was also alive, and his friend John Richmond; I would sometimes go to dinner with one or both and listen to tales of scandal. It was Buffy who taught me to eat hearts of palm, until I found out it killed the palm. Hugh Hood was there, and I think was once in my living room. Gwen MacEwen was there that winter. Clark Blaise taught at SGW and studied extra languages in his spare time. Before your very eyes he could turn himself into an Italian, a Russian, a Frenchman . . . he did the body languages too. Bharati Mukherjee was head of the graduate English programme at McGill. There seemed to be a lot of parties, a lot of eating.[5]

Blaise, who was married to Mukherjee, was also a writer teaching English at Sir George Williams. He and Atwood spent quite a bit of time together that year discussing literature and the developing Canadian literary scene. The second typescript of *The Edible Woman*, the one that Atwood was revising for publication, contains Blaise's scribbled comments.[6]

George and Angela Bowering were in Montreal as well, and they spent many evenings with Atwood and Polk. The Bowerings lived in a large Westmount apartment. Atwood became good friends with both George and the blonde and beautiful Angela.

In a short reminiscence entitled "Bowering Pie," Atwood suggests that George, a collector of photos, a man who discussed literary topics by quoting others, had developed a powerful mask that hid a deep and thoughtful poet. Certainly in their letters to one another he and Atwood address literary issues that they seem to have left unexplored when they were together. "I had a couple of poems I was going to show you," Atwood wrote in 1969 after having driven with Bowering through "Bowering territory" near a small "dot on the map called Okpatok or some such," where they ate "breaded veal cutlets" and watched "the locals smart-alecking at the waitress." "[F]unny how we never talk poetry when actually within speaking distance but substitute with remarks about how we look in jeans."[7] What their correspondence suggests to me, however, is that both writers are experts in the art of creating and using masks.

There was a series of poetry readings at Sir George Williams run by Stan Hoffman and Howard Fink. Many of the poets who came to read were American and well established: Anthony Hecht, Denise Levertov, Daryl Hine (who, although born in Vancouver, was then settled in Chicago). Department of English faculty members who also wrote poetry were asked to give readings as well, Atwood among them. After her reading she requested and received the same payment as the American poets.[8] At the time such behaviour seemed brash: this young Canadian expects to be treated on a par with the Americans. (Harrumph!) Today it would be seen very differently — the equivalent, for example, of a woman insisting on equal pay for equal work.

At night, Atwood revised *The Edible Woman* according to the rather conflicting suggestions made by McClelland and Stewart. The pace of her life was as hectic as it had been during her year at the University of British Columbia. Atwood's balancing act had quickly become a juggling act. But now that she was a little bit older, she could feel the effects of the self-abuse that act demanded. She wrote to Pachter: "Have lost much weight; 107 and going down. Don't eat, sleep, etc. Mostly it's just too many things. . . ."[9] But all of this didn't stop her. By December she was already thinking about her next novel. She was "writing poetry," she told Pachter, and "sharpening teeth and claws for the next prose effort, the camp novel."[10] She was also bracing herself for another move, this time to Edmonton.

★   ★   ★

The practical realities of a new marriage and strong loyalties she felt towards friends as well as members of the writing community were also putting a strain on Atwood — albeit one that she welcomed. Gwendolyn MacEwen, for one, depended upon Atwood as a kind of confidante during this year and the following one.[11] As well, Atwood continued to travel and to keep up with her friends in other cities. On 8 February 1968 she passed a "gruesome evening" ("gruesome," here, is meant to signal the Gothic theme of the evening) at Jay Macpherson's place; Pachter came bearing a copy of the illustrated *Speeches for Doctor Frankenstein*.

Still exhausted, even after spending some time during the summer of 1968 in northern Ontario and Quebec followed by a couple of weeks in Cambridge, where she met with her doctoral supervisor, Atwood went to join her husband in Edmonton. One of the things affecting her health, she discovered, was alcohol. "Liquor to you is poison," warned her doctor.[12] The other drain on her physical well-being was the condition of being torn between academic and creative worlds. Rather than complementing each other as she had imagined they would — and as Northrop Frye had suggested they would during their brief discussion of that subject in a Victoria College hallway — these realms seemed to be at odds with one another.

The life arrangement Atwood and Polk had made was a logical one: that first year in Montreal Atwood would teach and Polk would work on his dissertation; the roles would be reversed when Polk took up his teaching position at the University of Alberta in the fall of 1968. But Atwood's creative writing took a lot more time and energy than either of them had anticipated. And how could she give it up, even while teaching full time? It was also proving difficult for Atwood to focus her attention on a thesis that was becoming progressively distant from her immediate interests. Still, she worked at it diligently through the fall of 1967[13] and into the early part of 1968.

Atwood and Polk lived at number 8425, 107th Street, in Edmonton. It was an upstairs duplex. Atwood got to know the woman downstairs well; after all, in a winter of ice fogs ("if you breathe it, the fog cuts your lungs," Atwood explains[14]) and ice storms, people tend to stay inside. The woman's name was Jetske Sybyzma, and she taught art history at the university. Sybyzma was Dutch, an expert in mediaeval art, and was doing work on Hieronymus Bosch. Most believed his art to be loaded with Freudian symbolism, but she endeavoured to prove that it was astrological. Such an approach seemed to make sense when one considered it in relation to Bosch's view of the world. Sybyzma also worked with Renaissance portraits, pointing out the symbolism of hand position and rings.

Also skilled at palmistry, Sybyzma would instruct Atwood in it during that long, cold November and December. Atwood had already learned to read tarot cards (her knowledge of it emerges in *The Robber Bride*) and was intrigued with the art of reading palms. She made some good predictions. Poet Patrick Lane remembers that when he went through Edmonton, on the road after a "marriage breakdown," Atwood "read my tarot and told me I might die that year. I went on to have two near-fatal car accidents, one with Ray Fraser when we rolled eight times, topsy-turvey, on the 401 east of Toronto. Drunk again."[15]

Polk was having a difficult time at the University of Alberta. He felt ill at ease with the faculty and his own academic role and would return home from faculty parties in the deep winter with a mood to match the weather.[16] Canadian nationalism was on the rise, and it triggered anti-American sentiment. Polk, who was both an American and a professor of American literature, became a target. After berating Americans, people would add, "Oh, but I forgot — *you're* an American."[17] But the damage had already been done.

★   ★   ★

Cher Charlôt,

It's 28 below, going down to 35 below tonight with a wind chill factor of 75 below, and it's all coming in through the cracks in our apartment. We have blankets over the windows and our thermal underwear on, and I'm typing with a hot water bottle under my feet. It's fun in a way; going outside is a big adventure, but we hope it doesn't keep up much longer or we'll starve to death. We're barricaded in here with the turkey carcass left over from X-mas.[18]

★   ★   ★

Atwood and Polk had organized a series of poetry readings, held in the basement of their duplex. (Lane had been one of their invited readers.) Many of the participants were members of Edmonton's literary community, of which Atwood had quickly become part. Elizabeth Brewster went to the city in 1968 and spent two years working as a librarian before taking over Atwood's creative-writing class when she left. Although older than Atwood, Brewster remembers the younger poet as someone who influenced her thinking. In particular, Brewster writes in an autobiographical note, Atwood "influenced the choice and arrangement of the poems in my next book, *Sunrise North* (although this did not appear until 1972), and suggested the title." Brewster remembers Atwood's delight in reading palms and drawing horoscopes. "Perhaps the fact that she foretold that my later life would be happier and more prosperous than the early part," she muses, "and that I would have more fame, fortune, love, and friendship in the later part of my life, helped me to face the future cheerfully."[19] I wonder if she ever told Atwood this.

The Animals in That Country was published by the American house Atlantic-Little, Brown in 1968. All the poems it contained Atwood had written while living in Cambridge (from 1965 to 1967).[20] The Canadian edition, published by Oxford University Press, appeared the following year, at about the same time as *The Edible Woman*. In this early collection Atwood makes deft use of the precise image and works carefully with internal rhymes.

The Animals in That Country includes some of Atwood's most frequently anthologized early work — "Backdrop Addresses Cowboy," for example, and "Progressive Insanities of a Pioneer." In "The Reincarnation of Captain Cook," we catch a glimpse of Atwood's early preoccupation (soon to become a national preoccupation) with uninventing and reinventing Canada. "Now I am old," muses the speaker, "I know my / mistake was my acknowledging / of maps."[21] "Instant while Waking" anticipates some of the visions experienced by the protagonist of Atwood's next novel, *Surfacing*. "Astral Travel" suggests that Atwood was thinking about this subject well before the publication of *Lady Oracle*. We tend to forget that Atwood was still very young when she wrote the poems that form this collection until we reach the poem "Chronology." Here the poet traces her passage through childhood: "At 6 I was sly as a weasel," "At 12 . . . I was bored," "At 16 I was pragmatic . . . I wore my hair like a helmet," "But by 20 I had begun / to shed knowledge like petals / or scales." At twenty! Atwood, still in her twenties, was pondering what it would be like to be fifty. "Time," she writes, "wears me down like water."[22]

> At 50 they will peel
> my face away like a nylon stocking
>
> uncovering such incredible blank
> innocence, that even mirrors
> accustomed to grotesques
> will be astounded.
>
> I will be unshelled, I will be
> of no use to that city
> and like a horse with a broken back
> I will have to be taken out and shot.[23]

The Canadian edition of *The Animals in That Country* looked very different from the American edition. On the latter, the title was blocked above and below by two large rectangles: pink on the top, purple on the bottom. In each rectangle stood a stylized lion of the kind often found on crests. The Canadian cover was less conservative, as indicated by Atwood's letter to her editor, William Toye. "Are you really sure," she asked, "by the way — that you want a bull's rear end on the back cover?"[24]

★   ★   ★

The Edible Woman was also published — finally — in the fall of 1968 and also dedicated to "J." Atwood was quite worried about its dust-jacket blurb. In the Atwood Papers is a copy of a blunt letter to McClelland and Stewart's advertising and promotions department that Atwood composed and typed but never actually sent. It's all about that blurb.

> I feel *very strongly* that the copy as it stands manages to be both too serious and too coy; if you don't like my Dell-Mysteries format, please at least consider rewriting the original to remove some of the cutie-cutie nuances, especially that suicidal "However, if you really want to know . . . you will just have to read the book." My reaction, as a browser in bookstores of long standing, would be, No, I don't really want to know, and I won't read the book. Depending on a résumé of plot for such a book is treating a soufflé as though it were a steak. As you haven't read the book, you don't seem to realize what a put-on the whole thing is. M. & S. seems to be trying to make it into one of those serious books that treat modern life & female problems, whereas (if anything) it's a satire of the whole *genre*.
>
> I promise to write you a serious one next time; that is, unless you put me off novel-writing altogether by convincing me that if I do, you'll give it a jacket flap that will convince readers & reviewers they're about to enjoy a hilarious comedy.
>
> The jacket copy as it stands was based on suggestions by me, so I take the liberty of at least cleaning it up for you. I've said about 50 million times that surely the best advertisement is the title, and anything that gives away too

much — reveals the punch line, as it were — is a mistake. The cake should NOT be mentioned.[25]

What Atwood did send was a much more discreet letter with a different plot summary attached. She opens with "I've tried to include enough plot and thematic material while avoiding what I consider the unmentionables (the fact that Marian *does* get engaged to Peter, and the cake)." And she concludes with "Hope you like it; if not, I'll be forced into writing a 12 book epic in heroic couplets."[26] Atwood's version of the summary appears on the published edition.

In the final version of the manuscript, Atwood herself makes a cameo appearance. Just like Alfred Hitchcock did in his films, she appears in the novel just once, and briefly. Despite what many readers believe, Atwood is not the novel's protagonist, Marian; rather, she is the bedraggled English graduate student who tags along with Duncan and his two roommates, Trevor and Fish, to Marian and Ainsley's party. Marian "opened the door and found herself confronting Trevor's puzzled face. The other two were behind him, and an unfamiliar figure, probably female, in a baggy Harris-tweed coat, sunglasses and long black stockings."[27] There is Atwood.

When *The Edible Woman* at last appeared in print, Atwood became a celebrity in Edmonton, if not yet in the rest of Canada. In the spring of 1969 she attended book signings and appeared on local television shows. But it wasn't all glamorous. Her first book signing took place in the men's sock and underwear department of the Hudson's Bay Company store in Edmonton. (Why would a marketing representative station the author of a book entitled *The Edible Woman* there, of all places?) "Too terrifying," Atwood comments, laughing.[28] She sold two books.

Interviews were no more comfortable. During her first interview in support of *The Edible Woman*, Atwood fielded some rather awkward questions. Others were downright embarrassing: Do men find you attractive? Or sexist: How do you find time for the housework? One was even rather aggressive: Why should I read this novel?[29]

The Edible Woman was published in the United States by Atlantic-Little, Brown and shepherded through the process by Peter Davison. Davison had come to know Atwood at Harvard, just after the publication of *The Animals in That Country*, largely through his capacity as editor of the *Atlantic Monthly*. The American edition of the novel has a wonderful jacket designed by John Alcorn. A sketched nude woman, rendered in shades of yellow, brown, and pink, sits in what looks like a soup ladle. An edible woman. Her hair — white, and coifed like one of those eighteenth-century wigs — is done up elaborately with an ornament that bears a striking resemblance to a fleur-de-lis. The overall impression of the novel that the design gives us is that of a period piece; it signals a novel considerably more exotic and intellectual than the one signalled by the photograph of a nightie-clad young woman that appears on the Bantam-Seal paperback.[30]

★ ★ ★

In September of 1969, Atwood managed to secure a teaching position at the University of Alberta. She badly needed the financial security it would provide. With writer Rudy Wiebe she taught a creative-writing course (imaginative writing, that is, not composition). The course was structured as a seminar; every Tuesday night, groups of twelve to fourteen students would meet for close discussions of various texts and presentations by visiting speakers. Atwood asked Gwendolyn MacEwen to come and speak to the class at the end of October, but by then MacEwen's fear of flying had grown to the point that such a trip was impossible for her. She had agreed initially but, apologetically, had cancelled out at the last minute.[31]

Before the term began, Atwood had made significant progress on her thesis. She sent off a substantial portion to her typist, a Mrs. Kesson, and on 1 July 1969 felt confident enough to promise her another chapter in a couple of weeks.[32] By the end of the month, she had sent the manuscript to her trusted friend and advisor Jay Macpherson, who responded, in a letter dated 20 August, by furnishing Atwood with detailed commentary.

Her remarks were enthusiastic, with one exception: Macpherson thought that Atwood was refusing to acknowledge complications and inconsistencies. "Introduction," Macpherson wrote, "able and useful,"

> but worried me rather by its ruthless exclusion of anything not dead on the line you meant to follow. . . . The impression stayed with me as I read on: you're avoiding a lot of by-ways and illuminating observations you easily *could* make: in the end I'm apprehensive about your robbing the eventual book (suspect it's easier to write a fat thesis than thicken a thin — no insult intended — thesis up for a book: by fat I mean with asides & rewarding footnotes: the sort of thing you do awfully well in letters).[33]

Certainly, Atwood's letter to Professor Jerome Buckley of 1 July 1969 acknowledged that she had "narrowed the scope somewhat in order to keep within the 180-page limit."[34] Today, a 180-page doctoral dissertation would be considered a very short one indeed.

To earn some extra money, Atwood also signed a contract with the Department of English to serve as a marker for "Professor J. Polk," as of September 1969. In exchange for marking thirty-five freshman papers each month, Atwood would receive fifty dollars a month for six months.[35] Presumably Professor Polk was, at this point, earning considerably more from teaching than his wife.

Coordinating all these different activities — marking, thesis writing, teaching, and so on — took considerable energy. Atwood carefully planned her week in a logbook. Weekdays were divided into three chunks — morning, afternoon, and evening — all of which were subdivided into task slots. "Shopping" took the Wednesday between 11:30 and 2:00 slot, but all other tasks were related to writing and studying — "letters," "thesis," "article," "verse play," "read." Friday evenings and weekends were reserved for the "novel."[36]

Atwood never let her correspondence with friends and colleagues flag. Her letters to Pachter alternated quickly between news about life in general — cat talk in particular — to requests that Pachter look over poem translations. "I think 'Axiom' is probably O.K." she wrote. "As a matter of fact, I like it better in French. And 'Mid-Winter' doesn't look too bad, but there are problems with the third one. Should I be using the subjunctive anywhere?"[37] Pachter responded by sending "newly translated poems." He wrote, "attacked them for several hours this evg. to try and get them perfect. There were several stylistic maneyelas and grammatical gutmans to rectify. Have enumerated all the changes, so go over them and see if you follow them. O.K."[38] Although an artist by profession, throughout this correspondence Pachter shows himself to be a very capable writer and stylist as well.

Similarly, although a writer by profession, Atwood has a strong artistic bent. She designed the cover for *The Circle Game* (by hand, with letter transfers); did the collages and artwork for the Oxford edition of *The Journals of Susanna Moodie*; drew cartoons and comic strips, which appeared in various publications; and enjoys doing watercolours and sketches.[39]

★   ★   ★

Atwood devoted the spring of 1969 to completing *The Journals of Susanna Moodie*. Before she finally chose this title, however, she tried on a series of other ones: "Susanna Moodie: Autobiography from an Undetermined Location," "Susannah Moodie: Autobiographies from an Unknown Location," "Unspoken Poems of Susanna Moodie Recorded by Margaret Atwood," "Unspoken Poems of Susanna Moodie," and "Underskin Journals of Susanna Moodie." While her artwork embellishes the Oxford edition, Pachter's appears in the limited edition he put out in 1980 and in the 1997 reprint. As he worked on the project, he wrote to Atwood:

> I've just cut the typewritten manuscript of "Susanna" into
> pieces. Hope you don't mind but I had to in order to get
> some idea of space and pages. I've got the studio floor

littered in mock-ups and am now trying to figure out signature-to-page ratios. Each time I do any mock-up I get more mental ideas and I have to start again.

Already I can feel the excitement of being able to "compose" the character of the page myself without letting any machine do it. This is very important. I look at the poem for its visual shape as well as what it says. Cutting it out with scissors is like forming a snow ball. With one or two of them I've broken them up in what I think are logical division points in order to work better on a double-page spread.[40]

The idea of the creative potential inherent in cutting things out was, of course, central to the text itself, which opens with that powerful, and now famous, image:

I take this picture of myself
and with my sewing scissors
cut out the face.

Now it is more accurate:

where my eyes were,
every-
thing appears[41]

★   ★   ★

Atwood was now increasingly in demand as a writer, but she still managed to be very generous with her time. Rick Salutin, who was living in Quebec in 1969, asked her advice about where to submit his writing for publication. Atwood sent him a list. He had placed a poem in *Quarry*, he remembers, and Atwood was one of the only people to see it and comment. "She is the least selfish writer you could find," says Salutin, who has worked with Atwood on many projects associated with *This Magazine* over the years.[42]

At about this time, Atwood began to make carbon copies of her typed correspondence, realizing, perhaps, their significance as records of her involvement in the literary scene. Now she also felt the need to make some policy decisions, for the profession of being a writer involved many tasks beyond creative writing — book reviewing, for example, or writing letters to support funding applications. Was it really appropriate, Atwood asked herself, for her to review works written by good friends? After all, in the small Canadian literary community most writers knew one another. So the question was not only "Does a positive review of a good friend's work really serve the best interests of the reviewer and the book?" but also "Did it really serve the larger interests of Canadian literature?" And the same questions applied to negative reviews of any new book. When poet and *Quarry* editor Tom Marshall asked her to review MacEwen's new book, for example, she declined.

> But I would willingly review the work of someone I'm not in touch with on a personal level. Why not try me on someone else; male, preferably. (Women are still an ethnic minority group, & when one reviews another it looks like an "in-group" thing, bordering on the women's magazine.) Actually I'm better at more than one at once; suggest a group, why don't you? Then I'll say yea or nay. (I also have a thing about not reviewing people whose work I think I don't understand; I'd rather review* things I feel in touch with.) If it sounds like I'm a picky reviewer, you're right!
>
> (* things not people)[43]

Atwood had formulated such policies because, by nature and by upbringing, she would instinctively agree to give more than her fair share of time and energy to her community, yet the demands of the muse required her to set limits.

All the while, she wrote poems and sent them to publishers. To Tom Marshall she explained: "As for my own stuff — demand exceeds supply at the moment, but I have some untyped things

I'm working on; also a batch or two out at other magazines. If I like anything I'm working on, or if some things come back, I'll send you some. Would you like a human one or an inhuman one?"[44] Peter Davison, himself a poet and, at the time, both director of the Atlantic Monthly Press and a staff editor at the *Atlantic Monthly*, had developed a genuine appreciation for her work. He was delighted with the manuscript of a collection she sent to him in December. The few poems he did not like he thought were marred by the "patness of their endings." In this category he put "Cyclops" and "84th St. Edmonton." On the whole, Atwood abided by Davison's suggestions, requesting only that three poems on Davison's "doubtful" or "omit" list be included: "Game after Supper," "Descent," and "Dreams of the Animals." Noting Davison's objection, she asked William Toye to omit the last three lines of "84th Street Edmonton" from the edition of this collection that Oxford would eventually publish.[45] Davison also suggested a couple of titles for the new collection: "The Underland" and "Underworld and Later."[46] In a letter to Toye, Atwood declared her preference to be "Underground and Later," "since nothing better seems to have offered itself."[47] But something better did come up. The collection was published by both Little, Brown and Oxford, in 1970, as *Procedures for Underground*.

13

On the Rise:
Margaret Atwood and CanLit

Intellectual lady (you that is) I bow the head before that razor brain that could take me apart if it would and it might. Okay? Sure, why not (?), you're a sharp gal — and I sure hafta keep on respectin you while keepin one hand on guard over my softer and more vulnerable parts, as well as keepin any hint of the sentimental real self (which is the real me of course) from appearin on the surface. You see my predicament?

— Al Purdy[1]

ATWOOD AND POLK LEFT EDMONTON in 1970 and travelled to England. They left behind a country that had moved beyond the nationalist euphoria inspired by Expo '67 and was now moving into a darker phase. The year the young couple would spend across the pond was the year Prime Minister Pierre Trudeau would invoke the War Measures Act in response to the violence arising from the FLQ crisis in Quebec. The FLQ, or Front de Libération du Québec, a grassroots terrorist organization dedicated to securing Quebec independence, was planting bombs in Montreal and had kidnapped and murdered a cabinet minister.

Through a connection of Oscar Lewenstein's, Atwood and Polk found a large eighteenth-century house near Kew Gardens, "full of old harps, heavy furniture, and a mother-of-pearl coated *objet*."[2] They stayed there for three weeks. Lewenstein had taken an interest in *The Edible Woman*, and in April he asked Atwood and renowned film director Tony Richardson to develop a script.

Atwood, of course, was delighted. One aspect of the project that particularly pleased her was that Lewenstein wanted to shoot the film in Toronto. Charlie Pachter took Lewenstein on a tour of the city; this was so successful that Lewenstein's resolve to shoot there became even greater. Richardson now says that, although "slight," the script they wrote could have been "very funny."[3] Lewenstein was not actually entirely happy with it; but, nevertheless, he began casting the film, travelling with Atwood to meet with various actors. At one point, they were considering Donald Sutherland for a part, but he was too expensive.[4] Tony Richardson notes in his memoir that singer-actor Art Garfunkel was to play the role of Duncan.[5]

In July of 1970, Richardson and Atwood took another stab at rewriting the script, this time at Richardson's villa near St. Tropez. Richardson then followed Atwood and Polk to the Atwood family cottage in Quebec. But by October the word on the film was "delay."[6] Atwood didn't go into the details in her letters to Pachter, but a passage in Richardson's memoirs sheds a little light on the matter. It seems that Richardson and Lewenstein had a very generous offer from a "mystery banker" to finance the *Edible Woman* project, but the whole thing unravelled one evening at a party when, talking to Lewenstein, the "Maecenas" made a few "innocent" suggestions about how to cast the film. As Richardson explains it, "Oscar berated him in front of the man's wife: how dare he open his mouth? — it was privilege enough to have the chance of mere association with the likes of us." In a matter of moments, the tables were turned. All the funding disappeared and, when Richardson and Lewenstein tried to find the money elsewhere, they found that their Maecenas wielded considerable more power than they had given him credit for: the pair was "blackballed" by other producers.[7]

Richardson goes on to recount a few anecdotes about his time at Atwood's cottage and notes that it had "been fun and rewarding working with Peggy." Yet he only touches on his collaborative relationship with Atwood. She herself must have been very disappointed when the film deal fell through. Not for the last time the tarot cards had been proven wrong.[8]

When the time came to leave the Kew Gardens house, Polk and Atwood moved into a modest flat. It came with only a few pieces of furniture and a threadbare Persian rug. By October Atwood had written about a quarter of the "camp novel" — the fiction that would ultimately be *Surfacing*. "This time I'll finish," she wrote to Pachter. "I'm working like a bugger, writing a [chapter] a day and typing the one from the day before, so that by mid-November I should have a first, typed version."9 That prediction was optimistic. She and Polk spent part of November in France, at 63 rue de l'Octogone,10 and by December her energies had been diverted into short-story writing as well. Polk himself had moved from writing stories to working on an article. Now that they were both free of teaching commitments and able to focus on writing, the two settled into a daily rhythm that was relatively anxiety free. Then, on 14 January, Atwood reported to Pachter that the first draft of her novel should be done in "two weeks (ha, ha)."11

Atwood had told Pachter that the artist did not have to suffer, but with this new novel she was creating an artist-protagonist who represented a very different view. Although she had begun *Surfacing* in Edmonton, Atwood drafted the bulk of it in their small London flat, located in an area called Parson's Green (an "upmarket" neighbourhood now, but not then), working on a little secondhand German typewriter.12

The preliminary notes for *Surfacing* date back to the end of Atwood's year at the University of British Columbia, but the novel wasn't actually written until some six years later. "Some of the problems confronting me were formal," Atwood has said, "but some had to do with the nature of that material itself, and the difficulties I experienced in attempting to treat such material as what we call 'literature.' I have since found that many people from my generation who grew up in British colonies, or in countries that had recently been colonies, went through much the same process."13

The formal difficulty was, of course, what to make of the "great overwhelming empty landscape," the site of Atwood's childhood:

How to write about this childhood devoid of electricity, running water, movies, telephones and most other people — without making it sound like a verbal Christmas card, or like something out of Jack London or Robert W. Service, full of sourdoughs and huskies and gold prospectors and stage natives? (In fact I liked Jack London and Robert W. Service; but their Canadian North was definitely Boys-land, and I was not a boy.) I had yet another problem: the part of the North I spent a lot of time growing up in was practically devoid of people. I did not grow up surrounded by a layered social structure, with a long recorded history, many ancient buildings, varied social classes, extensive kinship networks and lots of diverse people to observe. It is rather hard to write a novel with no people or history in it. What for instance do you do for plot?[14]

It was ironic. Although the setting of *Surfacing* was the glacial-scrape region of childhood memory, Atwood created it while sitting in a London flat, wrapped in a comforter to ward off the cold (there was an electricity strike), with "mounds of garbage outside" (and there was a garbage strike). She started with some images from the end of the novel in her head and the assumption that this was to be a ghost story. The ghost stories her brother, Harold, used to tell her as a child had coloured her recollections of this northern locale for life, but Atwood also noted that "it is difficult," presumably for anyone, "to walk through these forests without starting to think that someone, or something, is watching you. What then could be a more appropriate genre for this raw material than a ghost story?"[15]

When *Surfacing* had been completed, Atwood explained more fully what she meant when she called the novel a "ghost story." She talked of three different kinds of ghost stories: first, the "straightforward" kind, in which the ghosts exist independent of their witnesses; second, one that might draw on "primitive myth" in that the dead return to life and seem to walk among the living; and, third, the "Henry James kind" in which the ghosts seem to be somehow related to, or extensions of, their witnesses' psyches.

Henry James's *The Turn of the Screw* is the best-known example of this third kind of ghost story. Atwood herself notes that she is most interested in this third, or "Henry James kind," of tale: it is, she explains, "obviously the tradition I'm working in."[16]

Of course, this distinction between the three different kinds of ghost story drew upon that undergraduate paper, "The Use of the Supernatural in the Novel," Atwood had written for Jay Macpherson. As I read that paper in the University of Toronto archives, I was immediately struck by the fact that it was Atwood writing about *writing* a story, rather than a reader's reaction to *reading* a story (which is what most undergraduate English papers record). Atwood herself told an interviewer, "I was going through my papers recently and I came across an old paper on ghost stories that I'd written in university. I'd forgotten all about it, but it contains the 'recipe' for the ghost story in *Surfacing*."[17]

The central problem with the original version of *Surfacing* was the same problem that had undermined her first unpublished novel: lack of plot. Originally, the narrator of *Surfacing* was conceived to be about forty, and the other characters were her sister and her sister's husband. But Atwood couldn't integrate the husband into the plot effectively. Speaking in the present tense to emphasize the fact that *writing* books is a process — only a reader can start with a finished product — Atwood has explained: "In fact, as I write along, I realize that there isn't a plot. There's a lot of scenery, but no action. I have written some very nice paragraphs, but there is nothing much in the way of events propelling them along."[18]

Significantly, given the emphasis on verbs and language experimentation in the published novel, Atwood describes her solution to the problem as a vision of action words:

> Gradually, over the nights, verbs moved in to animate the nouns, gradually a plot took form from the shadows. Even my early narrator, the forty-year-old, had been intended to achieve self-discovery by integration with her past, but her amnesia had not been as complete as the later one's became.

(The trick about integrating your past of course is that you have to forget it first.) I think that my fascination with forgetting and remembering the past had something to do with the way I had learned, or not learned, or had to dig up, the history of my own country. Canada, like most ex-colonial countries and most new-world ones, suffered from bouts of collective amnesia, and at that period its history had been, officially, conveniently forgotten. . . . The central push of the narrative in *Surfacing* is the speaker's discovery of her own forgotten past, which is less acceptable but more real than the false past she has invented for herself.[19]

Atwood mailed the novel's opening pages to her agent, Phoebe Larmore, in the late summer. When I spoke to Larmore, she described receiving those first pages; at this point in our conversation, she spoke more rapidly, and her sentences became clipped. Remembering that moment was exciting. Larmore, then living in Brooklyn Heights, says that "reading the magnificent opening of this book was astounding. It was one of the great moments of my agent life. I closed the office and walked the streets of New York to take it in, let it resonate."[20]

The novel was to be published by McClelland and Stewart (an American edition would be put out by Simon and Schuster the following year), but the copy editor the company engaged to work on the manuscript didn't know what to do about the unconventional punctuation. The overuse of commas in the novel, of course, was intended to indicate "a state of mind." The copy editor, anxious about such a violation of rules, went through the entire manuscript changing commas into periods or semicolons. Atwood, with magnifying glass in hand, changed them back. She then "wrote a dignified but pointed letter" explaining why.[21]

Surfacing was eventually made into a film, but not a very satisfying or successful one. Atwood was disappointed. This was her second film fiasco. Writer Timothy Findley remembers a reading Atwood gave at Harbourfront, the Toronto arts centre and exhibition space:

There was a Harbourfront event in which a few writers whose books had been made into films were invited to read from their relevant works. Atwood walked across the stage to the microphone, book in hand and deadpan firmly in place — facially and vocally. She addressed the audience: *I have been asked to give you the literary version of a scene from the film* Surfacing. *I want you to know that I spent all of last night leafing through the book, looking for a scene that was also in the film.* . . . There was then a very long pause, during which I began to think she was simply going to go back to her chair. But, she didn't. She read a scene that *should* have been in the film.[22]

14

The Rise of CanLit: Giving Blood

"What is the difference between Canada and yoghurt?" Pachter asked Atwood, and waited a beat. "Yoghurt has active culture." Atwood just roared.[1]

ATWOOD AND POLK made their way home after a year of travelling on the Continent. They settled in Toronto. Having moved about fifteen times in the course of the decade, Atwood was ready to buy a house and plant her feet firmly on home turf. She was naturally drawn to Toronto by family and friends, and Polk was willing. He was reluctant, in any case, to return to the United States now that the Vietnam War was looming and political unrest was mounting. A tide of Canadian nationalism, which Atwood had sensed and encouraged during her years at Sir George Williams University and at the University of Alberta, was rising. The stage was set for the blossoming of Canadian cultural identity. This was to occur over the next few years, and Atwood and her generation were going to be central to the process. The time was right for Atwood to come home — for good.

Stability presented itself to her in a number of forms. One of them was literary agent Phoebe Larmore, with whom Atwood would establish a strong and enduring relationship. Quite by chance, Larmore had come across a copy of *The Edible Woman*, and she was delighted and intrigued by it. "I had picked it up in a bookstore at the airport. When I read it on the plane I was captivated by the humour and piercing quality of the writing.

And I said to myself, who is this Margaret Atwood?"[2] That question would launch a partnership between the two women. At that point, Larmore was in New York City, working for John Cushman and Associates.

Ready to make professional commitments that would keep her in Toronto, Atwood accepted the offer of a position as assistant professor at York University (1971–72) and as writer-in-residence at the University of Toronto's Massey College (1972–73). Full-time work meant a steady income. The couple bought a house at 27 Hilton Avenue in a pleasant residential neighbourhood east of Bathurst Street, a little south of St. Clair Avenue, and just north of Toronto's landmark architectural folly, Casa Loma. Atwood would learn to drive in 1974 when she was living on a farm in Alliston, Ontario, but for now public transport would provide a convenient link between Hilton Avenue and Atwood's regular destinations: the university and downtown.

At York, Atwood taught a course called Canadian Women Writers. This was the first time that she had ever actually taught "Canlit," and it reflected both the growing impact of Canadian nationalism on university curricula and Atwood's own role in that reform. As well as examining the work of contemporary Canadian women writers — Margaret Laurence, Ethel Wilson, Sheila Watson, Adele Wiseman, Marian Engel, Gwendolyn Mac-Ewen, Miriam Waddington, and P.K. Page — Atwood initiated a project designed to determine whether Canadian reviewers betrayed a gender bias. Her class sent twenty-two form letters to male and female writers (eleven of each) asking if they had detected any such bias in the course of their careers. Of the eighteen responses received, only four women answered in the affirmative. Slim evidence. Nevertheless, Atwood wrote up a convincing and interesting report identifying gender bias in the assignment of reviews (women being assigned to review work by women); the sexual compliment or put-down; the "housewife" comment; the Emily Dickinson comparison ("when a male reviewer falls back on Emily Dickinson as the only person he can think of to compare the woman writer with . . . it usually indicates either that he's read no other women writer or poet or that he thinks of all women writers as introverted recluses or aberrations [i.e. not happily married wives and mothers]"); the she-writes-like-a-man comment; and the consignment of reviews of female-authored books to the women's page.[3] The project spoke not only to the times but also to Atwood's own perspective on gender bias in the profession. Not surprisingly, her report included comments that had been directed at her personally by a number of reviewers.

Equally interesting were the varied responses to the gender-bias question. Robertson Davies, one of the writers on Atwood's survey list, addressed the clash of the generations. He took offence not only at the question's implications but also at the way it was posed. It had been put to him in a letter signed by one of Atwood's students, Lori Tabachnick; she had apparently addressed him as "Robertson Davies." His rather intimidating reply was typed on Massey College stationery (Davies was master of the college at the time).

> Dear Sister in Christ Lori:
>
> As thou hast, without any previous acquaintance between us, addressed me by my Christian name, I judge thee to be one of the Society of Friends, vulgarly called Quakers, and shall try to reply fittingly. I know that thou wouldst not otherwise have the bloody gall to write as thou hast done.
>
> No, dear sister, I have never noticed any bias that might be attributed to sex in reviews of my work. As Christ died for us all, so is the redeeming work of the critic done without regard to sex or rank.
>
> Because of the frankness that must exist between us, as Friends, dear sister, I am impelled to say that I think thy question a foolish one. Circumcise the spirit, and forego such vain bibble-babble, or thou wilt end up a sociologist.
>
> Thine in the love and charity of Christ. . . .[4]

Al Purdy was another survey participant. His response was equally forceful, though far less . . . formal.[5]

*   *   *

For Atwood, coming home to Toronto was a pleasure; now she could reestablish contact with family and friends. For her nephews, Harold's children, David and Robert, she wrote and illustrated a small chapbook, *Confederation Incantation: A Nonsense Rhyme.* A copy of it, handwritten and with pen-and-ink illustrations, is kept in the University of Toronto archives.

What Atwood could not have known, however, is that by renewing old friendships she would be changing her own life dramatically. Instead of settling down, Atwood and Polk walked into the whirlwind that constituted House of Anansi, the small publishing house cofounded by Atwood's university friend Dennis Lee. Anansi — a force rather than a business — would draw Atwood and Polk into a world of intense creativity and high emotion, a world that was as much a product of the times as of the press itself. Anansi was one of several small presses whose lifeblood was a heady sense of intellectual adventure and a common spirit. Other such houses included Coach House and then New Press, Oberon, Talonbooks, and Breakwater.

For Atwood, the eye of the storm of social change that swept North America in the late 1960s and early 1970s was House of Anansi. It changed the course of her life not only in broad ways (which I can sketch out just vaguely) but also in one obvious and more concrete way: while both she and Polk became deeply involved in Anansi, they grew apart as a couple. By 1973, Atwood had entered into a relationship with writer Graeme Gibson, who, with his own former wife, Shirley, was also affiliated with the press. Although Gibson never actually worked at Anansi, he was a pillar of strength for those who did.

★   ★   ★

Dennis Lee and fiction-writer David Godfrey founded Anansi. Both taught at the University of Toronto, and when they established House of Anansi they had no plans to support themselves through it. The pair set up the press as a kind of cottage industry in 1967, naming it after the African trickster god (Ananse or Anansi) and running the enterprise out of Godfrey's home on Spadina Avenue. After about a year, Anansi's founders decided to try sharing quarters with New Press (near the University of Toronto). Godfrey subsequently joined New Press, and Anansi went on under the leadership of Lee.

Anansi initiated its Spiderline series of first novels in 1969, and this marked the real beginning of its intensive focus on fiction. However, it continued to publish poetry as well. Although small and lacking a distribution arm, Anansi was, at the time, one of the only publishing houses in Canada to concentrate on fiction — and for that it earned respect. Anansi publications were reviewed by some of Canada's top literary journals. Its list included a significant portion of key Canadian literary works of the period — fiction, poetry, and criticism. Among them were Atwood's *Power Politics* (1971) and *Survival* (1972), George Bowering's *The Gangs of Kosmos* (1969), Roch Carrier's *La Guerre, Yes Sir!* (1970), Northrop Frye's *The Bush Garden* (1971), Graeme Gibson's *Five Legs* (1969), George Grant's *Technology and Empire* (1969; perhaps the most important book Anansi ever published), Lee's *Civil Elegies* (1968), Michael Ondaatje's *Coming through Slaughter* (1976), P.K. Page's *The Sun and the Moon and Other Fictions* (1973), and Al Purdy's *Poems for All the Annettes* (1968; a slightly expanded reprint of the Contact Press edition). Because of the printing costs involved, Atwood's *The Journals of Susanna Moodie* went to Oxford. A host of other talented Canadian writers published with Anansi as well: Hubert Aquin, bill bissett, Austin Clarke, Matt Cohen, Marian Engel, Harold Ladoo, and Rachel Wyatt.

Those inhabiting the world of Anansi tended to be writers in the process of developing a niche for themselves in the Canadian literary landscape: Atwood, Douglas Fetherling, Shirley Gibson (author of the poetry collection *I Am Watching* [1973]), Lee, and Dale Zieroth. Over the next few years, Atwood, like many of the others associated with the press, gave copious amounts of time and energy to the Anansi project. In return, they all shared intimately in the excitement it generated. They also made a vital contribution to Canadian literature in general.

By 1970, Anansi had moved to 417 Jarvis Street — an old, three-storey brick building beside the Red Lion tavern. There was no secretary and no receptionist, just a bespectacled Dennis Lee greeting visitors with his quiet voice. Editorial meetings were informal and were often held over drinks at the Red Lion. "Anansi was the booze press," Lee chuckles.[6]

"The Death of Harold Ladoo" is Lee's long poem about Anansi and, more particularly, about Harold Ladoo, an Anansi writer of East Indian descent who was born in Trinidad and murdered on a visit there in 1973. The poem's speaker wrestles with the fact of Ladoo's death and with his own turbulent and varying responses to the Anansi enterprise in the hope of attaining some sense of the "high release" that the elegiac tradition can afford. Lee's is a poem of urgent need: Ladoo's need to write and to rage ("I'd / never seen the urge to write so / badly founded; nor so quiet, deadly, and convincing"[7]), and the speaker's need to grapple with his personal angel (a process enacted through the poem by what Lee calls an "accumulating series of ricochets"[8]). In one of the poem's early passages, Anansi is idealized as the speaker cries:

For I was drunk on the steady flood of talent,
the welter of manuscripts that kept
surfacing month after month, and often with lives attached.
    I'd seen
good sudden friends appear, two dozen savage hacks
descending like a tribe,
a shaggy new
community of rage where each had thought himself alone,
and claimed our heritage, not
by choice but finding it laced from birth through our being,
denial of spirit and flesh,
and strove we hoped to open room to live in, enacting
    in words
the right to ache, roar, prattle, keen, adore — to be
child, shaggy animal, rapt
celebrant and all in the one skin,
flexing manic selves in the waste of the self's deprival. And
    I was
flesh at last and alive and I cherished those

taut, half-violent women and men
for their curious gentleness, and also the need
in extremis to be.
They made good books,
and the time was absolute. And often we flirted with chaos
although it was more than that, for mostly I cherished
the ones who wore their incandescent pain
like silent credentials, not flaunting it,
and who moved into their own abyss with a hard, intuitive
    grace.
And the breakdown quotient was high, but
we did what had to be done and
we were young, Harold, and sitting there
on the porch of the Lion in sunlight, drinking beside you,
listening hour after hour,
I knew that you made one more among us, dragging old
generations of pain as perpetual fate and landscape, bound
to work it through in words;
and I relaxed.[9]

The Anansi years were charged ones, emotionally and cre-
atively, for those involved in the press's day-to-day operations:
David Godfrey and his wife, Ellen (who had left by the time
Atwood came on the scene); Dennis Lee and his wife, Donna; Ann
and Byron Wall; Shirley and Graeme Gibson; Polk and Atwood.
Those years were marked by some tremendous victories — both
financial and reputational — as well as some bitter professional
and personal disputes. It was intense. Electric. Bloody, even.
Writes Lee in "The Death of Harold Ladoo":

There was something in me that craved the welter of sudden
    friendships,
the unpurged intensity, booze, the all-night sessions,
even the breakdowns, the trials and suicides, and underneath
    it all,
half crazed,
the pressure of unremitting talent

revved up and honing in through
marathons of drafts.
It was a power source, it validated words
and the dubious act of writing.[10]

One of the worst tragedies associated with Anansi was the suicide
of writer Russell Marois. This brilliant, reserved, and deeply
troubled young man had lived in the Anansi basement when the
press was ensconced in Godfrey's home. He had written his
first novel, *The Telephone Pole*, there. It was a disturbing book,
largely because it presented dilemmas from which there was no
escape. In *Survival*, Atwood argues that the nihilistic and self-
destructive behaviour of Marois's characters serves to illustrate
that the loosening of puritanical taboos does not eliminate guilt
but rather exacerbates it.[11] Douglas Fetherling remembers Marois
as a "thin, blond, intense fellow, always chain-smoking. We
would talk and talk, and in a while I would stretch out on my cot
as he carved away at his tight surrealistic book about Montreal
street life, writing in longhand on canary copy paper."[12]

In 1971, while travelling from his hometown of Sherbrooke,
Quebec, to Toronto, Marois lay down in front of a train at Port
Hope. He was carrying no identification but had a slip of paper
with the Anansi phone number on it tucked into his breast
pocket. He had known that Shirley Gibson would answer the
phone when the authorities called with the news of his death. Lee
went to identify the body. Shirley Gibson wrote a poetry sequence
that both immortalizes the memory of Marois and attempts to
lay that memory to rest:

> You left no message,
>   only the one intrinsic in
>   my mailing address,
>   safe
>   in your left-hand pocket.
> But you never were much at
>   writing.
> Action was your way of getting
>   the word through.

And when you took that final action
    was it as sudden
    the impact painless as
    I had promised?[13]

But rest, at least in the Marois section of the collection *I Am Watching*, seems impossible to find.

there has always been
    blood between us
right from the start
    not the
quick hot spurt of the
    sudden wound or
beat of the heart pumping but

blood behind the eyes
    forcing the skull
nostrils tipped back to
    contain it.

we planned
    when it ended
to play it black apocalyptic
perform some clean amputation
    leaving
    tight bloodless wounds
but when did we conceive
this rat-grey hour
    slack with silence
minds running mazes clearly marked
    no exit?[14]

I think Marois's death, thinly disguised, was also probed in Ellen Godfrey's roman à clef *The Case of the Cold Murderer* (1976). The novel's obvious references to actual events were shocking — especially for those involved with House of Anansi. Robert Fulford wrote an article about it for *Saturday Night*, and Atwood responded to his piece; both agreed that Ellen Godfrey had gone too far.[15] Even the address of the small press in her novel was the same as Anansi's; also, her portrayal of the Shirley Gibson character is highly uncomplimentary. In the novel, though, the death is the result of murder, not suicide, and the murderer turns out to be the editor of the press. The "dithery gentle editor," Dennis Lee smiles, "was clearly intended to be me." He seems resigned — almost amused — as he reflects upon this. If it ever made him uncomfortable, it's no longer apparent.[16]

⋆　⋆　⋆

Speaking to me in a voice so soft that it was sometimes almost inaudible, Lee once more used blood metaphors to convey a sense of Anansi — of the need he'd had to "give blood" to the press, to labour, as editor, over each book. He also recalled the "blood-letting" that occurred in 1972, a process that ultimately led him to resign. "But make no mistake, Ladoo," the speaker in Lee's elegy cries during one of the moments in which Anansi is savagely undercut: "I was devouring you too, in the overall / carnage and we did feed off each other, / you gave your blood at last."[17] "Devouring," "carnage": such violent rhetoric from such a gentle man, beloved author of children's favourites such as *Wiggle to the Laundromat* and *Alligator Pie*. How ironic, I thought, when he arrived slightly late for our second appointment looking a bit pale, apologizing, saying he had just been to give blood.

　　To Lee, the Atwood who returned from abroad seemed different from the woman he had known at Vic, although she still had "buzzsaw wit." More famous, and with more demands on her time, she had learned to "do triage." Although "ferociously ambitious," she was "willing to put time into Anansi that she didn't have."[18] She must have seen this as a kind of duty, a community service. "We ran it on blood and enthusiasm," she told an interviewer in 1981.[19] In a 1976 interview she had commented that her role at Anansi was to "infuse some new blood into its veins." By the time Atwood returned to Toronto, the "revolution" had already taken place at Anansi: the heady atmosphere of enthusiasm arising from the early victories, through which the press had ignited a literary renaissance, had given way to an atmosphere of struggle. The press was, as Atwood put it, "embroiled in internal warfare." Dave Godfrey had left. Dennis Lee was thinking about leaving. It was with a certain sense of mission, then, that Atwood responded to Lee's invitation to join Anansi: she would serve the cause of a national literature and bring new energy to a flagging campaign. New blood. Upon her arrival, however, I don't think she quite realized how central her role would be in that campaign. As she later explained, her metaphor shifting from blood to water, "I was wrong. It was a whirlpool. Lots of people got sucked *in* and *down*."[20]

By infusing Anansi with their energy in this way, Lee and Atwood made the kind of commitment that extends far beyond mere loyalty. When he resigned in 1972, Lee sent a formal letter to the Anansi board (to which Atwood belonged) and an informal note to Atwood. Having known Atwood so long and so well, Lee needed to make things right between them. The disputes that had flared up as they had worked on *Survival* together needed to be put into perspective if the friendship they both wanted to preserve was to continue. Wrote Lee:

> We have very different ways of going about things, and — quite apart from our *Survival* ruckus — we've jangled each other at times at Anansi. I don't mean to sweep that under the carpet. But we have been mostly working for the same things. And most of our points of involuntary friction could have been dealt with, by organising decision-making so that my apparent amorphousness and your apparent brusqueness didn't have to clash. And — the man (sic) thing — our difference of wave-lengths is *not* the basic thing that brought me to this decision. So the decision is not something for which you need to feel fundamental responsibility (insofar as that response is in question at all).[21]

In answering Lee, Atwood again invoked the blood metaphor:

A reply to your note to me. It was good of you to write it.
As you know, I've made a similar decision re: Anansi, and
though mine was made for somewhat different reasons
(mine was partly because of the immense amount of time
& energy Anansi gobbles up, partly because of the personal
involvements and interrelationships, which I can only describe as bizarre) I feel that for both of us the decision was
the right one. . . . For a writer, it's really impossible, if you
are into any kind of long-term or large work, as you now
are & as I hope to be shortly. It's like the Rocking Horse
Winner — the more you give, somehow, the more is needed,
and there comes a point where there just isn't any energy
left. I think both of us need that energy for ourselves now
— you especially, as you have been giving that kind of blood
longer.[22]

But why so much blood? One answer has less to do with the
nature of the players — whether Lee was as soft-spoken then or
Atwood as controlled — as it has with the spirit of the age. Behind
the blue jeans, the long hair, the vulnerable and determined faces,
the familiar V formed by two raised fingers — the victory sign of
the 1940s transformed into the peace sign of the 1960s — lay an
urgent desire for social change. In the United States this desire
prompted challenges to the educational system and resistance to
American involvement in the Vietnam War. American draft dodg-
ers headed for Canada. Two members of the Anansi community,
Douglas Fetherling and Byron Wall, were among them. The story
goes that when Byron and Ann Wall crossed the border they had
a copy of Anansi's *Manual for Draft Age Immigrants to Canada*
with them. Twenty-five thousand copies of this small text were
given away; this distribution became part of Anansi's unspoken
mandate to perform community service.[23] Other small texts were
published primarily to make some money, although Anansi kept
its prices down — the press only wanted to charge what its
readers could easily pay. Two of these texts were *Law, Law, Law*
(which told you what to do if you were arrested) and *V.D.* (the
title is self-explanatory). And Atwood's *Survival: A Thematic*

Guide to Canadian Literature emerged from the same impulse.

> At one of our doleful board meetings, as we were staring
> glumly at the balance sheet, it struck me that a handbook
> on Canadian literature might be a welcome addition to this
> series. Such a thing did not exist, I reasoned; in fact, few
> critical works of any sort had then been produced on the
> subject, if indeed it was a subject. I knew from my travels
> about the country that many people were nevertheless
> interested in it. "Is there a Canadian Literature, outside of
> Stephen Leacock?" they would ask. "If so, why should we
> read it? Isn't it just rehashed English and American litera-
> ture really?" I thought a hundred-page leaflet squeezed
> from my lecture notes [from York] and my answers to such
> questions at poetry readings might fill the bill nicely and
> also keep the company from going broke. (Which fact,
> and my ingenuous avowal of it, led some later to comment:
> "She just wrote it to make money.")[24]

Dennis Lee edited the book. Ann Wall compiled the bibliog-
raphies and lists of source materials that appear at the end of each
section. By 1985, *Survival* had sold eighty thousand copies.

Fetherling describes the mood and sense of purpose that prevailed at House of Anansi during this period:

> There was no unspoken Anansi manifesto, beyond a kind
> of vague literary liberalism that was more of a sensibility
> than a philosophy (and in any case didn't necessarily even
> seem liberal some of the time). Anansi writers tended to be
> tortured by some enemy whose name they couldn't agree
> on. Dennis Lee spoke of *absence* as the fact of cosmology
> brought home to daily living. George Grant (one of Dennis's
> mentors) cited *technological empire* as the problem. Charles
> Taylor, the former China correspondent (and a Grant pro-
> tégé by way of Dennis), wrote of *radical Toryism* as the
> solution, while Margaret Atwood, for her part, was charac-
> teristically the most forthright and unambiguous in locating

the villain somewhere between patriarchy as a social system and maleness considered as a pathological condition. In fact, it seemed to me with certainty then, and still seems to me even now, that they were all, at some fundamental level, against more or less the same thing: Americanism, with its republican brutality and hatred of culture.[25]

Of course, Fetherling, a gifted prose writer, was very close at different moments to Atwood and to Anansi. He was also fired from Anansi and therefore has his own biases and bruises. Fetherling acknowledges: "I wasn't an important writer but I found a great sense of discovery in locating a group of people who hated the same enemy I did (even if, because I had been born there, they sometimes found it necessary to hate me in the bargain)."[26]

Canada, and Toronto specifically, was about to undergo a sustained bout of the kind of social unrest that was afflicting the United States. Lee would become a champion of local causes: the Stop Spadina movement (a grassroots movement to prevent the building of the Spadina expressway, originally intended to run from Highway 401 to the downtown core) and the Rochdale College experiment. The large concrete structure that was once Rochdale can still be seen at the corner of Bloor and Huron Streets near the University of Toronto. It was built as a cooperative student residence where an alternative kind of learning could take place. Soon, though, it became apparent that the project's lack of structure and regulations had allowed an enormous drug trade to take root. The Rochdale environment had become perilous rather than permissive. Lee, realizing that his vision of Rochdale was, in practice, dangerously naïve, withdrew his support and was left feeling deeply frustrated and disappointed.

Closely tied to the growth of Canada's left-wing grassroots movements was a mounting Canadian nationalism. To many, the United States now seemed to be dominating Canada's culture and economy to an alarming degree. Anansi, a Canadian publishing house for works written by Canadians and, to a large extent, *about* Canadians, was wholly committed to resisting this domination. Why, then, did the press publish Allen Ginsberg's *Airplane*

Dreams in 1968? Quite simply, Anansi's purpose was to prove a point about the unfairness of protective trade barriers. Publishing a high-profile American poet was a way of taking on Uncle Sam. Many copies of *Airplane Dreams* were seized and destroyed at the Canada-United States border before they could reach American markets because American law limited the number of books that could be distributed in the country by foreign publishers.[27] It was clear, in short, that Anansi conceived of itself as interested more in certain political ideals than in profits. The press had a social purpose, a mission.

★   ★   ★

Dennis Lee was a gifted editor but no businessman, and gradually the Anansi board began to demand a more pragmatic approach. Ann Wall took control of the press by buying out "all the minority shareholders" and funnelling some operating capital into the enterprise.[28] Jim Polk became the senior editor. The press moved to a cooperative publishers' building on Britain Street, "a little spit of a street around Sherbourne and Queen."[29]

> The Anansi books in this later period, through the 1970s and well into the 1980s, were much better chosen, better edited and better designed than the early ones — mostly thanks to Polk, I believe. The range continued to be broad, and the trend, already apparent, of showing more verve in fiction than in verse was exacerbated. And there were a few more bestsellers, such as Atwood's *Survival*, though of course bestsellers were never really the point. Social comment, the third force on its list, had always been a ragged, haphazard affair under the original team. Now, under Gibson, Wall, Atwood and Polk (later reduced to Wall and Polk), it took on a fresh sense of purpose: more realistic in its causes, more practical, more consistent. But for all that, Anansi books never again seemed so important. . . . In growing up, Anansi was somehow diminished.[30]

By 1973, Atwood had all but withdrawn from Anansi; she kept a hand in the poetry projects and maintained a nominal position on the board of directors. Lee remained one of her most trusted first readers. Writing about him in 1982, she praised him as an "almost mythical editor." "He lived and breathed the books he edited, and, in addition to his talent for perceiving a book's potential, he was able to generate the enthusiasm and energy that the writer often needed to finish." Years later, Atwood was able to transform the blood metaphor into one of healing: "The penalty, for [Lee], was the midnight-phonecall syndrome. Like a doctor he was always on call, though the blood he doled out was his own."[31]

But for all that, nearly everyone left Anansi with hurt feelings and a sense of disillusionment. It was inevitable. In "The Death of Harold Ladoo" Lee writes:

> We were a tiresome gang of honking egos:
> graceless, brawling, greedy, each one in love with
> style and his darling career. And images of liberation
> danced in our screwed-up heads, we figured
> aping those would somehow make us writers,
> cock and dash of the logos —
> oh, and Canada;
> but all it's done is make us life-and-blood clichés.
> Media fodder. Performing rebels. The works.
> Wack-a-doo!
> For this I tied my life in knots?[32]

But these low notes — they sound as though they are being pounded out on a piano — are only a few of the many that comprise Lee's poem. They combine to create the elegy's final chord, which, although played carefully, is resonant, almost triumphant: the speaker awaits the renewed call for "passionate awe" and "a high clean style."[33]

Anansi had made the initial gestures of liberation. Its writers had helped to invent a national rhetoric that moved beyond imitation of other traditions. Canadian literature had taken the first steps of its journey towards the institutionalization that would occur the next decade, and the central players on the Canadian literary scene would include many members of the Anansi crowd. And, yes, for this they all did tie themselves in knots. Which writers wouldn't have, given the chance?

15

Dodging the Flak

Following a nervous debut to Canadian poetry readers in the early 1960s as M.E. Atwood, Margaret Atwood has enjoyed a spectacular climb to the summit of Canadian letters. The period 1966 to 1973 in Canadian literature has to a great extent been dominated by her.

— Frank Davey[1]

SURVIVAL WAS BOTH a result of the rising tide of Canadian nationalism and a catalyst for it. Atwood intended it to be a general reader's introduction to Canadian literature, but the book was also prompted by the many questions she was being asked as she gave readings around the country. *Survival* helped to fuel an explosion of interest in Canadian literature and culture during the 1970s, a time that has been called the New Age of Canadian literature — it was certainly a period of literary rebirth.

The book created a stir. It was highly praised by most and harshly criticized by some,[2] but few failed to recognize its significance. *Survival* quickly became a landmark in the development of Canadian literature and culture.

Not surprisingly, its author was in demand as a speaker, but the cross-Canada reading tour she subsequently embarked upon was far from glamorous. Aboard a Greyhound bus, Atwood travelled through sleet and freezing rain to such places as North Bay and Renfrew, Ontario. "Question period: Do you have a message? Is your hair really like that, or do you get it done? Where do you get the ideas? How long does it take? What does it *mean*? Does it bother you, reading your poems out loud like that? It would bother me. What is the Canadian identity? Where can I send my poems? To get them published?"[3] Then there were the readings in New York. There Atwood had to explain what an outhouse was. There are some things that Canadians just *know*.

For Atwood, *Survival* was more than a book of criticism: it was a statement of belonging. She very firmly believed that her role was not to be just a writer; it was to be a *Canadian* writer. During the 1970s, to fulfil such a role entailed a struggle. It was still unusual and enormously difficult to make a decent living by writing full time in Canada. Both Margaret Laurence and Mordecai Richler had spent the previous decade in England in part because it was still important to make it outside Canada in order to make it inside Canada — a function of the country's perceived colonial inferiority. (Richler actually returned to Canada in 1972 just as the Canadian literary renaissance was gaining real momentum.)

Wrote Atwood at about this time: "Refusing to acknowledge where you come from . . . is an act of amputation: you may become free floating, a citizen of the world (and in what other country is that an ambition?) but only at the cost of arms, legs or heart. By discovering your place you discover yourself."[4] Over the course of the next decade, she would not only discover Canada but also become one of those who created it in myth and in narrative while striving to protect it from the cultural imperialism of the United States. Writing *Survival* was only one manoeuvre in the battle.

★   ★   ★

Many people thought that *Survival* owed a great deal to the influence of Northrop Frye (and the same was said of other literary-critical works of the period, including Doug Jones's *Butterfly on Rock*). As one commentator remarked soon after *Survival*'s publication, "Frye's teaching has also obviously contributed to much of the thinking in *Survival* — the denial, for example, of absolute standards in art, the need for an overall mythic approach in studying literature, and the necessity for personal involvement, even purgation, in experiencing art."[5] But while Atwood was undoubtedly influenced by Frye and George Grant, other factors came into play. The years she spent at Harvard (thinking of Canada from a distance, comparing the Canadian conception of Canadian literature to the American conception of American literature) and the Anansi experience contributed to the formation of *Survival* just as heavily. The very tone of *Survival* — Atwood adopted a voice that would appeal to the general reader, not just the scholarly one — reflected the influence of Anansi's social mandate and the insights Atwood had gained from her own lecture tours and teaching.

It was the early 1970s, and Canadian culture was exploding. All kinds of poetry were being published in the small literary journals — *Tamarack Review, Northern Journey, Vigilante, Blackfish*, and *Open Letter* — as well as in the more politically oriented *Canadian Forum* and *This Magazine*. For a time, it was possible to sell over one thousand copies of a poetry collection nationwide — an extraordinary number given the population of Canada. For a time, too, the sheer diversity of the poetry audience attested to the burgeoning popularity of the form. Wrote Atwood: "Trying to assess what is happening in Canadian poetry at the moment is like trying to assess an explosion, from the inside and while it is still going on: you can feel the energy, you can see the smoke and the fragments hurtling about, but you won't be able to determine what has been accomplished, or demolished, till afterwards. The best thing to do is to keep your head down and dodge the flak."[6]

*   *   *

If descriptions of Anansi are punctuated with blood metaphors, Atwood's evocations of what it felt like to be a key player in the Canadian literary renaissance feature a kind of battle rhetoric. It was "an explosion." The best thing for a writer to do was "dodge the flak." "Canadian literature," Atwood mused while extending her warring-factions metaphor: "the mere pronunciation of [the term] used to trigger a lightning epidemic of yawns and sneers, especially among Canadians [; it] is now a loaded phrase, like 'Women's Liberation.' To make any utterance on the subject is to divert both sides from their habitual pursuit of attacking each other and have them concentrate on you. Some would call this situation a lively literary climate; others a snake pit. Both would apply."[7]

Atwood has called the early 1970s her "dugout" years. She felt that she was being assailed by those who applauded *Survival* and the force of change it represented (teachers, critics, and the media — which were already recognized as a very powerful force in those post-Vietnam, post-McCarthy and Edward R. Murrow years). She also felt under attack by those who did not like the book. The need to hide herself away from it all — from the chaotic world of Anansi, from some of the strangely hostile Canadian responses to *Survival*,[8] from the fame that had started to erode her privacy and that had intensified still further with the 1972 publication of *Surfacing* — must have been ferocious at times. Yet Atwood never did surrender. Rather, in 1973 she moved to Alliston, a farming community about an hour's drive north of Toronto, with Graeme Gibson. There the couple would find the time to regroup and to establish a strong family relationship.

★   ★   ★

Graeme Gibson remembers that he first met Margaret Atwood in the spring of 1970 before she and Polk left for England. The occasion was a party at Grossman's Tavern in Toronto for poet Milton Acorn, who, disappointed that he had not won the Governor General's Literary Award that year, was being honoured that night with "the people's poet" award. At the party, Atwood complimented Gibson on his first novel, *Five Legs*, which had been published by Anansi and which had met with some success in Canada. On one level, *Five Legs* is the story of a man who has to choose between his marriage and academic career (portrayed as twin forms of entrapment within the stifling world of Anglo-Protestant southwestern Ontario) and freedom in its various forms: travel, another woman, a child, a different life. The funeral of a young friend, killed in a car accident outside Stratford, Ontario, provides the catalyst for Professor Lucan Crakell's self-exploration. "*Five Legs* was thought of as one of the first super modernist novels in the country," West Coast writer Brian Brett remarked to me, "a kind of cult hit for a while."[9] At this point, before the rush of celebrity triggered by *Surfacing* and *Survival*, Gibson's reputation was actually bigger than Atwood's. The first edition of his novel — twenty-five hundred copies — sold out in roughly three weeks.[10]

The relationship between Gibson and Atwood began at Anansi, amid the tumult. Graeme and Shirley Gibson eventually divorced, in 1976, but they had been estranged from one another long before the Anansi years. Shirley dedicated *I Am Watching*, which came out in 1973, to "G" and to her sons, but in it three different relationships the poet has with three different men are traced. Two of these men are clearly not Graeme Gibson, but they do bear a striking resemblance to other men in Shirley Gibson's own life. One, of course, was Russell Marois.

By 1973, Polk and Atwood had also agreed to go their separate ways. So for Atwood and Gibson the timing was right. Coming out of failed first marriages, both were a little older and wiser — they knew what they were getting into. Gibson knew that he was doing more than starting a new life with Peggy: he was taking on Margaret Atwood, a woman with considerable, even intimidating, talent and dedication, as well as a ready-made professional career. And Atwood, in turn, knew that with Gibson came his two boys, Matt (Thomas Matthew Mann) and Grae (Graeme Charles Alexander), who, in 1973, were already in their teens. It was to be a very happy match. The title of Atwood's next book of poetry, *You Are Happy*, reflects a change in mood and tone.

Graeme Gibson was born in London, Ontario, on 9 August 1934. His was a family of achievers with high expectations. Gibson's grandfather was a Toronto lawyer who owned an enormous house, complete with turret and ballroom. His father, Brigadeer

In the 1960s: cover for *The Circle Game*
PHOTOGRAPH BY CHARLES PACHTER. COURTESY CHARLES PACHTER.

Margaret Atwood reading at Harbourfront in Toronto (1978)
PHOTOGRAPH BY TIBOR KOLLEY. COURTESY *GLOBE AND MAIL*.

In farm country: Margaret Atwood in the Alliston years
PHOTOGRAPH BY R. BULL. COURTESY *TORONTO STAR*.

Margaret Atwood and her daughter, Jess (1980)

PHOTOGRAPH BY THOMAS VICTOR. COURTESY HARRIET SPURLIN.

Margaret Atwood speaking during El Salvador Week of Solidarity (1981)

PHOTOGRAPH BY D. BRAZAO. COURTESY *TORONTO STAR*.

The author of *Cat's Eye* with her cat (1988)

The politics of ventriloquism (circa 1996)

Margaret Atwood and Graeme Gibson (circa 1988)
PHOTOGRAPH BY BRIAN WILLER. COURTESY *MACLEAN'S*.

From left to right: Pierre Berton, Jack McClelland,
Margaret Atwood, Leonard Cohen, W.O. Mitchell
PHOTOGRAPH BY BRIAN WILLER. COURTESY *MACLEAN'S*.

Margaret Atwoods, junior and senior, with Charles Pachter and his mother, Sara

Thomas Graeme (Canada's youngest brigadeer), married an Australian opera singer named Mary Cameron. She was the daughter of a Brisbane doctor and a "Scots woman who loved the opera."[11] When, as an adult, Gibson travelled to Australia with his own family, he visited his extended family in Brisbane and recovered memories of childhood trips to Australia and Fiji. From his mother, Gibson inherited a beautiful, rich singing voice. He grew up on Gormley Avenue in residential Toronto. Five years older than Atwood, he can remember listening to the radio during the war with his younger brother, Alan. At age seven, he heard his brigadeer father send his sons a "special hello" from the front.[12] In 1955, at age twenty-one, Gibson was commissioned as a second lieutenant at the Royal Canadian School of Infantry at Camp Borden. But if soldiering was part of Gibson's heritage, it wasn't part of his nature. He attended the Collège Militaire Royal de Saint-Jean but did not do well.

Gibson was given the best education that Ontario could offer a young man: Upper Canada College followed by Trinity College School. He went on to the University of Waterloo for a year (1953–54) before transferring to the University of Western Ontario. He stayed at Western for a year (1954–55), spent a year studying at the University of Edinburgh (where he became engaged to a young nurse and broke it off twenty-eight hours later[13]), and then returned to complete his BA and to begin an MA (between 1956 and 1958). Soon after, he married Shirley Gibson and had two children with her: Matt in 1960 and Grae in 1962. From 1961 to 1966, Gibson taught English at Ryerson Polytechnic Institute on a full-time basis; he continued part time for another three years. When Ryerson Press was about to be sold to American interests, specifically McGraw-Hill, Gibson joined the protest; in fact, he climbed the statue of Egerton Ryerson and draped the American flag over it.[14]

Communion, Gibson's second novel, came out in 1971. It was not as well received as *Five Legs* had been. The first novel had sold about six thousand copies — a bestseller in Canada during that period.[15] His third novel was a long time coming, in large part because Gibson had become a driving force in community events. To these endeavours, Atwood lent both practical and moral support. Inspired by the 1971 Ontario Royal Commission meetings, where writers learned that they had some urgent and common concerns, Gibson began to set up a writers' union. Ron Evans, then of the Ontario Arts Council, provided the initial funding,[16] and in November 1973 the Writers' Union of Canada was founded. In an entry she wrote on the union for the 1988 *Canadian Encyclopedia*, Atwood explains the organization's mandate and rationale. The realization that writers had many common concerns and that literary agents were required to mediate between writers and publishers constituted the impetus for the union's founding.

> The union has done extensive work on contracts and retains a lawyer to give advice in negotiations; its Grievance Committee helps to resolve problems with publishers; it runs a manuscript-evaluation agency; it gives advice on tax matters; it acts as a clearing house for information and distributes a monthly newsletter. It organizes around particular issues, such as book dumping. . . . Union committees work on matters of COPYRIGHT protection, liaison with publishers and librarians, and CENSORSHIP and repression issues. One major objective — the establishment of a "Public Lending Right" fee which would reimburse writers for multiple use of their works through libraries — was achieved in 1986.
>
> But one of the most important achievements of the union is to have fostered a spirit of professionalism and self-respect among writers.[17]

Gibson, Marian Engel, and a small group of other writers provided the initiative and the elbow grease for the union project. The criterion for membership was (and still is) the publication of one book. Margaret Laurence was the union's first interim chairperson, and Engel became its first full-time chairperson. Gibson became the second chairperson in 1974 and served for a year. During his tenure, he took on the task of establishing a series of teachers' resource guides, which were distributed across Canada.

He also became involved with the Book and Periodical Development Council, first as vice-chairman, then as chairman (in 1976), and eventually as executive director. "What a job!" exclaims writer Frankish Styles. "Every member had a veto! Their two major concerns were persuading librarians to accept compensation for authors as a valid goal . . . and the physical distribution of books."[18] The first of these concerns has now been resolved: as Atwood points out, there is a public-lending-right fee for authors. The second concern has been partially addressed, the problem being an ongoing one, but computerization alone has made it much simpler for publishers to inventory their warehouse stock.

In 1977, Gibson became the moving force behind the Writers' Development Trust, with support from Laurence, Engel, Atwood, Pierre Berton, and David Young. Between 1977 and 1978 he served as the trust's first chairman. "His goals were far-reaching: to get the major writing organizations under one roof, to get funding to keep the [teachers'] Resource Guides alive, to [arrange for] gifted students [to be taught] by successful writers, to prepare for some type of pension plan to help aged and no-longer-producing authors, to produce a magazine with special emphasis on taking Canadian writing to distant parts of the English-speaking world."[19] For the most part, then, for Gibson the 1970s were gobbled up by literary activism. Although he would continue in these pursuits, particularly focusing his attention on PEN in the late 1980s (he was president of Canadian Centre, International PEN, from 1987 to 1989), he slowed his hectic pace during a time of personal crisis in the late 1970s; he did the same in the early 1980s while completing his third book. Gibson became a Member of the Order of Canada in 1992. His nomination was widely supported; the honour was clearly well deserved.

Gibson, says Brian Brett, "does a lot of the slogging in the trenches on those things. He's very smart at all of it. He always finds a way to deal." Together with Andreas Schroeder, he's one of the most respected people in the union. Brett explains that Gibson has "savvy." "He has a more hands-on approach. [Atwood] comes in for the cut and thrust."[20]

* * *

It was in September of 1973 that Atwood and Gibson moved north of Toronto, first to a rented farm near Beaton, and then to their own farm in Alliston. The rural atmosphere proved conducive to Atwood's work. "My post office box is in Alliston. That means I only have to collect my mail once a week. My working set-up there is very convenient. I have a room with two doors that close and I can't hear the telephone with both of the doors closed. My cats and dogs can't get in and that's good."[21] The chaos produced by the Anansi years, the constant demands on her time, receded.

As farmers, Atwood and Gibson had much to learn. Gibson began honing his machine-repairing skills, and together they set up a formidable vegetable garden. During their first year, 1973, they were plagued by slugs. By 1974, they had gained some insight into the minute workings of their new environment. Wrote Atwood:

> What defeats us, as always, is
> the repetition: weather
> we can't help, habits we don't break.
> The frogs, with their dud guitar-
> string throats, every spring, release
> their songs of love, while slugs breed
> in the rain under the hay
> we use for barricades;
> milkweed and pigweed, the purslane
> spreading its fleshy
> starfish
> at our feet,
> grabbing for space.
>
> We know the names by now;
> will that make anything better?[22]

But in an August 1974 letter to Dennis Lee, Atwood reported proudly: "we aren't *too* far behind everyone else around here, but it has taken a lot of time, energy & frustration."[23] Being "not too far behind" in the space of a year was no small feat.

They bought all their farm equipment secondhand at auctions. When an interviewer asked Gibson for anecdotes of that period, he spoke of the auctions he had attended, of how "very sad" they were. Most were held because someone had died, or because the farmer had grown too old and had no children to carry on the farmwork. But Gibson remembered one where the farmer had been involved in an accident, crushed by his own tractor. The machinery was in poor condition — so poor, in fact, that "neighbours were buying it when they didn't need it, and that's a very powerful spirit."[24]

Although separated from Toronto by miles of highway, Atwood was not entirely able to distance herself from the spotlight and the price that fame exacted. Like every other new celebrity, she was expected to have developed, overnight, a thick skin. Journalist Scott Young wrote a piece on her called "Making Hay" for the *Globe and Mail*, and it was riddled with barbs. Basing his column on a single remark Atwood had made between poems at a Bohemian Embassy reading — that she regretted being away from the farm because "it was a nice day for haying" — Young painted a particularly sexist portrait of Atwood as farmer. Either she had paid $200,000 for farm equipment, he wrote, or she had used her "feminine wiles" to obtain it.[25] By throwing down this gauntlet, Young invited Atwood to do battle in an arena she herself controlled: that of ironic wit. Atwood's response was feisty; she talked of "jackasses"; she called Young a "whipper-snapper" and a "treewaster."[26] These may have been her "dugout" years, but she was not contemplating surrender — just rethinking her strategy for survival.

Under siege, Atwood fielded incessant demands for her time and her words. She sponsored so many Canada Council applications in 1972 that by the end of the year she had composed a form letter to deal with them.[27]

As I read through Atwood's correspondence from the next couple of years, I realized just how much time and energy she was obliged to expend stating and restating and defending her position. For instance, in January of 1973, those involved in setting up the Writers' Union — Farley Mowat, Marian Engel, Austin Clarke, Margaret Laurence, Atwood, and Gibson — called a preliminary meeting and invited a number of fiction writers from across the country to attend. Subsequently, a committee was struck to draft a constitution. The endeavour attracted bad press almost immediately. Kildare Dobbs wrote a short *Toronto Star* column criticizing the "secretiveness" of the meeting and issued a warning: "anything that looks like domination by a small clique should be avoided."[28] Atwood's letter to the editor of the *Star*, written on the day Dobbs's piece appeared, points out that Dobbs had erred on six basic points.[29] But what had motivated Dobbs to make his charges in the first place? The answer, I think, had something to do with a typically Canadian discomfort at the growing prominence of the national literature and its main players. With the publication of *Survival*, Atwood had become a bona fide celebrity and, therefore, was wide open to attack. It was largely a question of timing. *Survival* was published just as Canadian nationalism was on the upswing, and Atwood became the spokesperson for a cultural moment. She was the woman of the hour.

★   ★   ★

In one way, Atwood's knack for anticipating a "paradigm crisis" was central to her success. The phrase itself comes from Brian Brett, who uses it to describe the way Atwood was "always just ahead of what culture was thinking. Always had that grace. Could sense what was going to be 'paradigm crisis.' "[30] But, for Atwood and for those closest to her, the rapid ascension to celebrity status that this knack had triggered had a very obvious downside.

Dobbs, in a 1973 *Books in Canada* column, noted wryly: "Everyone was watching Margaret Atwood. In the fall she had two new books in the best-seller lists. She was alert for insults to the IPA [Independent Publishers' Association]. She was helping to initiate a writers' union. It was not beyond possibility that she [would] get herself elected president of the IPA in 1973 and president of the projected writers' union as well. That way she could negotiate against herself."[31]

"What are you in Canada now anyway?" Atwood's New York editor asked her. "I mean, here you are a writer but what are you up there? Are you a 'thing'?" Speaking to the Empire Club of Canada in the spring of 1973, Atwood described this exchange, explaining that her answer to her agent's question was, of course, "yes." She was a "thing" — no longer a writer but a symbol. Cleverly, she started to take control of the rhetoric herself, working to deflate a balloon that was getting bigger and more unwieldy by the minute. "I used to be a writer," she continued,

> and the difference between being a writer and being a thing is that writers just write books and they write away and they write away and most of the time nobody pays much attention to them because they are either ahead of their time or behind it. But [when] what you happen to be saying coincides with what is going on in society; then you become a thing and this is what seems to have happened to me.[32]

The rest of this Empire Club address consists of a very deft summary and rebuttal of the various attacks on *Survival*.

One of the strongest attacks came from Robin Mathews. He charged that *Survival* privileged the struggle for individual liberation over the larger and — in Mathews's opinion — more important struggle for community liberation, while failing to make the distinction between the two. He also insisted that Atwood had relied too heavily on the Anansi writers at the expense of certain important Canadian literary figures. Mathews's article was published in *This Magazine Is about Schools*; the magazine's editors invited Atwood to respond in a subsequent issue.[33] "She handed Mathews his head," said Rick Salutin,[34] describing her rebuttal, in which she defends *Survival*'s victim thesis, arguing that it is a working hypothesis rather than a rigid conclusion, and maintaining that Mathews had misread a number of the book's points and arguments.

In 1974, Atwood moved quickly to defend herself on another front as well. The journal *Northern Journey* had published a story by William F. Wigle in which a character — named "Margaret Atwood" — behaves in a very un-Margaret Atwood-like manner. Nothing terrible — no vile or criminal acts — but the name "Margaret Atwood" had been used without her consent, and some details from a private conversation had been disclosed. The timing — the story came out in the midst of the *Survival* publicity storm — made matters even worse. To John (Buffy) Glassco, another Canadian writer who appeared as a character in the story, Atwood explained the swiftness and vehemence of her reaction. Quite apart from the distortion she perceived in the representation (her fictional counterpart spends two hours baring her soul to a stranger), Atwood objected to being used as a character in a work of fiction at all. She also pointed out that, according to American law, once you have allowed yourself to be used in a work of fiction, without objecting, then the "road is clear for anyone to use you in a similar way in other pieces of fiction." "I just don't relish," she concluded, "turning up as an axe murderess in the next . . . phantasmagoria."[35]

There's a wonderful passage in her letter to Glassco that further demonstrates how Atwood's sense of humour prevails, even when she is under pressure. "Did you know," she asks Glassco, as if introducing a piece of gossip, that "Earle Birney is considering suit against Dorothy Livesay, for a sentence in a critical article that might be interpreted that he pushed David off the cliff? Now *there's* a case. . . ."[36] "David" is a young man in a very well-known Birney poem who dies after falling from a precipice.

Glassco responded to Atwood's remarks about Wigle's story with surprise and amusement. "Let us all now be charitable," he began his reply to Atwood in an effort to calm the troubled waters.[37] Wigle himself wrote a conciliatory letter to Atwood: "If I have unwittingly invaded your private life, I apologize." Ultimately, though, he stood by his story: "I am sufficiently naïve to think that an anecdote told by a famous person [Fraser Sutherland, editor of *Northern Journey*] to three journalists is not *off the record* unless it is specifically prefaced as such. . . ."

He also asked Atwood to clarify the nature of his offence: "If you still feel that my story is damaging to you, I would like to know how and why."[38]

Quite simply, Atwood objected to both Wigle's use of her name and the inaccuracy of his portrayal of her. She thought they were evidence of his lack of good judgement and professional courtesy. As she explained to George Woodcock, the whole incident left her feeling exposed — and it was not a pleasant feeling.[39] The tempest also revolved around a secret — the "anecdote" to which Wigle referred in his letter — revealed by Fraser Sutherland to Atwood in Wigle's presence: apparently Sylvia Beare, who had written admiringly about Atwood for *Northern Journey*, was in fact a pseudonym for a well-known writer and friend of Atwood's. It was a joke, and it had been revealed in confidence. Wigle had failed to guide himself accordingly and had not paid close enough attention to the context and to Sutherland's tone. In its May 1974 issue, *Quill and Quire* looked at the Wigle affair in detail, but Atwood was not asked for her view.

Fraser Sutherland offered Atwood space in the next issue of *Northern Journey* to articulate her complaint. Instead, annoyed by the story and by *Northern Journey*'s refusal to offer her an apology, she sent her complaint to the Writers' Union. The union, then under the leadership of Marian Engel, Rudy Wiebe, and Harold Horwood, wrote to Sutherland on her behalf. In his response, dated 5 March 1974, Sutherland stood by his decision to publish the Wigle story.[40] People chose sides. George Woodcock called the story "absurd and unforgivable."[41] Another Atwood supporter, Margaret Laurence, refused to review Rudy Wiebe's new novel for *Northern Journey*. In a letter to Sutherland, Laurence stated that she had read the Wigle story and considered it "highly offensive. In my view, it is totally unethical to use anyone's real name in what purports to be a piece of fiction. This would be true even if the presentation of the person was accurate and favourable."[42]

The Wigle affair was widely publicized and quickly involved many of the central players in the Canadian literary community. Atwood never actually published an explicit reply to Wigle's story. However, there is a character in *Lady Oracle* — a reporter — who bears the name of Fraser, although the character's last name in the novel is Buchanan and not Sutherland. When Dennis Lee read the manuscript, he suggested that, depending upon how mischievous Atwood was feeling, she might call him "Will Fraser" — meaning, in the context of the novel, *will* Fraser reveal Joan Foster's "true" story.[43] The Wigle affair adds an extra twist.

⋆   ⋆   ⋆

A vicious attack on Atwood — thinly disguised as fiction — was published in the *Canadian Forum*. This time, Dennis Lee and Jay Macpherson came to her defence, taking on the *Forum* and the author of the article, identified only by the initials I.D. The piece was an allegory, a fairy tale about a young girl named Margaret who is forbidden to rise above the lake but aspires to airy heights nonetheless. Margaret is extremely clever, and she learns not only to survive in the lake in which she finds herself but also to beat the system — a power structure of older witches (or "Susannas"), sharks, and leprechauns. Margaret eventually understands that it is possible to sleep with leprechauns without either being reduced to their level (they think only about pots of gold and pretty girls) or making babies. But Margaret finds that sleeping with leprechauns is not half so much fun as eating them. This discovery eventually leads to her downfall. As the result of her rather odd eating habits, she is transformed into an octopus and forced to remain within the lake, never rising above it or moving beyond it. The fairy tale is called "How the Octopus Got Its Tentacles." The identification of Margaret with Margaret Atwood is clear: annoyed by the leprechauns' patronizing attitude towards girls, exemplified by their desire for a "sweet young thing" to cut their pie, she bakes a pie in the shape of a girl and cuts its head off; later she invents "The Circle Game" (sometimes simply called "Power Politics"). After becoming an octopus she declares, "I'm surfacing," and seems to echo Atwood's novel of that name by intoning, as she descends into the water, "The lake is quiet, the trees surround me, asking and giving nothing."[44] The moral of the story is obvious and very insulting: although more powerful and possessing a greater reach, the octopus is ultimately no better than the other lake dwellers.

Lee sent a long letter to the editor in which he argued that the real problem with the piece was not that it constituted an invasion of privacy, or that the quality of the writing was so poor ("the writing is so coy and lead-footed that one merely winces, and tries to forget those two pages of the magazine as quickly as possible"), but rather that the argument it presented was circular — in other words, I.D. "reads" the author through her writing and then explains the writing as a function of the author. "Freshman essays," said Lee, "get failed when they make this blunder."[45] In her own letter to the *Forum*'s editor, Jay Macpherson revealed the name of the writer hiding behind the initials. He was York University professor Ian Drummond.[46] Atwood herself actually knew the author's identity very early on.[47]

In a note to Lee, Atwood acknowledged how hurt she was by the piece and by the *Forum*'s decision to publish it. She was "stunned" by what Drummond had done. She was hurt not only by the "personal attack" his piece contained but also by its "rampant sexism" and *Forum* editor Mike Cross's decision to print it. Cross justified his decision, Atwood went on to say, "on the grounds that it would be good for circulation."[48]

*   *   *

Despite these skirmishes, Atwood's national and international success continued to grow throughout the 1970s. In fact, when Scott Symons challenged the legitimacy of her control over the national literary scene in a 1977 *West Coast Review* article entitled "The Canadian Bestiary," the sour grapes were evident: "who's going to risk his career and his neck, telling the current gaggle of Canadian feminist harridans that they'll last just as long as the trendy movement is 'women's glib.' I refer specifically . . . to such writers as Ms. Engel, Ms. Munro, Ms. Fraser, Ms. Atwood, et. al. Migod, what a blizzard of dry ice they are!"[49] Margaret Laurence responded to Symons in a letter published in the *Canadian Forum*. She took particular issue with the "reveal-ing" statement I have quoted: "*This* is literary criticism? This attack on women writers simply because they are women? . . . In this essay, Symons puts his cards on the table, and they are arrogant class cards all the way, as well as sexist and racist."[50] Laurence's rebuttal was strong, but it did not alter Symons's position. When he wrote another article in 1990, this one pub-lished in *The Idler* and called "Atwood-as-Icon," his theme was still control and his discomfort over the fact that Atwood had it.[51]

★ ★ ★

Throughout the 1970s Atwood continued to participate in an array of literary activities. In 1974, she became involved in *This Magazine*. Rick Salutin and the three other editors of *This* drove north to the Alliston farm on a mission to convince Atwood to become a contributing editor. During this, their initial editorial meeting, Salutin remembers that Atwood made "astute" com-ments about colour combinations for the magazine's cover. He decided soon afterwards that *This* should include political com-mentary, and some of it should take the form of cartoon strips. Salutin contributed many of these himself; his own strips paro-died the comics of the day, such as the dramatic serial *Rex Morgan, M.D.* Atwood joined in and, adopting the pseudonym Bart Gerrard, invented the campy heroine named Survival Woman, who quickly became a favourite of the magazine's readership. Her image adorned the magazine's subscription-renewal cards. "People loved that," Salutin recalls.[52]

Atwood concocted the *Barbed Lyres* project, a competition for the best short (maximum twenty lines) satiric verse on any topic. The more barbed the lyre the better. She convinced cultural critic and journalist (of the back page of *Maclean's* fame) Allan Fotheringham and musician-political satirist Nancy White to judge the competition with her. The best entries were published in a book, which was launched at the Horseshoe Tavern, a landmark Toronto drinking establishment. Atwood, to boost the sales, signed copies of the book at the event.[53]

In 1974, Atwood reviewed Laurence's *The Diviners* for the *New York Times*, Sinclair Ross's *Sawbones Memorial* for CBC Radio's *Sunday Supplement*, Iris Murdoch's *The Sacred and Profane Love Machine* for the *Globe and Mail*, and Susan Hill's *In the Springtime of the Year* and Cynthia Propper Seton's *The Half-Sisters* for the *New York Times Book Review*. Her assessments were fair, even, and generous. The attacks on her own work that she had endured that year seem not to have impaired her objectivity or her sense of literary value.

Her first honorary doctorate — a Litt.D. from Trent University in Peterborough, Ontario — came in 1973. It would be the first of many such honours. Ironically, at the same time Atwood was reviving her plans to finish the doctoral dissertation she had begun at Harvard. To some, this would seem unnecessary, a challenge that had become redundant. But to Atwood, the unfinished degree, the product of years of work, must have represented an enormous wasted effort. She wrote to Professor Jerome Buckley on 1 June 1973 to tell him of her plans and to confirm that all was well on the academic front.[54] His reply was warm and positive; it included his compliments on *Surfacing* and queries about the status of the film version of *The Edible Woman*. "Harvard," wrote Buckley, "thinks in eternities. Your time, as far as we are concerned, never runs out."[55] Atwood wrote to her typist, Mrs. Nellie Kesson, now married and living in Winnipeg, asking her to pick up where they'd left off.[56]

And Atwood was already planning the next step in her novel-writing career. In a letter to Marge Piercy, in which she thanked the American poet and novelist for her review of *Surfacing*, she made an interesting comment about the development of her heroines:

> I felt you had in the review yr fingers on a lot of the important pressure points . . . espec. the question of what then? what next? Obviously one can work out personal solutions or semi-solutions; social ones are much more difficult not only to bring about but to imagine. Marian's life [in *The Edible Woman*] will be circular (one more time

round) rather than spiral partly because I could see in 1965 (when book written; publisher lost ms for 2 yrs) no "out" for her provided by the society. Woman in *Surfacing* is left at the edge . . . all we know is that it will be different, but we don't know how. (Because I don't.) Next novel [*Lady Oracle*] won't resolve that, i don't feel (novels seem always about 2 yrs behind what I think when writing them) but the one after that will either have to or die.[57]

Atwood was right, of course: there was no easy way out for the heroine of *Lady Oracle*. It was to be a book about entrapment of various kinds, mostly of the heroine's own making, and about the impossibility of escape — personal, spiritual, or social.

During the early part of 1974, and during the whole Wigle episode, Atwood worked on *Lady Oracle*. On 16 January, she sent a list of requests to her research assistant, Donya Peroff, that make sense to anyone who has read the novel: a copy of *Jane Eyre*, an Italian *photoromanza*, a map of Italy, a dictionary, and a picture of a water fountain.[58]

Lady Oracle was written amidst the congenial hubbub that reigned at the Alliston farmhouse. Toronto friends who envied Atwood and Gibson their "restful" lifestyle had no idea what was really going on. The couple took on all the daily chores involved in maintaining the farm and the animals. They found themselves doing a lot of entertaining (there were twenty-four people to lunch on Labour Day). Neighbour people dropped by to borrow tools; neighbour pigs came to feast on rotting apples; and their own animals were inclined to wander — their cows were jumpers. Such distractions would deter most writers, but Atwood had taught herself to work on many different projects at the same time.

That skill was put to the test in 1974. That year the film script for *Surfacing* developed steadily;[59] *You Are Happy* was prepared for 1974 publication by Oxford in Canada and by Harper and Row in the United States in 1975; *The Servant Girl*, a drama based on a nineteenth-century murder trial (the precursor of *Alias Grace*), aired on CBC Television; Atwood received the Bess

Hopkins Prize from *Poetry* (Chicago); and for the poem "Songs of the Transformed" she was awarded another honorary degree, this time an LL.D. from Queen's University in Kingston, Ontario. In her spare time, Atwood obtained her driver's licence.

There are humorous pieces from this period as well. When accepting the LL.D. at Queen's, for example, she "provided," for the entertainment of her audience, a poem by one Maybelle Macfarlane, "The Warbler of the Upper St. Lawrence." One of Atwood's most fascinating send-ups of Canadian literature, however, is a series of regional romances she wrote around this time. The humour they radiate is reminiscent of the spirit that distinguishes the pieces she wrote with Dennis Lee for *Acta Victoriana* in her Vic days. "The Mundane and the Valley," for example, takes aim at Ernest Buckler's canonized novel *The Mountain and the Valley*. Buckler was a Maritimer, and Atwood's romance satirizes the rivalry between the Maritimes and central Canada (for many, embodied by the province of Ontario). Atwood's tale has Dorothy whispering "Ontario stinks" to Percy in an effort to excite him. The Quebec idyll is called "La Plume de ma tant pis," a play on the hackneyed French-class phrase "la plume de ma tante" and the dismissive "tant pis" ("too bad"). For Ontario, there's "Roughing It in the Bushes," a send-up of Susanna Moodie's sketches. Atwood takes on the prairie region by lampooning Sinclair Ross's novel *As for Me and My House*. Her version is called "As for Me and My Grain Elevator." Her spoof of British Columbian writing is written in poetry — "beecee poetry," a reference to that laid-back lowercase style of West Coast poets such as bpNichol and bill bissett. This piece, too, ends with the refrain "Ontario stinks," a perpetuation of the age-old rivalry between Canada's West and East.

★   ★   ★

Two major Atwood works came out in 1976: *Selected Poems* was published by Oxford in Canada (and by Simon and Schuster in the United States in 1978); *Lady Oracle* was published by McClelland and Stewart in Canada, Simon and Schuster in the

United States, and Andre Deutsch in Great Britain. The former was an important signal that Atwood's reputation as a poet in Canada *and* abroad was now solid. The latter, together with her earlier novel *Surfacing*, would ensure her a niche in the international canon of contemporary women's writing.

Lady Oracle had taken Atwood two years to write, partly because of technical difficulties. An early draft of the novel has Joan addressing most of her story to her husband, at that point named George. But the problem was that Joan would have to tell George things — in great detail, so that the reader could be furnished with the information — that he would already have known.

On 27 June 1975, Dennis Lee gave Atwood a detailed set of comments on this version of the novel. He began by praising her efforts — "it has done immoderate things to my adrenalin, kept my head in a buzz, and generally been a bloody good read" — and then moved on to deliver the critique that finally prompted Atwood to rework the manuscript. Besides noting her overuse of the "run-on comma" and her "tendency to switch back and forth between a very conversational diction and syntax, and an extremely formal syntax which in context usually seems mannered, even slightly pedantic," Lee pointed to the places where she had "boxed [herself] into a corner by writing in the present tense." He explained that "To have Joan say (think, write) 'I get up from the chair, I walk across the room, I open a can of sardines, I eat the first one, it goes down slowly . . .' starts to grate on the reader fairly quickly." Lee's other substantive comments had to do with characterization:

> But there are two characters who just aren't right yet; or rather, there are two characters-as-perceived-and-mediated-by-Joan.
>
> The first is Mum. She is a gorgon; fine. Gorgons do exist in real life, and I'm quite prepared to believe that she was one of them.
>
> The problem is that everything she says seems to be there to *demonstrate* her Gorgonish status. . . . Eventually you

end up rooting for her (in an abstract sort of way, mind you, since she is so recognizable a type, and so unsympathetic a person). One ends up disliking Joan for picking at the scab so relentlessly. . . . The second character I stumbled over, as you may have guessed, is "you," George. He's a total drag; or rather, Joan's version of him and feelings towards him are. He's clear enough as a type, that's not the problem. But she can scarcely bring him up for 2 sentences without getting her licks in, proving yet again what a self-righteous, tyrannical, prick he's been. . . . Who needs it?

Some critics of *Surfacing* asked a bright but finally wrong-headed question: what does the protagonist see in her boy-friend, when he's such a nerd? There, I presume that a good deal of the answer is that she doesn't see a fucking thing in him, and that is exactly the point. . . .

But what was appropriate there, isn't here. . . . [A]t the very least, we need to see enough of George to get some greater sense of what she dug in him. . . . Then there's the question, what sort of a book is this? Of course it's many sorts of book, and that *is* the sort of a book it is. What I feel you need to do now, though, having thrown all these glorious balls up into the air, is to go back and see which ones are still revolving & dancing there, and which have actually come down kerplunk, or (more difficult) which are in different atmosphere from the book. . . . Let me antici-pate myself, and say that I think what you have on your hands here is — wonder of wonders — a genuine comic novel. Bittersweet, eclectic, sophisticated; but finally a splendid comic novel. . . . Reading the book from that angle, some things fall away and others seem to be in the wrong key, or scored inappropriately. The first few chap-ters, for instance, are simply dull from that angle of vision . . . I suggest that both Joan's early days in the town, and her early recollections of life with George, be touched with particular daftness, that sense of a world that goes utterly out of control, like a Rube Goldberg machine, if you so much as poke a finger into it — and yet that, somehow, hasn't destroyed her and (we decide in the course of the book) won't destroy her, hurt her as it often does. To descend from such high-flown gabble, I think you need things to be shorter at the beginning, and also to have more comic incident. . . . Peggy, thanks muchly for letting me read this . . . of course, you'll take as much or as little of it as seems right for the book.[60]

This letter of Lee's was ten single-spaced typed pages long. It is a testament to his great editorial skill. But it wasn't intended to be an editor's response to a writer: Lee was writing to Atwood as one friend would to another.

Soon after *Lady Oracle*'s publication, Robert Fulford mentioned in an article on romans à clef that Douglas Fetherling, "the Toronto poet and *littérateur*, is reportedly pleased (though he refuses to comment) when friends suggest he is the model for the Royal Porcupine, an avant-garde artist in Margaret Atwood's new novel, *Lady Oracle*."[61] Charles Pachter told me that he believes the artist is "partly" Fetherling, but "the artist's loft is mine. It's 24 Ryerson. Atwood helped me with the down payment."[62] Atwood replied to Fulford:

> I was . . . shocked by the implication that I myself write *romans à clef*. I neither write them nor approve of them.
>
> Thus I must rush to defend the honour of my friend Doug Fetherling, a rather conservative Toronto journalist who does not have red hair or live in a warehouse or do concrete poems, and whose reaction to a dead dog would probably be to sick-up. (So would mine.) I must also rush to defend the honour of the other gentlemen who have been cast in the role of the Royal Porcupine by onlookers and ill-wishers. The Royal P. is not Charles Pachter, though Charles has a warehouse and has done a set of paintings featuring the Queen. He is not Mark Prent, Dr. Brute, Bill Bissett, or Flakey Rose Hips.
>
> But the most surprising claimant was my friend Alan Walker.

"I know who the Royal Porcupine is!" he proclaimed triumphantly.

"Oh, who?" I asked, intrigued, since I didn't know myself.

"Me!" he chortled.

"Urk," I replied. "Uh, Alan, why do you say that?"

"He collects Big Little books," Alan said, "and so do I."

"What can I say?" I said.

The fact that so many people have been identified as the Royal Porcupine should give the game away. There *is* no Royal Porcupine. He's not intended as a representation of any real person, living or dead. He's a character in a novel.[63]

In CanLit circles, a favourite game is matching Atwood characters to real people. And the game isn't complete until players have had a shot at matching Atwood to one of her own creations. The number-one choice is usually the protagonist. When Atwood would read a chapter from *Lady Oracle* to an audience, she would invariably be asked, "How did you lose all that weight?" Such misreading is anticipated by, and parodied within, the novel itself: the protagonist's husband — now called Arthur — reads her book *as though it were* autobiography. However, Atwood admits that the settings in her novels are more often than not very real, that the novels are "autogeographical." "I find it necessary," she explains, "in order to write about a place, to have actually been there. I can invent characters, but I am absolutely dependent on the details of the material world to make a space for my characters to move around in."[64]

16

Another Balancing Act: Fame and Motherhood

READING THROUGH THE COMMENTARY on Margaret Atwood (the writer rather than the work) published during the mid-1970s, I was struck by the absence of Graeme Gibson. For the first time I was looking at the material from a specifically biographical perspective, and suddenly this absence seemed glaring. Of course, the lack of references to Gibson was largely the result of Atwood's efforts to guard her private life very carefully. But, why, I wondered, did all those journalists who wrote about her not push a bit further? Was it merely their Canadian reticence? No. I think there was more to it than that. I think it was a reflection of the times.

Let me set the stage. In 1975, the world marked International Year of the Woman. The miniskirts and baby-doll dresses of the 1960s (yes, I have it on good authority that Atwood owned and wore one of these, as did many other women who might not admit to it now . . .) gave way to the menswear-for-women look; pin-striped power suits and flat shoes were in. On television, Marlo Thomas of *That Girl* fame passed the mantle to Mary Tyler Moore. A powerful role model, Mary showed her female audience that having it all in the 1970s didn't mean having a man. It was vital, however, to be thin, attractive, and — most of all — independent.[1] *Lady Oracle* emerged from this cultural shift. The media were now increasingly interested in Margaret Atwood specifically as a *woman* writer, a feminist, and a role model. The responsibility weighed heavily on Atwood's shoulders. Here she was, squarely in the spotlight with few role models of her own (of the contemporary-woman-writer variety) to call on for support.

★ ★ ★

It is 1948. One of a group of nine- and ten-year-old girls at a birthday party, Margaret Atwood sits in the darkness of a Toronto movie theatre. She is mesmerized. The film is *The Red Shoes*, and Atwood is watching Moira Shearer, playing the part of the ballerina Victoria, dance in ever-narrowing circles, trapped within a dilemma from which there is no escape. All of Atwood's terrified party companions know that for Victoria there can be no happy ending. Either she can give up dancing for the sake of her marriage and thereby destroy her soul, or she can dance and lose her husband. She chooses husband and marriage. This is 1948, after all. But of course her passion for dance can only be stifled for so long, and, in a fit of desperation, she puts on the red shoes and dances one last time. As the film ends, Victoria leaps into the path of an oncoming train. Atwood and friends emit a collective gasp. For me, Victoria's husband never seemed worth all the angst, with his small mind and small frame — but then, I suppose, he offered much more than just himself. He offered respectability. When a woman married in those days, she gained a position in society.[2]

In this film classic, the dilemma is mythic and monstrous in its proportions. But those little girls in the Toronto movie theatre knew that there was a hint of truth in it: at some point, their society would compel them to choose. Atwood remembers:

> the little girls watching fell into two groups: those who cheered on the husband, found the bleeding feet yucky, and swore never to get involved in anything more serious than needlepoint, thus forming the core of REAL women; and those who were on the side of the dancing and grew up to believe, not that Sylvia Plath was a real poet who committed suicide, but that Sylvia Plath was a real poet *because* she committed suicide. The trick for those of us of that generation

229

who wanted to be artists was to somehow do the art while keeping away from the train tracks.[3]

Making these observations forty years later (with eleven poetry collections, three short-fiction collections, seven novels, two children's books, three books of nonfiction, and numerous awards and honorary degrees under her belt), Atwood suggests that her own choice was inevitable. However, her success as an artist and as an individual may be attributed to the fact that she has never really made that choice — the choice that confronted her, for a moment, at that 1948 birthday party. Instead, she has become a master at establishing priorities, at juggling responsibilities, at identifying realistic goals, and at achieving them on schedule. Only on very rare occasions has she ever had to compromise or admit defeat. (And, just to be on the safe side, she has never danced near train tracks.)

* * *

By the mid-1970s Atwood had clearly achieved a level of excellence in her writing. And her reward was international recognition. She was also blessed with a happy family life and a certain stature in her community attained through activism. From the outside, it appeared that things — for women in general and for Atwood in particular — had changed dramatically.

But some problems persisted. In an article called "The Curse of Eve," Atwood bemoaned the lack of viable role models for women. She voiced her frustration, during a York University talk, at the notion — still alive and well in the 1970s — that

> women are still expected to be better than men, morally that is, even by women, even by some branches of the women's movement; and if you are not an angel, if you happen to have human failings, as most of us do, especially if you display any kind of strength or power, creative or otherwise, then you are not merely human, you're worse than human. . . . I could easily illustrate by reading from

my own clipping file: I could tell you about Margaret the Magician, Margaret the Medusa, Margaret the Man-eater, clawing her way to success over the corpses of many hapless men. Margaret the powerhungry Hitler, with her megalomaniac plans to take over the entire field of Canadian Literature. This woman must be stopped! All of these mythological creatures are inventions of critics; not all of them male. (No one has yet called me an angel, but Margaret the Martyr will surely not take long to appear, especially if I die young in a car accident.)

It would be amusing to continue with these excerpts, but it would also be rather mean, considering the fact that some of the perpetrators are, if not in the audience, employed by this university. So instead of doing that, I will enter a simple plea; women, both as characters and as people, must be allowed their imperfections.[4]

In an article she wrote at about this time, Atwood laid out some of the slots and categories that the media had created for women writers. Some of her ideas dated back to the survey she conducted with her Canadian-literature class while teaching at York — the one about gender bias in book reviews. The article was also an extended exploration of the red-shoes dilemma in a contemporary context. Earlier in the twentieth century, she explained, the woman artist could model herself on "suicidal Sylvia," a "dire" version of both "Recluse Rosetti" and "Elusive Emily." But now, she noted, there are new opportunities:

i) Happy Housewife
This one is almost obsolete . . . the attitude was, "Gosh, all the housework and you're a writer too!" Writing was viewed as a hobby, like knitting, that one did in one's spare time.
ii) Ophelia
The writer as crazy freak. . . .
iii) Miss Martyr, or, "Movie Mag"
Read any "movie mag" article on Liz Taylor, translate it

into writing terms and you've got the picture. The writer as someone who *suffers* more than others. Why does the writer suffer more? Because she's successful, and you all know Success Must Be Paid For. In blood and tears, if possible. If you say you're happy and enjoy your life and work, you'll be ignored.

iv) Miss Message

The interviewer who believes in Miss Message is incapable of treating your work as what it is, poetry and/or fiction. . . . Rare indeed is an interviewer who regards writing as a respectable profession, not as some kind of magic, madness, trickery or evasive disguise for a message; and who regards an author as a person engaged in a professional activity, not as a witch, boor, sufferer or messiah.[5]

*   *   *

If we skip ahead another couple of decades to 1996, we find Atwood penning her introduction to the revised version of the 1988 *Women Writers at Work*. She is still involved in the struggle that engages all women writers: breaking away from the "woman question" (Why must a woman be categorized first as a woman and *then* as a writer?); or, as Atwood puts it, "the trained-dog fascination with the idea of women writers" ("not that the thing is done well, but that it is done at all, by a creature that is not supposed to possess such capabilities").[6] Her point in writing this introduction is to underline — in red pencil — the overwhelming sense shared by all the writers interviewed in *Women Writers at Work* that they are, first and foremost, fighting to write well on their own terms. On this, Atwood speaks for herself as well.

*   *   *

Atwood again raised the woman question while interviewing Margaret Drabble in 1987 for *Chatelaine* magazine. Their conversation quickly turned to the difficulty of maintaining a writing career while coping with the practical realities of family life. The nitty-gritty of it. Who cooks the meals? Graeme Gibson in Atwood's case; Drabble said she shouldered the task in her house, although the family would eat out when she was working on a novel — "a very civilized thing to decide to do," commented Drabble. Interestingly, she went on to explain that she and her sister, novelist A.S. Byatt, were brought up in a very "feminist" way:

> My mother had been a very vocal feminist; she was very vocal but didn't do anything about it except to bring us all up to believe that we ought to do something about it. So I was brought up, as possibly you were, with this faith that one could do both, one could have a very full life. Of course what we hadn't realized was that it was absolutely exhausting. A lot of the 60s was spent figuring out that although in principle one could have children and work, in practice this was very, very hard.[7]

Drabble has three children — her first was born when she was twenty-one. Atwood, in a sense, has also raised three children: Jess, the child she had with Gibson in May of 1976, as well as Grae and Matt, Gibson's sons from his first marriage. But while Atwood's domestic circumstances might appear just about ideal from an outsider's perspective, a confession she has made during a couple of interviews — that she would have liked to have had more children — suggests that there may be some moments of regret.

★ ★ ★

Atwood completed *Lady Oracle* in the early part of 1976. That done, she and Gibson travelled to Mexico.[8] They had six weeks to rest and relax before they would again be plunged into a period of frenetic activity: they were expecting a baby. In mid-May Eleanor Jess Atwood Gibson was born.

Atwood's pregnancy had been an easy one.

> I kept expecting to have all these things you're supposed to
> get in pregnancy — varicose veins, sick to my stomach; but
> I never had any of them. . . . I kept wondering if I had
> mental dullness. It's very hard to tell. . . . The only problem
> I had was some pressure on a nerve in my leg which meant
> it would collapse every once in a while. So I was going
> around with this quite impressive-looking cane for a time.[9]

She and Gibson chose the name Jess because they liked it; later
they found out that it was a family surname on Atwood's side.[10]

Being writers, Mum and Dad were able to spend plenty of time
at home with Baby Jess. It was a luxury that few other professions
could afford. When Atwood first announced her desire to be a
writer, one of her mother's friends had said, "That's nice dear,
because it's something you can do at home."[11] To an ambitious
teenager that comment must have seemed tantamount to a dis-
missal of her serious writerly aspirations. But, when the time
actually came, Atwood remembered those words and recognized
their wisdom.

Soon after Jess's birth, Atwood sent a handwritten note to Bev
Hunter, her friend from Canadian Facts Marketing. She enclosed
an airplane ticket to Toronto from Vancouver, where Hunter was
now living. "Bev," wrote the new mother, "I don't know if you
remember this, but you said if I ever had a child, you would come.
This is it. Here's an airplane ticket." Still raising her own four
girls single-handedly, Hunter had just started a new job that she
badly needed to keep. Still, this kind of call was hard not to heed.
Armed with the note, she walked into her supervisor's office.
The supervisor said, "Go." She did.

Hunter described the atmosphere at the Alliston farmhouse to
me. She painted a picture of an extremely capable Atwood and
Gibson running a farming enterprise. Both she and I suspected
that she was remembering another visit. Surely Atwood couldn't
have been so active after so recently giving birth to her first child.
Said Hunter:

> I remember all of these little tiny jars of crabapple jelly,
> made from the tree outside. In the spare bedroom there was

a knitted counterpane made up of millions of squares all done in stocking stitch. The garden was filled with tuberous plants — melons. [Atwood] would weed and sprinkle. Out in the garage, she had the hugest dog known to mankind who had given birth to eight or twelve pups, which were at least as high as your hips. She had a pony. And the phone calls about what she wanted on the cover of her book. Upstairs there was a solarium filled with plants, and an eight-layered fruit-drying setup. At one point, Graeme, who was sitting in the kitchen reading the newspaper, talked about an article featuring a guy holding down more than one job and writing as well. From the other room Peggy said, in a low voice, "he's not the only one."[12]

Having attained a certain level of professional success, Atwood and Gibson were able to hire help. In that 1987 *Chatelaine* interview, Drabble commented that she had had her children very early on. "I didn't do it in that order," responded Atwood. "I waited until I had the money. I had the baby and hired the help." "Well," said Drabble, "you did it much, much more logically than I."[13]

Despite any regrets she may have over not having more children, Atwood knew that the practical advantage of having had Jess a bit later in life was that she could keep up a steady — if slightly slower — work pace. The promotional tour she undertook for *Lady Oracle* was less rigorous than it might otherwise have been, but Atwood did continue to produce new work. In fact, on 1 June 1976 she wrote a letter to Raymond Pannell of the Co-Opera Theatre expressing interest in, of all things, writing an opera libretto. She added, "could I have a little time to get over having the baby before we discuss this?"[14] Atwood wrote this letter about two weeks after Jess was born. Most new mothers would have allowed themselves six weeks to emerge from the haze.

Atwood's publication list reflects little evidence of a work slowdown. In 1977, she published a small book for schoolchildren called *Days of the Rebels, 1815–40*, part of the excellent

McClelland and Stewart Canada's Illustrated Heritage series. *Marsh, Hawk*, a broadside of her poems, was published by Dreadnaught as part of that small press's 52pickup series. *Dancing Girls*, Atwood's first collection of short fiction, was also published that year — by McClelland and Stewart in Canada and by Simon and Schuster in the United States; in 1979, Jonathan Cape brought it out in Britain.

Dancing Girls contained a couple of stories set in Boston — "Hair Jewellery" and the title story; "The Man from Mars," which, in some ways, anticipates *Lady Oracle*; "A Travel Piece," which heralds her 1981 novel *Bodily Harm*; and "Giving Birth." It won the Canadian Booksellers' Association Award and the Periodical Distributors of Canada Short Fiction Award.

The *Dancing Girls* stories were written between 1963 and 1977. A scrap of paper in the Atwood archives lists their dates of composition and publication. Some of these dates are surprising: "Dancing Girls," one of the Harvard stories, was written about ten years after Atwood left Cambridge. Other dates are as expected: "Giving Birth" was written shortly after Jess was born.

THE WAR IN THE BATHROOM 1963: 1964

THE MAN FROM MARS 1970: 1977

POLARITIES. 1970: 1971

RAPE FANTASIES. 1975: 1975

UNDER GLASS 1971: 1972

ENCOUNTERS WITH THE ELEMENT MAN 1971: 1972
   [which did not appear in the final collection]

THE GRAVE OF THE FAMOUS POET 1971: 1973

HAIR JEWELLERY 1975: 1976

WHEN IT HAPPENS. 1975: 1975

A TRAVEL PIECE 1975: 1975

THE RESPLENDENT QUETZAL 1976: 1977

TRAINING 1977

LIVES OF THE POETS 1977: 1977

DANCING GIRLS 1977

GIVING BIRTH . . . . 1977[15]

In April of 1977, Atwood and Gibson began work on a screenplay version of Margaret Laurence's Canadian classic *The Diviners*. On 26 January of that year, *Toronto Star* columnist Sid Adilman had announced: "What a powerhouse of writing talent! Margaret Atwood and Graeme Gibson, Can. Lit.'s favourite couple, are collaborating on the movie script of Margaret Laurence's bestselling novel, *The Diviners*. Producers Joyce Wieland and Judy Steed (the pair responsible for *The Far Shore*) and artist Charles Pachter [whose role was to help get the project off the ground financially] project an August or September start on a budget of $1.2 million."[16] But this project, like so many other film projects, became a source of frustration. "Peggy was quite straight thinking about what she felt it should be," explained Pachter, and Wieland and Steed "were pressured by so many outside influences in order to raise money" that there came a point, after Atwood had submitted the second draft of the screenplay, that Wieland and Steed decided to move on. The script was turned over to American writer Venable Herndon of *Alice's Restaurant* fame.[17] Pachter was also trying, with the help of agent Phoebe Larmore, to buy the film rights for *The Edible Woman* from Oscar Lewenstein. But by March of 1978 Pungent Productions (Pachter's company) had given up the fight to convince Lewenstein to relinquish control of the film rights.

In May, Atwood choreographed the All-Star Eclectic Typewriter Revue, which was staged by the Writers' Union before sellout audiences at Toronto's St. Lawrence Centre. In the *Toronto Star*, Robert Fulford praised Atwood for leading a rather inept, albeit well-intentioned, group of literati in an entertaining evening of song, skit, and dance. Fulford himself played the role of "God-Fulford," dancing to the tune "that was immortalized as the Chiquita Banana commercial." Fulford's point was not only that Atwood's camp-counsellor skills were still very much intact but also that there was a gentler side to the CanLit tribe: "Some of the evening was brilliant. But the tone was set by the Atwoodian comedy, and the tone was Ontario summer camp, circa 1955, at its finest. It was the kind of thing that is best done for the benefit of indulgent parents, and it convinced me once more that the writers of English Canada — for all their bickering and conniving and jealousy — have become a kind of family."[18] Did Fulford also imply, perhaps, that Atwood's role in the national literary "family" was that of a counsellor?

She can certainly dispense sage advice. When Atwood met Fulford in a restaurant to ask him to participate in the revue, she found him in a flustered state. In his memoirs, Fulford explains:

> I'[d] just been interviewed by a woman from the CBC. . . . Her first question was, "Mr. Fulford, you write the Note-book column and the Marshall Delaney movie column in *Saturday Night*, you write every weekend in the *Toronto Star* and some other papers, you give reviews on the radio and interview people on television — don't you think that's a bit too much Robert Fulford?" And all I could think of to say was something like "Well, of course, if you think so, then. . . ."
>
> "You should have said, 'It's not too much for me. Is it too much for you?'" [Atwood replied].
>
> Ever since, I've been hoping someone will ask me the same question again, so that I can give Atwood's answer.[19]

★   ★   ★

Motherhood was wonderful for Atwood. She managed to maintain the momentum of her work, to travel (to Venice and England that year), and to enjoy time with her young daughter. In some intangible way, too, motherhood was good for her public image. From the perspective of the Canadian public, the birth of Jess cast her in a new and more positive light.

The year 1977 also saw the publication of a special issue of the literary journal the *Malahat Review* devoted entirely to Atwood and her work. Atwood contributed a large number of photos to the issue, and many of her friends and literary colleagues wrote assessments and tributes, including George Bowering, Rick Salutin, Jane Rule, and Gwendolyn MacEwen. The issue was based on a symposium that had brought together a number of high-powered critics — Eli Mandel, George Woodcock, Francine du Plessix Gray — but there were also quite a few notable absences from the roster. Some of the people who knew Atwood and her writing best were not among the contributors: Charles Pachter, Dennis Lee, David Donnell, William Toye, Douglas Jones, Douglas Fetherling. A wide range of tone and genre is evident in this collection; as a whole, though, it attests to the prominence of Atwood in Canada at the time and celebrates her as a kind of presiding genius of Canadian letters. One photo collage featured in the issue is particularly striking. Atwood herself was "rather surprised": "I think the collage sequence was supposed to have been inspired by my work rather than by my finite personal being, which in this climate is usually swathed in wool. Even so???"[20]

By 1978, the siege had abated and Atwood had become more philosophical about her prominence. She remarked to Joyce Carol Oates, "as long as people are still attacking me, I'll know that I'm still saying something they find worth attacking. The career of a Canadian writer is usually, if initially successful, marked by a period of fervent attack and rejection." Atwood went on to say that she hadn't "achieved petrification yet," and hoped "not to for at least a few years. I'm still getting sneered at."[21] This attitude anticipates the reaction of one of Atwood's artist protagonists — Elaine Risley of her 1988 novel *Cat's Eye* — to a promotional poster featuring a photo of her own face. On it, someone has drawn a mustache just above the mouth. At fifty, Elaine finally comes to believe that such scribbles are a kind of compliment, a response to a public figure rather than to a private individual.[22] Atwood realized this in her thirties.[23]

17

Travelling

THE FOLLOWING YEAR, 1978, Atwood published a new collection of poetry, *Two-Headed Poems*, and a children's book, *Up in the Tree*. For the body of her work to date, she received the St. Lawrence Award for Fiction.

She says that she wrote *Up in the Tree* while working on *Surfacing*. "I know many will flinch in disbelief when I say that in some ways *Up in the Tree* was a much more painful book to work on than *Surfacing* was. Not that it was painful to *write*; but, in a fit of enthusiasm, I had said that I would illustrate it myself. And that was when the pain set it."[1] The book was illustrated by one "Charlatan Botchner" — yet another Atwood alias. It joined the list of pseudonyms and artist's signatures that Atwood had already employed: M.E. Atwood, Shakesbeat Latweed, and Bart Gerrard.

Up in the Tree, published by McClelland and Stewart, was originally meant to measure eight by ten inches and feature alternating two- and four-colour two-page spreads. That the finished product is actually four by five inches with two-colour illustrations is an indication of how complex the creative negotiation process turned out to be. Atwood hand-lettered the whole thing herself. She also did the line drawings. "Measured on the pain scale, *Up in the Tree* is my most serious book."[2] The protagonist of *Surfacing* is an illustrator; because Atwood worked on the two books at the same time, it is not surprising that the protagonist's ambivalent feelings about her work seem to anticipate Atwood's *Up in the Tree* tribulations.

Atwood sent an early version of *Two-Headed Poems* to Dennis Lee, who suggested that she tighten up the title poem because he saw it as a "centre of gravity" for the collection.

> This book is very interesting because it doesn't have the kind of *a priori* unity that *Susanna Moodie* or *Power Politics* had, and yet the core book . . . has a great deal of inner, organic, developing unity. . . . I guess I like the book so much because it has so many beautifully-defined centres of gravity — which don't combat or displace each other, but each of which animates the whole book with its own integral lines of force. "The Right Hand Fights the Left," "Marrying the Hangman," "The Bus to Alliston Ontario" are three other examples, and there are more. In each case, it's quite possible to read the whole book as imaginatively configured by that one poem; and then as you come to the next, the lines of force regroup themselves again so the whole book organizes itself around *that* poem. (That's what makes it so rich.) . . . Anyway, the public/authorial/private tensions reach one of their normative definitions in "Two-Headed Poems," and the difficulty of finding the context in which you want us to read that poem creates a blur which affects the whole book.
>
> I think the convention of the latter part of the book is just fine, by the way, with the mother running over all her life-concerns to find what wisdom she has, to pass on to her daughter. A very clean, almost invisible structural strategy. (I could imagine a short poem near the beginning in which the woman just asks herself what she can give her daughter, without any answers yet. That would suggest one more context for the painful, handsome, explorations of the middle section.) . . . Again, Peggy, bravissimo! Dennis.[3]

★ ★ ★

But these publishing milestones were not what made 1978 a year Atwood would never forget. It was the world tour. On 1 February, she, Gibson, and little Jess left home to spend about six weeks circling the globe. The adventure got under way in Paris, where Atwood and Gibson were part of a display put on by the Ontario government. Each of the participating Ontario artists — including photographers, weavers, painters, dancers, and musicians — was "boxed." That is, each was represented by a box measuring about six by three feet and papered with photos: a frontal view of the artist was displayed on the front of the box; profile views lined the sides; the back of the box bore the rear view. Inside each box was a set of appropriate artifacts. The box of renowned photographer Yousuf Karsh, for instance, contained his first camera and a few of his early portraits, among them the famous one of a pouting Winston Churchill, snapped just after Karsh had pulled the cigar from his mouth. Each box had a button that when pressed emitted a representative sound. Both Gibson and Atwood were boxed for the occasion and were in attendance when the exhibit was launched.[4]

As any parent knows, the logistics of travelling with a twenty-month-old child can be hair-raising. Although both Gibson and Atwood were experienced travellers — they had brought along an emergency kit of powdered-drink crystals, raisins, and dates for Jess and scotch for themselves — some problems were unavoidable. The kit was left on a plane. Gibson, bent on retrieving it, ran back through the airport and the security checkpoint; he finally made his way to the lost-and-found booth, where the precious property was waiting. What else could a father do?

Leaving Paris, they flew to Afghanistan via Tehran. In hindsight, the risk was probably too great, but how were they to know that they would be arriving in Afghanistan only weeks before the coup? The "via Tehran" part of the trip was also a mistake that Atwood and Gibson had plenty of time to ponder as they camped out at the airport, Jess shredding a paper plate and chattering at amused onlookers. They had obtained travel visas in Paris, but the airport officials seemed uneasy: they seemed to think the couple was planning to write an article on their trip (which, of course, they were). "Nothing political," the officials warned nervously. Gibson quickly switched the topic. At long last, the tired trio was admitted into the country.

Murphy's first law is that a bag will get lost on every trip. Murphy's second law is that a room reservation will go astray. It did. In Tehran. And, in the days leading up to demonstrations against the Shah of Iran that erupted in 1979, rooms were not easy to come by in that city. So, while Jess played with coins on the floor, Atwood haggled for an hour and a half with the desk clerks at the hotel where they had expected to stay before they agreed to find the young family a room in a different hotel. When they finally got there, it was 2:30 in the morning.

After Tehran, they flew to Kabul, in Afghanistan, where they spent a full week. There Jess and Atwood, in their Western clothes, stood out in the streets; Afghan women wear full purdah. Afghanistan adheres very strictly to Islamic ritual in general. The three were invited to tea by a man named Abdul, and Gibson remembers the surprise he felt when Abdul showed them his family photo albums: Abdul's wife was absent from her own wedding pictures; his daughters were missing from the family snapshots. "In fact there's no indication that women exist at all," Gibson writes in his article "Travels of a Family Man."[5]

The next stop was India, where they were overwhelmed by the Taj Mahal. Gibson's descriptions of the sublime moments he and his small family experienced on this trip are juxtaposed with commentary about the pressing realities of travelling with a child — frequent bathroom stops, for instance.

The Adelaide Poetry Festival was the official destination of the trip, so after India the trio made its way to Australia. As Gibson describes this high-profile literary event in "Travels of a Family Man," his frustration with what he discovered while attending it is palpable. He asks his readers to recognize a parallel between the patriarchal values that shape Afghan society and those that prevail in Australia. He recounts a conversation he had with two Australians, both of whom murmured something sympathetic about how difficult it must be for him to play second fiddle to Margaret and get left behind to look after Jess. Implicit in such a statement, Gibson points out, is a "fundamental feeling, very close to the surface here [in Australia], that there's something wrong when a woman achieves status, wrong because of the problem it creates for the male ego." Of course, this sexist attitude is not peculiar to Australia and Australians, as Gibson is quick to acknowledge. (It is certainly part of North American culture; that is why the disgruntlement that Arthur, of *Lady Oracle*, feels at his wife's literary sucess is so credible.) That said, Gibson must have encountered this notion just once too often during the Australia trip. "I've certainly never run into the assumption quite so frequently and crassly as I have here," he wrote, clearly annoyed.[6]

Atwood also wrote about their Australian sojourn: her piece appears in *Second Words* and details a week spent participating in a writing workshop. It focuses less on gender issues and more on national issues. But both Atwood's and Gibson's accounts of the trip, written for very different audiences, cover one particular aspect of their joint adventure: "In planning this trip," explains Gibson,

> we overlooked the problem of what we'd do with ourselves once Jess had gone to sleep in our hotel room. Since it's winter in Tehran, we can't stay on the balcony, so we've taken to squeezing a chair into the bathroom. At first it is an odd, claustrophobic situation, the two of us reflected in all those mirrors as we read and write, but we're used to it now and it's better than sitting in the dark.[7]

By the end of the trip they had become quite used to this system. Out of sheer necessity, it had been put into operation on a number of different continents.

Although they stopped in Fiji and Hawaii on their homeward journey, they were too tired and anxious to be back in Alliston to succumb to the allure of these tropical locales. But Atwood scarcely had time to settle back into farm life before she had to embark on a tour, arranged by Simon and Schuster, to promote *Selected Poems*. She travelled through the United States during the early part of April and ended up on the West Coast in May.

And, also in 1978, Atwood, Gibson, and Jess went to England. This time the family travelled in style, setting sail from New York on the legendary ocean liner the *Queen Elizabeth II*. They left

New York a day late, due to the ship's being detained in a horrendous storm a fortnight before. Sue Milmoe, Atwood's Harvard roommate, was living in New York and went to the pier where the ship was docked bearing some travel essentials — diapers for Jess and an Agatha Christie mystery for her parents. They fêted the occasion with coffee in styrofoam cups: gone were the days of champagne and streamers. After they got under way, Atwood joined the joggers who circled the deck each morning. The ship had a children's playroom as well, open from eight o'clock in the morning until seven at night; so, although they took Jess to meals, Gibson and Atwood had quite a lot of freedom while at sea.[8]

Atwood and Gibson's ultimate destination was Edinburgh. Gibson had been invited to serve as writer-in-residence at the University of Edinburgh. Quartered at 14 Belgrave Crescent, the trio spent the latter part of 1978 in the Scottish capital. Atwood managed to get Jess into a play group that met on Mondays and Fridays, and so two mornings a week she would settle her daughter into a stroller and make her way to the dusty hall where the group convened. It all sounds pretty normal: playtime, snack time, singsong time. Gibson went once and came back saying that it was like entering a "demented airport" — not a bad description for a group of active toddlers and their ride-on toys.[9]

One of the advantages of spending time abroad, for both Atwood and Gibson, was the relative privacy it afforded them. At Jess's play group, for example, when Atwood told the other mothers that she was writing a book, they were incredulous. "Do you have a publisher?" they asked. Remarks Atwood, "I'm amazed at how quickly the trappings, the public image, the assumed success, the right to say things such as 'I'm writing a novel,' unquestioned, fall away now that I'm in a strange country where only the literati have read my work and no one sees my face on subway posters."[10] A bit of a blow for her writerly ego. But also, surely, a relief. In any event, it was only a temporary hiatus from celebrity.

While the weather was still cold, Atwood's routine was to spend the mornings with Jess and, when a babysitter came on duty at lunch, to travel to an office she had rented. Here she would write for about four hours. The office itself was only about a fifteen-minute walk from Belgrave Crescent — just far enough away to facilitate the separation of work space and home space. "The office is a barren room up three flights of stairs, heated only by an electric heater, with a typewriter that jumps lines, bounces in from the margin, and periodically will not work at all. I sit in my coat, staring at the green blackboard on the wall opposite, and try to empty my head of everything."[11] There was a desperation to Atwood's writing at this point, a sense of panic. Not enough time to write and think. It wasn't going well. The chapters she produced were too short. Atwood, as a mother and a colonial, felt particularly isolated — to use the words of her title, "on the fringe of the empire." After all, the nucleus of her empire was Canada, not England; she was on the fringe indeed.

⋆ ⋆ ⋆

As Atwood and Gibson planned and undertook their travels, a political battle was being waged on the Canadian-literature front. At the end of 1977, the Writers' Union of Canada met to find strategies to curtail the importation of foreign remaindered editions of books by Canadian writers. This practice had cost writers a tremendous amount in royalty payments and Canadian publishers a great deal of revenue. The Coles bookstore chain was one of the major offenders. In part, the issue emerged because the shelf life of a hardback book in Canada was substantially longer than it was in the United States: up to two years in Canada versus six months south of the border. A book that was still selling well in Canada — particularly by one of the country's own authors — could find itself in the process of being remaindered in the United States. Some authors solved the dilemma by signing a contract directly with an American publisher; but this tactic, if it became widespread, would ultimately bring about the death of Canadian publishing. The Writers' Union decided to protest remaindered-edition dumping.

When Atwood published *Life before Man* in 1979, she did protect the novel from dumping by publishing it first with

McClelland and Stewart and then with Simon and Schuster in the United States and Jonathan Cape in Great Britain the following year. Of all her novels, this one is set in the most circumscribed geographical space; no character enters or leaves during the course of the narrative — except one, in a box. Ironically, Atwood produced this novel after a year of extensive and exhausting travel.

Working very hard to ground *Life before Man* in accurate details, Atwood dispatched Donya Peroff to clarify certain bits of information. Peroff talked to Jack Donnan at the Ontario Ministry of the Environment, for example, because Donnan and the character William have the same job. "Not interested in his personality," Atwood noted in her instructions, "just his job." She also asked Peroff to talk to several people who had Lithuanian Jewish grandmothers with the aim of collecting "domestic & family detail, ie. when did the grandmother come to Canada? Where did the family move? where did they live? what did they do for money? what did the grandmother wear? what was her house/apt. like . . . what was in it etc. Did they attend *shule*? Orthodox? any little expression you can pick up (Lithuanian Yiddish is quite different from other Yiddish dialects and the accent is different too.) that kind of thing."[12] Atwood provided Peroff with a contact name — someone who had "promised to get me some people with Lithuanian Jewish grandmothers." For information on Ukrainian grandmothers, Atwood gave her assistant a different name, but the instructions were the same.

Atwood's research for the novel, while characteristically meticulous, was anecdotal. To ensure that she had rendered nuances of speech and tone convincingly, she asked for the input of others. She sent an early version of the manuscript to her sister-in-law, Lenore, and her reaction was priceless. Lenore's reply is handwritten; her lines tilt optimistically upwards at the ends.

When I finished reading "Life Before Man" the first thing I said to myself was "How remarkable!! Peggy has managed to make all the people in the book ME!!" As a matter of fact I said it out loud even though everyone in the house was already asleep.

It wasn't until yesterday when I was packing the manuscript to return it to Jennifer that I found your letter and
realized what I was supposed to do. This was great as I
carefully had written a six page essay on what I thought,
the main thrust of which was that Jewish grandmothers
would be very unlikely to say "Gut in himmel" for so little
a reason. [As Lenore explained to me, she wouldn't say it
because it is a blasphemy to say "God." She might say
"Oy vais meer" or "Gevult."[13]] Also I felt Lesje would not
use the word "schul" but "synagogue." I was brought up
by immigrant parents who both spoke Yiddish (but not to
me) and I would say "synagogue" most of the time; maybe
sometimes "schul."

Elizabeth is my favourite person. I love her and so will all
of my friends. On the basis of my raving about her (never
mentioning her name or anything about what happens)
eight close friends have ordered the book from me provided
I personally autograph it.

[Overleaf.] I liked Elizabeth so much I had to write
something more. I think Elizabeth Taylor should play her
in the movie version. (Maybe I could be an extra in the ROM
cafeteria or at the Varsity or somewhere). I like her better
than Lesje because Elizabeth is almost 40, a little overweight, has 2 kids, and is going to be all right and Lesje is
too thin and young for my tastes.

Of course, being pregnant with Nate as a father, she's
going to get older and fatter and fast!

Lenore goes on to relate some family anecdotes (which she has
illustrated) and then returns to the subject of the manuscript:

I enjoyed this novel more than any of your others (I enjoyed
all of your others more than anyone else's others). It is SUPER!!

I also enjoyed William's environmental conversations with
Lesje and Elizabeth. I was eating a dish of ORO grown
rhubarb when he first started and laughed and choked on
the rhubarb.

I'm sure that someone by now has pointed out the difference between clockwise and counter clockwise [a diagram follows featuring a stick man running in the appropriate direction]. This is with reference to Nate's running path around Queen's Park.

After jotting down a few more family notes, Lenore fills Atwood in on her ceramic-elephant business: Lenore Atwood's whimsical clay sculptures — including an elephant series and a selection of menorahs and chanukiahs — are still popular in and around Toronto. "In your next novel," she adds, "is there any possibility that the heroine could see elephants over her partner's shoulder now and then??"[14]

Life before Man was originally called " 'Notes on the Mezaoic' — Mezaoic meaning 'middle life.' The novel is the middle of the lives of several people. And they're middle class. And it's mid-history. But the title was changed because everybody said, 'Notes on the What?' "[15]

In among the *Life before Man* papers in the Atwood archive are Atwood's travel itineraries for the book's promotional tour. A typical week on the road for Atwood, as it would be for many touring writers, is laid out in a hefty document. One such week, for example, takes fourteen pages to outline, and each page contains approximately eight different engagements — readings, interviews, or autograph sessions. Occasionally there is a note: "dates not available." Two or three days are reserved. These, presumably, are the weekends Atwood earmarked for rest and family time. And occasionally Atwood made a few entries herself, generally breakfasts and lunches with friends living in the towns she would be visiting. In Halifax she stayed with her aunt Joyce Barkhouse; the names of other Nova Scotia relatives were inscribed on the itinerary. But how much free time could Atwood have had to catch up with her extended family on a day (in Halifax) that looks like this on paper?

9:00 A.M.: Doug Murdoch, our Maritimes representative, will collect you. [She would be staying with her aunt Joyce Barkhouse.]

9:15 A.M.:	CBC Radio, "Information Morning," with Sue Dexter.	
10:00 A.M.:	Chronicle-Herald, Lorna Innis.	
11:00 A.M.:	CBC-TV, "High Noon," Augusta La Paix.	
12:30 P.M.:	Sanford Second Story Hollis Street [this is noted in Atwood's own handwriting].	
2:00 P.M.:	CBC, "Radio Noon Three," with Jim Bennett.	
2:30-4:00 P.M.:	CBC-TV, "Profile," Marilyn McDonald [full half-hour taping to be shown the following week, 10:30–11:00 P.M. in all three provinces; here Atwood has written "books signed"].	
8:00 P.M.:	Reading at Dalhousie, Canadian Book Information Centre.	

Judging from some notes written at the bottom of the page, including the names of Atwood's Maritime relatives and two restaurants (Five Fishermen and Clipper Cay), dinner was a family affair.[16]

This day sounds hectic, but the schedule for the evening and day Atwood spent in Montreal is positively daunting.

MONTREAL, OCT. 11-13, '79

Thurs., Oct. 11:

8:30 P.M.	CFCF TV McGowan & Co. Don McGowan	405 Ogilvy Ave.

Fri., Oct. 12:

9:00 A.M.	CBC Radio Daybreak Bob McKeown	1400 Dorchester E.
9:30 A.M.	CJAD Radio Sounds Like Montreal Helen Gougeon	1407 Mountain St.
10:00 A.M.	CJFM-FM Radio People Mary Lou Basaraba	1407 Mountain St.
11:00 A.M.	CHOM-FM Radio Hillary McLeod	1355 Greene Ave.

11:45 A.M.	Eaton autographing	677 St. Catherine W.
12:30 P.M.	CFQR-FM Radio	405 Ogilvy Ave.
	Ralph Lucas	
1:00 P.M.	Lunch	Airport Hilton
	Gordon Sinclair Jr.	
2:00 P.M.	CFCF Radio	Airport Hilton
	Best People	
	Gordon Sinclair Jr.	
3:00 P.M.	CBC International Service	359 Kensington Ave.
	North America	
	Gerard Rejskind	
8:30 P.M.	Saidye Bronfman Centre	
		5170 Cote St. Catherine Rd.
	Reading. Chairperson:	
	Rebecca Ougenfeld[17]	

Heaven help you if you happen to have a bad headache on a day like this. The American publicity tour took place in February, and Atwood spent three days in New York. Agent and friend Phoebe Larmore joined her on the interview and reading circuit.[18]

When I spoke to Jack McClelland of McClelland and Stewart, he pointed out that "promotion" was his real skill. "We offered a good imprint. Peggy never wanted to walk nude along the beach. She never liked promotional gimmicks. . . . Early on, she was very shy. Later, probably as a result of Graeme's influence, she promoted her work."[19] The Toronto launch for *Life before Man* — a formal cocktail party — was held at Jack McClelland's house on Dunvegan Road on 24 September.

★   ★   ★

It's typical of the cynicism of our age that, if you write a novel, everyone assumes it's about real people, thinly disguised; but if you write an autobiography everyone assumes you're lying your head off. Part of this is right, because every artist is, among other things, a con-artist.

We con-artists do tell the truth, in a way; but, as Emily

Dickinson said, we tell it slant. By indirection we find direction out.[20]

The reaction to *Life before Man* was curious. Internationally, the response was wildly enthusiastic; in Canada, it was mixed — roughly a third of the reviews were negative. On the American front, Phoebe-Lou Adams praised the novel lavishly in the *Atlantic Monthly*, and Marilyn French gave it a thumbs-up in the *New York Times Book Review* — she prononced it the best of the four novels Atwood had published to date. In Canada, reviewers posited two central objections to the book. The first, that it was (merely) a *women's* novel, was voiced by, among others, Barbara Amiel in *Maclean's*. The second objection was that *Life before Man* was essentially a roman à clef.[21]

Why was the novel received more negatively in Canada? One answer was supplied by Robert Fulford. In his *Saturday Night* column he posed this question: "Do Canadians fear excellence? Consider the case of Atwood." Fulford went on to suggest that it was a simple case of sibling rivalry on the national scale.[22] Atwood herself used a different metaphor: "We cut tall poppies."[23] In his memoirs, Fulford elaborates on the issue. He notes that one of Atwood's former friends considered suing her for libel after *Life before Man* appeared: "Again and again, Atwood has explained that it's an act of colossal ignorance and vulgarity to interpret her books as autobiographical; but in *Life before Man* she brilliantly reworked the pattern of her own and her friends' recent lives into her most compelling novel. (At least one of her ex-friends was muttering about a libel action months afterward.)"[24] The novel deals with the unravelling of two long-term relationships, one of which had been painfully tested by the suicide of a lover. Those who knew the inside story of the turbulent Anansi era, and particularly the events surrounding Shirley Gibson's affair with Marois and his subsequent suicide, would certainly have been tempted to draw parallels.

There is another, less-well-known link between a *Life before Man* character and a real-life figure. The gorgon-like Aunt Muriel is a watered-down version of an aunt who raised one of Atwood's

closest friends. Had Atwood faithfully depicted the real aunt —
"I didn't tell Peggy everything; so much more came to me in the
following years," Atwood's friend confided to me — nobody
would have found her particularly believable. Atwood sent a
copy of the novel to this friend with the relevant chapters marked.
The two had planned a visit during Atwood's promotional tour;
Atwood phoned in advance and said, "read the chapters before
I come tonight."[25] Aspects of the same cruel aunt may also be
glimpsed in the mother of *Lady Oracle*'s protagonist. Atwood
was careful only to use the material her friend had given her only
after the aunt's death.

In *Life before Man*, Atwood was working with several distinct
narrative voices — both male and female — for the very first time.
She had planned to create eight separate perspectives in her
Harvard-era novel, but that project had been abandoned. *Life
before Man*, then, was her most intrinsically constructed effort
to date. Written in the novelistic tradition of Jane Austen, it
surveyed the contemporary social scene and held up a rather
unflattering mirror to the values of the time. And some people
found the reflection too disturbing to contemplate.

18

Pressures and Crises

UPSET BY THE PERSISTENTLY biographical readings *Life before Man* was receiving and exhausted by its arduous promotion schedule, Atwood was at the end of her tether. A writer for *Chatelaine* reported:

> Margaret Atwood telephoned with the triumphant news that she was giving it all up: "No more interviews." Let someone else be fed to the media machine. Perhaps another female novelist could fend off such questions as "I understand you hate men and treat them like pieces of flesh," but Margaret Atwood was bowing out. She had talked it over with her mate, novelist Graeme Gibson, with her agent, and even over a sympathetic lunch with an out-of-town visitor, Swedish film director Mai Zetterling.[1]

But what, exactly, the "all" in "giving it all up" included remained unclear. She seemed just as busy as ever.

Atwood received her third honorary doctorate, this time from Concordia University, and the Radcliffe Graduate Medal. She was also elected vice president of the Writers' Union of Canada. As well, she continued to do small favours for others in the literary community. For example, for Jurgen Boden, who had hosted both Gibson and Atwood when they had visited Europe in May, she wrote a brief introduction to Catherine Young's first book of photographs, *To See Our World*. Atwood's name appears in bold letters on the front cover: the publisher was clearly using the Atwood cachet to sell the product. In February, Atwood participated in a tribute to Pierre Berton held at Toronto's Royal York Hotel. And she was still drawing *Kanadian Kultchur Komix*, her "Bart Gerrard" comic strip for *This Magazine*.

Her success was exhausting for the whole family. The indications were there — it was time to slow down and take a deep breath. This, however, was more easily said than done. The promotional tours and readings now had a momentum of their own that would be almost impossible to break.

Gibson was also struggling to find the time to produce his third novel. And the inspiration. As the years went by, that struggle was becoming more and more draining. "Robert's relationship to the machine," Gibson told journalist Roy MacGregor, referring to the protagonist of this troublesome third novel, "is rather like mine to the book." MacGregor had caught a glimpse of the manuscript when he visited the Alliston farm in 1979. He was writing a profile of Atwood, the second in three years. Looking for shelter from a rain shower, he entered a cabin at the end of Atwood and Gibson's property. There he caught sight of it.

> The room was spare, a chair, a desk with ancient typewriter, a table against one wall. On the wall was a small rectangle of yellowed, curling paper. It carried a quote from Franz Kafka: "If the book we are reading does not wake us, as with a fist hammering on the skull then why do we read it? . . . A book must be like an ice-axe to break the sea frozen inside us."
>
> The wind dying, I was about to leave when I noticed a thin mound of bone-white paper on the far table. It was a manuscript, the sheets squared perfectly; it seemed in waiting. The title was then *The Reckoning*, and though I was sorely tempted, I could not bring myself to invade Gibson's troubled privacy.[2]

Then, at about eight o'clock one November evening in 1979, while Atwood was in Windsor for a reading, she received a phone call from their Alliston friend and neighbour Peter Pearson.

Gibson, he told her, had collapsed with a perforated ulcer and had been rushed to the hospital. With no way to get home that night, she was trapped. "I will run a bath," she told Pearson, "call me back." Atwood will never forget waiting for that second call.[3]

The attack had been sudden, frightening, and painful — "I didn't know anything about pain until then," Gibson remarked later.[4] Somehow he had managed to finish reading a bedtime story to Jess. Then, before he could summon the live-in babysitter to take over, he keeled over. When the sitter finally found him, his face was grey, and he was lying on the floor. The farm was on a party line, and someone had left an extension off the hook. The sitter had to run to the next farm to get help. When Pearson arrived, he rushed Gibson to the hospital. Atwood got to the hospital the following day. "I knew he had been given something," she told me. "He looked at a very tacky copy of a painting and said: 'It's such a great painting. It has such depth!' "[5]

Gibson nearly died. The first threat to his life was the perforated ulcer, but then came surgery, peritonitis, pneumonia, and pleurisy. "Friends came and went," wrote MacGregor, "all of them stunned by this man they had always considered a rock in life lying strapped to machines, tubes running down his throat and into his arms. 'It was like staring at a draught horse that had been ploughed into the ground,' says David Young. On one of Young's final visits he pressed a note into Gibson's hand: 'Your body is sending you a message.' Gibson didn't need to be told."[6] MacGregor goes on to reveal that a month later Gibson was ready to burn the manuscript of his novel. Pearson asked whether he could keep it for Gibson for a month, and then, if Gibson still felt the same way, he would burn the stack of paper for him. Gibson didn't give the manuscript to Pearson; neither did he burn it himself. Instead, in 1980, he went alone to the Isle of Skye in Scotland and stayed there all summer. He began the book again, and this time he finished it. However, it would be another three years before it was published under the title *Perpetual Motion*.

★   ★   ★

In the spring, when the effects of Gibson's health scare had subsided, the family moved to Toronto and entered a period of calm. Jess was four and would soon be going to school. On 23 April, for $165,000, Atwood bought 73 Sullivan Street, a small house near the Art Gallery of Ontario and Chinatown. The eclectic urban neighbourhood they now found themselves inhabiting was dramatically different from Alliston, where the peaceful farm landscape had set the tenor of their days. They settled into a pleasing routine, balancing writing with public appearances and community work. Atwood's position at the Writers' Union was consuming quite a bit of her time. It seemed as if she had finally become more comfortable with being recognized; she had passed through a period of withdrawal into one of resignation, gracious acceptance.

Still, certain frustrations persisted for both Atwood and Gibson. It was hard for a writer like Gibson, for whom creation was a slow and painful process, to be married to someone whose literary output was as staggering as Atwood's. And it was becoming harder as time passed. On three occasions, Gibson told filmmaker Michael Rubbo, he had shown his work in progress to Atwood. He had done so because he was stuck and sensed in his heart of hearts that the quality just wasn't there. He needed to know for sure. Atwood was honest in her appraisal. "I should have said no," she admitted to Rubbo. "A close family member should only have to say 'you're wonderful. Have a cup of tea.'"[7] Gibson had another ulcer attack in May of 1980, and it, coupled with the fact that they were without a babysitter for the first few weeks of June, slowed both his and Atwood's work pace considerably.[8]

Atwood's frustrations had to do with film; although the rights had been sold to each one of her novels, the films themselves had met with either disaster or bad press. "The process is so elbows up," Peter Pearson explained to me, "and [Atwood] tends to be so gracious. *Lady Oracle* ripped her heart out."[9] Actress Margot Kidder had snapped up the rights to *Lady Oracle* and had quickly involved Atwood in the project. She had come to know Atwood through Pearson, a close mutual friend. Over the next few years,

Atwood would write and rewrite the screenplay, changing it drastically each time. Her early letters to Kidder were enthusiastic ("I'm so pleased you're going ahead with it"[10]), and Kidder's letters to her were even more so ("My work life is much brighter now that you're doing the script. . . . This is going to be fun"[11]). But then a chillier tone set in. Atwood's later letters are progressively more guarded, and in Kidder's handwritten replies the words sprawl across the page. Nevertheless, a type of friendship grew between these two creative individuals, and Kidder's warm and engaging personality emerges in her notes. Kidder was nearly always complimentary to Atwood, maintaining that her comments were "on the nose," but her compliments were generally accompanied by requests for script changes. "[P]lay up the 'love' part of Joan's relationship to Arthur," Kidder writes, and "stress the [Royal Porcupine] stuff a bit more than we've done."[12] Perhaps this particular note, dated "Mon. April ?" and expressing regret over what Kidder calls her "erratic emotional behaviour," prefigures some personal difficulties, wholly unrelated to the screenplay and the *Lady Oracle* project itself, that would trouble Kidder off and on through the 1990s. This letter of April 1980 also confirms that Atwood's friend and literary agent, Phoebe Larmore, had resigned as associate producer.

The first screenplay, written in 1980, emphasized the power, the passion, and the illicit nature of writing. In it, Aunt Lou writes a novel. The novel's title — *Dangerous Passion* — is apt, because its narrative is driven by the sense that writing is both dangerous and passionate. In this version of the screenplay, each stage of Joan's life is defined by a new discovery related to her emerging identity as a writer: Joan's mother kicks her out of the house when she finds her books; she has a sexual encounter with a librarian; she throws her books away when she marries Arthur but is forced to give him a copy of *Lady Oracle* when he suspects she has a lover; she admits to the Royal Porcupine that she writes "bodice rippers."

Atwood's second stab at writing a screenplay, dated July 1982, shifts the emphasis from writing to Joan herself and the various twists and turns her ineptness forces her to take. Whereas the first screenplay opens with Joan and Arthur locked in a passionate embrace, the second begins with Joan clad in her butterfly costume standing in her living room. It relies heavily on different images of Joan, including the fat lady. In this version, Joan manages to fake her suicide and then travel to England to spy on the Count and his new mistress. Arthur is jailed for Joan's murder; when she returns home, she has to spring him from jail. The final scene is set in a park. Joan flies a butterfly kite, which Arthur has earlier labelled an extravagant purchase. Letting the kite soar higher and higher, Joan declares she can love Arthur because now she feels "solid."

Stored with these two screenplays in the Atwood archive is a synopsis of yet another, Atwood's third attempt to tailor her novel for the screen. This time, she turned her attentions to retooling the happy ending — focusing specifically on Joan's attainment of a sense of self. Arthur is a more rounded and understanding fellow in this version. He is also a romantic in that he dons a bedspread cloak, goes down on one knee, and acts out Joan's fantasy for her. In return, she offers to give up her fantasy life. But it turns out that Arthur, all along, has been in love with this side of Joan: he adores her optimism, her desire for excitement and fun. Joan is a butterfly at last, and fantasy and reality turn out to be two necessary halves of one whole. In this version, Joan only contemplates staging her own suicide. Instead, she turns to writing as a means of escape. Arthur comes to find her, "a dark satin cape" flung around his shoulders. The whole thing ends with the two of them wandering through a museum admiring the fat ladies of the fifteenth-century Italian painters. They leave to share a meal of pasta and wine at a nearby restaurant. "It's going to be wine and pasta from now on!"[13]

Atwood wrote still more *Lady Oracle* screenplays, but Kidder was never entirely happy with any of them. Eventually, the project was shelved. It was one of the few times that Atwood was forced to admit absolute defeat. The hours and hours of work she had put into the project had amounted to nothing; her enthusiasm for the undertaking, which could have resulted in a wonderful film, had been squandered. As Pearson said, the experience "ripped her heart out."

In the realm of television, however, Atwood found consolation. *Snowbird*, a television drama that she had written with Pearson, was aired on CBC in 1981.

*   *   *

Breaking into film presented Atwood with one challenge. Her second challenge during this period lay in extending the boundaries of her fiction beyond the safe and the known. Atwood rose to meet it. Her next two novels pushed back those boundaries quite obviously by stepping outside the familiar milieu of contemporary Toronto: *Bodily Harm* is set in the Caribbean, and *The Handmaid's Tale* is set in the future. The second of these works posed the greatest risk for Atwood — how would her readers respond to this experiment with futuristic dystopia? — but the risk was well worth it. *The Handmaid's Tale* was a huge hit, and Atwood discovered that by extending her boundaries she had significantly extended her audience.

Bodily Harm drew its energy from two trips Atwood took in 1980. The first of these was to Portland, Oregon, where she gave a reading with American poet Carolyn Forché at the Portland Festival. The night before the reading, Mount Saint Helens, located not far from the state line in southwest Washington, had erupted for the second time, and grey ash was still falling from the sky. Some members of the audience wore surgical masks to protect themselves. When the engagement was over, Atwood and Forché found it hard to leave. Most other visitors to the area were trying to get out too; planes were grounded, presumably due to poor visibility, trains and buses were full, and Hertz, concerned about engine damage, was refusing to allow its cars on the road. The two women finally managed to arrange a lift to Eugene, Oregon, where cars were more readily available, and then drove south to San Francisco, where they boarded a plane. The drive took eleven hours. During that time, Forché talked of the situation in El Salvador; she spoke about the terror, the torture, and complained to Atwood about how difficult it was to get the word out. She also talked about political instability in the Caribbean and the horrors that would give rise to her collection of poetry *The Country between Us*.[14]

The second trip that inspired *Bodily Harm* took place in November. Atwood and Gibson spent six weeks on Saint Vincent, part of the Caribbean Windward Islands group. They were hosted by Atwood's old Leaside High School chum, Patricia (Pat) Parker, who had gone to live there with her husband, a senior government official.[15] Atwood and Gibson rented a house on the island. Atwood recalls that people would come, "under cover of night," to tell her their stories. In a letter to friend and publisher Arnulf Conraadi, she wrote that *Bodily Harm* had "a political background which is heavily based on fact."

> I have been collecting some of these scenes and images, but it didn't fall into place until I met somebody on a beach in the West Indies who told me the whole story of her life — none of which got into the book — but that story just made a few things fall into place. I suddenly saw how I was going to proceed with the novel, how all these disparate elements were going to start fitting together.[16]

Atwood worked on the novel steadily and finished it at the end of February 1981. She spent a month editing it and had a final version ready by the beginning of April. It was published soon afterwards by McClelland and Stewart in Canada, Simon and Schuster in the United States, and Jonathan Cape in Britain.

Bodily Harm has connections to some of Atwood's shorter works: to the story "A Travel Piece," most obviously, but also to some of the pieces in *True Stories* about politics and the West Indies. As Atwood puts it, they "fed" into the novel. "But," she adds, "I was going to the West Indies for years before I ever wrote a thing about it."[17]

★   ★   ★

While writing and promoting *Bodily Harm*, Atwood continued to nurture other aspects of her career. She attended numerous award ceremonies. In the spring of 1980, she received the Graduate Society Medal at Harvard from respected poetry critic and professor Helen Vendler. In her acceptance speech, Atwood confessed that she had written those very words over a "Frogurt and a cup of Sanka."[18] She probably had, and it indicated how little spare time she now enjoyed; any extra moments had to be used to maximum advantage. In 1981 Atwood also won the Molson Prize, was awarded a Guggenheim fellowship for the body of her work to date, became a Companion of the Order of Canada, and was nominated *Chatelaine* magazine's Woman of the Year. Atwood took her turn as chairperson of the Writers' Union from May 1981 to May 1982. She had been vice president the year before.

Notes towards a Poem That Can Never Be Written appeared in 1981. This new Atwood work, another small-press edition, was produced "in a limited edition of 200 copies, signed and numbered by the author. It was designed, composed, and printed by Glenn Goluska and hand-bound by Anne Goluska."[19] The chapbook bore the Salamander imprint, Atwood's own, and sold for sixty dollars a copy.

The poems in this sequence are "notes," because they allude to acts of torture that would be too horrifying to describe and to read about in more specific detail. They reference some of the atrocities Atwood may have read about as she leafed through the Amnesty International files, heard about during that long drive with Carolyn Forché, or listened to by cover of night in Saint Vincent. The sequence appears as a section of Atwood's 1981 poetry collection *True Stories*, published by Oxford University Press; "Notes towards a Poem That Can Never Be Written" is also the title of an individual poem in that section — one dedicated to Forché. "Don't ask for the true story," warns Atwood's speaker in the collection's opening lines.[20] To the reader's question "Why not?" the collection offers a variety of responses: because *the* truth can never be fully understood or articulated; or, as "Notes" proves, because some truths are just too painful. That Atwood turns to a literature of witness both in her novel *Bodily Harm* and in *True Stories* underlines her growing commitment to dealing with human rights issues in her writing and foreshadows her increasingly active involvement in human rights organizations during the decade.

In the early part of June, Atwood toured England and Sweden. She attended the Cambridge Poetry Festival and the Lahti Conference in Finland. At the beginning of this trip she lost all of her credit cards and learned that McClelland and Stewart had misplaced page 85 of her new novel, *The Handmaid's Tale*. The tone of the trip was set. By the time Gibson joined her, though, things had begun, at least temporarily, to go a bit more smoothly. Their Swedish sojourn was calm and enjoyable; they attended a luncheon hosted by the Canadian ambassador to Sweden and dined with members of the Swedish Writers' Union. Finland, however, was not such a pleasant experience. Throughout the Lahti Conference, the weather was cold and wet, and, to make matters worse, the talks were held in a field; participants retired to tents when the rain came down. Very few women speakers went to the conference, and the male participants were quite serious about their drinking. "It's a fairly relentless ordeal, especially in view of the fact that you don't get much sleep," wrote Atwood as a warning to others who might want to follow in her (by then) rather soggy footsteps.[21]

As 1982 unfolded, it became apparent that Atwood's productivity had not diminished. She coedited *The New Oxford Book of Canadian Verse in English* with William Toye. At the suggestion of Jim Polk, who was still with Anansi, she prepared and published *Second Words*, a collection of nonfiction articles, with that press. Polk oversaw the project. *Encounters with the Element Man*, a small-press edition of Atwood's poems published by Bill Ewert in Concord, New Hampshire, appeared. Ewert printed 150 copies to be sold at thirty dollars (American) each, and fifty deluxe copies to be sold at seventy-five dollars (American) each. Atwood received the Welsh Arts Council International Writer's Prize for her body of work and was given an honorary doctorate by Smith College in Northampton, Massachusetts.

But 1982 was really Gibson's year. In May he finally finished *Perpetual Motion*. It was published in the fall by McClelland and

Stewart. The novel's protagonist, Robert Fraser, is a nineteenth-century homesteader who inhabits a rocky piece of land near Toronto. Fraser is fascinated by the notion of a perpetual-motion machine. The novel was written to be read aloud; the prose is to be savoured. The rural setting, of course, owes much to the Alliston farm, but the novel is distinguished mainly by Gibson's effective use of myth.

★　★　★

Atwood's 1982 publication *Second Words* is a powerful amalgamation. It gathers together Atwood writings from a twenty-two-year period that cover a wide range of topics. It was Polk's encouragement that prompted her to produce this fascinating volume, a fact that attests to the strength of their working relationship — and to their mutual trust.

Atwood seems to have had some misgivings about the idea of collecting together so many discrete pieces; Polk, however, convinced her that, when read as a whole, the manuscript had a certain integrity: the individual pieces were linked by the themes (Atwood's themes, after all) of nationalism, writing, literature, and women. Polk also argued that the book had a kind of "plot" in that it showed Atwood's commitment to particular issues over a twenty-two-year period while also revealing the development of her perspective on those issues. And, to further assuage any misgivings Atwood might still have had, he promised her "secret rewards": "a cache of gold stars" when the galleys were ready, to be followed by the "incentive Mars bar."[22]

The tone of Polk's letter is warm and familiar, his razzing of Atwood amicable. When Atwood expresses some concerns about her 1982 essay "Writing the Male Character," Polk responds by telling her that it seems "fine" before teasing her about the spelling in the article (spelling is a point on which Atwood is consistently teased by family and friends). "[A]m sure it's your typist," he writes, who sticks an "e" on the end of Heathcliff and takes the "t" out of Kurtz.[23]

When the collection was published, Atwood sent a copy to Jerome Buckley, her Harvard supervisor. Of course, *Second*

Words more than fulfilled the requirements of a doctoral dissertation. Buckley's response was handwritten and congratulatory.

> It is a joy to read criticism as pungent as yours, and as free from pretentious jargon. Though I do not share all of your enthusiasms — e.g., for Adrienne Rich and Anne Sexton — I am constantly challenged by what you say. I find your essays a refreshing antidote to the new "new" American (or is it French at a long remove?) academic critics, who have almost decided that words are cruel deceivers and language has no meaning beyond the interior monologue. You keep up a spirited dialogue with a world that needs talking back to.[24]

One of the most fascinating reviews of *Second Words* was published in the *Globe and Mail* and was actually written by Atwood herself. Throughout it, she keeps her tongue planted firmly in her cheek. She demonstrates her self-confidence, her ability not to take herself too seriously; she also delivers a stinging rebuttal to some of the more offensive or silly critical takes on her work. As *Second Words* hit the stands she was no doubt recalling the reaction her first volume of criticism had elicited in the early 1970s. *Survival* had engulfed her in a wave of critical attention, a large portion of which was highly positive. She could not count on that happening again, but this time, if shots were to be fired, at least she could take the first. In writing her *Second Words* "review," Atwood seized her opportunity: she would lampoon that element of the media which was pursuing her relentlessly, bent on exposing the "real" Atwood. She signed her review "Margarets Atwood." Note the plural. "It has long been our opinion," she wrote,

> that "Margaret Atwood" ("Peggy" to her friends), purported author of some 20 odd books, does not really exist. It's true that there is an individual by that name who goes shopping, appears on the CBC and performs other mundane chores of this nature, but objective evidence supports the

conclusion that this person is merely a front for a committee.

To begin with, we have conflicting media sightings: can the motherly, cookie-baking, pussycat-loving comedienne described by Greta Warmodota in her May profile in The Griswold Examiner possibly be the same as the threatening succubus and man-devouring squid depicted by Alan Peevish and Frank Slug, among others? How to reconcile the author of Power Politics with the woman who was runner-up in the 1965 Consumer's Gas Miss Homemaker Contest? As the Celtic-Bilgarian ethnologist Gwaemot R. Dratora notes in his recent National Geographic piece, In Search of the Elusive Atwood, "Pinning down the real Atwood has a lot more in common with Pooh trying to catch the woozle: each time round the bushes, there's a whole new set of tracks." Wode M. Gratataro, noted Transylvanian architect, has commented less kindly, "Atwood is to literature what urban sprawl is to town planning," a sentiment echoed more elegantly by the Estonian-Italian postmodernist linguist and expert on metafiction, Trogwate d'Amorda: "Confronted by this gargantuan excrescence, one can only creep about, like Gulliver among the Brobdingnagians, recognizing a fingernail here, a nostril there, but at a loss to grasp the over-all form."

With the current book we find ourselves in the vicinity of what a nineteenth-century phrenologist would have called the Bump of Criticism. Second Words is a gathering of fugitive and occasional pieces pertaining more or less to literature and churned out by the Atwood committee over a period of 22 years.[25]

★　★　★

Within a two-year span, 1982 to 1983, two volumes of Atwood's short fiction were published: *Murder in the Dark* (from Coach House Press) and *Bluebeard's Egg* (from McClelland and Stewart). The paperback version of *Bluebeard's Egg* won the Periodical

Distributors of Canada Award and the Foundation for the Advancement of Canadian Letters Book of the Year Award. In 1983, Atwood received an honorary doctorate from the University of Toronto.

Unearthing Suite (from Grand Union Press) and *Snake Poems* (from Salamander) came into being in 1983 as well, joining the ranks of existing Atwood chapbooks. *Unearthing Suite* was one of three small-press books published that year by Glenn Goluska to aid the Writers' Development Trust. There were 150 copies for sale, signed and numbered by Atwood (175 copies in total). The other two books in the series were Jack Hodgins's *Beginnings* and Robert Kroetsch's *Letters to Salonika*. *Snake Poems* was published by Salamander, Atwood's own imprint. While living on the Alliston farm she had bought the equipment necessary to produce small-press books herself, but then her career took off and she didn't have time to make full use of it. She sold the equipment to Goluska, and he proceeded to operate Salamander as well as Grand Union Press.

During this period, Atwood was contemplating directions for her writing. The spring edition of the revue *Field* included a poem called "The Robber Bridegroom" — an early indication that Atwood was ruminating about a project that would develop into a novel in the course of the next ten years. (*The Robber Bride* was published in 1993.) The title story of *Bluebeard's Egg* encapsulates another version of this fairy tale, as does "Hesitations outside the Door" in *Power Politics*.[26]

★   ★   ★

In May of 1983, Atwood, Gibson, Jess, and Atwood's parents travelled to the Galapagos Islands on a birdwatching expedition, which had been organized by a friend named Marylee Stephenson. Atwood had met Stephenson in 1972 while speaking at the University of Windsor. A sociologist, Stephenson had been asked to attend the reading by a colleague in the English department. There was a silence when Atwood finished speaking: nobody wanted to ask the first question. "English teachers are awful with real writers," Stephenson remarked to me. Those attending that University of Windsor reading "all stood with their hands folded over their chests." So Stephenson filled the awkward void by telling the visiting speaker that she found the nature imagery in her poetry very accurate. "I spent a lot of my childhood in the bush," Atwood responded. And from that point on, the dialogue flowed more freely. Atwood and Stephenson next met at McMaster University in Hamilton, Ontario, where Stephenson had gone to teach. Stephenson had agreed to host Atwood during her visit. After discovering that Stephenson was an avid birdwatcher, Atwood invited her to Alliston to meet Graeme, a fellow birder. That was the beginning of a long friendship based on a mutual love of the outdoors. Stephenson remembers walking with Atwood and her mother in the bush north of Alliston. "They stopped," she said, "and sniffed, and said in unison: Fox!" Stephenson summed up her admiration for such a developed sensitivity to the natural world in a single word: "Remarkable!"[27]

Carl Atwood, of course, was similarly remarkable. And, as a zoologist, he was eager to visit the Galapagos, where he could retrace the development of Darwin's thought. "It's about time a reputable zoologist got down there and discovered the theory of evolution," he declared, and the trip was on.[28] There were twelve in the party; Jess, at age seven, was the youngest. They flew to Baltra, and from there a bus transported them to where their boat, the *Cachalote*, was moored. Visitors can't actually stay on the Galapagos Islands, as they constitute a protected area; those who want to explore them must retire to their ships at night. The condition of the ship, consequently, is an extremely important aspect of the trip. The *Cachalote*, a sailing vessel, had a crew of four: the captain (Hugo), a cook (also Hugo), a pilot (an American named Matt), and a guide named Pepe Salcedo whose mandate was to ensure that travellers in his care remained happy, safe, and environmentally aware. Everyone in the Atwood party fell in love with Pepe. Even Carl Atwood was moved to pronounce him a "good man" (a compliment he would never "bestow lightly") after hearing Pepe talk sensibly about grasshoppers. Pepe had a fine sense of humour too. One day he told them about a prank he'd pulled on a notch-on-the-bedpost kind of birdwatcher, the type who just wants to add another name to his list of conquests. " 'Quick,' [Pepe] said pointing to the sky. 'A flightless cormorant!' 'Where?' the guy said, swinging up his binoculars."[29]

It was an "El Niño" year, Marylee Stephenson told me, "warmer than usual; Jess could swim a lot." This was to be Stephenson's second trip to the Galapagos Islands, and it would be distinguished by some moments of high anxiety. One came when the group, travelling in a minivan, found itself just outside a town called Quevado in Ecuador. Quevado had been flooded by the runoff from rivers flowing down from the Andes Mountains. The roads in the area were built up, rising about twenty feet above the level of the surrounding land. These roads were also quite narrow. The minivan's driver crossed a bridge roughly half a city block long only to find the route blocked by a demonstration. A car had been overturned, and police were lobbing tear-gas canisters in an attempt to disperse the demonstrators, many of whom wore scarves over their faces. Stephenson's voice lowered as she concluded this story in clipped sentences:

> The bridge begins to clear. Three armed police are walking. In one hand, at their side, they have a tiny atomizer — mace. They didn't even draw guns. They righted the car, and just kept on walking, right past us.
>
> "Gee Peggy," I said, "I thought we might have another Bodily Harm here," thinking of the imprisonment of the novel's main character. The driver said that it was a good thing that the people weren't throwing rocks because then police would have shot. It was a teachers' demonstration.[30]

The group also endured an interval of tension on board the *Cachalote*. There was a violent storm. Endeavouring to comfort Jess, Stephenson says, "but really . . . ourselves too," everyone began to sing. "Peggy knows all the camp songs. I know fundamentalist church choruses. Jess wanted Graeme to sing." After the storm was over, a relieved Stephenson turned to Atwood and said: "we must have been singing for an hour and a half." Atwood replied, "No, five."[31] But for those among them suffering from seasickness, particularly Atwood's mother, the time must have dragged even more.

Cockroaches had infested the ship, a situation Atwood describes as normal. Her father would greet one by exclaiming "Ha!" The others were less "gleeful."[32] After returning to mainland Ecuador, the Atwood party spent four days in the cloud forest; there an abundance of insects delighted Carl Atwood.

★   ★   ★

A few months after they returned, in November, Carl Atwood had a stroke while driving on Highway 401 just north of Toronto. His car crossed four lanes of traffic and hit a guardrail. The stroke was a "transitory" one, there was no damage to the "thinking part of the brain," but Carl's left hand was affected.[33] In a story that appears in the American edition of *Bluebeard's Egg*, "In Search of the Rattlesnake Plantain," Atwood transforms this disturbing incident into compelling fiction — it was one rare instance in which she was willing to use strictly autobiographical detail as material for her art. The protagonist's father

> was driving his car, heading north. The stroke happened as he turned from a feeder lane onto an eight-lane highway. The stroke paralysed his left side, his left hand dragged the wheel over, and the car went across all four lanes of the westbound half of the highway and slid into the guard rail on the other side. My mother was in the car with him.
>
> "The death seat," she said. "It's a miracle we weren't mashed to a pulp."
>
> "That's right," I say.[34]

This story, which first appeared in *Harper's*, is also based on an orchid-hunting excursion in the woods near the Atwood family cottage. Marylee Stephenson, who is the character Joanne, described for me this particular trek, which she took with the

Atwoods. They were in search of a special orchid that Stephenson wanted to photograph. It was late. The light was bad. Stephenson knew that even if they were able to find the prized orchid the photo was unlikely to be a good one. But she went, nevertheless, out of consideration for Carl Atwood. Yet they did uncover the object of their search, and Stephenson captured it on film. "At the time, Peggy never said anything," Stephenson explains, "but when I read the story I realized that she had seen and understood everything." As a writer, "Peggy sees and registers in a way that you and I don't. It's just that it is not screened. Her threshold of screening is higher? Lower? It seems to register nearer consciousness."[35]

Atwood admitted to the close relationship between her father and the father in "Rattlesnake Plantain" to one interviewer, suggesting that the portraits of her parents in *Bluebeard's Egg and Other Stories* were a kind of "answer to people who mistakenly thought the heroine's parents in *Surfacing* were pictures of [her] own parents."[36] The collection is dedicated to Atwood's parents.

Like the daughter of the "Rattlesnake Plantain" protagonist, Atwood had been in England for a week when her father's stroke occurred. By this time, she and Gibson had established an escape routine — they were travelling abroad at fairly regular intervals. In November, Atwood told *Globe and Mail* columnist William French that she had gone to England "to get away" from Toronto. Wrote French, "it was increasingly difficult [for Atwood] to maintain privacy [at home], to get any writing done without being rude to people." She and Gibson chose to repair to Blakeney, Norfolk, explained French, because it is near a salt marsh "containing one of the great bird sanctuaries in Europe. They live in a fourteenth-century priory, just up the street from the fish market, and have rented another nearby cottage. Atwood works on her new novel there . . . and Gibson works on *his* new novel in the priory. 'It's better that way,' she says. 'We don't get in each other's way and we're not always interrupting each other for tea or something."[37] The priory was at 82 High Street, the town's narrow, cobbled main thoroughfare, which was, said Atwood, "lined with eighteenth century fishermen's houses . . . covered in round flints from the beach. Blakeney is surrounded by conservation land: miles of beaches on one side, farmland on the other." Atwood, Gibson, and Jess (who attended a local school) remained tucked away in this backwater from September until the end of March. For purely technical reasons alone, the temptation to call home frequently was not great. To place a call they had to go outside (remember this is winter in Norfolk) to a small cubicle built into the wall of the house — their potatoes-storage facility — and have a calling card handy. The building was originally, in the fourteenth century, the hospital of the local friary, but some sections of it dated from the Tudor period and the seventeenth century. The winter winds could blow the carpet off the bedroom floor. And the abode was haunted: the kitchen by a "headless woman," the dining room entryway by a "jolly cavalier," and the rest by nuns. The current owner didn't put much stock in the story of the headless woman; she had, after all, only been seen by North Americans.[38]

It may have been cold, and their home away from home may have been phantom-infested, but Gibson's ulcer was considerably better,[39] and by January 1984 Atwood had completed a large chunk of her novel.

> January 1, 1984. Blakeney, England. As of today, I have about 130 pp. of the novel done and it's just beginning to take shape & reach the point at which I feel that it exists and can be finished and may be worth it. I work in the bedroom of the big house, and here, in the sitting room, with the wood fire in the fireplace and the coke fire in the dilapidated Raeburn in the kitchen. As usual I'm too cold, which is better than being too hot — today is grey, warm for the time of year, damp. If I got up earlier maybe I would work more, but I might just spend more time procrastinating — as now.[40]

★   ★   ★

Xandra Bingley, whose house Atwood and Gibson lived in when they first arrived in Norfolk, offers this reminiscence: "Peggy went upstairs every morning to an icy bedroom and wrote on a typewriter missing the letter L. She stopped when Jess came home from school and they had toast and a drink and then Peggy and Jess would run round the two acre garden flying through the cold autumn early evening as if they were off to the moon. . . ."[41] But although Atwood was writing steadily (if not copiously), the novel wasn't working very well. She started to get distracted by the historical romances she had found on the bookshelves.[42]

The novel she was working on was called "Destroying Angels." Its central character was named Emma, the same character who figures in "Two Stories about Emma," a *Bluebeard's Egg* tale. The child of a Canadian father who blows himself up while trying to explode a beaver dam and a British mother, the novel's Emma must endure her parents' separation. The rupture occurs when her father's mistress confronts Emma's mother. Emma grows up perceiving her mother as cold and shrill — a "cardboard cutout of an Englishwoman" — until she goes to visit her later in life, in England. Suddenly, the mother is a cardboard cutout no longer; instead, Emma, who finds herself terribly out of place, becomes the two-dimensional figure.[43] Emma narrowly escapes death by drowning while rafting at Niagara Falls. We follow her through a couple of romantic relationships. As she etches her protagonist, it becomes evident that Atwood has never forgotten what she learned, during those childhood hours of voracious comic book consumption, about the power of transformation. Emma's choice is like Wonder Woman's: she may have superhuman powers or the love of a man. Convinced that she can only be granted one, she nevertheless wants both. She finally creates a third choice for herself: she walks away from responsibility.[44]

But "Destroying Angels" was not meant to be. Explained Atwood: "The novel that I started I'm going to let mulch for a while, until I can see another way of coming at it. I was trying to do too many things in it at once and it needs to be simplified."[45]

At about the same time, Atwood reviewed John Updike's novel *The Witches of Eastwick*. "These are bad Witches," she noted, implying that she had been reflecting upon the subject; "and Power-within, as far as they are concerned, is no good at all unless you can zap somebody with it."[46] This line of thought — on varieties and degrees of power and evil — would be a critical aspect of Atwood's next two novels.

At the end of March 1984, the family moved to West Berlin for three months. Atwood was the first Canadian to participate in a German Arts Council program for foreign artists. In Germany she finally began work on *The Handmaid's Tale*. In May of 1984, she, Gibson, and Jess journeyed on to Copenhagen, where they satisfied what remained of their travel urge before returning to Toronto. At home, Atwood settled down to a bout of very hard work: she finished *The Handmaid's Tale* and began a two-year term as president of International PEN, Canadian Centre (English Speaking).

19

Reflections on Society

I believe that fiction writing is the guardian of the moral and ethical sense of the community. Especially now that organized religion is scattered and in disarray, and politicians have, Lord knows, lost their credibility, fiction is one of the few forms left through which we may examine our society not in its particular but in its typical aspects; through which we can see ourselves and the ways in which we behave towards each other, through which we can see others and judge them and ourselves.

— Margaret Atwood[1]

ALTHOUGH ATWOOD DID NOT BEGIN writing *The Handmaid's Tale* until 1984, the initial idea struck just after she had finished *Bodily Harm* in 1981. One evening, she had dinner in Toronto with Eve Zaremba, "ex-*Broadside* editor and longtime family and personal friend." They chatted about "various things as we usually do, including some of the more absolutist pronouncements of right-wing religious fundamentalism. 'No one thinks about what it would be like to actually act it out,' said I (or someone). I was standing by the corner of the dining-room table, and the book came into my head. 'I think I'll write about that,' I said. Eve said, 'Do it!' "[2]

Atwood did "do it," but not until three years later, when she was in West Berlin. "More or less desperate" after having spent seven months labouring in vain over "Destroying Angels," she plunged into *The Handmaid's Tale* as soon as she got to Germany in the spring of 1984. Each day, she sat typing away on a heavy, rented, German carbon-ribbon typewriter.[3] "I discussed bits of *The Handmaid's Tale* with Graeme," she later admitted: "He thought I was going bonkers, I think. That's the problem with discussing works-in-progress. They always sound somewhat crazier than they may turn out to be. He kept saying, 'You're going to get in trouble for this one.' But he egged me on, despite that."[4]

Atwood recalls the fundamentals of her inspiration and how they began to coalesce. With this novel, she wanted to answer as concretely as possible two questions posed during that dinner:

> [I]f women's place is in the home, why aren't they in it, and how do you get them back in? And: if you were going to take over the United States, what slogans would you use? . . . I began with the hanging scene (which later migrated to the back of the book), and with the scene in which my character eats an egg. I did not yet have a name for her, or for the book. I remember writing a whole series of men's names down on a sheet of paper, and putting "Of" in front of each one. I chose "Offred" for about three different reasons, one of them being that it looked so strange and was not immediately recognizable for what it was — a simple first name with a simple patronymic added.
>
> From then on the book evolved in the usual way that books do — spurts of writing, discarded chunks, misgivings, interruptions, restructurings. The structure the book has now — named "daytime" sections alternating with sections all named "Night" — came when I saw that that was what I was doing anyway. The social details of the book came from observation, logical conclusions, and the reading of history over a period of many years. The voice is that of an ordinary, more-or-less cowardly woman (rather than a heroine), because I suppose I'm more interested in social history than in the biographies of the outstanding. (The only history book I've written is a work of social history, and it was from there that I probably got the white bags for

the hanging scene; woodcuts of rebels hanged in the 1837 Rebellion show the heads in white bags.)[5]

Apprehensive about how the product of such a radical shift would be received, Atwood phoned her British agent, Vivienne Schuster, and asked her if she could read what she had written so far. "It was a courageous book, a departure for her, and I felt she needed reassurance. She had it — in spades!"[6]

By the time Atwood and Gibson returned to Toronto in the late summer of 1984, most of the novel had been written. The final push came while Atwood was acting as honorary chair of the Master of Fine Arts Program in Tuscaloosa, Alabama; *The Handmaid's Tale* was published in 1985 by McClelland and Stewart (Houghton Mifflin also published it in the United States and Jonathan Cape in Great Britain). The novel expanded Atwood's reputation. With it, she gained what Phoebe Larmore calls a "more standard and mainstream audience."[7]

Atwood argues strenuously that *The Handmaid's Tale* is not science fiction: "Science fiction is filled with Martians and space travel to other planets, and things like that. That isn't this book at all. THE HANDMAID'S TALE is speculative fiction in the genre of *Brave New World* and *Nineteen Eighty-Four*. *Nineteen Eighty-Four* was written not as science fiction but as an extrapolation of life in 1948. So, too, THE HANDMAID'S TALE is a slight twist on the society we have now."[8] In fact, the novel grew out of a scrapbook that Atwood started to compile in 1983 during that chilly Norfolk winter. Items on "the religious right wing, on no-cash credit-card systems, on the low birth rate and prisons in Iran."[9]

One *Handmaid's Tale* reader proved that the novel was indeed based on probability rather than improbability by sending Atwood a newspaper clipping about a religious sect in the United States that referred to its "womenfolk" as "handmaids."[10] Certainly many of the novel's details have been extracted from contemporary daily life. For instance, when Atwood's Swedish translator asked "What cosmetics or medical remedies are [the Aunts] named after?" Atwood replied: "Aunt Elizabeth — Elizabeth Arden, Aunt Helena — Helena Rubenstein. Aunt Betty — Betty

Crocker, Aunt Sarah — Sarah Lee. The last two probably are not known in Sweden but substitute any name having to do with baked goods or cookery products that you can get away with. Aunt Lydia is a joke, it was a women's remedy called Lydia Pinkham."[11] It is also apparent that *The Handmaid's Tale* is set in an extrapolated Boston: "The Wall is the wall around Harvard yard," explains Atwood. "All those little shops and stores mentioned are probably there at this very minute." But despite the novel's New England setting, aspects of its plot were derived from Atwood's experiences in Iran and Afghanistan, "where women are treated in the same light as they are in [Gilead's] society — some ways better, some ways worse."[12] By drawing this parallel, of course, Atwood echoes observations Gibson made in his *Chatelaine* article about their time in these countries.

The Handmaid's Tale was an instant success. Nan Talese, Atwood's fiction editor at Houghton Mifflin, quickly extended her congratulations on the glowing reviews it was receiving: "Congratulations on being No. 1!" she wrote. "I always knew you were."[13] A week before the book's official publication date, Houghton Mifflin ordered a second printing. While the promotional schedule for this novel was as daunting as those for Atwood's earlier novels had been, something had happened to her reading fees: she would now be paid about $2,500 a reading — $1,000 more than she had got for reading from *Life before Man*.[14] (There were, of course, exceptions: for certain friends or groups Atwood would trim her fee substantially.)

The promotional tour for *The Handmaid's Tale* got under way in October. Atwood refers to such cross-country marathons as "kill-an-author-tours." Shedding some light on the mystery of how Atwood still managed to write articles and speeches while promoting her new work, her assistant Sarah Cooper confides, "Sometimes she comes back with poems, scribbled on napkins."[15] "She can write anywhere," confirms Peter Pearson.[16] The *Handmaid's Tale* itinerary speaks volumes. Between 27 September and 18 November, Atwood flew to Halifax, Winnipeg, Calgary, Edmonton, Vancouver, Ottawa, Montreal, London (Ontario), and Victoria. In Vancouver, the day went like this:

8:00 A.M.	Robert Mackwood will meet you in the lobby of the Denman Hotel (Joanne Blain of the *Vancouver Sun* will be travelling with us to the Webster show and will interview you following the Webster interview)
8:30 A.M.	Arrive at BCTV
9:00 A.M.	*LIVE* studio interview with Jack Webster BCTV (Scheduled for approx. 30 minutes)
10:30 A.M.	*TAPED* studio interview with Julie Brown Radio KISS-FM Vancouver (Scheduled for 10–15 minutes)
11:00 A.M.	*TAPED* studio interview with Viki Gabereau CBC Gabereau (Scheduled for 45 minutes with music selections)
12:00 P.M.	Lunch/interview with Max Wyman arts critic/columnist with the Vancouver Province (Binky's Restaurant on Robson Street)
12:50 P.M.	Robert Mackwood will take you to Duthies Books
1:00–1:30 P.M.	Autographing Duthies Books Owner: Celia Duthie/Manager: Kevin Williams (Mark Stanton will be on hand to return you to Denman Hotel)
2:00–4:15 P.M.	*BREAK*
4:15 P.M.	Robert Mackwood will meet you in the lobby and take you to:
4:50 P.M.	*LIVE* studio interview with Patrick Munro Radio CBC *The Afternoon Show* (Scheduled for 10 minutes)
5:00 P.M.	*TAPED* interview with Maureen McMorrow Radio CFMI Vancouver (Scheduled for 15 minutes: To be conducted in her apartment)
5:45 P.M.	Arrive at CKVU-TV
6:20 P.M.	*LIVE* studio interview with Laurier La Pierre CKVU-TV *Vancouver Live* (Scheduled for 8 minutes) Returned to Denman Hotel[17]

Although the task of promoting her work now seemed to Atwood, veteran of the "kill-an-author" circuit, unrelentingly onerous, alternatives were scarce:

> Every time I publish a book, I wonder how I can get out of promoting it. But the fact, sad or not, is that there is no central organ in Canada the equivalent of The New York Times, and full-page ads just don't seem to work. Book readers in Canada seem to want their authors live, right there on the local TV show and in the local bookstore. Out of every book a little blood must flow, and you ignore the trans-Canada-Wreck-an-Author tour at your peril, or at least at the peril of your sales. Informed sources estimate that tours inflate sales by 30 to 80 percent. Never mind the germ-laden TV makeup that makes you look like Medea, the planes that don't take off, the hotel reservations that aren't there when you breeze in at midnight, having done eleven interviews that day on nothing but a peach yoghurt eaten with a plastic spoon in the Regional Representative's car. It's all undergone in the name of Canadian publishing, and no-one has yet found another way.[18]

But there are a few small incidents that have occurred on the road that Atwood still savours. At one book signing, a man showed up dressed as a character in one of the novels; "that made my day," she says.[19] Another highlight was provided by the Nanaimo, British Columbia, hotel manager who left in Atwood's room the most enormous fruit basket she had ever seen.

The awards and accolades rolled in. For her body of work, Atwood won the Toronto Arts Award. For the novel specifically, she received a Governor General's Literary Award (her second) and the *Los Angeles Times* Fiction Award. She also shared the Philips Information Systems Literary Prize with Barry Callaghan, an annual award set up in 1984 to honour Canadian writers in midcareer. Previous winners had been Dennis Lee and John Robert Colombo. *The Handmaid's Tale* appeared on the annual list of twenty-six books that Queen Elizabeth took with her to read while holidaying at Balmoral Castle. It was no wonder that Fawcett Books of New York paid $605,000 for the American paperback rights to the novel.[20]

★   ★   ★

Throughout the months of September and October, Atwood received a string of telegrams from various publishing-industry figures:

THE HANDMAID'S TALE HAS BEEN SHORTLISTED FOR THE BOOKER PRIZE. WE ARE SO THRILLED AND SEND YOU WARMEST CONGRATULATIONS. THE PRIZE CEREMONY IS 22ND OCTOBER, WILL YOU COME? LOVE AND BEST WISHES, VIVIENNE [Schuster]

MANY MANY CONGRATULATIONS ON BEING SHORT LISTED FOR THE BOOKER, VERY WONDERFUL AND THOR- OUGHLY DESERVED. WE'LL AWAIT WITH BATED BREATH TILL OCTOBER. I BET YOU WIN. YOU SHOULD. LOVE FROM URSULA AND ALL AT VIRAGO.

SENDING YOU BOUQUETS OF BEST WISHES AS YOU ARE HERALDED IN ENGLAND AS THE LITERARY QUEEN YOU ARE. AM WITH YOU AS A BEAMING SPIRIT. LOVE, PHOEBE [Larmore].

PEGGY YOUR LISTING FOR THE BOOKER IS THE TALK OF FRANKFURT. CONGRATULATIONS. WILL TELEPHONE YOU NEXT WEEK FROM NEW YORK. LOVE NAN A. TALESE

BEVERLY WILSHIRE HOTEL
ATTN: GUEST MARGARET ATWOOD
CONGRATULATIONS ON THE TIMES BOOK REVIEW BEST SELLER NUMBER SIX. WHAT A GREAT WAY TO START — WHAT A BOOK — WHAT AN AUTHOR. LOVE NAN AND YOUR FANS AT HOUGHTON MIFFLIN COMPANY[21]

In September *The Handmaid's Tale* was short-listed for the prestigious Booker Prize. On 22 October, Atwood and Gibson flew overseas to attend the awards dinner, which was held in the Old Library of London's Guildhall. The competition for the Booker that year was very stiff. Atwood found herself up against another Canadian, Robertson Davies, who had been nominated for *What's Bred in the Bone*. The presence of two Canadians on the Booker shortlist was unprecedented in the award's seventeen-year history. The remaining nominees were Kingsley Amis, for *The Old Devils*; Kazuo Ishiguro, for *An Artist of the Floating World*; Timothy Mo, for *An Insular Possession*; and Paul Bailey, for *Gabriel's Lament*. Amis won. It was later reported that the contest had been very, very closely fought between Davies and Amis.[22] Ultimately, Davies was considered Amis's unofficial runner-up.[23]

From February to May of 1986, Atwood held the Berg Chair at New York University, teaching creative writing two days a week. Gibson and Jess stayed in Toronto so that Jess (by now age ten) could have an uninterrupted school year. Atwood also travelled occasionally during this time; she was still promoting *The Handmaid's Tale*. When she visited Los Angeles on 19 and 20 February, she stayed at the luxurious Beverly Wilshire Hotel. This information was published in the *Celebrity Service International Bulletin*. The signs were unmistakable — Margaret Atwood had become an international celebrity.

The media machine swung into action, supporting Atwood's new novel (as her publicists had planned) and Atwood herself (as her publicists must have hoped). Atwood received the red-carpet treatment during her travels (a warm letter of welcome came from the vice-president of the Beverly Wilshire) as well as plenty of encouragement (that same vice-president declared herself a "fan" of Atwood's writing and a supporter of the comments Atwood had made in favour of greater female delegate representation at a much-publicized PEN conference held in New York).[24]

On 14 March, Atwood stepped into a radio booth in New York City to record a commercial for *The Handmaid's Tale*.

ATWOOD: THIS IS MARGARET ATWOOD REPORTING FROM
THE REPUBLIC OF GILEAD, THE NEW THEOCRACY
THAT WAS FORMERLY THE UNITED STATES. I DON'T
KNOW IF THIS WILL EVER REACH THE AIRWAVES,
OR IF THIS WILL EVER END. . . .

ANNCR: *THE HANDMAID'S TALE*, MARGARET ATWOOD'S
BRILLIANTLY ACCLAIMED BESTSELLING NOVEL
ABOUT A FUTURE TOO TERRIFYING TO IGNORE. . . .

ATWOOD: READ IT WHILE IT'S STILL ALLOWED.[25]

Arriving at the studio, Atwood glanced at the ad copy she was to read, took out a pen, and quickly made a few changes. The result was a shorter ad (fifty rather than sixty seconds), and the spot was now crisper, more effective. Atwood promoted her novel in twelve American cities, using ads like this one, reading, giving interviews.

When an individual becomes interested in purchasing the right to convert a novel or story into a film, his or her name is added to a submission list. *The Handmaid's Tale* submissions list was long and star-studded. Twenty-seven names were inscribed on it, including Sissy Spacek, Julie Christie, Meg Tilly, Karen Allen, Donald Sutherland, Jane Fonda, and Stanley Kubrick.[27] In a letter to Daniel Wilson (who would eventually option the novel), Atwood suggested that Canadian Jackie Burroughs play Serena Joy in the film version of her novel: "[Burroughs] has a ravaged look that looks also as if she had once been beautiful and she is a fantastic actress." For the Commander — again thinking Canadian — she suggested Christopher Plummer, Donald Sutherland, or Gordon Pinsent. Helen Shaver, yet another Canadian, was Atwood's choice for the part of Moira.[28] Clearly, Atwood's desire to see her work on the big screen had been rekindled, despite past frustrations and disappointments. And this time the momentum seemed powerful enough to get such an enormous undertaking off the ground.

The Handmaid's Tale's star continued to rise. In 1987, the book was short-listed for France's illustrious Ritz Hemingway Prize, it won the Arthur C. Clarke Award for Best Science Fiction, and it was the regional winner of the Commonwealth Literary Prize. To receive the latter honour, Atwood was flown to London at the end of November. It wasn't until 2 July 1987, four years after its publication, that *The Handmaid's Tale* finally slipped off the *New York Times* best-seller list, where it had resided for twenty-three weeks.

20

Taking Action

AS *THE HANDMAID'S TALE* came into being and took on a life of its own, Atwood's world was changing and developing on other fronts. During the summer of 1984, she spent just enough time in Toronto to move into a new house — her current residence. Located in a residential neighbourhood near the University of Toronto, the house is large and fronted by a circular drive. The Sullivan Street place had been cramped and narrow — like most of the houses that share its downtown enclave — but in the new house everyone would have plenty of room to breathe: there would be space to entertain and roomy offices for Gibson, Atwood, and Atwood's full-time assistant. Decorated with the help of Charlie Pachter, the house is a comfortable, inviting haven.

It was at about this time that Atwood became even more actively involved in politics. A longtime supporter of Amnesty International, Atwood helped to found the Canadian English-speaking division of PEN (an international pressure group committed to freeing writers who are political prisoners). She remembers, as president, hosting meetings in her house. The organization's budget was nonexistent, and there was no executive assistant to help with the details. Members "raised their own startup money, licked their own stamps."[1]

During her term, Atwood worked to increase the profile of PEN within Canada as well as the profile of PEN Canada internationally. Consequently, she attended a number of PEN congresses. In 1986, the forty-eighth International PEN Conference was held in New York City. The organization's American president, Norman Mailer, was "at the helm." Atwood (who by then was no longer president of the Canadian division) made a strong statement about the lack of women present at the meetings. In an address to conference participants she said, "On the subject of quality: 'We need someone to do it who'll be equal to the men,' I was told. Which men? I wondered. And how many at once? I don't mind having to be equal to four or five men, but one hundred and fifty is a pretty tall order, and I wouldn't have minded having a little help."[2] Curiously, rather than apologizing for the gender imbalance, Mailer responded to her challenge by stating that most of the women he could have invited were mediocre, thereby sparking a debate that diverted media attention away from the central issue of the conference: writers in prison.[3]

In June of 1986, Atwood attended a PEN conference in Hamburg (before spending July in England). The following year, to raise funds for PEN, she compiled and edited *The Canlit Foodbook*, a compendium of recipes and food lore, poems, and prose pieces solicited from a range of literary luminaries. The project took a big bite out of Atwood's available time and energy.

Still, her efforts did not go unrecognized. In a letter to me, Timothy Findley, who took over from Atwood when her term as president ended in 1986, phrased this eloquent compliment:

> Few people remember that writers are always at work; if they're not actually writing, they're thinking about what they've just written — or about what they're going to write. And the more people who read what they've written, the more demands are made on their time, talent and energy. No writer in this country receives more demands than Margaret Atwood. When it came time to raise some money for International P.E.N. (the writers' equivalent of Amnesty International), it was Peggy who took on the unpaid job of collecting and editing all the contributions to one of the fund-raising projects, *The Canlit [Food]book*. And when there had to be a cocktail party for those whose money and

support we needed to stage a P.E.N. Congress in Toronto,
it was Peggy and Graeme who offered their home — and
their leadership — for the event. So, there we all were —
writers and representatives of governments, of funding
bodies and of corporations — with most of the guests eager
to meet and talk to Margaret Atwood. When everyone had
finally been canapéed, wined and chatted to, and only a few
P.E.N. members remained — I glanced across the room.
There were Peggy and Graeme — and just for a moment,
she closed her eyes, sagged and leaned against him. Yes, I
thought, you're tired. And no wonder. People ask you to do
this all the time, and none of your guests was given even
the slightest hint of the cost. That's class.[4]

Atwood's impulse to solve the problem, to take action, had
actually earned her deep and widespread respect — even from
those who hadn't "the slightest hint of the cost." Particularly
telling was the fact that she was unable to attend the Governor
General's Literary Awards ceremony, which took place that year
at Montreal's Place des Arts, because she had already promised
to be present at a different awards ceremony: on 3 June, at Queen's
Park, Toronto, Atwood was given the Ida Nadel Humanitarian
Award. In this instance, recognition of her political contribution
had eclipsed that of her literary endeavours. She was also nominated *Ms.* magazine's Woman of the Year. In 1987, she was
named Humanist of the Year and Fellow of the Royal Society of
Canada.

All the while, the academic honours rolled in. Atwood received
three honorary degrees in 1984: from Mount Holyoke College,
the University of Guelph, and the University of Waterloo. In
1987, she was awarded an honorary doctorate by her old alma
mater, Victoria College.

⋆   ⋆   ⋆

In 1986, Marian Engel died after a long illness. Atwood and
Gibson had lost an old friend, a colleague who had fought it out

in the trenches with them in the early days of the Writers' Union. Atwood wrote a tribute to Engel called "Stealing Time," which incorporates the anecdotes of others who had known her with Atwood's own recollections. Engel winking at Atwood during a crisis in a hospital. Engel advising Atwood, who was enduring a "fragmented period," to "steal time. Don't let other people take advantage of you."[5] In her friend's memory, Atwood established the Marian Engel Award, which consists of an annual ten-thousand-dollar prize for outstanding prose writing by a Canadian woman in midcareer.

Not surprisingly, 1986 was a slow publishing year for Atwood. Only one publication appeared: *The Oxford Book of Canadian Short Stories in English*, which she coedited with Robert Weaver, and which was published by Oxford.

⋆   ⋆   ⋆

During the latter part of 1987, Atwood became writer-in-residence at Macquarie University in Sydney, Australia. While there she spoke to an interviewer about her need to be away from Toronto because "the input is really somewhat ferocious these days."[6] Her uncharacteristically relaxed demeanour during this interview seems to support this assertion; she must have heaved a sigh of relief the moment she exited the Canadian spotlight. The pressure exerted upon her by the Canadian media — an extension of the assault begun in the early 1970s following the publication of *Survival* — was now constant. But Atwood, over the course of the decade, had gained perspective on this perpetual ordeal, and it was evident both in her public persona and her private self. Atwood and Gibson have a running joke with their friend writer Brian Brett that is part of the strategy to defuse the pressure, to get in a few digs at the success-obsessed media. It began with two project ideas that would leave most publishers cold: Gibson was thinking of writing a big book for birdwatchers, and Brett wanted to write a gardening book with no pictures. "I'm interested in the romance," Brett told me, in the "love" of gardening. The three like to talk about combining their efforts to create the ultimate unsaleable book. Atwood teases the two men, Brett especially, for writing for a very exclusive audience.[7]

If establishing a dugout was Atwood's coping strategy for the 1970s, then travelling (as a form of escape) was her strategy for the 1980s. Leaving the country for months at a time gave her enough room to breathe and to write. By 1987, she had attained the status of media icon. In his article "Kanada: The Miniseries," Guy Babineau lampooned this situation, casting actress Sigourney Weaver in the role of Margaret Atwood.

> "I am Margaret Atwood," says Sigourney Weaver. "Novelist, feminist and freedom fighter, and I'm here for the liberation of the Kanadian people. I may not have won the Booker Prize, but at least I'll win back my country."
>
> "Country?" says Joan Collins. "You call *this* a country? . . ."
>
> "Farley, get in here!" yells Sigourney Weaver. . . . "Farley, take the first hostage."
>
> "Which one?"
>
> At this point the camera comes in real close on Sigourney Weaver's face and she stares straight out at you with this real pained expression.
>
> "I don't know," she says. "They're Americans. It's so hard to tell them apart."[8]

★ ★ ★

During July of 1987, Atwood went canoe tripping in Temagami, an area north of Toronto, north even of Algonquin Park, where there are acid-rain lakes — crystal clear and breathtaking. As a child, Atwood would not have known why these bodies of water are so eerily beautiful; in this more environmentally aware era, the sinister answer is common knowledge. For canoe trippers, Temagami is a mythical place — more isolated than Algonquin, with portages that are narrower and more rugged. In July, the portages are dry and firm, and the blackflies have disappeared: conditions are generally favourable for a memorable trip. In recent years, though, this kind of wilderness area has come under increasing threat. What was once accomplished according to the honour system must now be strictly regulated: no garbage may be left; no cans may be brought in; no fires may be lit during dry periods.

Upon returning home, Atwood wrote about her Temagami holiday in an article called "Profiting by Our Wilderness," published in the *Toronto Star*'s Saturday magazine. In 1988, she wrote an entry for the McClelland and Stewart book *Save the Earth*. When Toronto's Rouge River Valley became the proposed site for a garbage dump, she addressed the city's Public Works Department.[9] She incorporated this issue into an allegory of the "Pristine family" who lives in "Peterson" (the name of Ontario's premier at the time) for an address she delivered to a group of lawyers at Toronto's Osgoode Hall.[10] A quick trip she took with Gibson and her stepson Matt to British Columbia was transformed into a travel piece with an environmentalist edge and a touch of nostalgia. Atwood, in other words, was entering another charged public arena, one she'd been at the fringes of for most of her life: environmental activism.

This activism had one unexpected consequence. Atwood was approached to challenge Art Eggleton and run for mayor of Toronto in 1988. She declined. Also that year, she received the YWCA Woman of Distinction Award and the National Magazine Award for Environmental Journalism. Atwood seems reticent when asked about such awards — the ones bestowed for humanitarian and environmental endeavours — but it's clear that she is pursuing these concerns because she is genuinely committed to them and because she is determined to give something back to her community. It's a question of a Girl Guide's honour, so to speak. Although these awards tended to come during the mid- and late 1980s, it is significant that her energy to support both political causes and environmental issues has never flagged. In 1990, for example, she wrote the introduction to McClelland and Stewart's *The Canadian Green Consumer Guide*. Recycling bins occupy a corner of her home office. Her letters are mailed in reused envelopes. The crushing of tin cans is standard practice at the Atwood cottage.

Environmental awareness became an explicit theme in Atwood's fiction during the late 1980s. She started to write the stories for her third collection of short fiction — *Wilderness Tips* — during a summer retreat to the cabin.[11] One of the collection's most striking stories is "The Age of Lead," which juxtaposes the tragedy of the third Franklin expedition (the crew was poisoned by the lead used to solder the tin cans in which their food was packed; this food-preservation technique was new and untested) with current technological hazards. Atwood explains her motivation for writing this story in an interview with her father's friend, the respected naturalist M.T. Kelly:

> [W]hat interested me about the story was the new evidence that's come up. That it was, in fact, man who did this to himself. It was the lead in the canned food that did him in. . . . We're at a peculiar time in history. Many other civilizations have hunted species to extinction, have brought about environmental catastrophe for themselves. The difference is that they didn't know what they were doing. We're now at a point in which we know what we're doing, we know what the results will be and the question is, Do we have the political will to stop ourselves in time?[12]

The three Franklin expeditions have captured the Canadian literary imagination. They figure in novels by Mordecai Richler and Rudy Wiebe, among others. Atwood herself documents the widespread treatment of the Franklin expeditions in one of her Clarendon lectures, the text of which is included in *Strange Things* (1995).

21

Reflections on the Artist

THE QUESTION "What's next?" never seems to remain answered for long. Part of being a writer is constantly devising new projects. In 1985, Atwood admitted that she had "lined up" about "three books." She told an interviewer: "I'm finishing one [*The Handmaid's Tale*], and I know what the next one is going to be [*Cat's Eye*]. Then I have another one I tried to write in 1968 and didn't complete. I'm going to do that one again." When asked "What is the difference in coming at it now after the gap? After it's been on the back burner all these years?" Atwood replied candidly: "It's been on the back burner, but my technical approach to it was wrong. I tried to tell the story from the point of view of too many characters at once. It became too unwieldy and large; it lost narrative momentum. In writing a novel you have to give the reader enough reason for turning the next page — apart from your delightful prose."[1]

"My problem," she explained on another occasion, "is that I get so fascinated by description and details I forget about anything happening; I have several unfinished novels with that problem. They have wonderful descriptions of things, but nothing actually occurs for a long time." Referring to the "back burner" novel, she added, "Once I tried to write a novel from the point of view of eight different characters. That was dandy and I had nice descriptions. But after 250 pages, no events had occurred. If I had followed out my scheme, the novel would have been about 1,500 pages long. It wouldn't have worked."[2] Atwood had begun to draft that troublesome piece of fiction while at Harvard, naming it, alternately, "Death of the Animals" or "The Nature Hut." She mapped the whole thing out on filing cards and planned to have each of the eight characters — four men and four women — articulate his or her own perspective. She never used filing cards again.

In May of 1986, Atwood published an article in the *New York Times Book Review* about "girlfriends" books. The subject would continue to grow in importance and popularity over the next decade, and it would become a crucial element of Atwood's next two novels, *Cat's Eye* and *The Robber Bride*. One reason that the dynamics of friendship in the universe of young girls had penetrated her imagination at this juncture was Jess. The central figures in *Cat's Eye* were girls of about ten — so were Jess and her friends, and, watching and listening carefully, Atwood was able to absorb their unique patterns of speech and behaviour. Perhaps this, combined with the international success of *The Handmaid's Tale* and her growing confidence in herself and her writing abilities, signalled to Atwood that it was time to write a novel of childhood. She had already sketched out the details in 1964 and 1965, the year she spent at the University of British Columbia. She returned to this material in the mid-1980s when she experimented with keeping a journal.[3] Among the Atwood Papers at the University of Toronto is a box containing an assortment of short pieces that form the basis of some of the novel's chapters. It is difficult to discern the exact relationship between these isolated and clearly autobiographical sketches and *Cat's Eye* itself. I do know that without the literary framework of the novel, the resonance of the novel's symbolism, the carefully controlled perspective of Elaine's eye, these fragments seem thin, certainly less "literary" than the finished product. They are in need of a context, or what Atwood calls "a literary home." Atwood has explained that with *Cat's Eye* she "wanted a literary home for all those vanished *things* from my own childhood — the marbles, the Eaton's catalogues, the Watchbird Watching You, the smells, sounds, colours. The textures. Part of fiction writing I think is a celebration of the physical world we know — and when you're writing about the past, it's a physical world that's vanished. So the impulse is partly elegiac. And partly it's an attempt to stop or bring back time."[4]

Five short fictions caught my eye as I perused the contents of this box in the archive: "Ox Eyes," a description of watching the Santa Claus Parade from a zoology-building window with a jar of ox eyes behind her on a shelf; "Balloons," a rather bleak depiction of postwar Toronto in winter; "Draft," a piece about quaffing draft beer in the King Cole Room below the Park Plaza Hotel; "Hazardous Experience," a brief account of her job at the Sportsman's Show renting out arrows at the archery game and of a trip to the Canadian National Exhibition with Charlie Pachter; and "Ravines." This last piece of writing clearly establishes the setting (and some of its implications) for the formative experiences of both Joan in *Lady Oracle* and Elaine in *Cat's Eye*. It is both a description of the ravine near Atwood's childhood home (the upper part of which is near the Mount Pleasant Cemetery) and a thought sequence on ravines in general. The piece describes a descent: literally a scramble past a decaying footbridge and then a walk down to the brickworks (a facility evoked in *The Edible Woman*), figuratively a slide into sleep, away from the "electrified life" of the world above the ravine. In the ravine there are strange men who hold bunches of daffodils or dandelions to conceal the flies of their pants (precursors of the Daffodil Man in *Lady Oracle*?). Also in this piece, Atwood portrays a brother who, when he wins "extravagantly" at marbles, puts his winnings of cat's eyes and water babies in a jar and buries them deep in the ravine.[5] Links to *Cat's Eye* are obvious: the ravine setting, the cat's-eye marble, the brother who inters a jar of marbles, the fear. Obvious, too, is the fact that Atwood, even in the space of a short fiction, could draw her readers into the ravine, could transport us from sleep to nightmare. But the full symbolic resonance of the ravine was not developed until Atwood wrote the novel itself; that the ravine existed outside the novel, in the Toronto of Atwood's childhood, is interesting but curiously beside the point.

"The Ravine" is also the title of an early story, one of four that critic Judith McCombs argues Atwood wrote while at UBC and identifies as precursors of the novel. Another of these stories,

"Cut-Out," details the relationship between "bossy Louise" (an early version of Grace Smeath), the "prudish" Susan, and a third, unnamed girl. This story was to become a scene in chapter 17 of the novel. Chapter 10 of *Cat's Eye*, McCombs maintains, is an extension of another unfinished story, "Scribblers," in which the girls attempt to draw pictures of the glamorous movie-style ladies they see in magazines. "Suffer the Little Children," writes McCombs, "is the intense and very recognizable early version of *Cat's Eye*'s chapters 18 and 23: of the self-righteous Grace Smeath, her bigoted mother and aunt, and the Smeaths' Sunday ritual of church, train-watching, dinner, and the father's indecent joke."[6]

The longest of the four stories, "The Ravine" features an omniscient narrator who follows the young Joan Blanchard, the "new girl" in the neighbourhood — a neighbourhood recognizable as the one Atwood grew up in and as the one depicted in *Cat's Eye*. Joan's three girlfriends are Cynthia, "clearly," says McCombs, "the early version of the novel's Cordelia: tall, adventurous, well-off, arrogant, disturbing"; Susan, the "early Cinderella-Rapunzel-Sleeping Beauty Susan [who] will become the novel's treacherous Carol Campbell, with the fairy-tale allusions muted, but with the same false, exaggerated femininity"; and Grace Grumwell, Grace Smeath of the novel.[7] McCombs describes the point at which this story ends:

Part "II. *Susan*" is only an eight-line beginning that mind-reads Susan's dream of being wrapped in piecrust, like the four-and-twenty blackbirds of the *Mother Goose* rhyme, to be "cooked and eaten" while she "lay there in the dish, inert, not wanting to move. . . ."

Does this broken-off parable of the edible girl mark the point at which "The Ravine" was abandoned because the November 1964 manuscript called "The Edible Woman," which is a first version of Atwood's first novel, intruded?

Perhaps; one cannot know for sure. But there is a parable, in holograph, saved for more than twenty years with the *Cat's Eye* notes, that is an adult version of Susan's dream of herself wrapped in piecrust, cooked and eaten. In this

. . . grotesque and surreal version of the feminine mystique, a "wife & mother [is] bound with string, an apple in her smiling mouth, on a huge roasting platter," and devoured by her husband and small children, who open "and drink the contents of her skull. Afterwards she gets up & dresses & goes to a bridge-club meeting." At the bottom of this page is an underlined title: "The Edible Woman."

Do the dream of the edible girl, and the parable of the edible woman, mark the point at which the earliest versions of these two novels began to assume their separate shapes? Perhaps; one cannot know for sure. (All puns on "know" and "no" intended.)[8]

We may glimpse another connection between *Cat's Eye* and Atwood's life by looking at a short piece published in *Murder in the Dark* called "Horror Comics." Its narrator is a twelve-year-old girl who is walking home from school with her friend "C." Their conversation, for a few blocks anyway, is decidedly Gothic. This young narrator — like *Cat's Eye*'s Elaine as she gains power over Cordelia — claims to be a vampire.

"I'm really a vampire, you know," I'd say in a conversational tone as we walked along, licking our lime popsicles. Those we paid for.

"No you aren't," C. said, her voice uncertain.

"You know I am," I said quietly. "You don't have to be afraid of me though. You're my friend." I dropped my voice an octave. "I'm really dead, you know."

"Stop it," said C.

"Stop what?" I said innocently. "I'm only telling you the truth."

This occupied the four blocks between the funeral parlour and the gas station. After that we would switch to boys.[9]

Another *Murder in the Dark* piece, "Fainting," also provides a sketch for *Cat's Eye* — it outlines the way a young girl can "slip sideways" out of time by fainting.[10]

*　*　*

Despite the fact that she had accumulated this cache of short prose sketches and stories beginning in the 1960s, Atwood didn't attempt to fashion a novel out of them until late 1987. In March 1988, she received a letter from writer Leon Rooke asking her to compose a brief commentary on postmodernism for a collection he was assembling. Atwood's reply was witty and revealing in its informality: "Truth is that I'm trying to finish a novel — almost there — going nuts. What use is critical theory when you're trying to figure out how to end ch. 44? Also — what use is a critical theory that tells you you don't exist? (Who wrote this?)"[11]

Cat's Eye was published by McClelland and Stewart in Canada in the fall of 1988 and the following year by Bloomsbury in Britain and Doubleday in America. As Peter Davison explains, Canadian publishers "think that people only buy (big expensive) books for Christmas."[12] Again, that year, *Cat's Eye* was found under many Christmas trees. Douglas Gibson, head of McClelland and Stewart, received thirty thousand orders for *Cat's Eye* before it was published.

The year after it was published, *Cat's Eye* won the Torgi Talking Book Award (from the Canadian National Institute for the Blind), the City of Toronto Book Award, the Coles Book of the Year Award, the Canadian Booksellers' Association Author of the Year Award, and the Foundation for the Advancement of Canadian Letters in conjunction with the Periodical Marketers of Canada Book of the Year Award. And, once again, Atwood was short-listed for the Booker Prize.

Almost immediately after it appeared, *Cat's Eye* was heralded as a triumph. *Maclean's* noted the personal content of the novel, the importance it attributed to family life. The magazine's reviewer also speculated about the impact the deaths of three central members of the Canadian literary tribe — Margaret Laurence, Gwendolyn MacEwen, and Marian Engel — had had upon *Cat's Eye*.[13] Certainly the tone of the novel is elegiac; it is permeated with a sense of loss — of innocence, of childhood, of youth. But I believe the novel's characters owe more to Atwood's childhood friends than to her fellow writers. Atwood, in mid-career, had written an elegy that makes direct reference to the settings and details of her childhood. She had created "a literary home" for them.

The completed novel is enriched by the inspiration of still more real-life figures. Mrs. Finestein, for example, embodies Atwood's tribute to one of her old neighbours: think of the warmth of Mrs. Finestein in the novel, of the welcome Elaine feels while in her home, of the exotic beauty of the oranges. As is the family in the novel, this family was Jewish; the mother could often be seen in her hoop earrings and mules. When Margaret was eleven, she had looked after this neighbour's young son. In fact, the other children in the neighbourhood, Margaret's classmates, also baby-sat for the family. But Margaret stopped babysitting for them rather abruptly, leaving the family to wonder why. Perhaps, they thought, it had to do with having too much schoolwork. But later, while reading *Cat's Eye*, they gained an additional insight: Had young Margaret come face to face with anti-Semitism and felt powerless to protect her young charge from the hostility she was beginning to sense around her?

Stephen, the protagonist's brother in the novel, also gains some dimension from a living person: Atwood's nephew, Harold's son, David Malcolm Atwood. When *Cat's Eye* was being written, David would have just completed his master's thesis, "Scalar Quark Production in Electron-Positron Collisions" (1986), and begun his doctoral research. He graduated from McGill University with a Ph.D. in physics, having written a dissertation called "Finding the Missing Pieces of the Standard Model" (1989).[14] Of course, there is something of Atwood's own brother in Stephen as well. The early rituals of dialogue and play Elaine and Stephen engage in were based on similar rituals shared by Margaret and Harold. Luckily, however, the parallel ends there. Harold is alive and well.

Why, then, the name Stephen? As a tribute to the world-renowned astrophysicist Stephen Hawking, who published a best-selling nontechnical explanation of his work, *A Brief History of Time*, in 1988. The novel's Stephen muses about the fluid nature of time — musings that are interpreted experientially by Elaine (when she finds that fainting is like "stepping sideways"), transformed visually through Elaine's paintings, and enacted by Atwood on a technical level (through flashbacks and fore-shadowing, for example). All are a timely response to Stephen Hawking's provocative theories.

And Cordelia. Isn't there a Cordelia in every girl's past? Or — even more disturbing — can we not recognize some aspect of Cordelia in our own childhood selves? *Cat's Eye*'s Cordelia appears as "C." in several of Atwood's short fictions — she is a childhood playmate, a partner, and a foil for the young protago-nists. She and her fictional companions are based on Atwood's own childhood friends. So when Atwood wrote the introduction to *Women Writers at Work* soon after completing *Cat's Eye*, it seems natural that she emphasized the acutely personal nature of writing. While "the dancer realizes someone else's dance," the writer inevitably draws from her own experience.[15] She wrestles with her personal angels each time she commits pen to paper.

Among Atwood's other large 1989 projects were coediting, with Shannon Ravenel, *The Best American Short Stories* (Houghton Mifflin); publishing a children's book called *For the Birds* (Doug-las and McIntyre); and publishing a new edition of *Selected Poems* (Oxford University Press). She also spent a term as writer-in-residence at Trinity University in San Antonio, Texas.

22

Reflections on Film

AT LONG LAST, Atwood was poised on the brink of motion-picture success. American producer Daniel Wilson had prevailed, scored *The Handmaid's Tale* option, and was proposing that Harold Pinter write the screenplay and Karel Reisz direct. While the renowned Pinter did go on to write, Reisz (of *French Lieutenant's Woman* fame) did not make the final cut: Volker Schlondörff would eventually be chosen to direct the film. A fan wrote to Atwood criticizing the choice of director. The note is undated, handwritten, and addressed to Atwood in care of her publisher:

> Dear Margaret;
>   I heard that the producer, director, and scriptwriter for the movie version of "A Handmaid's Tale" are all men.
>   When I read your book, I thought I was reading a woman's story. Of course, her life was completely manipulated by men in the book, so perhaps you planned it that the movie would be manipulated by men too. A cosmic joke, perhaps?
>   But — I think I really would rather see her perspective on the screen, not his.[1]

Atwood responded by explaining that she had received no offers from women producers, directors, or screenwriters during the six months before the deal was signed. She adds a few details about her experiences working with a woman producer on the film version of *Surfacing* and with Margot Kidder on *Lady Oracle*.

She notes that *Bodily Harm* and *Life before Man* — which had both been optioned in the rush for Atwood material — would have, retrospectively, a woman producer and a woman screenwriter chosen not because of their gender but because of their talent. Atwood goes on to defend her choice of director for *The Handmaid's Tale*, explaining how vital it is to her that the director be faithful to the book. Schlondörff, she writes, had been very faithful to Günter Grass's *The Tin Drum* when he had directed the film version of that novel in 1979. Bottom line: Atwood denies any necessary link between a director's gender and his/her faithfulness to the book — an author's primary consideration. "When you have gone a mile in my moccasins," she concludes, "you'll see what I mean."[2]

Although Atwood's reply is controlled, it betrays her weary frustration with the whole business. The movie version of *Surfacing*, directed by Quebec filmmaker Claude Jutra, had appeared in 1980. Jutra had stepped into the project after another director walked off. By then it was too late to change either the script or the casting — in other words, there was no longer leeway to improve the film in measurable ways. And Jutra, who would eventually succumb to Alzheimer's disease, was already in the early stages of his decline. The finished product reflects all these problems.

Three other Atwood novels had fallen into the hands of movie people, for better or worse. *The Edible Woman* had been passed through a number of hands, including those of John Kemeny and Oscar Lewenstein, Sir Tony Richardson, and British television director Alan Cooke. Atwood had written two screenplays of the novel: one with George Kaczender in 1970, another with Tony Richardson in 1971. But the film was never made. *Lady Oracle* had, of course, been optioned to Kidder, who, while in love with the book, was never satisfied with the scripts she received — including Atwood's. The project was finally derailed by this and by Kidder's desire to write, produce, direct, and star in the film herself. The plan for *Life before Man* came from Toronto-based Primedia Pictures. Scripted by Linda Griffiths (with a little bit of help from Atom Egoyan), the film was to be produced by Pat

Ferns, Annette Cohen, and Helen Shaver (who would also be taking a lead acting role). The director was to be Egoyan. Carla Singer optioned *Bodily Harm* and asked Vancouver writer Anne Cameron to write the script.[3]

That the film version of *The Handmaid's Tale* had gotten off to a rather rocky start, then, came as no surprise to Atwood. Wilson had originally met with her in New York in 1986, when she was promoting the novel. But it was only in 1988, when Wilson's production company, Cinecom, had received an "influx of money" and Wilson had found a new director, that the film became a practical reality. Originally, the "handmaid" herself was to be played by Sigourney Weaver, but, ironically, she was unavailable because she was shooting a film for Karel Reisz. Jodie Foster and Debra Winger were both offered the role, and both turned it down. Finally, Natasha Richardson (daughter of Vanessa Redgrave and Tony Richardson) signed on. Because they had lost Weaver, a major box-office draw, Wilson decided to strengthen the cast: as a result, Faye Dunaway (as Serena Joy), Robert Duvall (as the Commander), and Elizabeth McGovern (as Moira) came on board.

Atwood had elected to sell the rights to her novel to Wilson precisely because Wilson wanted Pinter to write the screenplay. Explained Atwood: "Pinter's very good at writing scenes which play against the dialogue: in which what people are saying is not what's happening in the scene. That was very much required for this film. And there are so many silences in his plays, and I thought that would be necessary for this as well. There are a lot of pauses in the book."[4]

With Schlondörff, a native of West Germany, in place, the film was shot between February and May at Duke University in Durham, North Carolina. The budget was thirteen million dollars. Atwood was on the set for one day only. In fact, her involvement with the film was minimal — she attended some preliminary meetings; she commented on the script, mainly suggesting small vocabulary changes ("hand lotion vs. hand cream etc.").[5] Atwood further insists that she did not influence the promotion of the film. Fortunately, Wilson was also adamant that the film not be labelled science fiction, supporting Atwood's own strongly held view.[6]

The Handmaid's Tale premièred at the Berlin Film Festival and immediately afterwards began runs in both East and West Berlin. The Berlin Wall had just come down (coincidentally, the film contains a shot — a hazy one, as there was a storm that day in North Carolina — of a replica of the wall). Also making their debuts that year at the high-profile festival were the American films *Steel Magnolias*, *The War of the Roses*, and *Music Box*. Two hundred East German directors attended the event; only thirty had come the year before. Also attending were Atwood, Gibson, and Jess. They came to the city where Atwood had begun writing *The Handmaid's Tale* for two premières on two consecutive nights. Atwood gave interviews, and they all went to receptions, news conferences, and photo sessions. The first première, held at the Zoo Palast, was preceded by a dinner with various film people and followed by a midnight reception at the smoky Paris Bar. Günter Grass showed up at the reception. Brian Johnson of *Maclean's* was in the audience at the West Berlin première. He remembers "light applause" after the film, which "warmed" as Atwood, Pinter, and Wilson walked on stage. When Schlöndorff joined them, however, his fellow West Germans emitted a chorus of boos. Because he had spent so much time working in the United States, his nationalistic peers had turned on him.[7]

The East Berlin première was at the Kosmos Cinema, "a strange hybrid of tacky art deco and swooping Soviet modernism." It started at eleven at night. The official itinerary for festival people proclaimed it absolutely necessary to come bearing a passport and accreditation: although the wall was down, there was still a border to cross.[8] At this screening, the audience sat "spellbound" throughout the movie and when it was over warmly applauded everyone involved — including Schlöndorff. "Here," the director said, "they think I'm a foreigner."[9]

*　　*　　*

The film of *The Handmaid's Tale* intensified the spotlight on Atwood's novels. And her poetry was celebrated when, in 1991,

Virago Press of Great Britain published a volume of selected poems entitled *Margaret Atwood Poems, 1965–1975*. Back at home, as well, Atwood seemed even more firmly imprinted than ever on the public consciousness — Atwood herself, that is. Not simply her work. Writer and critic Scott Symons, who had attacked Atwood in print in 1977, was among those who resented her rise to international fame. He pointed out that in July 1989 Atwood had appeared (and not for the first time) on the cover of *Saturday Night*. In August, she had graced the cover of *Toronto Life*; it was a special issue devoted to literature, the proceeds of which were earmarked for PEN; Atwood had agreed to autograph copies of the magazine. All of this, Symons maintained, proved that Margaret Atwood had gone from "celebrity, through icon-hood, to apotheosis."[10] The trend, in Symons's view, was not entirely positive.

That July issue of *Saturday Night* also contained a story called "Uncles" in which Robert Fulford appeared, in his own words, "under the thinnest possible disguise, as a disreputable and disloyal journalist." This portrayal, Fulford suspected, was a response to his depiction of Atwood in his memoirs, *Best Seat in the House*. Lending more weight to Fulford's suspicion was an anecdote someone had told him of Atwood walking into a shop called the Book Cellar in Toronto's Yorkville district and asking that her book not be displayed next to his. " 'Uncles' depicts a woman [named Susanna] a lot like Ms. Atwood," writes Fulford, a woman "who is profoundly wounded by the memoirs of a man a lot like me. She is so hurt, in fact, that the experience calls into question her image of herself and sends her mentally scurrying back to childhood in a panicky attempt to understand her feelings." The young Susanna grows up to become a reporter and is mentored by Percy Marrow, "a columnist and reviewer whose opinions and appearance are so like mine that five editors at Saturday Night recognized me instantly. Percy's secret nick-name is Vedge, for Vegetable Marrow, because he's shaped like one. He also looks like Humpty Dumpty, the Buddha, a walrus, and Mr. Weatherbee in the Archie comics — the author provides a rich panoply of images." When Vedge writes his memoirs, long after Susanna has gone on to become very famous and successful, he is critical of Susanna, and she feels betrayed.[11] As for a link between Atwood and the character of Susanna, Atwood denies that one exists.[12]

During the summer of 1991, Atwood gave four lectures at Clarendon College, Oxford, on topics of her choice relating to Canadian culture. (They were published by Clarendon Press in 1995 as *Strange Things: The Malevolent North in Canadian Literature*.) She had been told to expect a small audience the first day and progressively smaller audiences thereafter. But the pattern soon established itself as the opposite. Although Jay Macpherson, who attended those lectures, remembered a few empty rows at the very front of the hall in the sections cordoned off for VIPs, the place was filled to overflowing on the subsequent days. ("The main factor," a modest Atwood notes, "was that I spent 2 hours with the sound man ahead of time so people would actually *hear*."[13]) One reason for the success of the series was that the lectures were extremely well organized, accessible, and punctuated by moments of humour. Another was that Atwood, feeling the need for a little fun, had decided to draw the audience's attention to her earrings. For the first lecture, on the doomed Franklin expedition, her lobes were adorned with miniature skinning knives carved from Baffin Island bone. For the Wendigo lecture, a discussion of the legendary flesh-eating monster, Atwood sported earrings shaped like frogs devouring flies; explained Atwood, "for the eating motif, and also because when the Wendigo cannot find human flesh, its other choice is frogs." (Another reason, presumably, is that it is relatively hard to find Wendigo-motif jewellery.) She complemented the earrings with a Wendigo-theme outfit in black, like its teeth; red, like its eyes; and white, "like its icy heart."[14] Atwood adds that this earring escapade was intended to capture the attention of her English audience by "violating one of their central taboos (Never Refer to What You Have On.)[15] The Clarendon Lectures have already lead to two things: directly to *Strange Things*, and indirectly to an honorary Doctorate of Letters, awarded to Atwood in June of 1998. Some of the material from these lectures has already appeared in Atwood's fiction — I am thinking of the references to Franklin's failed third expedition in the short story "Age of Lead" — but I suspect that we will see more transformations of the material of the Clarendon Lectures in the future.

⋆   ⋆   ⋆

The *Cat's Eye* film project foundered in 1992, even after the well-respected Canada-based Atlantis Films had put massive resources behind it. Atlantis had hired Daniel Petrie to direct the movie (Seaton Maclean would have produced it). When this deal fell through over Thanksgiving weekend, Peter Pearson happened to be visiting Atwood. He suggested that they take on the task of bringing the novel to the screen together, as Pearson was familiar not only with the film media but also with the novel and its background. The neighbourhood of Atwood's childhood was also Pearson's, after all, and he was all too familiar with the landscape and, particularly, with the teachers from Whitney Public School, who were so "lovingly conjured" in the novel. Atwood agreed.

She did so in part, of course, because she and Pearson were good friends. But she must have also had the success of their past collaborative ventures in mind: specifically, the television productions *Snowbird* (1981; directed by Pearson, scripted by Atwood) and *Heaven on Earth*. The latter very fine series aired on CBC Television on 28 February 1987, receiving rave reviews. It was the first extended commentary on what are known as the "Barnardo children": approximately 120,000 children from orphanages and poor families in the British Isles who were sent to Canada between 1867 and 1914. The story is breathtaking in its enormity; one in ten Canadians, Pearson told me, is said to be a descendant of the indentured Barnardo children. These children did not find the better life for which they, their families, and their communities had hoped. Instead, they embarked on extremely hard lives, toiling unpaid, performing manual labour for adoptive families who never entirely accepted them. *Heaven on Earth* was comprised of six episodes scrutinizing individual home children;

the first episode introduced audiences to the situation and to the characters who would star in the subsequent episodes. The idea for the project came from Peter Pearson, who gathered an enormous amount of information — and some wonderful photographs — from the families of home children. Pearson and Atwood worked on the first draft of the script in 1979, and Pearson sold the project to Pat Ferns in the early 1980s; hence, the final version of the script, written by Atwood, was edited by (director) Allan Kroeker and Nancy Botkin.[16] All the episodes were filmed outside Toronto in 1986.

In terms of the *Cat's Eye* project, Petrie had wanted to treat the material in a realistic style and had intended to focus on the present time of the novel. As he conceived it, the film would not attempt to re-create the past visually. Atwood and Pearson's concept revolved around a background (Elaine, the eight-year-old child in 1947 or 1948) and a foreground (Elaine, the fifty-year-old woman in 1992). The conundrum they faced was how to make it possible for the eight year old to solve the problems of the fifty year old on film. Should the eight year old be shot standing in front of a painting? Should the audience watch the twenty-one year old Elaine as she paints? Or, said Pearson, his tone of voice indicating a breakthrough idea, "if the present voice runs all through the past in the novel, why can't the child's voice colour the present?"[17] By 1 September 1993, Atwood and Pearson had taken the script through five drafts, each time coaxing another layer of the novel's reflections — on childhood, on the artist, on the artistic process — closer to the screen.

23

Death: Some Reflections

Every once in a while, Graeme and I look at each other and say the life we're leading is nuts. We should be going to a croft somewhere in upper Scotland and be sedentary for a while. . . . But we do like to travel.

— Margaret Atwood[1]

ATWOOD AND GIBSON settled into a steady routine of travelling for pleasure (usually birdwatching) and travelling for work. In order to create an uninterrupted space in time to write, they were spending four months out of the country each year; during these sojourns they did nothing but write. At the same time, their pleasure travel was gradually evolving into a business. Through the mid-1980s Gibson owned and operated The Great Auk, a company that ran birdwatching tours to the wilderness of Cuba. The enterprise allowed him to defray some of the enormous costs involved when he and Atwood flew to out-of-the-way locations.

The winter of 1991 to 1992 Atwood and Gibson spent in France. There Atwood wrapped up *Good Bones* and began writing *The Robber Bride*.[2] Shortly after arriving in France, Atwood read at the Canadian Embassy in Paris with Anne Hébert. William Toye, there visiting expatriot Canadian writer Mavis Gallant, was in the audience. He remembers Atwood reading her poems first in French and then in English and wondering whether it should have been the other way around since most people in the room would have understood English and caught her nuances of tone and meaning.[3] But Atwood had decided to work on her French. Throughout the winter her facility with the language improved, and there was no question of relinquishing that momentum. By 1996, she was able to tape an extended sequence of radio interviews — in French — with Quebec writer Victor-Lévy Beaulieu. Although Atwood's French is carefully enunciated, deliberate, and heavily accented in those interviews, it is strong enough to communicate wit, humour, and some keen insights into Canadian politics.

In 1992, *Good Bones* was published by Coach House Press in Canada and Bloomsbury in Great Britain (in 1994 Doubleday published it in the United States). Resolving the final details involved in bringing the manuscript to press was tricky: Atwood was in France; her backup team (assistants Joan Sheppard and Donya Peroff, as well as those at Coach House Press) was in Canada; and there was a postal strike. At one point, the contents of a Chronopost package — including an original cover design — went missing between France and Toronto.[4] Faxes flew fast and furious across the Atlantic as Atwood tied up loose ends.

Between such anxious moments as these, Atwood enjoyed the balmy Provençal winter, savouring truffles procured at a local fair.[5] Atwood and Gibson rented three houses in France at different points during that winter; at this juncture they were inhabiting one that had once belonged to the village wolf catcher. Two stuffed wolves were stationed on either side of Atwood's desk.[6] But it was at a different desk, belonging to her friend Doris Heffrom, that she began work on *The Robber Bride*. At one point, during a hurricane, Atwood used an array of candles to light her way when the electricity went off. Other sections of the novel were written in a compartment (equipped with a table and a computer outlet) of a trans-Canada train while the Rocky Mountains rolled past and at a desk belonging to Phoebe Larmore in California. "Once I've got going, I just try to write at it every day."[7] Such statements, say Atwood's friends, roommates, and assistants, may be taken quite literally. "She can be sitting in the kitchen," remarks Pearson, "turning the grocery list into a poem."[8]

On 1 June 1993, Sarah Cooper came to work for Atwood as her assistant and, as Atwood notes, "improved life greatly!"⁹ Before Cooper came on board, Atwood had employed two part-time workers: one had done the bookkeeping and typing; the other took care of the day-to-day office work. Cooper had worked at Coach House Press and while there had organized the tour for Atwood's *Good Bones*, so the two had already worked together when Cooper submitted her application for the position Atwood was offering. As Cooper explains it, her job is to organize the office in such a way as to free Atwood up for writing. Generally, if Atwood is at home, she spends the morning writing (from 9:30 A.M. until about 1:00 or 1:30 P.M.). In the afternoon, she has meetings with various people or discussions with Sarah and answers her mail. Although Cooper keeps regular hours — she works about forty hours a week — Atwood herself often works into the evening. Dinner is usually between 7:00 and 8:00 P.M. "She has a strong desire to write," says Cooper, and "is very, very motivated."¹⁰

When Atwood is travelling to promote a book, she does not designate specific chunks of time for writing; instead, she works spontaneously whenever a small interval crops up. Cooper reports that when Atwood returned from the *Robber Bride* promotional tour she "plunked down a draft of *Morning in the Burned House*" on her assistant's desk. "She writes on place-mats," Cooper adds. As well as "home" time and "away" time, there is what Cooper calls "limbo time," when Atwood is neither writing a major work nor touring. These periods can be extremely busy: the phone rings off the hook while Atwood tries to catch up with her correspondence, visit friends, and fulfil various obligations. "Off time" seems to be limited to a couple of weeks at the cottage or on a canoe trip, or maybe a week of bird-watching.¹¹

★ ★ ★

In March of 1992, Carl Atwood had another stroke. Then, in September, he suffered a severe heart attack and almost died.

On 5 January 1993, after a long, sad fall and early winter, he did pass away.

A sequence of poetry in Atwood's 1995 collection *Morning in the Burned House* suggests the range of emotions that such a personal watershed evokes. I heard Atwood read from *Morning in the Burned House* at Harbourfront in late 1995. Before each poem, she took the time to set the stage for the narrator. But before the last poem she read, the only one from the sequence about her father's death, Atwood made no transitional statement to orient the audience. She moved from a poem spoken in the voice of Cordelia (to her father, King Lear) to a poem that was clearly a deeply and directly personal creation. Audience members were forced to come to terms with this abrupt shift on their own. Atwood left the stage as soon as she finished reading the poem. The audience sat silently for a moment.

> The memory is no friend.
> It can only tell you
> what you no longer have:
>
> a left hand you can use,
> two feet that can walk.
> All the brain's gadgets.[12]

The decline of her father's physical condition, his slow and painful deterioration, had prompted Atwood to reappraise memory. One poem in the sequence dedicated to him, "Bored," compares the young Atwood's frustration with the repetitive tasks of daily life with the older Atwood's sense of the larger value of those tasks. It closes on a note of regret:

> . . . Why do I remember it as sunnier
> all the time then, although it more often
> rained, and more birdsong?
> I could hardly wait to get
> the hell out of there to
> anywhere else. Perhaps though

boredom is happier. It is for dogs or
groundhogs. Now I wouldn't be bored.
Now I would know too much.
Now I would know.[13]

The poems in this sequence form a moving tribute as they trace
the steady decline of the man who was, once, the capable father
of the poet's memory:

. . . the same father I knew before,
the one who carried the green canoe
over the portage, the painter trailing,
myself with the fishing rods, slipping
on the wet boulders and slapping flies.[14]

The sequence seems intensely personal, strikingly so. But the
poems it contains, while written for the poet's father, are also
carefully framed by a larger context — the rituals of memory and
forgetting. The fourth section of *Morning in the Burned House*
contains poems on cultural rituals ("Oh"), historical artifact
("Man in a Glacier"), myth ("King Lear in Respite Care"), and
dream ("Two Dreams"). Together, these reflections on personal
and cultural memory and memory loss insist on being taken
personally; they ensure that we, as readers, recognize the steady
march of time and our inability to stop it. These poems articulate
our need for ritual, myth, and dream and *our* realization that they
are somehow just not enough.

⋆　⋆　⋆

Personal loss dominated 1993 for Atwood, but there was a
professional high point: the publication of *The Robber Bride*.
Atwood's British business manager, Vivienne Schuster, tells one
anecdote about the *Robber Bride* "book-fest" (a meeting held in
Toronto), at which Atwood and a core group of her editors
discussed the book and its launch; the first such "fest" was held
at Phoebe Larmore's suggestion (for *Cat's Eye*). Remembers

Schuster: Atwood showed up at breakfast the first morning carrying copies of her new novel tucked into gift bags with a "different colour of tissue paper spilling out the top." Schuster got the "bright scarlet paper." Phoebe Larmore got "lavender and pale blue." Continues Schuster: "Now what could be the significance of all this, we all wondered, but Margaret was giving nothing away. You will recall [the *Robber Bride* character] Charis sees people's aura in colours and so, as we disappeared to our rooms to begin the pleasure of reading the new novel it soon became apparent [that] Margaret . . . had decided my aura is a decided red! As was Zenia's. Hmm — food for thought!"[15]

One member of Atwood's professional "inner circle" is her trusted McClelland and Stewart editor, Ellen Seligman. She is "exquisite," declares Larmore.[16] Seligman is also Jim Polk's partner, and the strong relationship she and Atwood share is a testament to the maturity and professionalism of all three. Within the Canadian publishing industry, Seligman is very widely respected. In a recent *Toronto Life* profile, Stephen Smith points out that in 1992 "four of the five books in the running for the fiction [Governor General's Literary Award] were Seligman's." Still more of the books she has edited have been short-listed for significant literary awards in the past few years. Atwood says that working on a book with Seligman can be intense: "Usually it's punctuation we argue over. We'll horse-trade: she'll say, I'll give you a semicolon here if you give me a dash there. And I'll say, Only if you give *me* another semicolon over there. I'll go into her office and we'll talk over a manuscript this way and then we'll go downstairs and get a sandwich and a lottery ticket. We haven't won yet — well, a couple of new tickets."[17]

Gibson's fourth novel, *Gentleman Death* was published in the spring of 1993; *The Robber Bride* came out in the fall (published simultaneously by McClelland and Stewart in Canada, Bloomsbury in Great Britain, and Doubleday in the United States). The following year, *The Robber Bride* garnered a number of honours: the Trillium Award for Excellence in Ontario Writing, the Canadian Authors' Association Novel of the Year, and the *Sunday Times* Award for Literary Excellence. Also in 1994, the government of

France awarded Atwood a Chevalier dans l'Ordre des Arts et des Lettres.

On the basis of *The Robber Bride*, Atwood was the regional winner (Canada and the Caribbean) of the Commonwealth Writers' Prize. Since the first time she won this award (in 1987, for *The Handmaid's Tale*), the structure had been changed. Then, there was only one award; so, rather strangely, the runner-up in the regional category (second to Atwood's novel) was actually the winner of the Commonwealth Prize that year. (One wonders if the popularity of Atwood's novel — and, therefore, its financial success — might have adversely influenced the adjudication committee.)

Atwood had known for a long time how to read tarot cards, but reference to them had never crept into her writing before. In *The Robber Bride*, the reading of tarot cards — and the casting of horoscopes — are part of the symbolism of the narrative itself. These occult arts provide a fascinating keyhole through which to glimpse the novel's intricate patterns. As does the notion of ghosts — they, or what Tzvetan Todorov has called the realm of the "uncanny," had fascinated Atwood since her Victoria College days. In her acknowledgements, Atwood notes that she has drawn from a story told by poet P.K. Page the idea of "the ghost as dry rice." Page told me that story:

> It was the first death in my life. A friend of mine died when I was about twenty or so. We had been talking about what happens after death. She always said you just went. I said I had a feeling that there just might be something. A few days later she died, I was in bed. It was dark, people said I was dreaming. I saw a sort of light in the room — made up of a kind of molecular dance — and it formed the figure of the friend. "So I was right," I said.
>
> "That's what I came back to tell you."
>
> "So, what's it like?" I asked.
>
> "I can't tell you. Each death is personal. My death is of no use to you." I balanced myself — leaned forward to kiss her, leant on her arm — and it was almost solid. It was a dry rice feeling. And then the molecular dance came back.

It changed my life. I don't know what it was, but it changed my life.[18]

Atwood employed this story not in depicting the return of Zenia but in adding dimension to the return of a much more positive and magical force: Karen's grandmother.

> She walks towards Karen and Karen feels a cool wind against her skin, and the grandmother holds out both of her knobby old hands, and Karen puts out her own hands and touches her, and her hands feel as if sand is falling over them. There's a smell of milkweed flowers and garden soil. The grandmother keeps on walking; her eyes are light blue, and her cheek comes against Karen's, cool grains of dry rice. Then she's like the dots on the comic page, close up, and then she's only a swirl in the air, and then she's gone.[19]

★　★　★

What other sources of inspiration were there for *The Robber Bride*? As her poem "The Robber Bridegroom" suggests, Atwood was thinking about this fairy-tale frame of reference during the 1980s. And, of course, her *Witches of Eastwick* review suggests that she was exploring the potential of a quintessentially powerful femme fatale like Zenia years before Zenia was written into this novel. Aspects of Zenia may also be traced to early drafts of the Emma stories.

But are the novel's characters based on real people? When the book was undergoing its initial rush of popularity, everyone was longing to know, and the character they wanted to have identified for them first and foremost was, of course, Zenia. Atwood again strenuously dismissed all such reductive readings of the novel, especially the rumoured link between Zenia and columnist Barbara Amiel. She was still drawing comics — they appeared in diverse organs such as *Publishers Weekly* and *Brick* — and they proved to be a wonderful vehicle for venting the frustration such clamour provoked in her. In one cartoon, she drew herself as a short little woman seated on a chair; her toes dangle vulnerably above the floor; she is being asked by an interviewer the "which-character-are-you" question. The answer is "Zenia" — to the interviewer's puzzled amusement — and the bubble above the little cartoon Atwood contains an image of the wonderfully voluptuous Zenia she images herself to be.[20] When the real Atwood is asked the same question, she explains that "the only real, living person in this book is Saddam Hussein." She adds: "Of course I'm Zenia-like. She's a liar. And what do novelists do? . . . They lie."[21]

★   ★   ★

After promoting *The Robber Bride* throughout the United States in the spring, Atwood spent the summer focusing on other pursuits. In the fall, she toured Sweden, France, Denmark, Finland, and Norway. Hans Nygren, Atwood's Swedish publisher, remembers that both she and Gibson were "dead beat" at the outset of this European tour:

> But she bore up, as always, lectured at the [1994 Gothenburg Book] Fair (drew twice as big a crowd as Norman Mailer, which he drily commented on), made a minibus tour through Sweden with us, lecturing at two universities, the last one Uppsala, and full houses everywhere — and always calm and composed, never complaining. However, at the end of the day, surrounded by friends at private dinner-parties, when coffee is served and singing occurs, Margaret has shown herself quite capable of matching any Swedish challenge in the light repertoire. A memorable rendering of a song about the shaving habits of rugged Canadian lumberjacks comes to mind.[22]

("My lover was a logger . . ." Atwood has scribbled in the margins of my manuscript.)[23]

Given this account, it comes as no surprise that in 1995 Atwood won the Swedish Humour Association's International Humorous

Writer Award. Although this honour coincided with the publication of her light-hearted children's book, in which the letter *p*
figures rather prominently, *Princess Prunella and the Purple
Peanut* (published by Key Porter in Canada, by Workman Publishing in the United States, and by Barefoot Books in Great
Britain), the humour award was really for the Swedish translation
of *The Robber Bride*.

24

Of Past and Present: Some Reflections

THE "SUFFERING ARTIST" figure invoked at the beginning of this exploration seems to have been eclipsed by Margaret Atwood's rise to national and then international prominence, by the way her professional ascent has coincided with her establishment of a stable family and community life.

Implicit in any writer's biography is the comparison between life and art. In Atwood's case, that comparison is often initiated by one rather blatant question: Is Margaret Atwood like her fictional heroines? The assumption here can be a rather unflattering one, depending upon which heroine the questioner has in mind. But it is prompted by a simple observation that is not mean-spirited. Atwood's heroines and their surroundings *seem* real, the thinking goes, so real that they *must* be drawn from real life. (And this is where the questioner gains momentum.) So what, then, *are* the details of Atwood's real life? As the pointed questions are posed, as the artist faces her interlocutors, the "suffering" comes into focus. Is it required as the muse's due?

So many of Atwood's protagonists are Canadian writers and/or artists who live in Toronto; the question of whether Atwood has modelled them on herself can't help but take shape as we read an Atwood novel. But, when asked out loud, the question's intrusive nature becomes all too apparent. An unsuppressible curiosity makes readers want to peek behind the stage curtain, to scrutinize the flesh-and-blood Peggy Atwood as well as her creation. And compare.

All this means that Atwood must dress to camouflage herself as well as to express her taste in fashion. It means that after a speech, when the queries flood in, Atwood must field a few personal ones, such as "Were you overweight as a child (like Joan Foster)?" "Did you live near a ravine (like Elaine)?" And then there are the unspoken questions, those detectable in furtive glances: "Uh . . . that uncomfortable young woman in *Surfacing* — the one who never tells us her name — were you, you know, a bit like her? As . . . hmmm . . . bad as that awful Zenia?" (For the sake of biographical accuracy: No to the overweight question. Yes to the ravines — everyone who grows up in Toronto lives near one. No. And No.)

For Atwood, the worst aspect of such probes is that the questioner, in assuming that writing a novel merely involves cutting and pasting bits and pieces of real people and events to the page, devalues the creative act itself. Readers who pursue such thinking have discounted the writer's imagination.

The larger the audience at an Atwood reading, the more such questions pop up. And, despite her obvious discomfort, Atwood continues to be surprisingly open and honest in her responses. In recent years, she has even included quite a bit of autobiographical material in her speeches and articles. Why? One reason is, simply, that people want to know, and Atwood is generally responsive to her audience. Another reason is that, accepting that the demand for this type of information must be filled, Atwood wants the facts to be presented as accurately as possible. Ironically, then, she provides this autobiographical information in order to limit speculation and to protect her privacy.

Most of those "Are you like your heroines?" questions Atwood has answered — as well as she can — over the years. She has replied to a host of "how" questions as well. Such as "How do you write? shorthand? longhand? in pencil? How can you continue to accomplish so much?" But the "why" questions — the ones I keep asking myself, the questions that are central to this biography because they are the important ones in the long term — are harder. Why did she become a writer? Why did she become the kind of writer she is? Why does this writer, a skilled speaker and performer who is uncomfortable with the kind of scrutiny performance provokes, continue to undertake such a huge number of public engagements?

These "why" questions tend to have "should" answers. Because Atwood thought, and still thinks, she *should*. But there is more. So let me back into the "why" questions by answering some "what" questions. Atwood, who will probably be remembered longest for her poetry, who is best known to her contemporaries for her novels, whose face has become a Canadian icon, whose name lends support to such causes as PEN and Amnesty International, whose wit is legendary, and whose laugh is infectious, is a writer committed to the exploration of contemporary ethics. She is concerned, in her writing, in her speeches, in her professional dealings, with defining what it means to be ethical. At particular moments in time. (Should Offred of *The Handmaid's Tale*, in order to protect herself, sleep with one man and pass off the child she conceives with him as another man's?) In practical terms. (How should an employee handle a customer who finds a housefly in a product she is being paid to help sell?) Atwood writes and speaks about *should*, and that is what wins her the respect of her audiences, what allows her to lead them into the complex realm beyond the wit, humour, and entertainment dimension of her writing, what leads them to reread her work, what leads them to want to know more about its author.

Given all this, then, how *do* we answer that primary question, "Is Atwood like her fictional heroines?" Sometimes. She stands behind some of their decisions — especially those made in their more courageous moments. But perhaps a better answer is, "Only in relatively insignificant ways." Some protagonists share a cultural history with their creator; they have lived in the same cities as she during the same decades. And they're female. But while Atwood's heroines are underdogs, victims of the forces around them, she herself is not. Through her writing she articulates a genuine sympathy for those who have drowned in the treacherous social currents that she, by and large, has managed to navigate.

If Atwood writes about contemporary morals, what important lessons does she impart? Respect the individual. Respect the individual's freedom of expression. Don't judge a person too quickly or too easily. (In other words, don't judge a book by its cover.) And, above all, recognize that there is much more to a person than meets the eye. Atwood, in her work and in person, proves this truism time and time again.

★ ★ ★

If Atwood is a contemporary moralist, though, what accounts for *Alias Grace*, her most recent novel, published in 1996? It is a historical novel. The answer is that strangely, in some ways, *Alias Grace* drives home Atwood's moral stance more forcefully than any of its precursors; while the novel draws readers into the social and intellectual attitudes of the mid-nineteenth century, it also prompts them to ponder larger, timeless issues. And ponder them they have, because the publication of *Alias Grace* coincided with media storms surrounding the murder trials of O.J. Simpson and Paul Bernardo. The novel's effect, then, was to inspire its readers to view contemporary news stories within a broader context.[1]

Alias Grace is Atwood's ninth novel. It was eagerly anticipated and well publicized. The face of Margaret Atwood was emblazoned on Barnes and Noble shopping bags during the fall of 1996, heralding the novel's arrival on this American bookstore chain's shelves later that season. Barnes and Noble also sold Margaret Atwood mugs and canvas tote bags. In Canada, *Toronto Star* columnist Beverley Slopen revealed the setting and historical context of the novel back in May — but she didn't give away the plot.[2]

When *Alias Grace* finally appeared, few were disappointed. Nominated for the Booker, short-listed for a Governor General's Literary Award, and awarded Canada's coveted Giller Prize, the novel won critical acclaim. It also became an instant international bestseller and was quickly adopted as the *Reader's Digest* Book-of-the-Month Club main selection. Atwood's characteristic attention to detail (What would a female prisoner wear in the Kingston Penitentiary during the nineteenth century? What would she eat? What expressions would she use when speaking to others? Or

321

thinking to herself?), combined with historical research of the highest calibre (much of it conducted by her sister, Ruth) and a sex-blood-and-intrigue plot, makes *Alias Grace* a compelling read. That Doubleday made available a "reader's companion" to the novel, containing a note from Atwood, an interview transcript, and a list of topics for group discussion, indicates both the powerful interest the book has generated as well as its ability to prompt further exploration, discussion, and research. Scholars will be delving into this narrative for years to come. Jodie Foster's company, Egg Pictures, has optioned the film rights, winning the spoils of a bidding war that pitted Egg against such contenders as Miramax, Fox Searchlight, and Nicole Kidman's production company.[3]

Alias Grace is based on historical accounts of, and surrounding, the 1843 trial of Grace Marks, a sixteen-year-old girl convicted, with her lover James McDermott, of the murder of their employer and his girlfriend. It is a work of fiction woven from historical events that have been developed through a writer's intuition. Names taken from the trial transcripts become fully rounded characters in the novel. Early drafts involved two time schemes: past and present. Gradually, though, Atwood realized that there was no need to keep one foot in current time. That decision eliminated the first hundred pages. She then transformed the third-person Grace into the first-person Grace and linked her narrative to other passages in the novel — letters, poems, journalistic accounts, and interviews — thereby creating the narrative patchwork that comprises the published version.[4]

I first read *Alias Grace* in galleys during the summer of 1996. I was thrilled to be one of the first people invited to read the book that everyone was waiting for. The handwritten note attached to the package said "please keep hush re: the plot," increasing my excitement at being let in on the secret. As I rushed through the work, anxious to find out how the story was going to end, I was stunned by how different it was from Atwood's other work. What had triggered this radical directional shift towards the nineteenth century, towards recorded historical events? In hindsight I was way off the mark. Rather than being a new departure, *Alias Grace* was a logical extension of Atwood's writerly interests. As for the nineteenth-century setting, there was nothing new about it. Atwood specialized in Victorian literature as a graduate student; later she wrote a radio drama about Grace Marks and a historical primer on Canada in the early part of the century, *Days of the Rebels*. Stir into this mix her love of Gothic literature and murder mysteries and her exploration of paranoid schizophrenia in *The Journals of Susanna Moodie* and suddenly it all seems quite clear. *Alias Grace* is the product of a mature writer who, at the height of her career, returns to a story that has been at the back of her mind since the early days and looks into it more deeply. Could I have seen it coming? I would be lying if I were to say I could. And then I would have to come up with some prediction about what kind of a novel Atwood's tenth will be. I can't, of course. And that's what makes waiting for the novel Atwood is working on at the moment so exciting.

In the case of *Alias Grace*, I even had the advantage of a few hints contained in the working list of epigraphs to the novel. Seeing that list in January of 1996, I anticipated a contemporary novel that would explore Atwoodian themes: false memory, duplicity, the power relations of truth telling.

> Silence has its laws and its demands. . . . Is there more of what is said or of what is not said?
> — Ryszard Kapucinski, *The Soccer War*

> There is no language without deceit.
> — Italo Calvino, *Invisible Cities*

> I have no Tribunal.
> — Emily Dickinson, *Letters*[5]

Only the last of these epigraphs appears in the final text, but the first two still strike me as appropriate — both to the contemporary novel I had envisioned in my mind's eye and to the historical novel that finally appeared.

I see *Alias Grace* as a sophisticated articulation of some of the central and long-standing concerns of Atwood's career: Canadian culture and Canadian women, identity construction and gender bias, and the power dynamics of truth telling. In this novel, Atwood takes up many of the concerns of her early work and expands on them. Most obviously, although *Alias Grace* is an international bestseller, it is explicitly a Canadian book by a Canadian writer about a Canadian heroine. If Atwood hesitated to make the Canadian setting of her earlier novel, *The Edible Woman*, explicit, by the time she wrote *Alias Grace* such hesitation had vanished. As she did in *Survival*, in *Alias Grace* Atwood brought Canadian culture to her readers' attention; but while her initial premise in *Survival* was that her readers didn't know about Canadian literature, perhaps didn't even know that it existed as a discrete entity, in *Alias Grace* Atwood assumed that her readers either already knew of Grace Marks through the writings of Susanna Moodie or would come to know her through *Alias Grace* itself. Whereas *Survival* put Canadian literature on the map in the early 1970s, in the late 1990s *Alias Grace* assumed that Canadian literature was already on the map. Atwood, of course, played a vital role in putting it there.

Another issue that emerges throughout Atwood's fiction involves the various roles society expects women to play and the ways in which women respond to those roles. All of Atwood's female characters are acutely aware of social expectations. They are concerned about them. Unable to ignore them. Not all of these women comply, though, and it is through their refusal to play along that we come to learn about them and, in some ways, to judge them. A few do comply absolutely and completely, but they are seldom protagonists. Think of Anna, in *Surfacing*, who puts on her makeup, "her face," before her husband wakes up in the morning. We meet a character such as this from the outside. We meet Atwood's protagonists from the inside. An Atwood protagonist's thoughtfulness generally leads to her noncompliance with society's norms. The "Surfacer" and the "Edible Woman," for example, are temporarily debilitated by their own rebelliousness, but their actions are philosophically sound. Offred and Ofglen in *The Handmaid's Tale* actually risk their lives through noncompliance. Other Atwood protagonists are undecided. Witness Joan Foster: deciding not to fulfil society's expectations, she somehow *does* fulfil them. All of them. Simultaneously. What Atwood's fiction suggests is that external expectations play a large part in women's identity construction. Grace Marks proves the point. Whether Grace is ultimately a villain or a victim, we will never know. Perhaps she is both, purely as a result of the way she is perceived.

As I have said, the publication of *Alias Grace* coincided, coincidentally, with the media frenzy surrounding the O.J. Simpson trial in the United States and the Paul Bernardo trial in Canada. Bernardo and his wife, Karla Homolka, were accused of murdering at least two young women. Simpson was accused of murdering his estranged wife and a companion. The media decided that Bernardo and Simpson were guilty before they were even tried. When it came to Homolka, however, the pundits seemed torn: was she victim or villain? Homolka's lawyers exploited this moment of media uncertainty to its fullest. They plea bargained, and Homolka received a reduced sentence. Bernardo was punished to the full extent of the law and vilified in the press. Simpson, as the world knows, was declared innocent by the criminal-court jury but found guilty in "the court of public opinion" and, later, in civil court. In short, Homolka, as a woman, was treated differently than Simpson and Bernardo.

The same discrepancy occurs in the case of Grace Marks and her partner in crime, James McDermott. McDermott is hanged; Marks is sent to prison. Also, interestingly, several of the novel's male characters strive to prove Grace's innocence; their female counterparts are generally more suspicious. This phenomenon, some theorists suggest, occurs in contemporary trials as well. Atwood points to this observation in a number of interviews.[6] The timing of the novel's publication, then, gives rise to a provocative question: Have expectations of women really changed so much?

A few months after the publication of *Alias Grace*, Canadians found themselves caught up in yet another related news item: the advent of DNA testing, the subsequent release of some wrongly convicted criminals, and the resulting challenge to the judicial system. Criminals, it suddenly appeared, were not as easy to identify as we had previously thought. But of course that is precisely the lesson learned by those who argued to free Grace Marks in the nineteenth century and by those who have read about her ordeal in Atwood's twentieth-century novel: the act of judging a person is fraught with difficulty, uncertainty; in fact, it is practically impossible. The novel refuses to, cannot, disclose whether Grace is guilty or innocent of this brutal crime. Instead, it suggests that she cannot be so reduced. "The fullness of Grace is the point," explains Atwood.[7]

Can one individual understand another? Can I grasp your motives? Can you share my experience? No. No. No. On this score, Atwood is definite. That we are always tempted to try, however, is the basis upon which we, as Atwood's audience, are drawn to her work and to the protagonists who, at some level, Atwood invites us to know. And this simple, unalterable fact — that one individual can never really know and understand another — has daunting implications for the biographical project. For *this* biographical project.

Conclusion:
Reflecting Back

THIS BIOGRAPHY BEGAN with a description of the moments when Atwood decided and declared that she would be a writer; what shaped her writing drove the subsequent chapters. Nurtured by a supportive family of high achievers, taught to respect the individual, introduced to causes worthy of her time and energy (maintaining the natural world, supporting Canadian culture, furthering the rights of women), Atwood refined the objectives of her writerly vocation: to hold a mirror up to her society and her times and, by doing so, to play a part in reshaping them. As a result of her profession (the force with which she pursues and hones her craft) and her vocation (her forcefulness of purpose), Atwood has gained international respect both as a writer and as a "standard bearer."[1]

Atwood is motivated by something beyond the desire for recognition, awards, and prizes; otherwise, would she not have put her pen down long ago? I believe, and have argued throughout this book, that her writing is motivated by a strongly didactic impulse. But there are, of course, other reasons why Atwood writes. She says that she wrote *The Robber Bride* "to Delight" (I like that delight-full capital D)[2] her audiences, something she has done for audiences all over the world with this and other works. More generally, as she once mused, writing gives her the chance to lead a "double life." By way of Margaret, that is, Peggy Atwood is able to "examine" and "explore," "come to know people in ways, and at depths, that are otherwise impossible."[3] Margaret offers Peggy another dimension. (I should add that Atwood does not see herself as unique in leading such a doubled existence; rather, as her profiles of fellow writers suggest — particularly those of Dennis Lee, Marie-Claire Blais, and George Bowering — she sees it as an integral part of the writer's existence.)[4]

Perhaps she continues to write, as she once explained to CBC's Pierre Castonguay, "out of the fear of never producing anything"[5] — a fear that, in darker moments, must plague all writers. But at another level I expect that she is not really sure why she writes,[6] just that the alternative is, for her, unthinkable.

One other possibility. It has to do with a figure of the artist, neither Margaret nor Peggy, against whom and in defiance of whom Atwood writes. She is not so much a darker twin as a negative transparency, Atwood's relationship to her being like the one between a figure in a photograph and the same figure in the photograph's negative. This negative figure appears in Atwood's writing, and her outline is visible behind the decisions that have shaped Atwood's career; she is fed by the idea, the fear, that there may be a causal link between suffering and creativity. "Is it true that artists have to suffer to be creative?" asked Pachter in 1968.[7] Atwood's answer, as I have illustrated throughout this book, in the life she eventually scripted for herself, was a vehement "No." "[E]veryone has neuroses," she explained in her response, "but the artist has a way of working them out ([her] art)."[8]

But art, for Atwood, is neither tonic (a kind of therapy) nor laxative (a vehicle for the unmediated expression of the self); it cannot be so devalued. The artistic process involves the *transformation* of experience rather than the mere *expression* of it. "I believe in artistry," she tells one interviewer; "I believe that there's a difference between true confessions and writing a novel."[9] The former is a kind of therapy — whereby self-expression can be an end in and of itself. But, as Timothy Findley points out, art is not therapy, although it may be cathartic (both for the reader and for the writer).[10] For Atwood, it is precisely the element of artistry in art — the distance afforded by the artistic process, the construction of the aesthetic artifact — that is of value.

Cat's Eye is perhaps the best case in point: a tightly controlled novel that transforms a slice of the author's own childhood by tracing the protagonist's journey towards catharsis. In that novel, some demons are laid to rest — not merely because they are named but also because they are contained. It is a novel about artistic transformations (visual and verbal), and it enacts transformation.[11]

During the 1970s, many would have rejected Atwood's conviction that art was a way of doing battle with neurosis rather than a method for its expression. The tragic deaths of Sylvia Plath and Anne Sexton, as well as the popularity of confessional poetry more generally and what it revealed about the confessional poets, meant that the figure of the suffering artist loomed large and came to represent an incredibly strong link between creativity and suffering — even self-destruction.

In 1977, Atwood wrote a poem for Pat Lowther, a Vancouver poet who died tragically — murdered by her husband — in 1977. "Which stone / are you in?" Atwood's poem asks, echoing the title of one of Lowther's own poetry collections, *The Stone Diary* (the title is, of course, now well known in a slightly altered form as the title of Carol Shields's award-winning novel). Although Lowther's mouth is "sealed over" like a "jar / closed," this poem affirms the power of her "blood," her still-smouldering "fire."[12] Originally intended for inclusion in Atwood's 1978 collection *Two-Headed Poems*, the poem didn't make the final cut.

That year, Atwood also reviewed a collection of letters written by American poet Anne Sexton, who committed suicide in 1974. She seemed puzzled that Sexton had allowed these fifty thousand assorted personal expressions to survive her. "Do any of us, really, want strangers reading our mash notes to high school boyfriends, our petty gossip and our private love letters after we are dead? For some reason, perhaps not unconnected with her final act, Anne Sexton did."[13] Atwood concludes that "two Annes" emerge from the collection: the "good Anne," who wrote the letters, and the "bad Anne," the owner of the bleaker voice that speaks in Sexton's poems. As Atwood read through Sexton's letters and penned her description of the "bad Anne" with the "bleaker voice," was she thinking about her own experience as a poet, realizing that she possessed a much more positive sense of the creative process and its transformative, healing power?

Underlining her response to Pachter a decade earlier, Atwood subsequently remarked to fellow writer Joyce Carol Oates: "I certainly don't feel that all art is a consequence of neurosis. I tend to see it as the opposite. Not that some artists aren't neurotic . . . but that the art, the making or creating, is made in spite of the neurosis, is a triumph over it."[14] She echoes the sentiment of American poet Denise Levertov, who, in a 1974 speech given a few weeks after Sexton's death, argued passionately for the need to redirect attention away from the darkness (by which she meant a destructive and almost a cult-like fascination with suffering as source and prerequisite for creativity) to the light (the "romantic" aspects of artists' "tenacity" and "devotion" to their art, as well as the "self-affirming" potential of art).[15] "The artist, the poet," explained Levertov, "needs the stamina of an astronaut and the energy derived only from being passionately in love with life and with art."[16] By recasting art as a gesture of defiance rather than an articulation of surrender, both Levertov and Atwood consciously invert the equation of art and suffering.

Although Atwood dismissed that causal link very early in her career, the sad reality was that she would be made all too aware that suffering was part of many writers' lives. Many of Canada's best writers, some her closest friends, would be faced with terrifying struggles. And through her involvement in Amnesty International and PEN, Atwood has been instrumental in launching initiatives to support writers who have suffered as a result of their writing. Fate would have it that, in large measure, Atwood was spared in order to become, in the last part of the twentieth century, one of the most respected critics and chroniclers of our times. That is, during the 1980s and 1990s, Atwood's professional and personal success — her incredible ability to compartmentalize her time; to juggle the demands of writing, family, and professional responsibilities; to balance personal, professional, and vocational objectives; to keep her priorities straight; and even, simply, to keep her head while enduring promotional tours and media attention — are testament to the strength of her position. Or, perhaps, to the sheer strength of her character.

Either way, a detailed record of Atwood's career provides enough evidence to defy some of the most deeply held myths about writers and their lives.

Afterword:
On Words and Ever Onwards

Sue Walker: "No chosen biographer?"
Margaret Atwood: "Oh no, what would they put in?"[1]

MARGARET ATWOOD BROUGHT A NUMBER OF BOOKS to my attention during the course of this project — all of them related in one way or another to biography in particular and to writing in general. In the beginning came Lewis Hyde's *The Gift*[2] (a book, an article of faith, to which I have subsequently returned time and time again). Hyde argues that art is a gift. It *can* (and Atwood's work is a case in point here) exist at the intersection between two different exchanges — a commodity exchange and a gift exchange. But it does not have to. Art can be art without a market; it can't be art without a gift — that of the artist's talents. Hyde goes on to say that artists labour in the service of their talent. They have a responsibility not only to receive the gift but also to use it, to keep it in motion. (I cannot help but think here of Atwood's poem "Owl and Pussycat, Some Years Later," in which the two artist figures "polish" their talent, rubbing it like "silver / spoons,"[3] driven by the desire, the need, to "sing on."[4])

Then there was Alain de Botton's *Kiss and Tell*[5], a wonderfully witty send-up of the biographical enterprise. It's a novel dressed up to look like a biography (adorned with family tree, index, and photos), and the biographical subject is the narrator's twenty-eight-year-old girlfriend. The narrator's asides, his oh-so-obvious subjectivity, as well as his too-earnest attempts to pursue the implication of every single hair and thread and trivial incident are all part of the fun and quite to the point. Equally self-conscious was Ronald Searle's *The Rake's Progress*,[6] in which sketches and their ironic titles laugh out loud at the sheer pretension of anyone who sets out to present the whole picture or (and I'm thinking of the title's reference to John Bunyan's *The Pilgrim's Progress* here) its allegorical significance and moral implications. Rather, Searle's pen opts for swift and stylized, self-consciously "authoritative," as he sketches milestones in the lives of his various rakes — "The Poet," "The Novelist," "The Painter."

In Jack Miles's Pulitzer Prize-winning *God: A Biography*, the impossibility of the biographer's task announces itself even in the title. By acknowledging this impossibility in the book's opening, and by establishing parameters for his study with absolute precision (an exploration of God as the central character of a "classic of world literature"[7]), Miles clears a path wide enough for the sophisticated interpretive machine he brings to it. By furnishing me with this title, by leading me to a work that harbours the poststructuralist assumptions that what we know of individuals is a function of their currency in a media-dominated world, was Atwood suggesting that this biography would inevitably deal with Atwood-as-fictional-representation rather than as private individual?

There were other offerings as well: Doris Anderson's *Rebel Daughter*,[8] suggested because of its detailed description of Canadian women in the earlier decades of this century as well as for Anderson's sheer strength of spirit and clarity of vision, and Janet Malcolm's *The Silent Woman*,[9] an intelligent metabiography of Sylvia Plath as told — or not told — by Plath and her biographers (moral: take more than one version of a story into account). Atwood also supplied the titles of articles on biography by James Atlas,[10] then in his seventh year of writing Saul Bellow's biography, and by Phyllis Webb,[11] who speaks in a poet's voice of her fear of psychobiography and in a reader's voice of its haunting power (moral: if you are going to attempt a biography, be responsible).

And Atwood sent me two passages from works she had enjoyed; each made an interesting point. In the first one, taken from *Robertson Davies: Man of Myth*, Davies discusses the relationship between fiction and the imagination. The moral? Don't make too crude an equation between a writer's life and his or her art. Take imagination into account:

> *My books are works of imagination.* Every time one appears I receive letters explaining to me that I have made mistakes about this, that and the other, as though historical accuracy were my principal aim. Of course I try not to make mistakes in matters of fact, but if I were a better historian I would be a lesser novelist. The imagination is a cauldron, not a filing cabinet. But in most of the criticism of my work I read I find that imagination is the quality that appeals least to the majority of critics. To compare small things with great, I would infinitely rather have *Twelfth Night*, in which Illyria has a seacoast, than Hakluyt's *Voyages*. Imagination is all I have to work with; take it from me, and I am rotten meat for any critic with a pocket-knife.
>
> Imagination is in short supply in Canada. Whenever I meet with students I invariably hear the question: 'Where do you get your ideas from?' and whenever I read criticism I know that many of the critics will be hog-wild for *research* and consider imagination a rather sneaky trick. It is the NOTHING BUT attitude toward literary art. . . . Admittedly I try, like a good conjuror, to persuade my readers, for as long as they read, that I am offering them reality. I bring in Sir Wilfrid Laurier and King George V as front-men for illusion. But in the end the illusion is the best I have to offer.[12]

The second passage comes from the introduction of Javier Marias's book *Todas las Almas*, translated as *All Souls*. In it, Marias explains just how specific the personal pronoun must be — specific to a time and place, as well as to an individual. The lesson here? Statements have particular contexts.

If I call myself "I" . . . it is simply because I prefer to speak
in the first person and not because I believe that the faculty
of memory alone is any guarantee that a person remains the
same in different times and different places. The person
recounting here and now what he saw and what happened
to him then is not the same person who saw those things
and to whom those things happened; neither is he a prolon-
gation of that person, his shadow, his heir or his usurper.[13]

Taken together, the insights offered were rich and various, but
there were two common threads: most obviously, a self-conscious
awareness of the impossibility of the biographical enterprise;
and, less obviously, but equally significant, an absolute fascination with it. Fear and fascination.

★   ★   ★

Marias's point — that there is more than one "I" — parallels the
point of *Alias Grace* about the "fullness" of Grace, that there is
more to her than meets the eye. Similarly evasive was Atwood's
insistence, throughout this exercise, that "I am not who you think
I am" (the quote is actually from Laura, speaking to Petrarch).[14]
And, of course, she's right; there *are* more and different Atwoods
than the ones I have outlined. Other variations and reflections.

★   ★   ★

People don't realize that she's a Scorpio. So much emotion,
a dark, deep river with a strong current.
— Hélène Holden[15]

★   ★   ★

MA is always just ahead of what culture was thinking.
Always had that grace. Could sense what was going to be
"paradigm crisis."
— Brian Brett[16]

*   *   *

Certainly her intensity and brilliance have always fright-
ened many of her contemporaries. . . .

— Robert Fulford[17]

*   *   *

From her novels it is hard to know what a truly warm,
sympathetic and kind person she is. Her patience and
courtesy with strangers at book-signings, readings, public
appearances [are] never failing. She will stay on the task till
every last reader has been greeted and sent away happy with
an Atwood autograph even after a long reading, a longer
question-and-answer session, and probably days of arduous travel before and after. She has an enormous zest for
life and for new experiences.

— Mary Irving Campbell[18]

*   *   *

She can be difficult. That "buzzsaw" wit. People do find
her difficult. Refusing to acknowledge that is pussyfooting.
Emphasizing it too much is unnecessary. There has to be a
balance.

— Dennis Lee[19]

*   *   *

In the seventies, Peggy and Graeme came to the Townships
to stay over and to give a talk at Bishop's. They arrived late,
having stopped, I think, to watch birds and been caught up
in a driving rain, so that by the time they arrived the
students were having their own party. And, after a rushed
dinner, we went off to Bishop's. There, at one point, Peggy
explained she had written a comedy, and then a quest

romance, and then a gothic romance, and next she would write a tragedy or was it a satire — the trouble is that I don't remember if any of these specific terms are indeed the ones she used. Sitting behind her on the stage, I remarked that this procedure seemed somewhat cut and dried. Peggy whipped around and said, in her somewhat withering way, "And how do you organize *your* life?"

— Doug Jones[20]

*　★　★

Representing Margaret Atwood is like representing a dynasty of writers. I am always racing to keep up with her. There are some important things that have to be said. This woman is larger than life. This woman is a genius, she is magnificent in what she creates and the expanded and exquisite way she lives her life.

— Phoebe Larmore[21]

*　★　★

I find Peggy's work pure strength. Most especially her poetry. And for me that's because she is a fearless presenter of the dark side of things. Not fearless herself but as a witness. That's a particular kind of courage that is hard to come by. It's always gorgeous to find that she can take us to such awful places and say it's ok to laugh as well as to scream no . . . don't let that happen to me, I'm not going to let it. If I play the where would I be without her game, I'd have had less fun, be less wary, think less well of myself, think less fiercely about myself, I'd be here but I wouldn't be here so well. Pure strength is hard to come by and if someone has it they're not usually generous to share it out. I think it's pretty much excellent that Peggy is, for me anyway, so a million blessings go on her wild curly head from me.

— Xandra Bingley[22]

And, as Robert Fulford explains, there are also "many more Atwoods to come."[23]

★   ★   ★

Michael Rubbo: "Where do you go from here?"
Margaret Atwood: "Ever onward."[24]

Notes

INTRODUCTION

1 Qtd. in Charles Pachter, interview with the author, 4 Nov. 1997.

2 Margaret Atwood, letter to Charles Pachter, 28 Dec. 1968.

3 Margaret Atwood, "A Taste of Squalor," selections from a ms., 1991, box 148: 8, Margaret Atwood Papers, U of Toronto, 3. Sections were later published as "Where Is How," *Publishers Weekly* 8 Aug. 1991.

4 Margaret Atwood, "Why I Write Poetry," *This Magazine* Mar.–Apr. 1996: 44.

5 Kay Cogswell, letter to the author, 26 Jan. 1998.

6 Lois Gould, "The Margaret Factor," *New York Times Sunday Magazine* 24 Nov. 1996.

CHAPTER I: LITERARY APPRENTICESHIP

1 Margaret Atwood, "Travels Back," *Second Words: Selected Critical Prose* (Toronto: House of Anansi, 1982), 107–13.

2 Margaret Atwood, "My Mother Would Rather Skate than Scrub Floors," with Joyce Carol Oates, *Conversations*, ed. Earl Ingersoll (Princeton, NJ: Ontario Review, 1990), 70.

3 Margaret Atwood, "Most Influential Books," ms., n.d., box 146: 32, Margaret Atwood Papers, U of Toronto.

4 Margaret Atwood, "Defying Distinctions," with Karla Hammond, *Conversations*, 100.

5 Sara Eaton, *Lady of the Backwoods: A Biography of Catharine Parr Traill* (Toronto: McClelland, 1969).

6 Jerome H. Rosenberg, *Margaret Atwood*, Twayne's World Authors Series: Canadian Literature 740 (Boston: Twayne, 1984), 4.

7 Margaret Atwood, "Margaret Atwood," with Eleanor Wachtel, *Writers and Company*, by Eleanor Wachtel (Toronto: Knopf, 1993) 196.

8 Margaret Atwood, "An Interview with Margaret Atwood," with Betsy Draine, *Interviews with Contemporary Writers*, ed. L.S. Dembo, 2nd ser., 1972–82 (Madison: U of Wisconsin P, 1983) 368.

9 Margaret Atwood, "The Curse of Eve — Or, What I Learned in School," *Second Words* 223–24.

10 Sharon Rose Wilson, *Margaret Atwood's Fairy-Tale Sexual Politics* (Toronto: ECW, 1993).

11 Margaret Atwood, "Addictive Habits," ms., n.d., box 148: 10, Margaret Atwood Papers, U of Toronto, 2.

12 Atwood, "Addictive Habits" 3.

13 Margaret Atwood, "More Room for Play," with Catherine Sheldrick Ross and Cory Bieman Davies, *Conversations* 154; Atwood, "Addictive Habits"; Margaret Atwood, notes to the author, 1 Sept. 1996.

14 Atwood, "Addictive Habits" 2.

15 Atwood, "Addictive Habits" 4.

16 Margaret Atwood, notes to the author, 1 Sept. 1996.

17 Atwood, "Addictive Habits."

18 Atwood, "More Room for Play" 153–54.

19 Margaret Atwood, "The Empress Has No Clothes," with Elizabeth Meese, *Conversations* 182.

20 Atwood, "Addictive Habits" 7.

21 Margaret Atwood, "Nine Beginnings," *New Essays in New Territory* (New York: Norton, 1991) 156, vol. 2 of *The Writer on Her Work*, ed. Janet Sternberg.

22 Margaret Atwood, "Skipping Tea with Margaret Atwood," with Barbara Yost, *Bloomsbury Review* Sept.–Oct. 1994: n. pag., box 76: 22, Margaret Atwood Papers, U of Toronto.

23 Margaret Atwood, "An Interview with Margaret Atwood," with J.R. Tim Struthers, *Essays on Canadian Writing* 6 (1977): 20. See also Atwood, "Defying Distinctions" 109; and Atwood, "An Interview with Margaret Atwood" (with Draine) 368.

24 Margaret Atwood, interview with the author, 1 May 1996.

25 Margaret Atwood, letter to the author, 28 Nov. 1995.

26 Atwood, "Skipping Tea."

27 Atwood, notes to the author, 1 Sept. 1996.

28 Margaret Atwood, interview with the author, 1 May 1996.

29 Margaret Atwood, interview with the author, 1 May 1996.

30 Joe Kronick and Doreen Kronick, interview with the author, 25 July 1995.

31 Margaret Atwood, "A Flying Start," *That Reminds Me: Canada's Authors Relive Their Most Embarrassing Moments*, ed. Marta Kurc (Toronto: Stoddart, 1990) 12.

32 Margaret Atwood, "Managing Time for Writing," with Sue Walker, *Conversations* 176.

33 Atwood, "Defying Distinctions" 100.

34 Atwood, "The Empress Has No Clothes" 182.

35 Atwood, notes to the author, 1 Sept. 1996.

36 Atwood, notes to the author, 1 Sept. 1996.

37 Margaret Atwood, "Theology," *Now* 26 Sept.–2 Oct. 1985: 29.

38 Atwood, interview with the author, 1 May 1996.

39 Margaret Atwood, "English Teacher's Speech," *Indirections* Mar. 1986: 8.

40 Atwood, "English Teacher's Speech" 11.

41 Margaret Atwood, "Margaret Atwood Interview," with Barbara Wade, *Maclean's* In Class Program, 1981, box 56, folder 58, Margaret Atwood Papers, U of Toronto.

42 Margaret Atwood, "Northrop Frye Observed," *Second Words* 399.

43 Margaret Atwood, "Why I Write Poetry," *This Magazine* Mar.–Apr. 1996: 47.

44 Atwood, letter to the author, 28 Nov. 1995.

45 Atwood, notes to the author, 1 Sept. 1996.

46 Atwood, interview with the author, 1 Sept. 1996.

47 Margaret Atwood, "Travels Back," *Second Words* 109.

48 Margaret Atwood, "Armenian Association Award Speech," n.d., box 148: 25, Margaret Atwood Papers, U of Toronto.

49 Margaret Atwood, "Three Cheers for Corona!" *First Words*, ed. Paul Mandelbaum (Chapel Hill, NC: Algonquin, 1993) 11.

50 Atwood, "Synesthesia," 1956, box 3: 3, Margaret Atwood Papers, U of Toronto.

51 Atwood, "Addictive Habits" 3.

52 Atwood, "Nine Beginnings" 135–36.

53 Atwood, "The English Lesson," *First Words* 14.

54 Atwood, notes to the author, 1 Sept. 1996.

55 Atwood, "The English Lesson" 15.

CHAPTER 2: FAMILY VALUES

1 Margaret Atwood, letter to Peter Miller, 19 Oct. 1965, box 1: 16–17, Contact Press Papers, U of Toronto.

2 Margaret Atwood, "Witches," *Second Words: Selected Critical Prose* (Toronto: House of Anansi, 1982) 331.

3 Margaret Atwood, "Canadian-American Relations: Surviving the Eighties," *Second Words* 371.

4 Margaret Atwood, "Great Aunts," *Family Portraits: Remembrances by Twenty Distinguished Writers*, ed. Carolyn Anthony (New York: Doubleday, 1989).

5 Margaret Atwood, "Bluenosers," box 74, folder 7, 1983, Margaret Atwood Papers, U of Toronto. (Published as "Landfall: Nova Scotia," *New York Times Magazine* 18 Mar. 1984: 89, 100–03.)

6 Atwood, "Bluenosers" 2.

7 Atwood, "Bluenosers" 3.

8 Atwood, "Great Aunts" 4–5.

9 Atwood, "Great Aunts" 4.

10 Margaret Atwood, "The Empress Has No Clothes," with Elizabeth Meese, *Conversations*, ed. Earl Ingersoll (Princeton, NJ: Ontario Review, 1990) 181–82.

11 Atwood, "Bluenosers" 2.

12 Margaret Atwood, interview with the author, 1 May 1996.

13 Atwood, interview with the author, 1 May 1996.

14 Margaret Atwood, "My Mother Would Rather Skate than Scrub Floors," with Joyce Carol Oates, *Conversations* 70.

15 Margaret Atwood, "Growing Up Lucky under the Union Jack," speech for Wheaton College, 10 Nov. 1984, box 90: 51, Margaret Atwood Papers, U of Toronto.

16 Margaret Atwood, interview with the author, 1 Sept. 1996.

17 Margaret Atwood, "Using Other People's Dreadful Childhoods," with Bonnie Lyons, *Conversations* 221.

18 Atwood, "Great Aunts" 9.

19 Atwood, "Great Aunts" 7.

20 Atwood, "Great Aunts" 7–8.

21 Margaret Atwood, "For Uncle O., Banker, Dec'd.," n.d., box 11, folder 9, Margaret Atwood Papers, U of Toronto.

22 Atwood, "Great Aunts" 10.

23 Margaret Drabble, "Margaret Atwood Talks to Margaret Drabble," *Chatelaine* Apr. 1987: 73, 124–30.

24 Margaret Atwood, "More Room for Play," with Catherine Sheldrick Ross and Cory Bieman Davies, *Conversations* 155–56.

25 Margaret Atwood, letter to Joyce Barkhouse, 26 Oct. 1997.

26 Joyce Barkhouse, letter to Margaret Atwood, 26 Oct. 1983.

27 Atwood, "Great Aunts" 5.

28 Margaret Atwood, "Biographophobia: Some Personal Reflections on the Act of Biography," *Nineteenth-Century Lives*, ed. Laurence S. Lockridge, John Maynard, and Donald D. Stone (New York: Cambridge UP, 1989) 1.

29 Atwood, "Great Aunts" 14–15.

30 Margaret Atwood, "Five Poems for Grandmothers," *Two-Headed Poems* (Toronto: Oxford UP, 1978) 37.

31 Atwood, "Five Poems for Grandmothers" 36.

32 Margaret Atwood, letter to the author, 28 Nov. 1995.

33 Margaret Atwood, "While I Was Growing Up," *Chatelaine* May 1985: 93–94.

34 Atwood, interview with the author, 1 May 1996.

35 Atwood, "Witches" 331.

36 Margaret Atwood, "Lady Oracle," with John Goddard, *Books in Canada* Nov. 1985: 8.

37 Margaret Atwood, "Witch Craft," with Camille Peri, *Mother Jones* Apr. 1989: 28.

38 Atwood, interview with the author, 1 May 1996.

CHAPTER 3: PROFESSIONAL TRAINING

1 Margaret Atwood, "Dire Things: An Interview with Margaret Atwood," with Mark Abley, *Poetry Canada Review* 15.2 (1995): 28.

2 Margaret Atwood, "Metamorphosis: From Bedbug to Artist in

Twenty-Five Years," Duthie Lecture, Vancouver, 1988, box 148: 18, Margaret Atwood Papers, U of Toronto.

3 Margaret Atwood, "Poetry and Audience," n.d., box 56: 3, Margaret Atwood Papers, U of Toronto.

4 Margaret Atwood, "A Taste of Squalor," selections from a ms., 1991, box 148: 8, Margaret Atwood Papers, U of Toronto.

5 "Atwood, Harold Leslie," *Canadian Who's Who*, 1994 ed.

6 Margaret Atwood, "The Empress Has No Clothes," with Elizabeth Meese, *Conversations*, ed. Earl Ingersoll (Princeton, NJ: Ontario Review, 1990) 187.

7 Dennis Lee, interview with the author, 13 Nov. 1995.

8 Margaret Atwood, notes to the author, 1 Sept. 1996.

9 Jay Macpherson, interview with the author, 1 Mar. 1996.

10 Margaret Atwood, foreword, *Charles Pachter*, by Bogomila Welsh-Ovcharov (Toronto: McClelland, 1992) 2.

11 Elizabeth Renzetti, "Convention Becomes Carol Shields," *Globe and Mail* 18 Sept. 1997: D1.

12 Douglas Fetherling, *Travels by Night: A Memoir of the Sixties* (Toronto: Lester, 1994) 238.

13 Atwood, notes to the author, 1 Sept. 1996.

14 Qtd. in Lee, interview with the author, 13 Nov. 1995.

15 David Knight, interview with the author, 1 Mar. 1996.

16 Margaret Atwood, "Fifties Vic," Nov. 1979, box 56: 51, Margaret Atwood Papers, U of Toronto, 2.

17 Atwood, "Fifties Vic," 2.

18 Alexandra Johnston, interview with the author, 22 Mar. 1996.

19 Margaret Atwood, "Jay Macpherson: Poems Twice Told," *Second Words: Selected Critical Prose* (Toronto: House of Anansi, 1982) 407.

20 Macpherson, interview with the author, 1 Mar. 1996.

21 Margaret Atwood, "Into the Fields of Light," *Books in Canada* Apr. 1982: 15.

22 Margaret Atwood, "The Use of the Supernatural in the Novel," 25 Mar. 1961, box 3: 13, Margaret Atwood Papers, U of Toronto.

23 Margaret Atwood, "Dancing on the Edge of the Precipice," with Joyce Carol Oates, *Conversations* 74.

24 Atwood, notes to the author, 1 Sept. 1996.

25 Johnston, interview with the author, 22 Mar. 1996.

26 Another Bill was part of the crowd: a graduate student by the name of Bill Martyn. He received his MA from Victoria College in 1961.

27 Macpherson, interview with the author, 22 Mar. 1996.

28 Knight, interview with the author, 1 Mar. 1996.

29 Atwood, "Fifties Vic" 1.

30 Margaret Atwood, "Northrop Frye Observed," *Second Words* 399–400.

31 Atwood, "Northrop Frye Observed" 403.

32 Atwood, "Fifties Vic" 4.

33 Atwood, "Fifties Vic" 5.

34 Knight, interview with the author, 1 Mar. 1996.

35 Margaret Atwood, "Northrop Frye 1912–1991," *Canadian Literature* 129 (1991): 242–43.

36 Shakesbeat Latweed (Margaret Atwood and Dennis Lee), "The Expressive Act," n.d., box 3: 6, Margaret Atwood Papers, U of Toronto.

37 Latweed, "The Expressive Act" 3–4.

38 Atwood, "Fifties Vic" 3.

39 Margaret Atwood, "A Cliché for January," *First Words*, ed. Paul Mandelbaum (Chapel Hill, NC: Algonquin, 1993) 18–20.

40 Robert Graves, *Conversations with Robert Graves*, ed. Frank Kernowski (Jackson: UP of Mississippi, 1989) 110.

41 Margaret Atwood, "Great Unexpectations," *Ms.* July–Aug. 1987: 79.

42 Margaret Atwood, "Introduction to Sylvia Tyson Concert," box 56: 52, c. 1979, Margaret Atwood Papers, U of Toronto.

43 Atwood, notes to the author, 1 Sept. 1996.

44 John Robert Colombo, interview with the author, 8 May 1996.

45 Margaret Atwood, "For *Some*," 3 Oct. 1975, box 56: 23, Margaret Atwood Papers, U of Toronto.

46 John Robert Colombo, autobiographical entry, *Contemporary Authors*, Autobiography Series 22, ed. Joyce Nakamura (New York: Gale, 1996) 38.

47 Margaret Atwood, "Margaret Atwood," with Eleanor Wachtel, *Writers and Company*, by Eleanor Wachtel (Toronto: Knopf, 1993) 193.

48 Charles Pachter, interview with the author, 11 Sept. 1995.

49 Judith McCombs, letter to the author, 11 Sept. 1996.

50 Margaret Atwood, "Isis in the Dark," *Wilderness Tips* (Toronto: McClelland, 1991) 61–62.

51 Atwood, "Isis in the Dark" 65.

52 Qtd. in Rosemary Sullivan, *Shadow Maker: The Life of Gwendolyn MacEwen* (Toronto: HarperCollins, 1995) 103.

53 Publicity flyer, 17 Nov. 1960, box 1, file 9, Margaret Atwood Papers, U of Toronto.

54 Margaret Atwood, "Why I Write Poetry," *This Magazine* Mar.–Apr. 1996: 48.

55 Jay Macpherson's influence on Atwood's poetic voice has been noted by Sandra Djwa, "The Where of Here: Margaret Atwood and a Canadian Tradition," *The Art of Margaret Atwood: Essays in Criticism*, ed. Arnold Davidson and Cathy Davidson (Toronto: Anansi, 1981) 15–34; and "Letters in Canada, 1981: Poetry," *University of Toronto Quarterly* 51 (1982): 345–47. See also Jerome H. Rosenberg, *Margaret Atwood*, Twayne's World Authors Series: Canadian Literature 740 (Boston: Twayne, 1984) 7.

56 Macpherson, interview with the author, 1 Mar. 1996.

57 Margaret Atwood, "Some Sun for This Winter," *Acta Victoriana* Jan. 1961: 19.

58 Margaret Avison, letter to Margaret Atwood, 8 Sept. 1961, box 1: 11, Margaret Atwood Papers, U of Toronto.

59 Margaret Atwood, "The Way They Were," *Books in Canada* May 1991: 12.

60 David Knight, interview with the author, 1 Mar. 1996.

CHAPTER 4: GROWING CONCERNS ABOUT NATURE

1 Margaret Atwood, "True North," *Saturday Night* Jan. 1987: 304.

2 Atwood, "True North" 313.

3 Henri Audet, interview with the author, 1 Mar. 1996.

4 Margaret Atwood, "The Empress Has No Clothes," with Elizabeth Meese, *Conversations*, ed. Earl Ingersoll (Princeton, NJ: Ontario Review, 1990) 181.

5 Atwood, "The Empress Has No Clothes" 182.

6 Joe Kronick and Doreen Kronick, interview with the author, 25 July 1995.

7 Rick Salutin, interview with the author, 5 Apr. 1996; Julian Geller, interview with the author, 2 Feb. 1996.

8 Margaret Atwood, "Capering," *The Great Canadian Anecdote Contest*, ed. George Woodcock (Madeira Park, BC: Harbour, 1991) 28.

9 Margaret Atwood, "More Room for Play," with Catherine Sheldrick Ross and Cory Bieman Davies, *Conversations* 160.

10 Kronick, interview with the author, 25 July 1995.

11 Charles Pachter, interview with the author, 8 Sept. 1995.

12 Kronick and Kronick, interview with the author, 25 July 1995.

13 Atwood, "Capering" 29.

14 Atwood, "Capering" 28.

15 Atwood, "Capering" 29.

16 Margaret Atwood, notes to the author, 1 Sept. 1996.

CHAPTER 5: A CANADIAN NATIONALIST ABROAD

1 Margaret Atwood, "Dancing on the Edge of the Precipice," with Joyce Carol Oates, *Conversations*, ed. Earl Ingersoll (Princeton, NJ: Ontario Review, 1990) 77.

2 Mary Irving Campbell, letter to the author, 17 July 1996.

3 Jerome Buckley, letter to the author, 13 Sept. 1995.

4 Buckley, letter to the author, 13 Sept. 1995.

5 Jerome Buckley, letter to the author, 17 May 1996.

6 John Ayre, "Margaret Atwood at the End of Colonialism," *Saturday Night* Nov. 1972: 26.

7 Campbell, letter to the author, 17 July 1996.

8 Margaret Atwood, letter to Charles Pachter, 28 Oct. 1996.

9 Campbell, letter to the author, 17 July 1996.

10 Campbell, letter to the author, 17 July 1996.

11 Margaret Atwood, interview with the author, 1 May 1996.

12 Atwood, letter to Pachter, 28 Oct. 1961.

13 Campbell, letter to the author, 17 July 1996.

14 Margaret Atwood, letter to Charles Pachter, 22 May 1962, box 1: 59, Margaret Atwood Papers, U of Toronto.

15 Margaret Atwood, notes to the author, 1 Sept. 1996.

16 Margaret Atwood, "If You Can't Say Something Nice, Don't Say Anything at All," *Language in Her Eye*, ed. Libby Scheier et al. (Toronto: Coach House, 1990) 3.

17 Atwood, "Dancing on the Edge of the Precipice" 77.

18 Margaret Atwood, "Growing Up Lucky under the Union Jack," 10 Nov. 1984, box 90: 51, Margaret Atwood Papers, U of Toronto, 2.

19 Margaret Atwood, "The Empress Has No Clothes," with Elizabeth Meese, *Conversations*, ed. Earl Ingersoll (Princeton, NJ: Ontario Review, 1990) 185.

20 Margaret Atwood, "After Survival . . . ," *Encounters and Explorations: Canadian Writers and European Critics*, ed. Franz K. Stanzel and Waldemar Zacharasiewicz (Würzburg: Königshausen, 1986) 132.

21 Atwood, "Dancing on the Edge of the Precipice" 77.

22 Atwood, "Dancing on the Edge of the Precipice" 78.

23 Campbell, letter to the author, 17 July 1996.

24 Margaret Atwood, "My Poetic Principles on Oct. 29, 1962," 29 Oct. 1962, box 1: 6, Margaret Atwood Papers, U of Toronto.

CHAPTER 6: FEMINISM

1 Margaret Atwood, "Case of the Crazed Cashier," *Toronto Life* Mar. 1990: 46–47.

2 Margaret Atwood, notes to the author, 1 Sept. 1996.

3 Atwood, "Case of the Crazed Cashier" 46–47.

4 Margaret Atwood, "Margaret in Marketland," selections from a ms., c. 1984, box 90: 37, Margaret Atwood Papers, U of Toronto.

5 Margaret Atwood, "Tightrope-Walking over Niagara Falls," with Geoff Hancock, *Conversations*, ed. Earl Ingersoll (Princeton, NJ: Ontario Review, 1990) 208–09.

6 Chris Lloyd, interview with the author, 26 Apr. 1996.

7 Lloyd, interview with the author, 26 Apr. 1996.

8 Bev Hunter, interview with the author, 9 Aug. 1996.

9 Hunter, interview with the author, 9 Aug. 1996.

10 Hunter, interview with the author, 9 Aug. 1996.

11 Mary Sims, letter to the author, 2 Apr. 1996.

12 Margaret Atwood, "A Taste of Squalor," selections from a ms., 1991, box 148: 8, Margaret Atwood Papers, U of Toronto.

13 Margaret Atwood, "Where Is How," *Publishers Weekly* 8 Aug. 1991: 9.

14 Margaret Atwood, letter to Hope Leresche, 7 Dec. 1965, box 92: 1, Margaret Atwood Papers, U of Toronto.

15 Hope Leresche, letter to Margaret Atwood, 1 Dec. 1965, box 92: 1, Margaret Atwood Papers, U of Toronto.

16 Margaret Atwood, interview with the author, 1 Sept. 1996.

17 Margaret Atwood, "An Interview with Margaret Atwood," with Betsy Draine, *Interviews with Contemporary Writers*, ed. L.S. Dembo, 2nd ser., 1972–82 (Madison: U of Wisconsin P, 1983) 373–74.

CHAPTER 7: THE RIGHT BALANCE

1 Chris Lloyd, interview with the author, 26 Apr. 1996.

2 Margaret Atwood, "Margaret in Marketland," c. 1984, box 90: 37, Margaret Atwood Papers, U of Toronto.

3 Lloyd, interview with the author, 26 Apr. 1996.

4 Mary Sims, letter to the author, 2 Apr. 1996.

5 Atwood, "Margaret in Marketland."

6 Sims, letter to the author, 2 Apr. 1996.

7 Sims, letter to the author, 2 Apr. 1996.

8 Margaret Atwood, interview with the author, 1 May 1996; Margaret Atwood, notes to the author, 1 Sept. 1996.

9 Margaret Atwood, "Tightrope-Walking over Niagara Falls," with Geoff Hancock, *Conversations*, ed. Earl Ingersoll (Princeton, NJ: Ontario Review, 1990) 207.

10 Margaret Atwood, interview with Margaret Kaminski, *Waves* 4.1 (1975): 8–13.

11 Margaret Atwood, "A Taste of Squalor," selections from a ms., 1991, box 148: 8, Margaret Atwood Papers, U of Toronto, 1.

12 Margaret Atwood, *The Edible Woman* (Toronto: McClelland, 1969) 51.

13 James Ford, interview with the author, 23 Jan. 1998.

14 Ford, interview with the author, 23 Jan. 1998.

15 Sims, letter to the author, 2 Apr. 1996.

16 Lloyd, interview with the author, 2 Apr. 1996.

17 Lloyd, interview with the author, 26 Apr. 1996; Chris Lloyd, interview with the author, 9 Jan. 1998.

18 Margaret Atwood, "Dancing on the Edge of the Precipice," with Joyce Carol Oates, *Conversations*, ed. Earl Ingersoll (Princeton, NJ: Ontario Review, 1990) 75.

19 Ford, interviews with the author, 23 Jan. 1998; 9 June 1998.

20 John Robert Colombo, memo, 14 Feb. 1966, box 95: 5, Margaret Atwood Papers, U of Toronto.

21 Report, n.d., box 95: 5, Margaret Atwood Papers, U of Toronto.

22 Report, n.d., box 95: 5, Margaret Atwood Papers, U of Toronto.

23 Report, n.d., box 95: 5, Margaret Atwood Papers, U of Toronto.

CHAPTER 8: THE DEMANDS OF THE MUSE

1 Rosemary Sullivan, *Shadow Maker: The Life of Gwendolyn MacEwen* (Toronto: HarperCollins, 1995) 148.

2 Sullivan, *Shadow Maker* 150, 149.

3 Doug Jones, letter to the author, 1 Apr. 1996.

4 Margaret Atwood, "The Grunge Look," *Writing Away: The PEN Canada Travel Anthology*, ed. Constance Rooke (Toronto: McClelland, 1994) 3.

5 Margaret Atwood, "Returns: Paris," *New York Times Sophisticated Traveler* 7 Oct. 1984: n. pag.

6 Atwood, "The Grunge Look" 11.

7 Jane Rule, interview with the author, 27 Mar. 1996.

8 Judith McCombs, "From 'Places, Migrations' to *The Circle Game*: Atwood's Canadian and Female Metamorphoses," *Margaret Atwood: Writing and Subjectivity*, ed. Colin Nicholson (New York: St. Martin's, 1994) 51–67.

9 Margaret Atwood, letter to George Woodcock, 20 May 1974.

10 McCombs, "From 'Places, Migrations' to *The Circle Game*" 54, 62.

11 McCombs, "From 'Places, Migrations' to *The Circle Game*" 61.

12 Peter Miller, "Contact Press: The Later Years," *Canadian Notes and Queries* 51 (1997): 4.

13 Peter Miller, letter to Louis Dudek and Raymond Souster, 15 July 1965, Contact Press Papers, U of Toronto.

14 Miller, "Contact Press" 9.

15 John Robert Colombo, interview with the author, 8 May 1996.

16 Margaret Atwood, libretto, *Trumpets of Summer*, music by John Beckwith, 1964, box 41: 2–8, Margaret Atwood Papers, U of Toronto.

17 Margaret Atwood, "Margaret Atwood," with Eleanor Wachtel, *Writers and Company*, by Eleanor Wachtel (Toronto: Knopf, 1993) 202–03.

18 Margaret Atwood, letter to Charles Pachter, 23 Sept. 1964.

19 Margaret Atwood, "Metamorphosis: From Bedbug to Artist in Twenty-Five Years," Duthie Lecture, Vancouver, 1988, box 148: 17, Margaret Atwood Papers, U of Toronto.

20 Margaret Atwood, letter to Charles Pachter, 17 Oct. 1964.

21 Rule, interview with the author, 27 Mar. 1996.

22 Atwood, "Metamorphosis."

23 Margaret Atwood, interview with the author, 1 May 1996.

24 Atwood, "Where Is How," *Publishers Weekly* 8 Aug. 1991: 9.

25 Margaret Atwood, "Metamorphosis."

26 Rule, interview with the author, 27 Mar. 1996.

27 Rule, interview with the author, 27 Mar. 1996.

28 Chris Lloyd, interview with the author, 26 Apr. 1996.

29 Jones, letter to the author, 1 Apr. 1996.

30 Al Purdy, "An Unburnished One-Tenth of One Per Cent of an Event," *Malahat Review* 42 (1977): 62.

31 Jones, letter to the author, 1 Apr. 1996.

32 Al Purdy, letter to the author, 15 Nov. 1997.

33 Jones, letter to the author, 1 Apr. 1996.

34 Purdy, letter to the author, 15 Nov. 1997.

35 Margaret Atwood, "Dancing on the Edge of the Precipice," with Joyce Carol Oates, *Conversations*, ed. Earl Ingersoll (Princeton, NJ: Ontario Review, 1990) 80.

36 Judith McCombs, "Early *Cat's Eye* Stories: Atwood's 1964–5 'Cut-Out,' 'Scribblers,' 'Suffer the Little Children,' and 'The Ravine,' " American Association of Canadian Studies in the United States Conference, Seattle, 16 Nov. 1995.

37 Margaret Atwood, "Who Created Whom? Characters That Talk Back," *New York Times Book Review* 31 May 1987: 36.

CHAPTER 9: ATWOOD AS MUSE

1 Charles Pachter, interview with the author, 11 Sept. 1995.

2 Margaret Atwood, "Owl and Pussycat, Some Years Later," *Paper Guitar: 25 Writers Celebrate 25 Years of* Descant *Magazine* (Toronto: HarperCollins, 1995) 15–21.

3 Charles Pachter, interview with the author, 8 Sept. 1995.

4 Pachter, interview with the author, 11 Sept. 1995.

5 Charles Pachter, letter to Margaret Atwood, 2 May 1962, box 1: 59, Margaret Atwood Papers, U of Toronto.

6 Judith McCombs, "From 'Places, Migrations' to *The Circle Game*: Atwood's Canadian and Female Metamorphoses," *Margaret Atwood: Writing and Subjectivity*, ed. Colin Nicholson (New York: St. Martin's, 1994) 62.

7 Raymond Souster, letter to Margaret Atwood, 14 Dec. 1963, box 1: 74, Contact Press Papers, U of Toronto.

8 Bogomila Welsh-Ovcharov, *Charles Pachter* (Toronto: McClelland, 1992) 11.

9 Charles Pachter, letter to Margaret Atwood, 8 Oct. 1964.

10 Margaret Atwood, letter to Charles Pachter, 17 Oct. 1964.

11 Margaret Atwood, letter to Charles Pachter, 9 Nov. 1964.

12 Charles Pachter, letter to Margaret Atwood, 11 Nov. 1964.

13 Margaret Atwood, letter to Charles Pachter, 18 Nov. 1964.

14 Charles Pachter, letter to Margaret Atwood, 8 Dec. 1964.

15 Margaret Atwood, letter to Charles Pachter, 12 Dec. 1964.

16 An official receipt, issued to UBC acquisitions librarian Rita Butterfield and dated 12 Mar. 1965, indicates that the per-copy price of a Cranbrook *Circle Game* was $150. Those interested in tracking down a copy (and paying today's price of about $12,000) should contact Janet Fetherling at Annex Books in Toronto.

17 McCombs, "From 'Places, Migrations' to *The Circle Game*" 65.

18 Atwood, letter to Pachter, 12 Dec. 1964.

19 McCombs, "From 'Places, Migrations' to *The Circle Game*" 58.

20 Margaret Atwood, *The Circle Game* (Toronto: Contact, 1966) 40.

21 Atwood, letter to Pachter, 12 Dec. 1964.

22 Margaret Atwood, letter to Peter Miller, 19 Oct. 1965, box 1: 16–17, Contact Press Papers, U of Toronto. See also box 1: 50, Margaret Atwood Papers, U of Toronto.

23 Margaret Atwood, *Alias Grace* (New York: Talese-Doubleday, 1996) 358.

24 Margaret Atwood, letter to Charles Pachter, 16 Jan. 1965.

25 Charles Pachter, letter to Margaret Atwood, 23 Jan. 1965, box 1: 61, Margaret Atwood Papers, U of Toronto.

26 Pachter, letter to Margaret Atwood, 23 Jan. 1965.

27 Margaret Atwood, letter to Charles Pachter, 24 Feb. 1965.

28 Charles Pachter, letter to Margaret Atwood, 10 Feb. 1966.

29 Charles Pachter, end portion of letter to Margaret Atwood, 23 Feb. 1966.

30 Margaret Atwood, letter to her grandmother, n.d., box 17: 3 (in the notebook "The Deaths of Animals"), Margaret Atwood Papers, U of Toronto.

31 Atwood, letter to Charles Pachter, 24 Feb. 1965.

32 Pachter, interview with the author, 11 Sept. 1995.

33 Bogomila Welsh-Ovcharov, *Charles Pachter* (Toronto: McClelland, 1992) 30.

34 Charles Pachter, letter to Margaret Atwood, 19 Dec. 1968.

35 Charles Pachter, letter to Margaret Atwood, 9 Apr. 1969.

36 Charles Pachter, letter to Margaret Atwood, 12 May 1969.

37 Welsh-Ovcharov, *Charles Pachter* 134.

38 Qtd. in Pachter, interview with the author, 11 Sept. 1995.

CHAPTER 10: WRITING AND HARVARD

1 Margaret Atwood, letter to the author, 28 Nov. 1995.

2 Margaret Atwood, letter to Miss Billings, c. 1967, box 12: 3 (in the notebook "Early Drafts of 'Journals of Susanna Moodie' and Personal Notes, Letters"), Margaret Atwood Papers, U of Toronto.

3 John Robert Colombo, letter to "Dear Fellow Poet," 1 Jan. 1967, box 92: 2, Margaret Atwood Papers, U of Toronto.

4 Margaret Atwood, letter to Charles Pachter, 16 Feb. 1967.

5 Rick Salutin, interview with the author, 5 Apr. 1996.

6 Peter Miller, memo to Raymond Souster and Louis Dudek, 15 July 1965, box 1, Contact Press Papers, U of Toronto.

7 Raymond Souster, note to Peter Miller and Louis Dudek, c. 1965, box 1: 15, Contact Press Papers, U of Toronto.

8 Peter Miller, letter to Louis Dudek and Raymond Souster, 15 July 1965, box 1, Contact Press Papers, U of Toronto.

9 Dennis Lee, letter to Margaret Atwood, c. 1966, box 1: 44, Margaret Atwood Papers, U of Toronto.

10 Margaret Atwood, letter to Peter Miller, Jan. 1966, box 1: 15–17, Contact Press Papers, U of Toronto.

11 Margaret Atwood, letter to Charles Pachter, 9 Oct. 1965.

12 Margaret Atwood, letter to the author, 28 Nov. 1995.

13 Margaret Atwood, letter to Charles Pachter, 9 Oct. 1966.

14 My thanks to Sheri Weinstein for her description of Harvard and vicinity.

15 Margaret Atwood, "The Landlady," *The Animals in That Country* (Toronto: Oxford UP, 1968) 14.

16 Margaret Atwood, interview with the author, 1 May 1996.

17 Margaret Atwood, letter to Hope Leresche, 7 Dec. 1965, box 92:1, Margaret Atwood Papers, U of Toronto.

18 Margaret Atwood, letter to Wynne Francis, 24 Sept. 1966, box 1: 35, Margaret Atwood Papers, U of Toronto.

19 Margaret Atwood, sketch, 1965, box 17: 4, Margaret Atwood Papers, U of Toronto.

20 Margaret Atwood, letter to John Newlove, 24 Sept. 1966, Margaret Atwood Papers, U of Toronto.

21 Margaret Atwood, letter to Charles Pachter, 23 Sept. 1966.

22 Sue Milmoe, interview with the author, 26 June 1996.

23 Milmoe, interview with the author, 26 June 1996.

24 Judy Wright, letter to the author, 21 July 1996.

25 Milmoe, interview with the author, 26 June 1996.

26 Judy Wright, letter to the author, 21 July 1996.

27 Milmoe, interview with the author, 26 June 1996.

28 Margaret Atwood, letter to Daryl Hine, 13 Jan. 1967, box 1: 38, Margaret Atwood Papers, U of Toronto.

29 Margaret Atwood, letter to John Newlove, 5 Jan. 1967, box 1: 52, Margaret Atwood Papers, U of Toronto.

30 Margaret Atwood, letter to Al Purdy, 7 Jan. 1967, box 92: 2, Margaret Atwood Papers, U of Toronto.

31 Margaret Atwood, letter to Charles Pachter, 27 Feb. 1967.

32 Milmoe, interview with the author, 26 June 1996.

33 Wright, letter to the author, 26 July 1996.

34 Margaret Atwood, letter to Charles Pachter, 27 Mar. 1967.

35 Margaret Atwood, interview with Joyce Carol Oates, selection from a ms., c. 1978, box 56: 31, Margaret Atwood Papers, U of Toronto.

36 William Toye, interview with the author, 15 July 1995.

37 Margaret Atwood, "Writing Utopia," c. 1989, box 148, Margaret Atwood Papers, U of Toronto, 3.

38 John Robert Colombo, interview with the author, 8 May 1996.

39 Margaret Atwood, letter to Roy MacSkimming, 16 Feb. 1967, box 92: 2, Margaret Atwood Papers, U of Toronto.

40 Margaret Atwood, letter to Charles Pachter, 18 July 1967.

41 Margaret Atwood, handwritten draft of letter to Hope Leresche, c. 1967, box 95: 6, Margaret Atwood Papers, U of Toronto.

CHAPTER 11: A WEDDING

1 Margaret Atwood, letter to Charles Pachter, 16 May 1967.

2 Sue Milmoe, interview with the author, 26 June 1996.

3 Judy Wright, letter to the author, 21 July 1996.

4 Milmoe, interview with the author, 26 June 1996.

5 Milmoe, interview with the author, 26 June 1996.

6 Margaret Atwood, letter to Charles Pachter, 18 July 1967.

CHAPTER 12: AND TEACHING TOO

1 Margaret Atwood, "Sir George Piece," c. 1977, box 56: 28, Margaret Atwood Papers, U of Toronto, 1.

2 Atwood, "Sir George Piece" 2.

3 Atwood, "Sir George Piece" 2.

4 David Sheps, interview with the author, 10 Apr. 1996.

5 Margaret Atwood, "Bowering Pie . . . Some Recollections," *Essays on Canadian Writing* 38 (1989): 4.

6 Margaret Atwood, notes to the author, 28 Nov. 1995.

7 Margaret Atwood, letter to George Bowering, 6 July 1969, box 2: 1, Margaret Atwood Papers, U of Toronto.

8 Sheps, interview with the author, 10 Apr. 1996.

9 Margaret Atwood, letter to Charles Pachter, 18 Nov. 1967.

10 Margaret Atwood, letter to Charles Pachter, 7 Dec. 1967.

11 Rosemary Sullivan, *Shadow Maker: The Life of Gwendolyn MacEwen* (Toronto: HarperCollins, 1995) 207, 215.

12 Margaret Atwood, letter to George Woodcock, 20 May 1974.

13 Margaret Atwood, letter to Charles Pachter, 8 Dec. 1967.

14 Margaret Atwood, interview with the author, 1 May 1996.

15 Patrick Lane, e-mail to the author, 13 Feb. 1996.

16 Margaret Atwood, letter to Charles Pachter, 20 Nov. 1968.

17 Margaret Atwood, letter to Robin Mathews, 17 July 1969, box 2: 1, Margaret Atwood Papers, U of Toronto.

18 Margaret Atwood, letter to Charles Pachter, 28 Dec. 1968.

19 Elizabeth Brewster, autobiographical entry, *Contemporary Authors*, Autobiography Series 15, ed. Joyce Nakamura (New York: Gale, 1992) 158.

20 Margaret Atwood, letter to Peter Davison, 26 Oct. 1967, box 92: 4, Margaret Atwood Papers, U of Toronto.

21 Margaret Atwood, "The Reincarnation of Captain Cook," *The Animals in That Country* (Toronto: Oxford UP, 1968) 61.

22 Margaret Atwood, "Chronology," *The Animals in That Country* 54–55.

23 Margaret Atwood, "Time," *The Animals in That Country* 55.

24 Margaret Atwood, letter to William Toye, 11 Mar. 1968, box 1: 57, Margaret Atwood Papers, U of Toronto.

25 Margaret Atwood, letter (unsent) to Scott McIntyre, 28 Aug. 1967, box 95: 8, Margaret Atwood Papers, U of Toronto.

26 Atwood, letter to Scott McIntyre, 28 Aug. 1967, box 95: 8, Margaret Atwood Papers, U of Toronto.

27 Margaret Atwood, *The Edible Woman* (Toronto: McClelland, 1969) 249.

28 Margaret Atwood, letter to the author, 28 Nov. 1995.

29 Margaret Atwood, "A Taste of Squalor," selections from a ms., 1991, box 148: 8, Margaret Atwood Papers, U of Toronto.

30 I am grateful to Peter Davison for lending me copies of the American editions of Atwood's books.

31 Sullivan, *Shadow Maker* 237.

32 Margaret Atwood, letter to Mrs. Nellie Kesson, 1 July 1969, box 50: 4, Margaret Atwood Papers, U of Toronto.

33 Jay Macpherson, letter to Margaret Atwood, 20 Aug. 1969, box 50: 5, Margaret Atwood Papers, U of Toronto.

34 Margaret Atwood, letter to Jerome Buckley, 1 July 1969, box 50: 5, Margaret Atwood Papers, U of Toronto.

35 Department of English, University of Alberta, contract, 1969, Margaret Atwood Papers, U of Toronto.

36 Margaret Atwood, logbook, 1969, box 12: 3, Margaret Atwood Papers, U of Toronto.

37 Margaret Atwood, letter to Charles Pachter, 6 Nov. 1969.

38 Charles Pachter, letter to Margaret Atwood, 10 Nov. 1969.

39 Some of these watercolours and sketches appear in *Margaret Atwood's Fairy-Tale Sexual Politics* by Sharon Rose Wilson (Toronto: ECW, 1993).

40 Charles Pachter, letter to Margaret Atwood, 5 Mar. 1969.

41 Margaret Atwood, *The Journals of Susanna Moodie* (Toronto: Oxford UP, 1970).

42 Rick Salutin, interview with the author, 5 Apr. 1996.

43 Margaret Atwood, letter to Tom Marshall, 16 July 1969, box 2: 1, Margaret Atwood Papers, U of Toronto.

44 Atwood, letter to Tom Marshall, 16 July 1969.

45 Margaret Atwood, letter to William Toye, 27 Jan. 1970, box 11: 11, Margaret Atwood Papers, U of Toronto.

46 Peter Davison, letter to Margaret Atwood, 2 Dec. 1969, box 11, Margaret Atwood Papers, U of Toronto.

47 Atwood, letter to William Toye, 27 Jan. 1997.

CHAPTER 13: ON THE RISE:
MARGARET ATWOOD AND CANLIT

1 Al Purdy, letter to Margaret Atwood, 6 Dec. 1965, box 1: 67, Margaret Atwood Papers, U of Toronto.

2 Margaret Atwood, letter to Charles Pachter, 6 Sept. 1970.

3 Tony Richardson, *Long Distance Runner: A Memoir* (London: Faber, 1993) 231.

4 Margaret Atwood, letter to Charles Pachter, 1 Oct. 1970.

5 Richardson, *Long Distance Runner* 231.

6 Atwood, letter to Charles Pachter, 1 Oct. 1970.

7 Richardson, *Long Distance Runner* 231–32.

8 Margaret Atwood, letter to Charles Pachter, 11 Apr. 1971.

9 Atwood, letter to Charles Pachter, 1 Oct. 1970.

10 Margaret Atwood, letter to Charles Pachter, 11 Nov. 1970.

11 Margaret Atwood, letter to Charles Pachter, 14 Jan. 1971.

12 Margaret Atwood, "A Taste of Squalor," selections from a ms., 1991, box 148: 8–9, Margaret Atwood Papers, U of Toronto.

13 Margaret Atwood, "Self-Discovery through Integration with One's Past," paper presented to the Shastri Institute Conference, 1988, box 148: 28, Margaret Atwood Papers, U of Toronto.

14 Atwood, "Self-Discovery" 2A.

15 Atwood, "Self-Discovery" 6–7.

16 Margaret Atwood, "Margaret Atwood," with Graeme Gibson, *Eleven Canadian Novelists*, by Graeme Gibson (Toronto: Anansi, 1973) 18.

17 Margaret Atwood, "A Question of Metamorphosis," with Linda Sandler, *Conversations*, ed. Earl Ingersoll (Princeton, NJ: Ontario Review, 1990) 43.

18 Atwood, "Self-Discovery" 7.

19 Atwood, "Self-Discovery" 7–8.

20 Phoebe Larmore, interview with the author, 25 Apr. 1996.

21 Margaret Atwood, home page 1996 (http://www.io.org/~toadaly).

22 Timothy Findley, letter to the author, 23 Feb. 1996.

CHAPTER 14: THE RISE OF CANLIT: GIVING BLOOD

1 Charles Pachter, interview with the author, 11 Sept. 1995.

2 Phoebe Larmore, interview with the author, 25 Apr. 1996.

3 Margaret Atwood, "Sexual Bias in Canadian Reviewing: A Preliminary Report," submitted to the Division of Humanities, York University, 1970–71, box 95: 10, Margaret Atwood Papers, U of Toronto.

4 Robertson Davies, letter to Lori Tabachnik, 17 Nov. 1971, box 95: 15, Margaret Atwood Papers, U of Toronto.

5 Al Purdy, letter to Barry Steele, 28 Nov. 1971, box 95: 15, Margaret Atwood Papers, U of Toronto.

6 Dennis Lee, interview with the author, 13 Nov. 1995.

7 Dennis Lee, "The Death of Harold Ladoo," *Nightwatch* (Toronto: McClelland, 1996) 46–47.

8 Lee, interview with the author, 13 Nov. 1995.

9 Lee, "The Death of Harold Ladoo" 48–49.

10 Lee, "The Death of Harold Ladoo" 53–54.

11 Margaret Atwood, *Survival: A Thematic Guide to Canadian Literature* (Toronto: House of Anansi, 1972) 139.

12 Douglas Fetherling, *Travels by Night: A Memoir of the Sixties* (Toronto: Lester, 1994) 154.

13 Shirley Gibson, *I Am Watching* (Toronto: House of Anansi, 1973) 17.

14 Gibson, *I Am Watching* 11–12.

15 See Robert Fulford, "Thrills," *Saturday Night* Nov. 1976: 38; and Margaret Atwood, "Royal Porcupine Identikit," *Saturday Night* Jan.–Feb. 1977: 3.

16 Lee, interview with the author, 13 Nov. 1995.

17 Lee, "The Death of Harold Ladoo" 54.

18 Lee, interview with the author, 13 Nov. 1995.

19 Joyce Wayne, "The Atwood Generation: Notes on Surfacing from the Underground," *Quill and Quire* Feb. 1981: 4.

20 Margaret Atwood, "A Question of Metamorphosis," with Linda Sandler, *Conversations*, ed. Earl Ingersoll (Princeton, NJ: Ontario Review, 1990) 56.

21 Dennis Lee, letter to Margaret Atwood, 22 Nov. 1972, box 1, Dennis Lee Papers, U of Toronto.

22 Margaret Atwood, letter to Dennis Lee, n.d., Dennis Lee Papers, U of Toronto.

23 Jon Krampner, "House of Anansi Press," 12 May 1977, ms. of a *Detroit Free Press* article, box 17, House of Anansi Correspondence, U of Toronto.

24 Margaret Atwood, "After Survival . . . ," *Encounters and Explorations: Canadian Writers and European Critics*, ed. Franz K. Stanzel and Waldemar Zacharasiewicz (Würzburg: Königshausen, 1986) 133.

25 Fetherling, *Travels by Night* 113.

26 Fetherling, *Travels by Night* 113.

27 Krampner, "House of Anansi Press" 6.

28 Fetherling, *Travels by Night* 162.

29 Fetherling, *Travels by Night* 162.

30 Fetherling, *Travels by Night* 162–63.

31 Margaret Atwood, "Dennis Lee," n.d., box 74: 2, Margaret Atwood Papers, U of Toronto, 2.

32 Lee, "The Death of Harold Ladoo" 50.

33 Lee, "The Death of Harold Ladoo" 66.

CHAPTER 15: DODGING THE FLAK

1 Frank Davey, "Margaret Atwood," *From There to Here: A Guide to English-Canadian Literature since 1960*, Our Nature — Our Voices 2 (Erin, ON: Porcépic, 1974) 30.

2 The most scathing of these is Robin Mathews, "Survival and Struggle in Canadian Literature: A Review of Margaret Atwood's *Survival*," *This Magazine Is about Schools* 6.4 (1972): 109–24.

3 Margaret Atwood, "Travels Back," *Second Words: Selected Critical Prose* (Toronto: House of Anansi, 1982) 109.

4 Atwood, "Travels Back" 113.

5 John Ayre, "Margaret Atwood and the End of Colonialism," *Saturday Night* Nov. 1972: 26.

6 Margaret Atwood, "The Buffer Zone," TLS 26 Oct. 1973: 1306.

7 Atwood, "The Buffer Zone."

8 Margaret Atwood, draft letter to "Dear Sir" [Frank Davey], c. 1973, box 92: 8, Margaret Atwood Papers, U of Toronto.

9 Brian Brett, interview with the author, 3 May 1996.

10 Norman Mackenzie, rev. of *Five Legs*, by Graeme Gibson, *Dalhousie Review* 49 (1969): 436–39.

11 Roy MacGregor, "Novelist-in-Progress," *Toronto Life* Dec. 1982: 76.

12 MacGregor, "Novelist-in-Progress" 44.

13 MacGregor, "Novelist-in-Progress" 76.

14 Frankish Styles, "Canadian Writers' Engineer," *Canadian Author and Bookman* 56.4 (1981): 13.

15 MacGregor, "Novelist-in-Progress" 76.

16 Styles, "Canadian Writers' Engineer" 13.

17 Margaret Atwood, "Writers' Union of Canada," *Canadian Encyclopedia*, 1988 ed.

18 Styles, "Canadian Writers' Engineer" 13.

19 Styles, "Canadian Writers' Engineer" 13.

20 Brett, interview with the author, 3 May 1996.

21 Margaret Atwood, "Thinking about the Techniques of Skiing . . . ," with Mary Ellis Gibson, *Conversations*, ed. Earl Ingersoll (Princeton, NJ: Ontario Review, 1990) 37–38.

22 Margaret Atwood, "Nothing New Here," *Two-Headed Poems* (Toronto: Oxford UP, 1978) 24–25.

23 Margaret Atwood, letter to Dennis Lee, 5 Aug. 1974, box 1: 13, Dennis Lee Papers, U of Toronto.

24 Graeme Gibson and Margaret Atwood, interview, with Allan Anderson, 27 July 1977, Margaret Atwood Papers, U of Toronto.

25 Scott Young, "Making Hay," *Globe and Mail* 12 Aug. 1974: 25.

26 Margaret Atwood, letter to the editor, *Globe and Mail* 30 Aug. 1974; qtd. from copy of the letter, courtesy of Margaret Atwood.

27 Margaret Atwood, "Dear ——," n.d., box 27: 1, Margaret Atwood Papers, U of Toronto.

28 Kildare Dobbs, "Birth Pangs of a Union," *Toronto Star* 30 Jan. 1973.

29 Margaret Atwood, letter to the editor, *Toronto Star*, 30 Jan. 1973.

30 Brett, interview with the author, 3 May 1996.

31 Kildare Dobbs, "Toronto Daily Star," *Books in Canada* Jan.–Feb. 1973: 11.

32 Margaret Atwood, "Getting Out from Under," address to the Empire Club of Canada, 15 Apr. 1973, box 56: 19, Margaret Atwood Papers, U of Toronto.

33 See Mathews, "Survival and Struggle in Canadian Literature"; and Margaret Atwood, "Mathews and Misrepresentation," *This Magazine Is about Schools* 7.1 (1974): 29–33.

34 Rick Salutin, interview with the author, 5 Apr. 1996.

35 Margaret Atwood, letter to John Glassco, 8 Apr. 1974.

36 Atwood, letter to John Glassco, 8 Apr. 1974.

37 John Glassco, letter to Margaret Atwood, 5 May 1974.

38 William F. Wigle, letter to Margaret Atwood, 31 Jan. 1974.

39 Margaret Atwood, letter to George Woodcock, 20 May 1974.

40 Fraser Sutherland, letter to Marian Engel, 5 Mar. 1974.

41 George Woodcock, letter to Margaret Atwood, 15 Mar. 1974.

42 Margaret Laurence, letter to Fraser Sutherland, 19 Feb. 1974.

43 Dennis Lee, letter to Margaret Atwood, 27 June 1975, Dennis Lee Papers, U of Toronto.

44 I.D., "Fairy Tales of Canada. The Lady of the Lake: Or, How the Octopus Got Its Tentacles," *Canadian Forum* May–June 1974: 68–69.

45 Dennis Lee, letter to the editor, *Canadian Forum* Sept. 1974: 40.

46 Jay Macpherson, letter to the editor, *Canadian Forum* Sept. 1974: 40–41.

47 Margaret Atwood, letter to Sam Solecki, 22 Dec. 1979, box 2: 9, Margaret Atwood Papers, U of Toronto.

48 Atwood, letter to Dennis Lee, 5 Aug. 1974, box 1: 13, Dennis Lee Papers, U of Toronto.

49 Scott Symons, "The Canadian Bestiary: Ongoing Literary Depravity," *West Coast Review* Jan. 1977: 3, 10, 15.

50 Margaret Laurence, letter to the editor, *Canadian Forum* Nov. 1977: 31.

51 See Scott Symons, "Atwood-as-Icon," *Idler* May 1990: 36–39.

52 Rick Salutin, interview with the author, 5 Apr. 1996.

53 Salutin, interview with the author, 5 Apr. 1996.

54 Margaret Atwood, letter to Jerome Buckley, 1 June 1973, box 50: 5, Margaret Atwood Papers, U of Toronto.

55 Jerome Buckley, letter to Margaret Atwood, 11 June 1973, box 50: 5, Margaret Atwood Papers, U of Toronto.

56 Margaret Atwood, letter to Mrs. Nellie Kesson, 25 June 1973, Margaret Atwood Papers, U of Toronto.

57 Margaret Atwood, letter to Marge Piercy, 2 Aug. 1973, Margaret Atwood Papers, U of Toronto.

58 Margaret Atwood, note to Donya Peroff, 16 Jan. 1974, box 27: 1, Margaret Atwood Papers, U of Toronto.

59 Margaret Atwood, letter to George Woodcock, 23 Mar. 1974, Margaret Atwood Papers, U of Toronto.

60 Dennis Lee, letter to Margaret Atwood, 27 June 1975, Dennis Lee Papers, U of Toronto.

61 Robert Fulford, "Thrills," *Saturday Night* Nov. 1976: 38.

62 Charles Pachter, interview with the author, 11 Sept. 1995.

63 Margaret Atwood, letter to the editor, *Saturday Night* Jan.–Feb. 1977: 3.

64 Margaret Atwood, "My Mother Would Rather Skate than Scrub Floors," with Joyce Carol Oates, *Conversations* 72.

CHAPTER 16: ANOTHER BALANCING ACT: FAME AND MOTHERHOOD

1 I am indebted to Sandy Tomc for these insights. See Sandra Tomc, "Dieting and Damnations," *ESC* Dec. 1996: 441–60.

2 Margaret Atwood, "The Curse of Eve — Or, What I Learned in School," *Second Words: Selected Critical Prose* (Toronto: House of Anansi, 1982) 224.

3 Margaret Atwood, "Science and the Novelist," Wiegand Lecture, 1989, box 148: 22, Margaret Atwood Papers, U of Toronto.

4 Margaret Atwood, "The Curse of Eve — Or, What I Learned in School," *Women on Women*, ed. Ann B. Shteir (Toronto: York UP, 1978) 25–26.

5 Margaret Atwood, "Paradoxes and Dilemmas: The Woman as Writer," *Women in the Canadian Mosaic*, ed. Gwen Matheson (Toronto: Martin, 1976) 268–69.

6 Margaret Atwood, introduction, *Women Writers at Work: The Paris Review Interviews*, ed. George Plimpton (New York: Penguin, 1989) 8.

7 Margaret Drabble, "Margaret Atwood Talks to Margaret Drabble," *Chatelaine* Apr. 1987. (In its unpublished form, this interview is "The Three Margarets," selections from a ms., c. 1987, box 146: 25, Margaret Atwood Papers, U of Toronto.)

8 Margaret Atwood, "Thinking about the Technique of Skiing," with Mary Ellis Gibson, *Conversations*, ed. Earl Ingersoll (Princeton, NJ: Ontario Review, 1990) 39.

9 Margaret Atwood, "Interview with Margaret Atwood," with Helen Slinger, *Maclean's* 6 Sept. 1976: 4.

10 Margaret Atwood, letter to the author, 28 Nov. 1995.

11 Margaret Atwood, "Why I Write," *Quill and Quire* Aug. 1993: 1.

12 Bev Hunter, interview with the author, 9 Aug. 1996.

13 Drabble, "Margaret Atwood Talks to Margaret Drabble" 130.

14 Margaret Atwood, letter to Raymond Pannell, 1 June 1976, box 113: 1, Margaret Atwood Papers, U of Toronto.

15 Margaret Atwood, story list, Margaret Atwood Papers, U of Toronto.

16 Sid Adilman, "Laurence Novel Movie Script in Top Hands," *Toronto Star* 26 Jan. 1977.

17 Charles Pachter, interview with the author, 2 Oct. 1995.

18 Robert Fulford, "Ever a Camp Counsellor, Atwood Directs a Review," *Toronto Star* 14 May 1977: H5.

19 Robert Fulford, *Best Seat in the House: Memoirs of a Lucky Man* (Toronto: Collins, 1988) 202.

20 Margaret Atwood, "Dancing on the Edge of the Precipice," with Joyce Carol Oates, *Conversations* 82.

21 Atwood, interview (with Oates).

22 See Margaret Atwood, "Another Night Visit," c. 1977, box 14: 2, Margaret Atwood Papers, U of Toronto. This poem, dedicated to a Canadian poet who had just died very tragically, posits such stony silence as a far worse alternative.

23 Not only does Atwood articulate a newfound resignation to media scrutiny in the interview with Oates, but she also articulates a very strong sense of vocation when she talks of the power and purpose of writing.

CHAPTER 17: TRAVELLING

1 Margaret Atwood, "Production Problems," *Canadian Literature* 78 (1978): 13–15.

2 Atwood, "Production Problems" 4.

3 Dennis Lee, letter to Margaret Atwood, 5 June 1979, box 32: 7, Margaret Atwood Papers, U of Toronto.

4 Margaret Atwood, interview with Joyce Carol Oates, selection from a ms., c. 1978, box 56: 31, Margaret Atwood Papers, U of Toronto.

5 Graeme Gibson, "Travels of a Family Man," *Chatelaine* Mar. 1979: 134.

6 Gibson, "Travels of a Family Man" 136.

7 Gibson, "Travels of a Family Man" 132.

8 Margaret Atwood, "Playgroup at the Fringe of Empire," box 56: 37, Margaret Atwood Papers, U of Toronto.

9 Atwood, "Playgroup at the Fringe of Empire" 2.

10 Atwood, "Playgroup at the Fringe of Empire" 3.

11 Atwood, "Playgroup at the Fringe of Empire" 3.

12 Margaret Atwood, note to Donya Peroff, n.d., box 32: 7, Margaret Atwood Papers, U of Toronto.

13 Lenore Atwood, interview with the author, 5 Nov. 1997.

14 Lenore Atwood, letter to Margaret Atwood, 5 June 1979, box 32: 7, Margaret Atwood Papers, U of Toronto.

15 Margaret Atwood, "Just Looking at Things That Are There," with Alan Twigg, *Conversations*, ed. Earl Ingersoll (Princeton, NJ: Ontario Review, 1990) 123.

16 Itinerary for *Life before Man* promotional tour, c. 1979, box 128: 14, Margaret Atwood Papers, U of Toronto.

17 Itinerary for *Life before Man* promotional tour, c. 1979, box 128: 14, Margaret Atwood Papers, U of Toronto.

18 Itinerary for *Life before Man* promotional tour, c. 1979, box 128: 15, Margaret Atwood Papers, U of Toronto.

19 Jack McClelland, interview with the author, 22 May 1996.

20 Margaret Atwood 1996 home page 4.5.

21 See Phoebe-Lou Adams, rev. of *Life before Man*, *Atlantic Monthly* Apr. 1980: 123; Marilyn French, "Spouses and Lovers," *New York Times Book Review* 3 Feb. 1980: 1, 26; Barbara Amiel, "Life after Surviving," *Maclean's* 15 Oct. 1979: 66–67.

22 Robert Fulford, "Notebook," *Saturday Night* May 1980: 12.

23 Margaret Atwood, "Diary Down Under," *Second Words: Selected Critical Prose* (Toronto: House of Anansi, 1982) 305.

24 Robert Fulford, *Best Seat in the House: Memoirs of a Lucky Man* (Toronto: Collins, 1988) 193.

25 Friend of Margaret Atwood, interview with the author, 9 Aug. 1996.

CHAPTER 18: PRESSURES AND CRISES

1 Judith Timson, "Magnificent Margaret Atwood," *Chatelaine* Jan. 1981: 60.

2 Roy MacGregor, "Novelist-in-Progress," *Toronto Life* Dec. 1982: 75.

3 Margaret Atwood, interview with the author, 1 May 1996.

4 MacGregor, "Novelist-in-Progress" 76.

5 Atwood, interview with the author, 1 May 1996.

6 MacGregor, "Novelist-in-Progress" 76.

7 Michael Rubbo, dir., *Once in August*, Canadian Writers Series, National Film Board of Canada, 1984.

8 Margaret Atwood, letter to Margot Kidder, 20 May 1980, box 95: 28, Margaret Atwood Papers, U of Toronto.

9 Peter Pearson, interview with the author, 3 May 1996.

10 Margaret Atwood, letter to Margot Kidder, 6 Dec. 1979, box 95: 28, Margaret Atwood Papers, U of Toronto.

11 Margot Kidder, letter to Margaret Atwood, 3 Feb. 1980, box 95: 28, Margaret Atwood Papers, U of Toronto.

12 Margot Kidder, letter to Margaret Atwood, c. Apr. 1980, box 95: 28, Margaret Atwood Papers, U of Toronto.

13 Margaret Atwood, draft of outline, screenplay synopsis for *Lady Oracle*, 1982, box 87: 5, Margaret Atwood Papers, U of Toronto.

14 Lorna Irvine, letter to the author, 18 Feb. 1996; Margaret Atwood, "Introduction to the Work of Carolyn Forché . . . ," July 1981, box 56: 59, Margaret Atwood Papers, U of Toronto.

15 Margaret Atwood, letter to Margot Kidder, 5 July 1980, box 95: 28, Margaret Atwood Papers, U of Toronto.

16 Margaret Atwood, "Witness Is What You Must Bear," with Beatrice Mendez-Egle, *Conversations*, ed. Earl Ingersoll (Princeton, NJ: Ontario Review, 1990) 164.

17 Atwood, "Witness Is What You Must Bear" 170.

18 Margaret Atwood, "Witches: The Strong Neck of the Favorite Ancestor," *Radcliffe Quarterly* Sept. 1980: 4.

19 Margaret Atwood 1996 home page 5.7.

20 Margaret Atwood, "True Stories," *True Stories* (Toronto: Oxford UP, 1981) 9.

21 Margaret Atwood, report to the Department of External Affairs, Ottawa, regarding a trip to England, Sweden, and the Lahti Conference in Finland, 3–19 June 1991, box 90: 7, Margaret Atwood Papers, U of Toronto.

22 James Polk, letter to Margaret Atwood, 7 Apr. 1982, box 67: 1, Margaret Atwood Papers, U of Toronto.

23 James Polk, letter to Margaret Atwood, 15 Apr. 1982, box 67: 1, Margaret Atwood Papers, U of Toronto.

24 Jerome Buckley, letter to Margaret Atwood, 30 Jan. 1983, Margaret Atwood Papers, U of Toronto.

25 Margaret Atwood, "Second Words," *Globe and Mail* 20 Nov. 1982: L2.

26 I am indebted to Sheri Weinstein for this insight.

27 Marylee Stephenson, interview with the author, 27 Feb. 1996.

28 Margaret Atwood, "Islands of the Mind," *Quest* Apr. 1984: 38.

29 Atwood, "Islands of the Mind" 40.

30 Stephenson, interview with the author, 27 Feb. 1996.

31 Stephenson, interview with the author, 27 Feb. 1996.

32 Atwood, "Islands of the Mind" 40.

33 Margaret Atwood, letter to Michael Enright, 6 Jan. 1984, box 74: 8, Margaret Atwood Papers, U of Toronto.

34 Margaret Atwood, "In Search of the Rattlesnake Plantain," *Bluebeard's Egg and Other Stories* (New York: Fawcett Crest, 1987) 264.

35 Stephenson, interview with the author, 27 Feb. 1996.

36 Margaret Atwood, "Using Other People's Dreadful Childhoods," with Bonnie Lyons, *Conversations*, ed. Earl Ingersoll (Princeton, NJ: Ontario Review, 1990) 225.

37 William French, "Not All Atwood's Stories Are for Those with Healthy Appetites," *Globe and Mail* 3 Nov. 1983: E1.

38 Margaret Atwood, "North Norfolk Coast," 1984, box 90: 39, Margaret Atwood Papers, U of Toronto.

39 Margaret Atwood, letter to Charles Pachter, 23 Jan. 1984.

40 Margaret Atwood, "Nine Beginnings," *New Essays in New Territory* (New York: Norton, 1991) 153, vol. 2 of *The Writer on Her Work*, ed. Janet Sternberg.

41 Xandra Bingley, letter to the author, 30 July 1996.

42 Margaret Atwood, "A Taste of Squalor," selections from a ms., 1991, box 148: 8–9, Margaret Atwood Papers, U of Toronto.

43 Margaret Atwood, "Death by Beaver," n.d., box 106: 22, Margaret Atwood Papers, U of Toronto, 11–12.

44 Margaret Atwood, "Eccentric Flints," n.d., box 106: 17, Margaret Atwood Papers, U of Toronto, 3–4.

45 Qtd. in Mary Battiata, "A Canadian Cassandra," *Winnipeg Free Press* 20 July 1986: 67.

46 Margaret Atwood, "Wondering What It's Like to Be a Woman," rev. of *The Witches of Eastwick*, by John Updike, *New York Times Book Review* 13 May 1984: 1.

CHAPTER 19: REFLECTIONS ON SOCIETY

1 Margaret Atwood, "An End to Audience?," *Second Words: Selected Critical Prose* (Toronto: House of Anansi, 1982) 346.

2 Margaret Atwood, "If You Can't Say Something Nice, Don't Say Anything at All," *Language in Her Eye*, ed. Libby Scheier et al. (Toronto: Coach House, 1990) 17.

3 Margaret Atwood, "A Taste of Squalor," selections from a ms., 1991, box 148: 8–9, Margaret Atwood Papers, U of Toronto.

4 Margaret Atwood, "Tightrope-Walking over Niagara Falls," with Geoff Hancock, *Conversations*, ed. Earl Ingersoll (Princeton, NJ: Ontario Review, 1990) 200.

5 Atwood, "If You Can't Say Something Nice" 18–19.

6 Vivienne Schuster, letter to the author, 26 Mar. 1996.

7 Phoebe Larmore, interview with the author, 10 Apr. 1996.

8 Margaret Atwood, interview, Houghton Mifflin publicity release, Feb. 1986, box 149: 4, Margaret Atwood Papers, U of Toronto.

9 Margaret Atwood, "A Writer's Road from Wilderness to Wealth," *Independent* 6 Feb. 1987: 12.

10 Marilyn Linton, "Atwood's New Tale: It's Fiction So Close to Fact It Scares Her," *Sunday Sun* 2 Feb. 1986: C17. On this subject, see also Margaret Atwood, "An Interview with Margaret Atwood," with Sue Matheson, *Herizons* Jan.–Feb. 1986: 20–22.

11 Margaret Atwood, letter to Maria Ekman, 10 Apr. 1986, box 151: 8, Margaret Atwood Papers, U of Toronto.

12 "Margaret Atwood," interview, *Quill and Quire* 1 Sept. 1985: 66.

13 Nan Talese, letter to Margaret Atwood, 4 Dec. 1985, box 149: 1, Margaret Atwood Papers, U of Toronto.

14 Itinerary for *The Handmaid's Tale* promotional tour, c. 1985, box 149: 3, Margaret Atwood Papers, U of Toronto.

15 Sarah Cooper, interview with the author, 10 May 1996.

16 Peter Pearson, interview with the author, 3 May 1996.

17 Itinerary for *The Handmaid's Tale* promotional tour, c. 1985, box 149: 2, Margaret Atwood Papers, U of Toronto.

18 Margaret Atwood, "Flogging It in the Frozen North," n.d., box 56: 8, Margaret Atwood Papers, U of Toronto.

19 Atwood, "Flogging It in the Frozen North."

20 Ken Adachi, "Governor General's Award Was a Surprise for Atwood," *Toronto Star* 4 June 1986: F1.

21 Telegrams, Sept.–Oct. 1986, box 150: 12, Margaret Atwood Papers, U of Toronto.

22 Leslie Plommer, "Kingsley Amis Beats Davies . . . ," *Globe and Mail* 23 Oct. 1986.

23 "Amis Edges Out Davies to Win Literary Award," *Toronto Star* 23 Oct. 1986.

24 Helen V. Chaplin, letter to Margaret Atwood, 19 Feb. 1986, box 149: 3, Margaret Atwood Papers, U of Toronto.

25 Radio commercial transcript, 14 Mar. 1986, box 149: 3, Margaret Atwood Papers, U of Toronto.

26 Adachi, "Governor General's Award Was a Surprise."

27 Submissions list for film rights to *The Handmaid's Tale*, c. Feb. 1986, box 149: 3, Margaret Atwood Papers, U of Toronto.

28 Margaret Atwood, letter to Danny Wilson, 9 Feb. 1987, box 152: 2, Margaret Atwood Papers, U of Toronto.

CHAPTER 20: TAKING ACTION

1 Margaret Atwood, letter to the author, 28 Nov. 1995.

2 Margaret Atwood, "Foreign Women," 1986, box 91: 23, Margaret Atwood Papers, U of Toronto.

3 See Robert Collison, "Margaret Atwood Takes N.Y.C.," *Chatelaine* June 1986: 64–65, 99–100. See also Joyce Johnson, "Margaret Atwood's Brave New World," *Washington Post Book World* 2 Feb. 1986: 1–2; and Ellen Vanstone, "Prize Writer," *Toronto Life* Mar. 1987: 10–11.

4 Timothy Findley, letter to the author, 23 Feb. 1996.

5 Margaret Atwood, "Stealing Time: Marian Engel," *Encounters and Explorations: Canadian Writers and European Critics*, ed. Franz K. Stanzel

and Waldemar Zacharasiewicz (Würzburg: Königshausen, 1986) 34.

6 Michele Field, "Margaret Atwood's Colonial Days," *Good Weekend*, c. 1987, box 130: 13, Margaret Atwood Papers, U of Toronto.

7 Brian Brett, interview with the author, 3 May 1996.

8 Guy Babineau, "Kanada: The Miniseries," *Canadian Forum* Feb. 1987: 42.

9 Margaret Atwood, address to the Toronto Public Works Department, 11 Jan. 1989, box 148: 24, Margaret Atwood Papers, U of Toronto.

10 Margaret Atwood, "Laying down the Law," 10 Jan. 1989, box 148: 20, Margaret Atwood Papers, U of Toronto.

11 Margaret Atwood, "A Taste of Squalor," selections from a ms., 1991, box 148: 8–9, Margaret Atwood Papers, U of Toronto.

12 Margaret Atwood, "In the Field," with M.T. Kelly, *One on One: The Imprint Interviews*, ed. Leanna Crouch (Toronto: Somerville House, 1994) 157.

CHAPTER 21: REFLECTIONS ON THE ARTIST

1 Margaret Atwood, "Managing Time for Writing," with Sue Walker, *Conversations*, ed. Earl Ingersoll (Princeton, NJ: Ontario Review, 1990) 176.

2 Margaret Atwood, "Tightrope-Walking over Niagara Falls," with Geoff Hancock, *Conversations* 203.

3 Margaret Atwood, "Nine Beginnings," *New Essays in New Territory* (New York: Norton, 1991), vol. 2 of *The Writer on Her Work*, ed. Janet Sternberg.

4 Margaret Atwood, "Waltzing Again," with Earl Ingersoll, *Conversations* 236–37.

5 Margaret Atwood, "Ravines," box 90: 22, Margaret Atwood Papers, U of Toronto. (This is not the short story entitled "The Ravine.")

6 Judith McCombs, "Early *Cat's Eye* Stories: Atwood's 1964–5 'Cut-Out,' 'Scribblers,' 'Suffer the Little Children,' and 'The Ravine,' " American Association of Canadian Studies Conference, Seattle, Nov. 1995.

7 McCombs, "Early *Cat's Eye* Stories."

8 McCombs, "Early *Cat's Eye* Stories."

9 Margaret Atwood, "Horror Comics," *Murder in the Dark* (Toronto: Coach House, 1983) 13.

10 Margaret Atwood, "Fainting," *Murder in the Dark* 16.

11 Margaret Atwood, letter to Leon Rooke, 29 Mar. 1988, box 124: 9, Margaret Atwood Papers, U of Toronto.

12 Peter Davison, interview with the author, 22 May 1996.

13 Judith Timson, "Atwood's Triumph: With a New Novel and International Acclaim, Margaret Atwood Is a World Celebrity," *Maclean's* 3 Oct. 1988.

14 David Malcolm Atwood, home page.

15 Margaret Atwood, introduction, *Women Writers at Work: The Paris Review Interviews*, ed. George Plimpton (New York: Penguin, 1989) xvii.

CHAPTER 22: REFLECTIONS ON FILM

1 Unnamed fan, letter to Margaret Atwood, c. 1989, box 152: 3, Margaret Atwood Papers, U of Toronto.

2 Margaret Atwood, letter to unnamed fan, 2 Feb. 1989, box 152: 3, Margaret Atwood Papers, U of Toronto.

3 Martin Knelman, "Lights! Camera! Atwood!" *Toronto Life* Apr. 1990: 33.

4 Qtd. in Myra Forsberg, "Makers of 'Handmaid's Tale' Analyze a Grim Fantasy," *New York Times* 2 Apr. 1989: 13. See also insert entitled "Journey to the Screen."

5 Margaret Atwood, letter to the author, 1 Sept. 1996.

6 Sheldon Teitelbaum, "The Handmaid's Tale," *Cinefantastique* Mar. 1990: 16.

7 Brian Johnson, "Returning to a New Berlin," *Maclean's* 26 Feb. 1990: 45.

8 Itinerary, Anke Zindler Filmpresse, c. 1991, box 152: 5, Margaret Atwood Papers, U of Toronto.

9 Johnson, "Returning to a New Berlin" 45.

10 Scott Symons, "Atwood-as-Icon," *Idler* 28 May 1990: 36.

11 Robert Fulford, "Facts and Arguments," *Globe and Mail* 25 June 1990: A14.

12 Margaret Atwood, notes to the author, 1 Sept. 1996.

13 Atwood, notes to the author, 1 Sept. 1996.

14 Val Ross, "I've Always Been Funny," *Globe and Mail* 24 Aug. 1991: C2.

15 Atwood, letter to the author, 1 Sept. 1996.

16 Jim Bawden, "Fine Script Moves Heaven on Earth Right to Heart," *Toronto Star* 28 Feb. 1987: F1.

17 Peter Pearson, interview with the author, 3 May 1996.

CHAPTER 23: DEATH: SOME REFLECTIONS

1 Qtd. in Ed Haag, "International Atwood," *Canadian* Sept. 1988: 58.

2 Margaret Atwood, "A Taste of Squalor," selections from a ms., 1991, box 148: 8–9, Margaret Atwood Papers, U of Toronto.

3 William Toye, interview with the author, 30 Aug. 1995.

4 Margaret Atwood, "Skipping Tea with Margaret Atwood," with Barbara Yost, *Bloomsbury Review* Sept.–Oct. 1994: n. pag.

5 Margaret Atwood, "Provence: Romans vs. Celts," *New York Times Magazine* 12 Sept. 1993: 72.

6 Atwood, "Skipping Tea with Margaret Atwood."

7 Atwood, "Skipping Tea with Margaret Atwood."

8 Peter Pearson, interview with the author, 17 June 1996.

9 Margaret Atwood, notes to the author, 1 Sept. 1996.

10 Sarah Cooper, interview with the author, 10 May 1996.

11 Cooper, interview with the author, 10 May 1996.

12 Margaret Atwood, "A Visit," *Morning in the Burned House* (Toronto: McClelland, 1995) 88.

13 Margaret Atwood, "Bored," *Morning in the Burned House* 92.

14 Margaret Atwood, "Flowers," *Morning in the Burned House* 95.

15 Vivienne Schuster, letter to the author, 26 Mar. 1996.

16 Phoebe Larmore, interview with the author, 10 Apr. 1996.

17 Qtd. in Stephen Smith, "The Good Editor," *Toronto Life* Oct. 1995: 52.

18 P.K. Page, interview with the author, 27 Mar. 1996.

19 Margaret Atwood, *The Robber Bride* (Toronto: McClelland, 1993) 302.

20 Margaret Atwood, "Book Tour Comics . . . The Radio Interview," *Publisher's Weekly* 24 Jan. 1994: 14.

21 Qtd. in Val Ross, "I've Always Been Funny," *Globe and Mail* 24 Aug. 1991: C1.

22 Hans Nygren, letter to the author, 23 May 1996.

23 Atwood, notes to the author, 1 Sept. 1996.

CHAPTER 24: OF PAST AND PRESENT: SOME REFLECTIONS

1 Joan Thomas, "Atwood Jogs a Murderous Memory," *Globe and Mail* 7 Sept. 1996: C20.

2 Beverley Slopen, "Atwood Probes a 19th-Century Murder Mystery," *Toronto Star* 18 May 1996: L16.

3 Barbara Wickens, "People," *Maclean's* 17 Feb. 1997: 71.

4 Margaret Atwood, "The Patchwork Quilt Called Grace," *Reader's Showcase* Oct. 1996: 12–13.

5 Qtd. in Sheri Weinstein, letter to the author, 10 Jan. 1996.

6 See Mark Abley, "States of Grace," *Gazette* [Montreal] 29 Sept. 1996: D1, D4.

7 Margaret Atwood, unpublished interview with David Wiley, csint.html@www.daily.umn.edu

CONCLUSION: REFLECTING BACK

1 I am indebted to Sally Jacobsen for this notion of Atwood as an example of "intellectual engagement" (as articulated in the nomination letter Jacobsen sent to the Modern Language Association in 1990). However, it was Robert Fulford who referred to Atwood as "emblem" and "standard bearer" for English Canadian political movements (Fulford, *Best Seat in the House: Memoirs of a Lucky Man* [Toronto: Collins, 1988] 187). Here I use the term more broadly.

2 Margaret Atwood, "Why I Write," *Quill and Quire* Aug. 1993: 21.

3 Atwood, "Why I Write" 21.

4 See Margaret Atwood, "Bowering Pie . . . Some Recollections," *Essays on Canadian Writing* 38 (1989): 3–6. See also Atwood's "Dennis Lee Revisited," *Descant* 3.9 (1982); and "Marie-Claire Blais Is Not for Burning," *Maclean's* Sept. 1975: 26, 28–29.

5 Margaret Atwood, letter to Pierre Castonguay, 20 Feb. 1984, box 74: 15, Margaret Atwood Papers, U of Toronto. Author's translation.

6 Atwood, 'Why I Write,' 21.

7 Qtd. in Charles Pachter, interview with the author, 4 Nov. 1997.

8 Margaret Atwood, letter to Charles Pachter, 28 Dec. 1968.

9 Qtd. in Camille Peri, "Witch Craft," *Mother Jones* Apr. 1989: 31.

10 Timothy Findley, *Inside Memory: Pages from a Writer's Workbook* (Toronto: HarperCollins, 1990) 181.

11 See also Cooke, "Reading Reflections: The Autobiographical Illusion in *Cat's Eye*," *Essays on Life Writing*, ed. Marlene Kadar (Toronto: U of Toronto P, 1990) 162–70; and for additional discussion of Atwood's aesthetic transformations, "The Politics of Ventriloquism," *Various Atwoods: Essays on the Later Poems, Short Fiction, and Novels*, ed. Lorraine M. York (Toronto: House of Anansi, 1995) 207–28.

12 Margaret Atwood, "Another Night Visit," c. 1977, box 14: 2, Margaret Atwood Papers, U of Toronto.

13 Margaret Atwood, "Monument to a Dead Self," *New York Times Book Review* 6 Nov. 1977: 15.

14 Margaret Atwood, interview with Joyce Carol Oates, selection from a ms., c. 1978, box 56: 31, Margaret Atwood Papers, U of Toronto.

15 Denise Levertov, "Light Up the Cave," *Light Up the Cave* (New York: New Directions, 1981) 81. My thanks to Susan Glickman for bringing Levertov's article to my attention.

16 Levertov, "Light Up the Cave" 85.

AFTERWORD: ON WORDS AND EVER ONWARDS

1 Margaret Atwood, "Managing Time for Writing," with Sue Walker, *Conversations*, ed. Earl Ingersoll (Princeton, NJ: Ontario Review, 1990) 173.

2 Lewis Hyde, *The Gift: Imagination and the Erotic Life of Property* (New York: Vintage, 1979).

3 Margaret Atwood, "The Owl and the Pussycat, Some Years Later," *Paper Guitar: 27 Writers Celebrate 25 Years of* Descant *Magazine* (Toronto: HarperCollins, 1995) 17.

4 Atwood, "The Owl and the Pussycat, Some Years Later" 20.

5 Alain de Botton, *Kiss and Tell* (New York: Picador, 1995).

6 Ronald Searle, *The Rake's Progress: The Immoral Tales* (London: Perpetua, 1955).

7 Jack Miles, *God: A Biography* (New York: Vintage, 1996).

8 Doris Anderson, *Rebel Daughter: An Autobiography* (Toronto: Key Porter, 1996).

9 Janet Malcolm, *The Silent Woman: Sylvia Plath and Ted Hughes* (London: Vintage, 1995).

10 James Atlas, "People Are Talking about Books," *Vogue* Aug. 1996: 142, 144.

11 Phyllis Webb, "Poetry and Psychobiography," *Brick* 46 (1993).

12 Judith Skelton Grant, *Robertson Davies: Man of Myth* (Toronto: Viking, 1994) 585.

13 Javier Marias, *All Souls* (London: Harvill, 1995) opening paragraph. Originally published as *Todas las Almas* (Barcelona: Anagrama, 1989).

14 Margaret Atwood, notes to the author, 1 Sept. 1996.

15 Hélène Holden, interview with the author, 13 Feb. 1996.

16 Brian Brett, interview with the author, 3 May 1996.

17 Robert Fulford, *Best Seat in the House: Memoirs of a Lucky Man* (Toronto: Collins, 1988) 200.

18 Mary Irving Campbell, letter to the author, 17 July 1996.

19 Dennis Lee, interview with the author, 13 Nov. 1995.

20 Doug Jones, letter to the author, 1 Apr. 1996.

21 Phoebe Larmore, interview with the author, 25 Apr. 1996.

22 Xandra Bingley, letter to the author, 21 May 1996.

23 Robert Fulford, "The Images of Atwood," *Malahat Review* Apr. 1977: 98.

24 Michael Rubbo, dir., *Once in August*, Canadian Writers Series, National Film Board of Canada, 1984.

Index